T5-BBA-978

HANDBUCH DER ORIENTALISTIK
HANDBOOK OF ORIENTAL STUDIES

ERSTE ABTEILUNG
DER NAHE UND MITTLERE OSTEN
THE NEAR AND MIDDLE EAST

HERAUSGEGEBEN VON

H. ALTENMÜLLER, B. HROUDA
B.A. LEVINE, K.R. VEENHOF

SIEBZEHNTER BAND

JUDAISM IN LATE ANTIQUITY

PART TWO
HISTORICAL SYNTHESES

JUDAISM IN LATE ANTIQUITY

PART TWO
HISTORICAL SYNTHESES

JUDAISM
IN LATE ANTIQUITY

EDITED BY

JACOB NEUSNER

PART TWO

HISTORICAL SYNTHESES

E.J. BRILL
LEIDEN · NEW YORK · KÖLN
1995

The planning and organization of this book were supported by the University of South Florida, the Max Richter Foundation and the Tisch Family Foundation.

The paper in this book meets the guidelines for permanence and durability of the Committee on Production Guidelines for Book Longevity of the Council on Library Resources.

Library of Congress Cataloging-in-Publication Data

Judaism in late antiquity / edited by Jacob Neusner.
     p.   cm. — (Handbuch der Orientalistik, Erste Abteilung, der Nahe und Mittlere Osten, ISSN 0169-9423 ; 17. Bd.)
    Includes bibliographical references and index.
    Contents: — pt. 2. Historical syntheses.
    ISBN 9004101306
    1. Judaism—History—Post-exilic period, 586 B.C.-210 A.D.–
–Sources.   I. Neusner, Jacob, 1932–   .   II. Series: Handbuch der Orientalistik.   Erste Abteilung, Nahe und der Mittlere Osten ; 17. Bd.
BM176.J8   1994
296'.09'015—dc20   94-30825
                                        CIP

Die Deutsche Bibliothek – CIP-Einheitsaufnahme

Handbuch der Orientalistik / hrsg. von B. Spuler unter Mitarb. von C. van Dijk ... – Leiden ; New York ; Köln : Brill.
Teilw. hrsg. von H. Altenmüller. – Teilw. mit Parallelt.: Handbook of oriental studies
Abt. 1, Der Nahe und Mittlere Osten = The Near and Middle East / hrsg. von H. Altenmüller ...
NE: Spuler, Bertold [Hrsg.]; Altenmüller, Hartwig [Hrsg.]; Handbook of oriental studies
Bd. 17. Judaism in late antiquity.
   Pt. 2. Historical syntheses. – 1994

Judaism in late antiquity / ed. by Jacob Neusner. – Leiden ; New York ; Köln : Brill.
   Handbook of oriental studies : Abt. 1, The Near and Middle East ;
   ...)
NE: Neusner, Jacob [Hrsg.]
Pt. 2 Historical syntheses. – 1994
   (Handbook of oriental studies : Abt. 1, The Near and Middle East ;
   Bd. 17)
   ISBN 90-04-10130-6

ISSN   0169-9423
ISBN   90 04 10130 6

© *Copyright 1995 by E.J. Brill, Leiden, The Netherlands*

All rights reserved. No part of this publication may be reproduced, translated, stored in a retrieval system, or transmitted in any form or by any means, electronic, mechanical, photocopying, recording or otherwise, without prior written permission from the publisher.

Authorization to photocopy items for internal or personal use is granted by E.J. Brill provided that the appropriate fees are paid directly to The Copyright Clearance Center, 222 Rosewood Drive, Suite 910 Danvers MA 01923, USA. Fees are subject to change.

PRINTED IN THE NETHERLANDS

CONTENTS

PREFACE

This volume introduces the religious systems of Judaism in late antiquity to scholars in adjacent fields, such as the study of the Old and New Testaments, ancient history of Classical Antiquity, earliest Christianity, the ancient Near East, and the history of religion. Here we offer factual answers to the two questions that study of any religion in ancient times must raise. The first, covered in the companion-volume, is, what are the sources—written and in material culture—that inform us about that religion? The second, treated here, is, how do we understand those sources in the reconstruction of the history of various Judaic systems in antiquity. These chapters set forth in intelligible systems the facts the sources provide. Because of the nature of the subject and acute interest in it, in part two, we also raise some questions particular to the study of Judaism, those dealing with its historical relationship with nascent Christianity.

In the companion volume, on the sources of Judaism in late antiquity, specialists in each of the types of sources on Judaism set forth the principal sources for the study of the Judaism of the dual Torah in its formative age, the first seven centuries C.E. [=A.D.] Here specialists in the types of Judaism present what they deem to be syntheses of the sources; and, further, specialists in the study of formative Christianity provide consensus-views of the character of Judaism in the first century and the relationship of Jesus to that Judaism. We conclude with a proposed periodization of the history of Judaism in its formative age.

In these descriptions of the state of the evidence, we mean to provide a first step in guiding readers toward what is known, and how they may examine the evidence. We mean to set forth a starting point for further work on a variety of topics. The sources that provide information on ancient Judaism, discussed in the companion-volume, are presented in these chapters: Judaism Outside of Rabbinic Sources: Non-Rabbinic Literature, Gœnter Stemberger, University of Vienna; Targumim, Paul Flesher, University of Wyoming; Archaeology and Art, James F. Strange, University of South Florida; Rabbinic Sources: The Mishnah, Tosefta, and the Talmuds, Alan J. Avery-Peck, College of the Holy Cross; The Midrash-Compilations, Gary G. Porton, University of Illinois; Written Evidence of Synagogue Life: Liturgy, Lawrence Hoffman, Hebrew Union College-Jewish Institute of Religion, New York.

Matching the account of the sources for the study of Judaism, in these essays, the authors of the several syntheses turn from fact to interpretation. Scholarship today ordinarily recognizes that in antiquity there was not a single Judaism but rather diverse Judaic systems set forth each its own Judaism. We therefore provide syntheses that describe four Judaic systems or types of Judaism. We begin with Judaism of the mystical type, which is to be treated both on its own and also in relationship to the culturally- or socially-distinctive Judaic systems. The mystical is represented only by writings that give slight indication of their origin or whom they represented. It may be characterized as a different style, modifying or modulating the Judaic systems represented in Rabbinic writings, or in the Dead Sea library, or in Greek. What we want to know is modified, therefore, by the character of the sources classified as mystical. On that account we commence with a type of Judaic system that we know differently from those that in the nature of their evidence we can identify with particular times, places, and circumstances.

Of these, the first, the Hellenistic, refers to the religious system put forth by Jews who spoke and wrote in Greek; the second, the Judaic system set forth in the Dead Sea Scrolls, speaks for a different kind of community altogether, a specific one, located in one place and represented by its diverse writings. Finally, the Rabbinic Judaic system is the most cogent of the set , since it everywhere is characterized by a single myth, which maintains that at Sinai God reveqaled the Torah to Moses in two media. These are the written Torah, now, the Hebrew Scriptures or Old Testament, and the oral Torah, now written down in the Mishnah and in exegetical writings attached to the Hebrew Scriptures, called Midrash-compilations. The picture of Rabbinic Judaism is in two parts, first, a systematic definition, concerning the definition of "the Torah" in Rabbinic Judaism, then an account of the history and the hermeneutics of the Rabbinic literature.

The work of interpretation proceeds to three special problems, with special attention to Christianity in the setting of Judaism. We note, to be sure, that the sources and syntheses in this handbook address Judaic systems after 70, while the issue of Christianity represented by the Gospels addresses Judaic religious affairs prior to that time. But it is entirely a propos to include the Gospels here, since, while speaking of earlier times and deriving from traditions commencing at the beginning of the faith, still, they reach us in the form given them after 70. The first concerns New Testament scholarship, one of the principal neighboring fields of learning to the

study of Judaism: what do we know about Judaism in the time of
Jesus and the founding of Christianity? The Gospels, particular the
Synoptics, provide evidence nearly contemporary to the period of
which they speak concerning the religious life of Jews in the Land
of Israel, a glimpse into the perspective of a complex community in
that, at that time, saw itself as part of that same "Israel" of which
ancient Israel's Scriptures speak and which was then comprised by
the Jews of their time and place. The second provides a definitive
picture of the relationship of Jesus to Judaism. Since, we realize, no
single "Judaism" corresponded to a single "Christianity," simple
answers on the Judaic system(s) to which Jesus related and responded no longer prove accessible. The third brings us to the interests of
historians and historians of religion, another important contiguous
area of learning. Here we want to know how the history of not the
various Judaic formations or systems, but of Judaism in ancient
times seen as a complete religious entity, is periodized and so organized in a coherent way.

Each of the chapters of the syntheses is joined to an account of
several approaches to that same problem of synthetic representation of the sources. In that way readers gain access to a diversity of
viewpoints, while considering the presentation of one of the participants in contemporary scholarly debate. The intent throughout
therefore is to address colleagues interested for their own reasons in
the character of ancient Judaism in late antiquity. This book means
to guide readers in taking the first steps in the study of Judaism in
the time of the beginnings of Christianity and the formation of the
Bible, Old and New Testaments together. It does not compete with
two other, valuable introductions to the study of ancient Judaism,
one bibliographical, the other centered on "the state of the question." Indeed, because these other works are available, we were
able to conceive the present book in the way we have, as a fundamental introduction to a considerable subject, a first step for outsiders with special rreason to find their way into the field.[1]

---

[1] Readers in need of a bibliographical account of what has been done in the
area of special interest to them, will find in the superb updating of Strack by
Gœnter Stemberger, published as H.L. Strack, G. Stemberger, *Introduction to the
Talmud and Midrash. Foreword* by Jacob Neusner (Minneapolis, 1992: Fortress), a
compendious and thoughtful, definitive bibliography. Second, for absolutely first
class introductions to the state of numerous specific questions, the current work of
Lester Grabbe, *Judaism from Cyrus to Hadrian.* I. *The Persian and Greek Periods.* II. *The
Roman Period* (Minneapolis, 1992: Fortress Press), provides precisely what one needs
to know about issues of sources, syntheses, and methodological considerations, to
proceed further. Finally, for annotated bibliographical essays on the special problems of the paramount Judaism treated here, Rabbinic Judaism, now there is

A brief definition of the terms of this book, including those that have already been used, will help readers grasp the conceptual framework of this work. What, first of all, do we mean by "Judaism" or "a Judaic system" or "a type of Judaism"? All descriptive (as distinct from theological) scholarship recognizes out of the diversity of sources not a single Judaism, but a set of Judaic systems or Judaisms, which account for the character of the sources themselves. All of these "systems" or "Judaisms" have to be characterized in their own evidence and terms, as is the case in this introduction to their sources and their synthesis.

A Judaism presents a world view (ethos), a way of life (ethics), and an account of the social entity, Israel (ethnos), that appeals to the Pentateuch in setting forth a (to the faithful) self-evidently valid answer to an urgent question. A Judaism addresses its social entity, its "Israel", and identifies its canonical writings, always including the Pentatreuch, commonly extending to the entirety of the Hebrew Scriptures of ancient Israel or "Old Testament". A Judaism will select a central symbol and will present a generative myth, which, in narrative form, accounts for the system as a whole and all of its parts as well. We know one Judaism from some other by comparing and contrasting the generative myth and central symbol

---

available a new printing of the work edited by me, *The Study of Ancient Judaism.* N.Y., 1981: Ktav. Second printing: Atlanta, 1992: Scholars Press for South Florida Studies in the History of Judaism. I. *The Study of Ancient Judaism: Mishnah, Midrash, Siddur.* II. *The Study of Ancient Judaism: The Palestinian and Babylonian Talmuds.* It remains to note that this writer has edited *The MacMillan Dictionary of Judaism. The Biblical Period* (N.Y., 1994: MacMillan Publishing Co.) and has also written *The Doubleday Anchor Reference Library Introduction to Rabbinic Literature* (N.Y., 1994: Doubleday). For Rabbinic Judaism, I call attention also to the following: John Bowker, *The Targums and Rabbinic Literature. An Introduction to Jewish Interpretations of Scripture* (Cambridge, 1969: Cambridge University Press); Hyam Maccoby, *Early Rabbinic Writings* (Cambridge, 1988: Cambridge University Press). *Cambridge Commentaries on Writings of the Jewish and Christian World, 200 BC to AD 200.* Edited by P. R. Ackroyd, A. R. C. Leaney, and J. W. Packer. Volume III; Shmuel Safrai, editor; Peter J. Tomson, Executive Editor, *The Literature of the Sages.* First Part: *Oral Tora, Halakha, Mishna, Tosefta, Talmud, External Tractates* In the series, *Compendia Rerum Iudaicarum ad Novum Testamentum.* Section Two. *The Literature of the Jewish People in the Period of the Second Temple and the Talmud* (Assen/Maastricht and Philadelphia, 1987: Van Gorcum and Fortress Press). These articles are briefly summarized at the chapters that deal with their topics. Note also the announced continuation, Shmuel Safrai, editor; Peter J. Tomson, Executive Editor, *The Literature of the Sages.* Second Part. *Midrash, ggada, Midrash Collections, Targum, Prayer,* which, as of the date of the publication of this book has not yet appeared. A further important starting point is the entries on each document in *Encyclopaedia Judaica* (N.Y. and Jerusalem, 1971: MacMillan and Keter). These are cited under the names of the various authors and cover every document treated here. The entries by M. D. Herr are noteworthy for their consistent plan; the others are haphazard and not always illuminating.

that characterizes one but not another. That definition permits us
to accommodate as equally interesting and important all of the
types of sources—written, archaeological, and external in origin—
as well as all of the syntheses that the respective sources yield. The
conception of "Judaisms" also relieves us of the obligation of harmonizing all of the sources, on the one side, or eliminating as
"inauthentic" or "marginal" sources that do not cohere with the
ones we maintain are "normative." That theological account of
matters is entirely valid in its context, but that context is not the
one defining the work of description and analysis that is undertaken
here.

The reason that people who are not theologians may think about
one unitary, harmonious Judaism, standing in a single, linear relationship with the Hebrew Scriptures ("Sinai"), and forming the incremental statement that is authentic, normative, orthodox, and
classical, is simple. Later on, speaking descriptively, we may say
that there was only a single unitary, linear, and incremental
Judaism ("Jewish tradition"). Looking backward, we know that of
the Judaisms of the time, one turned out to predominate later on. It
is the Judaism that appeals to the symbol of the Torah and relates
the myth of the revelation by God to Moses, called our rabbi, at
Sinai, of the Torah in two media, written and oral.

But when that Judaism took shape between the first and the
seventh centuries of the Common Era (C.E. = A.D.), other Judaic
systems existed, and within the Judaism of the dual Torah accom-
modation was made for points of emphasis, e.g., mystical religious
experience, that the principal systemic documents do not stress.
Earliest Christianity falls well within the definition of (a) Judaism;
the Judaism attested by the Dead Sea writings certainly does as
well; and there is no doubt that the Hellenistic Judaic writings adumbrate a distinct system as well.

The approach to the study of ancient Judaism taken in these
essays, with its emphasis upon the diversity of Judaic systems of
Judaisms, is not the sole current way of viewing matters. Another
approach asks all evidence to tell about a single Judaism, which
everywhere predominated. That approach begins in the requirement of the theology of Christianity to define that Judaism out of
which Christianity emerged. Since, some hold, to begin with there
was one single, harmonious Christianity, so,therefore, we have to
describe one single, equally uniform Judaism. Books about Judaism
in modern times derived first from Protestant, and only later from
Judaic theologians, and only now have historians of religion addressed the task. So it is to begin with Christian theological interest

that accounts for interest in the historical description of another religion altogether, namely, Judaism. Since Christianity is seen to emerge as a single religion, so too Judaism is described as a single, unitary religion. That conception then allows historians to compare and contrast one religion with another, a single Christianity with a single Judaism.

The reason a different approach, represented in these pages, has taken over is simple. A considerable obstacle to the presentation of one unitary, harmonious Judaism, however, confronts us when we examine the diverse positions concerning a common agenda of topics set forth various Judaic writings. If we ask Philo, the Essenes of Qumran, Josephus, and authors of diverse extant writings—apocalyptic, pseudepigraphic, for instance—of the first centuries B.C. and A.D. to define for us what they mean by the shared categories, e.g., "God," "Torah," and "Israel," each document, whether standing for an individual or an entire community, presents its own answers, and these conflict with those of all others. Since not all can be right, precisely what we mean by a systematic statement about Judaism as a single religion is hardly clear. Describing "the Judaism of Jesus," therefore proves exceedingly uncertain. That fact hardly surprises historians of earliest Christianity, who have to contend with a Jesus fully set forth in his life by the Evangelists as against a Jesus with no biography and only a few authoritative sayings defined by Paul; a Church governed by the Torah based in Jerusalem and a Church not governed by the Torah and free of locative authority altogether, among numerous contradictory allegations set forth by authoritative writings. Some, including this writer, have formulated matters in terms of a plurality of Judaic or Christian systems, hence speaking of "Judaisms" or "Christianities."

Four solutions to the broadly-acknowledged fact that various sources of Judaism conflict now circulate, of which the fourth forms the basis for the essays here. The first is the nominalist, seeing Judaism as the sum and substance of what diverse Jews said about this and that; the second is essentialist and harmonistic, seeing Judaism as the lowest common denominator of all evidences; the third is a theological definition, based upon a canonical selection of the writings that attest to the faith, all else dismissed as sectarian or heretical; and the fourth is historical-documentary. The first is represented by S. J. D. Cohen, whose *From the Maccabees to the Mishnah* (Library of Early Christianity. Philadephia, 1987: Westminster Press) gives us as many Judaisms as there were Jews; the third position is represented by the well-known names of George Foot Moore, Ephraim E. Urbach, and most currently E. P. Sanders essentialist-harmonistic approach, taken in his *Paul and Palestinian Judaism. A Comparison of Patterns of Religion.* (London: SCM Press, 1977. Pp. xviii+627), and the fourth by this writer, with the results now fully summarized in *Rabbinic Judaism: An Historical Introduction* (Minneapolis, 1996: Fortress Press).

Is there no Judaism that transcends the various Judaisms, e.g., represented by the prayers that people said in the synagogues? That is, in this same context, we have to ask ourselves about the interpretation, within the systemic approach, of the liturgy of the synagogue, so far as we have access to it. The brief reference to the problem of classifying the liturgy in relationship to Judaic religious systems requires amplification. The liturgical writings are not so readily classified as other bodies of writings that represent (a) Judaism. On the one hand, it is clear from rabbinic literature, the sages of ancient times took responsibility for the regulation of the liturgy, as they did of much else. But the same sources that portray sages as defining the wording of prayers and the conduct of synagogue life also indicate that the liturgy is broadly accepted and in no way representative of the sages in particular, on the one side, or the result of their authorship, on the other. The recitation of the Shema ("Hear O Israel, the Lord our God, the Lord is one") for example cannot be assigned to either the authorship or the sponsorship of the authorities who produced the Mishnah, but long antedates them. The Targums, or translations of Scriptures into the Aramaic vernacular that Jews in the Near and Middle East spoke, finally, are diverse at least one of them, that of Onqelos, cites the Mishnah and must be classified as rabbinic in origin and program; the classification of others is hardly so clear.

Therefore the generality of scholarship prefers to take account of the diverse character of the sources and the contradictions in both detail and in general that they yield by formulating our picture in the categories used here: various Judaisms or Judaic systems, the evidence of each to be examined in its own terms. That preference accounts for the character of both parts of this handbook on Judaism.

I got the idea for this book when pursuing research on Zoroastrianism in connection with my *Judaism and Zoroastrianism at the Dusk of Late Antiquity.*[2] Working in the substantial collection of Cambridge

---

[2] *Judaism and Zoroastrianism at the Dusk of Late Antiquity. How Two Ancient Faiths Wrote Down Their Great Traditions.* Atlanta, 1993: Scholars Press for South Florida Studies in the History of Judaism.

University Library, I looked in vain for basic, clear introductions to the history, literature, and religion of Zoroastrianism in antiquity. What I found was scattered, diffuse, and often not entirely clear. Few specialists in the field write with outsiders to the field in mind, and much that they produce is incoherent and subjective. Not only so, but interests of historians predominated, and only a few works on Zoroastrianism as a religion are to be found. Asking myself how matters would appear to scholars in fields adjacent to my own, I realized that, for the study of ancient Judaism too, there is need for an exercise in explanation to scholars in cognate areas now becoming aware of what they need to know concerning Judaic religious life. I turned to specialists on various problems to address colleagues in other fields, as well as lay readers. Their task is defined in a simple, practical way: to provide an entry to a rich and complex body of data, which bears important points of relevance to the study of religion in general, and religion in antiquity, in particular. When I proposed to E. J. Brill a volume to explain precisely what sources tell us about ancient Judaism and how scholars have formed of those sources a clear account of that Judaism, I found a positive response. The ready collaboration of some of the best scholars at work today underlined the widespread recognition that a book such as this would serve a useful purpose.

I express my continuing thanks to the University of South Florida for providing ideal conditions—including a generous research expense fund—in which to pursue my research, and to my colleagues in the Department of Religious Studies and in other departments for their collegiality. They show me the true meaning of honesty, generosity, and sincerity. In the long, prior chapter in my career, now closed, I never knew such people of character and conscience. While a Visiting Fellow at Clare Hall, Cambridge, I planned this book with my editor at E. J. Brill, Elisabeth Erdman-Visser. I found her work professional and responsible. The humble facilities of that research center on the fringes of Cambridge conceal the wealth of spirit and intellect that flourish there; to the President and staff of Clare Hall and to the many friends and colleagues who accorded a warm welcome to my wife and myself, I express thanks. My thanks go, also, to the collaborators in this project, who minded deadlines and produced their best work for the book.

Jacob Neusner

MAJOR ISSUES IN THE STUDY AND UNDERSTANDING OF JEWISH MYSTICISM

Ithamar Gruenwald
(Tel Aviv University)

A

The modern study of Jewish mysticism is primarily connected with the name of Gershom Scholem (1897-1982). In his life-work,[1] Scholem laid the foundations of the historical-critical study of Jewish mysticism. Scholem saw himself principally a historian, and applied the historical-philological method or approach to his studies. Jewish mysticism was presented as one of the major factors in the history of religious ideas and events in Judaism. Scholem's interests were largely focused on historical events and thematic correspondences between ideas as manifested in the philological study of texts. Lesser emphasis is given to the personal activities and experiences of the mystics themselves. Even when their biographies became the centre of interest, that was a by-product of the general concern for historical issues rather than an actual attempt at penetrating the nature of the mystical mind and experience, subjects that should by no means be neglected in any comprehensive study of mysticism. When writing his great book on Sabbatai Zevi,[2] the false Jewish Messiah of the seventeenth century who allegedly was influenced by mystical ideas, Scholem's major interest was with the Sabbataean movement, its ideology and historical development. In this respect, the title of the book induces a wrong impression: It bears the name of the person, not of the movement.

In spite of the fact that criticism can be raised against certain points in Scholem's work,[3] it must be admitted that his work still serves as a major scholarly tool and solid point of departure for all scholars in the field. There is nothing but great admiration that can

---

[1] A comprensive bibliography of Scholem's writings was published on the occasion of his eightieth birthday: *Bibliography of the writings of Gershom G. Scholem*, Magnes Press: Jerusalem, 1977. A few more writings were added till his death in 1982. Some of his writings were published posthumously, and there are plans to publish more of them in the future.

[2] See G. G. Scholem, *Sabbatai Sevi: The Mystical Messiah*, E.T. by R.J. Zwi Werblowsky, Bollingen Series XCIII, Princeton Univ. Press: Princeton, 1973.

[3] See the discussion below.

go with the voluminous output of a scholar who has substantially
transformed the science of Judaism in the twentieth century. Notwithstanding this acknowledgment, it must be admitted, too, that
an increasing sense of critical dissatisfaction with some of the results
of Scholem's research, even of his methodological and historiosophical presuppositions, slowly finds its way into academic circles.[4]
In fact, a major shift in the methodological approach in the study of
Jewish mysticism is already well under way. It has become evident
to the scholarly community that with new perspectives and directions in mind, other centres of interest will be opened and new
modes of thinking will develop in the study of Jewish mysticism.
Scholarly perspectives are vital factors in turning attention to matters that deserve study and exploration.[5] Scholarly directions, however, are mainly a matter of applying principles of organizing information in a manner that bestows a sense meaningful coherency on
the subjects under study.

Scholem was certainly right when recognizing the fact that any
conclusion reached in regard to the various trends of Jewish mysticism has significant implications for the study and understanding of
Judaism at large. Consequently, any change of perspectives and
directions in the study of Jewish mysticism will naturally result in
correspondingly establishing new perspectives and directions in the
study of Judaism. In this respect, Scholem contributed more than
anyone else to redeeming Qabbalah, and Jewish mysticism in general, from the status of heresy that was so often attached to it,
particularly in Jewish orthodox circles. As a result of Scholem's
research and strong historiosophical positions, Mysticism, at large,
could once again be viewed as an integral part of Jewish religiousness. As indicated above, however, Scholem was inclined to view
Jewish mysticism as part of an esoteric enclave within Judaism. This
view can now undergo substantial changes. It is, therefore, conceivable that our new understanding of Jewish mysticism will eventually
result in a new assessment of our knowledge and understanding of
Judaism at large.

In the framework of this newly developing orientation, it is expected that greater attention will be given to matters relating to

---

[4] Recently, that criticism has been linked to the the name of the Israeli scholar
Moshe Idel, but he is certainly not the first and the only one that criticized
Scholem's work. In fact, another Israeli scholar, the late Isaiah Tishby, was one of
the most outspoken critics of some of Scholem's conclusions. My own criticism will
be mentioned in due course; and in so far as it was previously published, the
necessary bibliographical details will be given when necessary.

[5] See M. Idel, *Kabbalah: New Perspectives*, Yale Univ. Press: New Haven and
London, 1988.

mystical experience and practice. The greater attention given to the more "personal" issues in the study of mysticism will focus our attention in the direction now commonly referred to as "religious spirituality," that is, those components in religion that reflect and activate the spiritual life of people. In this respect, too, it now becomes evident that the separation between mysticism and other forms of Jewish religiousness and spirituality was in reality not as definitive and binding as it was considered to be by scholars in the past. It was common to speak about esoteric and exoteric forms of religiosity, that is, about open and public *versus* secret and sectarian social and ideological configurations in the Jewish world.[6] Admittedly, esotericism flourishes in separatist movements, and in as much as these movements intensified their religious activities by seeking extraordinary psychical experiences, mysticism may well be said to be connected with esotericism.[7] In addition, several of the major mystical treatises in Judaism contain directions to the readers to keep secret the information contained in these books.[8]

What matters most in our eyes, however, is the fact that there is a clear mystical, or spirituality enhancing component, in Jewish religiousness, as such. That component should not be viewed only as a split-enhancing factor. There were indeed times, about which more will be said later on, in which major splits occurred within the world of Judaism in connections with mystical and other extreme forms of spirituality. But there were also times of convergence and cultural fusion between the various, sometimes conflicting, cultural components. In other words, we consider it an overstatement when people argue that mysticism and other forms of spirituality are universally amounting to social fractionizing and ideological separatism.[9]

In other words, it can well be said that the study of Jewish religiousness and mysticism is undergoing serious transformation.[10]

---

[6] In one way or another my own discussion of the theory of esotericism was influenced by the same trend. See I. Gruenwald, *Apocalyptic and Merkavah Mysticism*, Brill: Leiden and Koeln, 1980, pp. 3-28.

[7] In fact, it was quite common to speak, interchangeably, of esotericism and mysticism. The two terms are very often used synonymously. See, M. de Certeau, *The Mystic Fable*, Vol. I: "The Sixteenth and Seventeenth Centuries", University of Chicago Press: Chicago and London, 1992, pp. 94 *seq.*: "'Mystical' as the Adjective of a Secret".

[8] Here *Daniel* xii:4 can serve as a model-formulation of that principle: "But you, Daniel, shut up the words, and seal the book, until the time of the end...." [RSV].

[9] See S. E. Ozment, *Mysticism and Dissent*, Yale Univ. Press: New Haven and London, 1973.

[10] There are several publications in press now which will exemplify and underline this statement.

Another important issue which is affected, in this respect, is the assessment of the place Halakhah used to occupy in the Jewish world. It can now be safely said that the "orthodox" view, according to which Halakhah is the major and dominant feature in Judaism, can no longer be sustained. In one way or another, Scholem himself was advancing ideas which were pointing in the same direction. In the eyes of several of his readers this implied his intellectual preference for a secular type of Judaism. But Scholem himself, in a series of lectures and interviews, emphasized the vital place Halakhah used to, and must, play in Jewish life.[11] He evidently was not, however, singularly fascinated with the type of Judaism represented by the *Shulhan Arukh*, the most widely accepted Code of Jewish Law.

It should be noted, however, that the *Shulhan Arukh* was composed by Rabbi Yosef Karo (1488-1575), a famous Talmudic scholar *and* mystic, who lived in Safed.[12] In this respect, he is a significant example to the fact that Halakhah and mysticism cannot so easily be separated from one another as some orthodox Halakhists, and for that matter even some secularly oriented scholars, would wish. We can also mention here the early Tannaim, the first Mishnah sages, who were deeply involved in the mystical speculations about the Merkavah. In fact, four generations of such scholars, from Rabban Yohanan ben Zakkai to Rabbi Aqiva, are listed in Talmudic sources as carrying on the Merkavah tradition from master to student.[13]

Scholem's scholarly and historiosophical positions were based on his own life-experience and upon some cultural trends in the Jewish world in the last three hundred years. Being one of the strongest exponents of a liberal, secular line in modern Judaism (alias, Zionism), Scholem was inclined to fight Jewish traditional orthodoxy for its lack of concern for the *res mysticae*.[14] Scholem had a bitter fight

---

[11] For that see the selected essays by G. Scholem, *On Jews and Judaism in Crisis*, Schocken Books: New York, 1976.

[12] See R.J.Z. Werblowsky, *Joseph Karo: Lawyer and Mystic*, Jewish Publication Society: Philadelphia, 1977.

[13] See I. Gruenwald, *Op. Cit.*, pp. 73-97.

[14] Scholem's views on these issues were variously discussed in recent years. See particularly D. Biale, *Gershom Scholem: Kabbalah and Counter-History*, Harvard Univ. Press: Cambridge, MASS. and London, 1982. See further, R. Alter, *Necessary Angels: Tradition and Modernity in Kafka, Benjamin and Scholem*, Harvard Univ. Press: Cambridge, MASS., 1991. There are a few discussions of these issues written in Hebrew, but we shall limit ourselves here, as much as we can, to publications in English.

on two fronts: the above mentioned orthodox view and the tendency of the nineteenth century scholars of the Wissenschaft des
Judenthums (Heinrich Graetz being one of their most formidable
exponents) to discard mysticism as the dark face of Judaism.
Scholem was certainly right in criticizing the arguments brought
forward by these nineteenth century scholars. As we have just observed, the picture was neither as dark, nor as one-sided as it appears when viewed in a polemical context. Paradoxically speaking,
since Scholem's name is also associated with the characterization of
Judaism in terms of the separation between its exoteric and esoteric
phases, he may in an indirect way be associated with the view that
esotericism occupies the reverse side of the cultural palette, with all
the implications that such a view carries. However, in maintaining
larger terms of reference than allowed by Scholem for the study of
Jewish mysticism, one is likely to gain more clarity and precision of
observation, and hence reach less rigid conclusions in regard to the
overall nature of Judaism and its mystical inclinations.

Furthermore, Scholem also proceeded from a point of departure
that assumed the incomparable nature of Jewish mysticism. Admittedly, every spiritual phenomenon must be studied *sui generis*, that is,
within its own frame of references. If one wishes to address an
international community of scholars, however, greater efforts than
those hitherto made, must be accomplished. An ongoing and open
dialogue between researchers in the same field is one of the major
goals of academic research. In this regard, Scholem placed the
study of Jewish mysticism on a shelf on which it was not immediately accessible to non-Jewish students of mysticism.

Scholars of Jewish Studies, or Judaic Studies, in the twentieth
century have all too often placed themselves at a place where an
international community of scholars find it difficult to carry out an
exchange of views and ideas. With few exceptions, this is also true
of studies in the area of Jewish Mysticism, which as a matter of
general rule, neither display the necessary efforts at arousing international interest nor stimulate comparative work. Jewish mysticism
is by all standards a very rich and illuminating point of comparison,
particularly to those engaged in the study of its Christian kin and
counterpart. It is therefore to be deplored that too little of the
intrinsic nature of Jewish mysticism has been made available by
non-Jewish scholars.

It has yet to be asked why the famous Eranos-lectures which
Scholem used to give, and which were initially addressed to a wider
intellectual audience than scholars of Judaism, did not succeed in

having the expected impact on the scholarly world.[15] Was the subject matter of those lectures too specialized and threatening in the
eyes of people who, for various reasons, preferred to maintain their
image of Judaism as a legalistically oriented religion in which mysticism had no place? Indeed, instead of using the Jewish perspective as a natural point of comparison in the study of [Christian or
Western forms of] mysticism, many scholars have gone to places as
far off as India and Japan for their points of reference and orientation. In many cases that move involves great methodological and
contextual problems which are somehow ignored by the scholars in
question. We shall return to this point later on.

The present study aims at presenting the Jewish material in a
comparative framework that, hopefully, will make several aspects of
Jewish mysticism more available to non-Jewish scholars than in the
past. We hope that in doing so, the intellectual gains will be worth
the price of avoiding detailed discussions of points that deserve
more attention and greater depth of investigation than are given to
them here. The various aspects and trends in Jewish mysticism are
very rich in factual material and spiritual contents.[16] No justice can
be done to a religious phenomenon that is contained in hundreds of
books and in thousands of manuscripts, many of which are still
unpublished, in a short survey the nature of which is dictated by
limited space and the desire to address as wide an audience as
possible.

There is hardly any aspect of Jewish religiousness that is not in
one way or another touched upon by mystical writings and addressed in a mystical manner. A full realization of the multi-faceted
contributions of Jewish mysticism to the world of Jewish religiousness will involve many years of study. For, the study of Judaism at
large, in light of the various cross-references that exist between its
mystical and non-mystical manifestations, will involve a re-exami-
nation and a new study of all sources at our disposal. It will be eye-
opening in every aspect possible and will radically change not only
our understanding of Judaism but also of Jewish mysticism. Among
other things to be accomplished in this new study of Judaism is the
inevitable elimination of the commonly held view that there always
was a clear cut distinction between the exoteric types of Jewish
religiousness and its esoteric counterparts. When viewed on a large

---

[15] These lectures were published in a number of volumes. See particularly G.
Scholem, *On the Kabbalah and its Symbolism*, Schocken Books: New York, 1965.
[16] In this respect G. Scholem's *Major Trends in Jewish Mysticism*, first published in
1941, is still an undisputed classic of its kind.

scale, this distinction will in all likelihood turn out to be one of the great fictions of the modern scholarly mind. We have already mentioned this fact above and we shall return to it later on. We do consider it important, however, to mention it as emphatically as we can so as to give the reader a clear notion of perspectives and directions which set the overall nature of the present study.

B

It is only natural to expect of a study discussing the general characteristics of Jewish mysticism to begin with a general definition of mysticism, and then qualify its specifically Jewish character. As many who are basically informed about mysticism and its scholarly discussion know, however, it is indeed very difficult to satisfactorily fulfill that expectation. Mysticism is a label which is easily attached to a variety of religious experiences and doctrines; and, apart from giving them all one and the same label, it is rather difficult to come up with one comprehensive and definitive characterization that will do justice to each of them. The same holds specifically true of Jewish mysticism. It houses many trends, forms of experience, doctrines, and notions; and there is hardly one unifying factor which ties all of them coherently together.

For the sake of a very general orientation, however, we would here suggest viewing mysticism as the diversified forms of direct realizations of divine presences, whether on earth or in heavenly domains.[17] In the course of such realizations, or as a result, substantial changes of human consciousness are likely to occur. Such changes or transformations are often viewed as the ultimate condition for those realizations. Without entering a state of ecstasy, so a common and widespread belief has it, no mystical experience can be fully realized. In many cases people envision themselves as being overcome (or technically speaking, "possessed') by something which they can hardly account for, and as a result of which they believe unusual things happen to them. In other cases, people would report that they experienced something that in normal religious life is conceived of as ideas or notions.[18] It is, indeed, one thing to speak about God and the love of God (=theology), and another one to

---

[17] In this we follow the characterization of [Christian] mysticism as suggested by B. McGinn, *The Presence of God: A History of Western Christian Mysticism*, Vol. I: *The Foundations of Mysticism*, Crossroad: New York, 1991.

[18] Here the discussion in Lectures XVI and XVII ("Mysticism") of W. James, *The Varieties of Religious Experience*, first published in 1902, is still relevant.

experience His presence and to be able to show one's love to Him in a most intensive manner (=mysticism).[19] In this respect, mysticism may be described as a live realization of theological notions or entities.

What makes the definition, or the overall characterization, of mysticism such a difficult task is the fact that every religion has its own particular types of mystical realizations. It has been argued with some justice that mystical experiences are embedded in the basic notions of the particular religion in which they occur.[20] What makes the mystical experience so unique in this respect is the conscious desire on the mystic's part to either restore previous—mostly scriptural—states of theophany or go beyond ordinary realms of religious experience as maintained under normal conditions, whether personal or historical. Mysticism, more than just telling something about the nature of a specific religion, tells about what that religion normally fails to accomplish for those who desire to live their religious lives in modes that transcend the ordinary ones. Mysticism penetrates beyond the world of ordinary religious phenomena and practice. In many cases it even utterly changes the commonly accepted surface-structure of religious experience. In other cases, mysticism is likely to transform, from its roots up, everything that looks democratically established and organized in the world of religion.

One example is the fact that, although the notion of union with the figure of the Christ is a dogmatic issue in Christianity, its actual mystical realization on an intensively personal level was quite often viewed as breaking established norms and rules of the Church. This by no means is a scholarly observation only, but something about which the relevant pages of Church history tell long stories. Many mystics found themselves excommunicated by the Church and their writings put on the *Index*, if not actually burned. On the Jewish side of the story we find that mystical ideas and notions very often replaced previously accepted attitudes to the written word of Scripture. The plain sense of Scripture is dispensed with in Jewish mysticism, and a variety of secret, or esoteric, meanings is introduced by way of so-to-speak interpreting it. In doing so, Jewish mysticism, or Qabbalah as its medieval and post-medieval manifestations are called, creates a situation in which the word of God is so-to-speak

---

[19] See, B. McGinn, "The Language of Love in Christian and Jewish Mysticism", in: S.T. Katz (ed.), *Mysticism and Language*, Oxford Univ. Press: New York and Oxford, 1992, pp. 202-235.
[20] See S.T. Katz (ed.), *Mysticism and Religious Traditions*, Oxford Univ. Press: Oxford, 1983. Katz's own position on the subject will be discussed below.

forced to undergo substantial and radical changes. Needless to say, such radical transformations of meaning were sufficient cause for tension and strife. In this respect, Jewish history, too, wrote its unique pages of sharply-pointed polemics against the Qabbalah. And there were unpleasant moments at which excommunication and burning of books were the inevitable results of a fierce power game.[21]

As a matter of common practice, mysticism is associated with visions and auditions. Mystics are said to enjoy all kinds of supernatural experiences. Meditation, contemplation, and to a significant extent even possession by spirits and speaking in tongues are credited with being important manifestations of mystical experience. It is less common, though, to associate mysticism with interpretative activities in the course of which mystics believe that God and the celestial world can be revealed to them in a variety of ways. It should be recognized, however, that mystics are very much inclined to meditate on Scriptural texts (the *Song of Songs* is one famous example),[22] and to develop in the course of those meditations spiritual stances that are unique in their essence and nature. In this respect, *lectio divina* is one preliminary stage of a mystically oriented contemplative reading of Scripture. Those who read mystical writings, which are interpretations of Scripture, in a cursory manner are likely not to discover the presence of active mystical experiences in those writings. Consequently, there exist views held in relation to Qabbalah according to which it is not a fully developed kind of mysticism. We need not go into the details of such views here. M. Idel has collected interesting material that amply illustrates the use of mystical techniques in relation to the study of sacred texts.[23] Consequently, the one-sided emphasis on the speculative elements in Qabbalah, and—complementarily—the arbitrary neglecting of the experiential components in it must give way to a new way of

---

[21] There was a fierce controversy over the *Zohar*, the major mystical text of the Qabbalah, in Italy of the sixteenth century. I. Tishby published an extensive article (in Hebrew) on that chapter in the history of the Qabbalah. See his *Studies in Kabbalah and its Branches: Researches and Sources*, Vol. I, Magnes Press: Jerusalem, 1982, pp. 79-130.

[22] In this respect Jews and Christians seem to have shared the same tradition. See, E.E. Urbach, "The Homiletical Interpretations of the Sages and the Expositions of Origen on Canticles and the Jewish-Christian Disputation", *Scripta Hierosolymitana*, Vol. XXII (1971), pp. 247-275. See further D.J. Halperin, *The Faces of the Chariot*, Mohr (P. Siebeck): Tuebingen, 1988, pp. 322-358.

[23] See, *Kabbalah: New Perspectives*, passim; *Studies in Ecstatic Kabbalah*, SUNY: Albany, 1988; *The Mystical Experience in Abraham Abulafia*, SUNY: Albany, 1988.

treating those issues. This will evidently result in the characterization of the mystical qualities of Qabbalah in a new way. We would
like to repeat that the more experiential aspects of Qabbalah should
be evaluated on the same level of significance as the doctrinal ones.
In order to achieve this, however, one must sometimes go beyond
the surface of the words used by the mystics and find the code
which gives access to the layers of mystical experience that are not
always as explicitly described as one would wish them to be. This is
particularly true when it comes to the treating of the Qabbalists'
interpretative oeuvre.

There is one caveat, however, that needs be taken into consideration at this point. Those engaged in the comparative study of
mysticism should become aware of the fact that there is no word in
Hebrew for mysticism. Jewish mystics could call themselves by any
name but that of mystics! "Qabbalah" means "reception," or technically speaking, oral religious tradition. Qabbalah is the major
mystical movement of the Jews. Its first major manifestations can be
located in Southern France and in Spain and dated in the thir-
teenth century; since then it developed in various ways and took
many directions.[24] Thus the Merkavah mystics of Talmudic times
(2nd to 6th centuries of the C.E.) who practiced an intensive type of
experiential mysticism cannot be included, historically speaking, in
the rubric of Qabbalah. In their activities, those mystics preceded
the Qabbalah, and they represent a completely different type of
mysticism than that of the Qabbalah. Some essential qualities of
this mysticism will be highlighted later on. We may still mention the
fact that the turning point in the history of Jewish mysticism is *Sefer
Yezirah* ("The Book of Formation\Creation"), the date of which can
be fixed only in a general manner, and not later than the ninth
century C.E. In inaugurating the Sephirot-terminology, *Sefer Yezirah*
opened a new era in Jewish mysticism. When people came back,
later on, to the Merkavah-terminology, they more often than not
did so by harmonizing the two kinds of terminology.

C

It is a question of a different order whether mystical experiences as
such can be properly assessed by people who do not possess the

---

[24] See, G. Scholem, *Origins of the Kabbalah*, Jewish Publication Society: Princeton,
1987.

capacity or the willingness of sharing them.[25] These people may be referred to as the unintended or unimplied audience, i.e., people who are not addressed by the documents in question or see themselves reluctant to share them. Moreover, not every person that believes in the possibility of divine interaction with human beings is also able, or ready, to become part of those events. The very awareness, however, of the possibility or the mere existence of such an interaction is almost a *sine qua non* for the understanding of the mystical realms, or dimensions in religion. We say this, since the language used by mystics can look like sheer gibberish in the eyes of people approaching the texts in question from a distance or a point of spiritual alienation. The more "mystical" the text is the more inaccessible and idiosyncratic it becomes, both in terms of its forms of expression and the essence of its contents. In some cases of Jewish mystical expression, mostly prayers, the page is filled with letters and signs which, practically speaking, make no sense to the outsider. There is also a special script which mystics and magicians shared in antiquity. More than just intellectual empathy is required here on the part of the reader or student.[26]

One reason for this rather annoying state of affairs is that, paradoxically speaking, mystics communicate in a manner which makes their modes of communication a matter of deciphering codes. If mystics are at all inclined to give expression to their uneasiness about the nature of their own experiences, this happens in many cases, when they are so-to-speak disturbed by their own inability of fully accounting for the unique nature of those experiences. To use a famous example, Paul was not sure whether his vision(s) had happened "in the body or out of the body" (*2 Cor.* 12:2-3). In other words, Paul was not sure whether his experience(s) had been phys-

---

[25] In the following pages I take issue with several positions which are differently outlined in the three collections of papers edited by S.T. Katz: (1) *Mysticism and Philosophical Analysis*; (2) *Mysticism and Religious traditions*; (3) *Mysticism and Language*; Oxford Univ. Press: New York and Oxford, 1978, 1983, 1992, respectively. It would be too tedious for the reader to check references and follow detailed debates with individual scholars whose papers are included in those three volumes. However, points of agreement as also of divergence will be easily recognized by those familiar with the subject matter.

[26] In this respect, it would be of great interest to study Qabbalistic iconography and pictorial imagery. There is very little done on these subjects in modern scholarship, and the whole area awaits scholarly attention. In this context mention should be made of the fact that another desideratum in the area is a close study of the way Qabbalists, or people who worked on their behalf, depicted the "tree" of the Sephirot. Moshe Idel has informed me that he collected a lot of material, mostly derived from manuscripts, and that he intends publishing it in the near future.

ical or spiritual ones. To begin with, one of the most tantalizing
questions in the area of apocalypticism and mysticism (and prior to
that in Prophecy) whether the people who experienced visions and
other kinds of supernatural phenomena did so as a matter of physical reality or merely as part of an inner, dreamlike vision or hallu-
cinatory event. As indicated above, no conclusive answer can be
given to that question. But what is of even greater interest in this
respect is the question of whether we could have imagined that Paul
was writing out of some kind of mystical experience, unless he said
so himself? I consider it as highly inconceivable that we would have
done so.[27]

It is indeed interesting to notice that mystics too were bothered
by such questions. In fact, there is a rather astonishing variety of
problems that relate to the inner perspectives from which visionaries view their own experiences. Mystics, like St. John of the Cross,
would torture themselves with endless deliberations on account of
the indeterminate nature of the source of their visions. Some mystics would waste much psychic and intellectual energy on such
questions as whether their visions have a divine or a diabolic origin.
To be true, no mystic should feel himself exempt from the need to
ask himself such questions. The first who must trust the mystics in
their visions and auditions are the mystics themselves. Understand-
ably, this cannot be accomplished unless an process of relentless
introspection occurs. This in no way is a sign of mental queasiness,
but a token of salutary staunchness.

In another context, we find Rabbi Aqiva admonishing his colleagues not to call out "There is Water, There is Water," when
approaching the heavenly marble stones (*Bav. Hagigah*, 15/b).[28] In
fact, one of the major ordeals of the Merkavah mystics was connected with a test of nerves. When those mystics stood at the gate of

---

[27] See, A. Schweitzer, *The Mysticism of Paul the Apostle*, London, 1953. It should
be noticed, though, that Schweitzer's book is mainly dealing with theological issues. In fact, it is a book on the theology and Christology of Paul's writings. It is
noteworthy, too, that in Bernard McGinn's discussion of the subject, only a few
pages are devoted to "Pauline Writings". See, *Op. Cit.*, pp. 69-74. See now C.R.A.
Morray-Jones, "Paradise Revisited (2 Cor. 12: 1-12): The Jewish Mystical Background of Paul's Apostolate", *Harvard Theological Review*, Vol. LXXXVI (1993), pp.
177-217; 265-292.

[28] This passage has given rise to endless debates in modern scholarship on the
nature of the mystical experience of the Mishnaic or Talmudic sages. Basically,
two positions have been taken on that issue: (1) The sages were aware of the
material incorporated in the Hekhalot writings, and actually influenced by it; (2)
The kind of mysticism of which we learn in the rabbinic writings is of a completely
different nature than the one of the Hekhalot tractates. In any event, this is a
passage that comes very close to the Hekhalot material, and cannot be explained
away as being metaphorical in nature.

the sixth heavenly palace, they were asked what they saw. Looking at the glistening marble stones, they had to resist the temptation of crying out: "There is Water, There is Water!" When they failed the test and did cry out the forbidden words, however, they were inflicted with a rush of waters threatening to devour them.

Although mystics were inclined to ask questions relating to the validity of their visions, as indicated above, their way of questioning should not be confused with that of the skeptical critic. While the skeptical critic would give expression to doubts as to the real occurrence of what mystics describe, no mystics would say that they did not experience their vision(s). Again, mystics cannot be deprived of their respective experiences. What they would insist on verifying is the divine nature and origin of those experiences. At the other end of the spectrum, the skeptic would relentlessly argue against the validity of the mystical "narrative," as such. But mystics should not be worried by that, nor should those who study their writings do so.

D

As indicated above, mysticism consists of live experiences of what, in the eyes of many religious people, are only conceptual entities. However, it often so happens that the realization of the divine presence actually crystallizes in conceptual, intellectual, realms.[29] The people who think that mystical experiences necessarily evolve in what may be described as emotional—rather than conceptual—realms may find it difficult to follow this line of argumentation.[30] In a general sense, distinctions between mystical and conceptual forms of realization make sense only when and where both entities are not viewed on the same level. When conceptual modes of intellection are preferred, some people would argue that this passes as a negative judgment on all forms of emotionalism. Rationalistic habits of evaluation apparently leave no room for something that is of a more emotional essence. Some would even go so far as maintaining that when mystical forms of expression are preferred, irrationality inevitably sets in. It must be admitted that material and psychic experiences are generally viewed as inferior to those described as intellectual, conceptual and ideational. Apart from being a key issue in philosophical phenomenology and epistemology, however, this is

---

[29] This is particularly true of the Qabbalah and its literary and conceptual offshoots.

[30] For a general background for the ensuing discussion and the various positions taken by philosophers and scholars on these questions see B. McGinn, *Op. Cit.*, pp. 291 ff.: "Philosophical Approaches to Mysticism".

not what is universally held as true and binding in mystical circles. Mystics would in all likelihood argue that psychic activity and experiences are not less valid for them than are those created in intellectual and conceptual frames of mind. Psychic activity is as real in their eyes as any other kind of human activity. Thus, mystical imagination, which may really take idiosyncratic forms, may not be less valid, epistemologically speaking, than other forms of intellection and expression.

Mystical realizations usually evolve in realms that may be described as extra-intellectual. Apart from the ones mentioned above, we can mention here those that evolve in the course of prayer, as a result of apocalyptic visions, and in the course of shamanistic experiences. Shamanism would involve a translocation of the human spirit to other (geographical) realms in order to obtain some kind of information on behalf of a group.[31] Ezekiel's travels in the spirit from Babylonia to Jerusalem and back would exemplify a shamanistic type of experience. A certain shamanistic element is also present in the heavenly trips of the apocalyptic visionaries and Merkavah mystics.[32] In relatively rare cases, however, does the mystical experience involve a sense of actual fusion with a divine being. Technically called "mystical union" this fusion is generally conceived of as the highest stage of mystical realization. We shall return to this point later on; at the moment suffice it to say that it is quite difficult to decide in each case whether a certain text actually entails a mystical union or not. Scholars are at variance among themselves as to how to evaluate the texts in question. Distrust is not always identical with intellectual skepticism. It is therefore a matter of good advice when told that when mystics speak of their experiences, we should at least give them the benefit of the doubt.

Since mystics are likely to use formalized types of expression, people may after all be justified in their hesitations concerning the virtual occurrence of what is described. It is indeed one thing to use the language of mystical exhortations and another one to experience something of real mystical nature. There are no clear cut criteria on the basis of which it can be decided which occurrence is which in this respect. In some cases, the detailed description of the

---

[31] This is the essence of M. Eliade's handling of the subject. See, M. Eliade, *Shamanism: Archaic Techniques of Ecstasy*, Bollingen Series LXXVI, Princeton Univ. Press: Princeton 1964.

[32] A discussion of the possible shamanistic qualities of apocalypticism and Merkavah mysticism can be found in I. Gruenwald, *From Apocalypticism to Gnosticism*, pp. 105ff.

mystical practice may induce the impression that those who pre-
scribe the means are also those who have experience to support
their words. But we should be aware of the fact that when texts
speak of desired experiences, the language used may reflect less
than is actually said. It is equally right to say that when mystics, like
so many other kinds of speculative thinkers, use the language of
actual experience, they mean what they say. Mystics are prone to
seeking modes of concretely realizing their notions about the divine. For that reason, as we said above, mystics deserve to be given
the benefit of the doubt.

This brings us to a point where once again a word must be said
about the nature of the mystical experience, particularly in its relationship to interpretation.[33] The questions have been raised in modern scholarship as to whether the mystical experience is at least
potentially identical with interpretation, or whether mystical experience, almost by definition, must be viewed as distinct from interpretation. As a rule, in the case of a diversified and multi-cultural
phenomenon as mysticism, room must be left for a rather large
range of categorizing options. There are cases in which one view
can be substantiated—some of these will be discussed below—and
there are cases in which that view can be rightly called into question. In any event, Jewish mysticism in the Middle Ages
(=Qabbalah) by and large evolved in a seemingly interpretative
context. As indicated above, however, interpretation-linked mysticism does not exclude the existence of other forms of mysticism in
which interpretation does not play a central role. We have already
mentioned that fact above, and we shall come back to it in a different context later on.

Another point to be considered at this juncture is that made by
S. Katz to the effect that religious mysticism is preconditioned by
previous cultural experiences and doctrines. According to S. Katz,
mysticism grows out of a previously shaped doctrinal framework.[34]
Admittedly, mysticism has to be viewed in the context of a given
and specific religious system.[35] However, its overall indebtedness to
previously formulated doctrines and beliefs should not be stretched

---

[33] The reader is here referred to the collection of essays by G. Scholem, *On the
Kabbalah and Its Symbolism*, Schocken Books: New York, 1965. In many of these
essays and studies, Scholems discusses in an eye-opening manner various points
that will be discussed in the following pages. My emphases, though, are slightly
different than those of Scholem.
[34] See, S.T. Katz, "The 'Conservative' Character of Mystical Experience", in:
S.T. Katz (ed.), *Mysticism and Religious Tradition*, pp. 3ff.
[35] This is a point made by G. Scholem, *Major Trends in Jewish Mysticism*, p. 6.

beyond factual limits. Many forms of mystical expression venture into new conceptual and experiential territories or take a marked critical stance over against traditional views and theological frameworks. In this respect, it may be safe to say that if tradition also means its criticism, then Katz's view can be sustained. When we see in criticism an act of disengaging a position from the grip of tradition, however, then at least a paradox must be tolerated in the study of mysticism. Thus, once again, in the study of mysticism—as also in other branches of knowledge—one should avoid postulating theories and positions that involve filling vessels to the point of overflowing.

E

Yet another point deserves consideration in the present context. It relates to the question whether the mystical quest necessarily involves a substantial transformation of human consciousness (usually referred to as ecstasy). If we maintain, regardless of the question raised above concerning the relationship of the mystical experience to previous cultural models and patterns, that many of the mystical experiences known to us in one way or another try to relive scriptural modes of theophany, even when substantially deviating from them, then the following question comes to mind: Can it be argued that those original theophanies already entailed such changes of human consciousness, or do those changes happen only on the rather late mystical level? The answer to this question is not an easy one for two reasons: (1) There is very little in the nature of the autobiographical self-exposure in the writings of the scriptural figures whose utterances we study in this context. Although there are scattered pieces of information which can give us a fair cumulative picture of the various types of prophetic experiences, there are many prophets about whom nothing is said by way of exposing the nature of their respective experiences; (2) Mystics are notorious for their reluctance to speak about their experiences. These two reasons, when put together, render any potential comparison between mystical experiences and notions on a rather speculative level. Consequently, it is also too risky to make generalizations regarding the nature of the mystical experience. Some mystics may indeed have had experiences in which ontological changes of consciousness came over them; in the cases of other mystics this must not necessarily hold true.

When it comes to mystics active outside of the Jewish-Christian-Islamic triangle, matters become even more complicated. Eastern and other mystics are hardly aware of the need to terminologically align their perceptions and experiential descriptions with those known to mystics and scholars in the West. However, too many scholars believe that the language commonly used in Eastern religions is very close to mystical forms of speech known from the so-called Western religions. The religious mentality of the East (Buddhism and Shintoism, being only two of the more familiar examples) is so different from anything known to us in the West that comparisons really run the risk of falling into the traps of redundancy.[36] We are often warned, when told of the religions of the East, that the term "religion" does not apply to those systems. Consequently, any talk about the so-called *mysticism* of the East should be taken with due mental reservation.

It is very common to find people who think that one can easily identify modes of mystical expression in contexts that we would not generally associate with mysticism. Thus Timothy Leary, who used to advocate the use of hallucinogenic drugs such as psilocybin (the chemical derivative of a certain type of mushroom, often qualified as "sacred"), spoke of ecstatic experiences that he considered to be "closer to the mystics than to the theologians".[37] People with mystical inclinations would generally agree with the statement that in order to achieve higher, or trans-subjective, states of cognition one must expect, and even strive to attain, ontological transformations of consciousness. If we ask ourselves, however, what kind of such transformations one must expect or presuppose when mystical awareness is connected with the so-called mystical interpretation of Scripture, the answer can only be a rather evasive one. We know for instance that among the Qumran sectarians there prevailed a belief that their interpretation of Scripture, particularly in its eschatological dimensions, was helped along by some kind of divine revelation. We shall later on see how mystical interpretations of Scripture can be realized in connection with, or in the framework of, some kind of ontological transformation of human consciousness.

Indeed, it is not unusual to find in all kinds of esoteric and mystical writings statements to the effect that they were divinely

---

[36] In my opinion too many modern scholars engage in those comparative studies. R. Otto was one of the first that ventured into those distant territories. It sometimes appears that the sheet that is spread in his *Mysticism East and West* is too small to cover all areas of comparison.

[37] See T. Leary, *The Politics of Ecstasy*, Paladin: St. Albans, Herts, 1973, p. 15. For a serious and academic approach to the question of mysticism and drugs, see, F. Staal, *Exploring Mysticism*, University of California Press: Berkeley...,1975.

inspired. People looking for an ultimate justification for their rather idiosyncratic modes of writing and ideas would have no second thoughts about superscribing their utterances with divine labels. Modern critical scholars would evidently argue that several books in the Hebrew Scriptures actually profess a status of divine inspiration whereas, in reality, they are products of anonymous writers. In this respect, Jewish apocalypticism of Second Temple times, which fictitiously attributes books and revelations to biblical figures, does not exhibit a novelty of literary genre. The technique is known by the term "Pseudepigraphy" which with many people implies a token of criticism. So-called insiders, however, saw nothing wrong in the practice, and thus it was widely in use even among Qabbalists. For instance, the concluding paragraph of *Sefer Yezirah* ends with a statement tracing its lineage to Abraham, the Patriarch. Pseudepigraphy is not limited to scriptural figures. The *Zohar*, for instance, was attributed to Rabbi Shim'on bar Yohai, one of the Tannaitic followers of Rabbi 'Aqiva, who lived in the second century C.E. With all its voluminous, multi-layered material, this book contains almost no information about the actual identity of the people who took part in its composition and about their mystical states of mind. Recently, attempts have been made to put the finger on the biographical, or historical, identity of those people as a group, and this beyond the commonly accepted theory that Rabbi Moshe Di-Leon wrote the major parts of the *Zohar*.[38] What stands clear is the fact that, phenomenologically speaking, mystical experiences recorded in absolute anonymity and presented in the literary form of pseudepigraphy, should feel no constraints or inhibitions in relation to the subject matter and its manner of presentation. And if any kind of information about those books is assumed, it must be accepted as bookish, and for that matter, also categorized as untargeted and inconclusive.

Needless to say, the mystical type of experience is an intensively personal one, and the fact that many aspects of Jewish mysticism are presented to the reader in an absolutely depersonalized manner constitutes one of its most peculiar characteristics. This fact holds true in relation to the apocalyptic visionaries, the Hekhalot writings, *Sefer Yezirah*, *Sefer Ha-Bahir*, *Sefer Ha-Zohar*, and some other books that constitute most important phases of medieval Jewish mysticism. Matters significantly change in this respect, when we

---

[38] See, Y. Liebes, *Studies in the Zohar*, SUNY Press: Albany, 1993, pp. 85-138.

come to the writings of Abraham Abulafia, the various members of
the Lurianic circle in Safed and the Hasidic sages in East Europe in
the eighteenth century. Here we find more identifiable and person-
alized forms of expression. However, they cannot change the general impression one gets to the effect that essential phases of Jewish
mysticism are shrouded in mystery and obscurity; in this respect,
they give no hope for clarity and informative validity.

F

It must be clear by now that we consider it vital for the discussion
of our subject to present it in as wide a context as possible. In this
respect, comparative considerations of the various epistemological
and phenomenological problems involved in the presentation of our
subject matter seem to us to be of great importance. Comparative
ways of study are in themselves divided into multi-cultural and
mono-cultural phenomena. "Multi-cultural" here qualifies comparable phenomena that are present in a number of cultures, while
"mono-cultural" here qualifies comparable phenomena in the same
cultural context. We consider both cultural perspectives to be of
relevance to the discussion of Jewish mysticism, since they are instrumental in bringing about a substantial reorientation in its study.
Although the study of Jewish mysticism is in the first place an-
chored in the study of Judaism and should be understood in a
mainly Judaic context, it is equally important to realize the relevancy of non-Judaic, that is, multi-cultural, perspectives to the
study of Jewish mysticism. As we argued above, this observation
should be complemented by another one: Jewish mysticism is relevant to the study on non-Jewish forms of mysticism. All this has
recently been demonstrated in an admirable way by Bernard
McGinn who opened his, above-mentioned, historical survey of
Christian mysticism with a chapter on "The Jewish Matrix" of
Christian mysticism. In our eyes the term "matrix" is a considerably valuative one, and for that matter it makes a stronger case
than another term that could suggest itself in the same context,
namely, "background". Contextual affiliations can be described in
many ways: Those that emphasize the generic, even "maternal"
(i.e., "matrix'), aspects of those affiliations make more emphatic
claims than those stating the mere circumstantial ones.
    What is likewise of great importance in this particular context of
our discussion is the fact that in fully realizing the presence of a
mystical component in a certain religion one is likely to change

one's way of looking at the very essence of that religion.[39] This fact holds true in the cases of Jewish Mysticism and Judaism, and its full acceptance in the community of scholars is likely to change basic assumptions prevalent in the general area of Jewish Studies. For all too many scholars still share the routine of ignoring the relevance which the study of Jewish mysticism may have for a full understanding of Jewish religious life and creativity. This holds true of academic areas such as Jewish History, Literature/Poetry, Law/Halakhah and Linguistics. To give one example out of the many, we would mention the study of Jewish religious poetry and liturgy. In these subjects there prevails an intentional suppression of any kind of scholarly interest in a serious and systematic study of the influence which Jewish mysticism had on the contents and nature of the liturgical poetry and the prayer book. The same holds true of other quarters of academic scholarship where the best that is done is paying formal lip service to the various subjects touching upon Jewish mysticism. Instead of showing serious interest in the relevant material and the bearing it has on a proper understanding of the various aspects of Jewish religiousness, its history and creative manifestations, scholars prefer to see in the mystical aspects of Judaism a side issue relevant for the understanding of isolated, elite circles only. It must be said in as clear and loud a voice as possible: modes of religious experience involving extraordinary states of consciousness—such as Prophecy, Apocalypticism and Mysticism—are as much a part of Jewish religiousness as are Theology and Law/Halakhah! Knowledge and study of them is as important as any other predominant feature in Jewish life, its intellectual world and religious predispositions.

What we have in mind here is not a simple recognition of a *de jure* status, but a virtual and resolute *de facto* recognition of the vital interaction between mystical and non-mystical forms of religious life. It has recently been shown how influential Qabbalistic ways of thinking were in Jewish everyday practice and Halakhah.[40] In re-

---

[39] In this respect we cannot join H.H. Penner, "The Mystical Illusion", in: S.T. Katz (ed.), *Mysticism and Religious Tradition*, pp. 89-116, who argues that in many religious systems mysticism does not constitute a separate entity.

[40] See, J. Katz, *Halakhah and Kabbalah* (in Hebrew), Magnes Press: Jerusalem, 1984. However, Katz who is a social-historian subtitles his book in the following manner: "Studies in the History of Jewish Religion, Its Various Faces and Social Relevance"! In other words, the title of the book is, from our point of view, two sizes too large considering the measures given in the subtitle. There are a few studies written by scholars of Jewish mysticism which take up the subject referred to in the title of Katz's book; however, we preferred to refer to that book because of its symptomatic position.

cent years it became clear, also, that even in medieval Jewish philosophy modes of mystical (non-Qabbalistic!) thinking and experience were a neatly integrated component. Thus, the example of
Maimonides (1134/5-1204) who is commonly identified with trends
of philosophical rationalism, shows a clear inclination toward mystical thinking.[41] This is particularly true of his characterization of
the peaks of the philosophical undertaking. Medieval Jewish philosophy is in this respect influenced by its Islamic counterpart
which, in turn, shows a clear Neoplatonic influence. What is of
particular interest here is the fact that those philosophers who
adapted the so-called Neoplatonic model saw the unification of the
Passive Intellect of man with the Active One of God as the afore-
mentioned peak. That unification can happen in the course of the
philosopher's life or as a special, so to speak eschatological, bonus
in his afterlife. What matters here is the fact that a mystical type of
language is used in our case, even though the "Active Intellect" of
God is only the tenth, and for that matter the lowest, of a series of
ten divine emanations. From that point of view, then, there is no
substantial difference between the goals of the *via philosophia* and
those of the *via mystica*.

G

This connection between philosophy and mysticism brings us back
to a point already discussed above, namely the relationship between
interpretation and mysticism. Since language is the most ready-at-
hand mode of thinking, and Hebrew allegedly is the language of
God in which Scripture is written, it is only natural that Jewish
mysticism would evolve in the framework of scriptural texts. In this
way, God Himself or His metaphysical essence, can most readily be
realized. We make this point here because, in the minds of many
Christian readers, mysticism is believed to evolve in other conceptual modes, such as pictorial imagination and emotional identification. As we saw, Christian mysticism is predominantly Christ-ori-
ented. In principle, the mystical identification with His figure does

---

[41] See, D.R. Blumenthal, "Maimonides: Prayer, Worship and Mysticism", in:
D.R. Blumenthal (ed.), *Approaches to Judaism in Medieval Times*, Vol. III, Scholars
Press: Atlanta, 1988 pp. 1-16. See also the contributions of Steven Harvey and
Ithamar Gruenwald in J. L. Kraemer (ed.), *Perspectives on Maimonides*, Oxford Univ.
Press: Oxford, 1991. I miss in Alfred L. Ivry's contribution to that volume the
Neoplatonic mystical-strain as pointed out, for instance, by Fazlur Rahman, *Proph-
ecy in Islam: Philosophy and Orthodoxy*, The University of Chicago Press: Chicago and
London, 1958.

not necessitate the presence of an actual text, although the details of Jesus' life derive from texts and are enacted mainly in the Eucharist. The passion story—which in Christian life, practice and theology figures as the culmination of the messianic way of life—principally unfolds in spiritual domains and not *in* texts. Although the Gospel stories unfold in texts, their actual wordings in the minutest details are not made to count in the same manner as do the various texts of the Hebrew scriptures in any Jewish mystical, or Qabbalisitc, context. For, as Nahmanides (1194-1270) argues in the Introduction to his Pentateuch Commentary, the Torah (the Pentateuch) is actually composed of a long sequence of divine names. These are not identifiable unless the *text* is transposed to another mode of consonantal readings. The knowledge of those readings is the (secret) art of the mystic. If the text itself is an embodiment of the divine essence, any mystical interaction between a human being and God conceivably unfolds in that realm. The text actually facilitates interaction with God who, on philosophical premises, is beyond human cognition. The scriptural text renders God in a mode that is cognitively accessible to man. The Christ figure, the object of mystical contemplation in Christianity, is never conceived in transcendental terms and, *per definitionem*, is always accessible to human perception and cognition. He may therefore become part of human cognition in as immediate a form as possible. Once again, what matters for the Christian mystic is the narrative, not its exact verbal configuration. A Christian mystic can read his "texts" in any language, while the Qabbalist is totally dependent on the Hebrew text in its minutest grammatical, syntactical, and verbal details.[42]

In conceiving of God in linguistic modes, one bypasses the risk of treating Him in a manner that many a traditional Jewish theologian and halakhist would view as dogmatic anathema. For, according to the view held by many a theologian and halakhist, any corporeal presentation and configuration of God is downright blasphemy. It would run counter to the second of the Ten Commandments, namely, that no pictorial images of God and of any other divine beings should be created by humans. Jewish mystics and visionaries, however, did not always take along that injunction on their mystical trips. Neither did they seriously consider God's words to Moses, to the effect that no human being can survive a facial

---

[42] I miss this comparative characterization in W.R. Inge, *Christian Mysticism,* Meridian Books: New York, 1956.

theophany (*Exodus* xxxiii: 20-23).[43] In Jewish apocalypticism and Merkavah mysticism, there exists an undisguised propensity to achieve visual experiences of God. The *Shi'ur Qomah* sections of the Hekhalot literature go to such conceptual extremes as measuring the various parts of the *Corpus Dei* and giving them mystical names!

As G. Scholem has rightly observed in his discussion of the *Shi'ur Qomah*, there are in Judaism two conflicting attitudes towards the corporeality of God: one that maintains a rather lax attitude towards the issues involved in that corporeality and another one that sees in any corporeal presentation or vision a matter of gross profanation. Some people would speak of the bodily appearances of God, while others would ostensibly avoid and even forbid doing so. This is already characteristic of biblical religiousness. It should be noted, too, that there are sections in the *Zohar* that engage in mystical speculations about the bodily appearances of God.[44] In one way or another, the linguistic characteristics of the *Shi'ur Qomah* speculations emerge time and again in the course of the historical and literary developments of Jewish mysticism. It must be admitted, however, that when this so happens, it is not always in relation to visual experiences, but as a form of organizing and systematizing mystical notions in the rather peculiar terminology of *Shi'ur Qomah*. Those who engage in these speculations in relation to scriptural texts, like the writer of the *Zohar*, that is, those who present their subject matter as an interpretative oeuvre, make it clear that they incline to formulate their notions within the limits of what scriptural texts would allegedly allow; however, this was not always the case. As Professor Shaul Lieberman has shown, many of the daring *Shi'ur Qomah* speculations in Talmudic times and literature were formulated in relation to the text of the *Song of Songs* and the scriptural narrative of the Exodus and the theophany on Mount Sinai.

If we move on from the sphere of general scholarly deliberations to that of actual occurrences, then we must observe that scholars quite recently began to pay attention to materials in the writings of the medieval Qabbalists which show that it was not unusual for

---

[43] See. G. Scholem, *On the Mystical Shape of the Godhead*, Schocken Books: New York, 1991, pp. 15-55: "*Shi'ur Komah*: The Mystical Shape of the Godhead"; I. Chernus, "Visions of God in Merkabah Mysticism", *Journal for the Study of Judaism*, Vol. XIII (1982), pp. 123-146; D. Boyarin, "The Eye in the Torah: Oracular Desire in Midrashic Hermeneutic", *Critical Inquiry*, Vol. XVI (1990), pp. 532-550.

[44] A good and comprehensive overview of the *Zohar*-literature, its structure and contents, can be found in I. Tishby, *The Wisdom of the Zohar*, Vols. I-III, Oxford Univ. Press: Oxford, 1989. Tishby's is one of the best introductions to the literature and ideas of the Qabbalah-literature.

those Qabbalists to conceive of themselves as having some kind of
mystical experience in the course of their contemplative performance of the Halakhah. To give one interesting example which has
been studied extensively by Elliot Wolfson, Qabbalists thought that
a vision of God could be achieved if the act of circumcision was
performed according to the Qabbalistic ritual.[45] It is interesting to
notice how the Qabbalistic way of conceiving of the circumcision
ritual crystallized. First we have the scriptural passages relating to
the act of circumcision; then came the rabbinic (and for that matter
also the Geonic, or post-rabbinic) interpretations—both ideological
and Halakhic; on top of that all came the Qabbalistic interpretation
which transformed previous notions and brought about substantial
changes in the manner in which details were conceived of as a
coherent whole in that ritual. Here we enter the domains of magic
and theurgy which were, until very recently, somewhat underrated
in the study of the essence and the nature of Jewish mysticism. We
shall return to this point later on.

It must be noted that Qabbalists often speak about desired or
expected states of mystical union with the Deity.[46] These usually
come in relation to, and as a culmination of, the study of the Torah
and the performance of the Law. What counts here is not the normative performance of the divine laws, but the actual realization of
the divine essence as it is encapsuled in the words used by the texts
in question. We can only repeat here the notion to the effect that in
many cases the mystical contacts between man and God are effected in the course of the mystical or the speculative handling of
scriptural texts. Those texts are not studied for their information-
conveying components as straightforwardly contained in the plain
text of Scripture, but for the divine essence that their actual wording carries. In this respect it may be said, with Scholem, that the
Qabbalistic way of reading Scripture entails strong anti-nomistic,
even anarchistic, tendencies.[47] In point of fact, there *are* clear signs
of radical ways of thinking in medieval Qabbalah and its historical
offshoots. Even when Qabbalists do not seek radical positions for

---

[45] See, E.R. Wolfson, "Circumcision and the Divine Name: A Study in the
Transmission of Esoteric Doctrine", *The Jewish Quarterly Review*, Vol. LXXVIII
(1987), pp.77-112; "Circumcision, Vision of God, and Textual Interpretation:
From Midrashic Trope to Mystical Symbol", *History of Religions*, Vol. XXVII
(1987), pp. 189-215.
[46] See, M. Idel, *Qabbalah: New Perspectives*, pp. 59-73: "Unio Mystica in Jewish
Mysticism".
[47] See, G. Scholem, *On the Kabbalah and Its Symbolism*, pp. 5-31.

their own sake, they often find them, almost inadvertently, in the course of their mystical interpretation of Scripture. That interpretation does everything to the text except clarify its plain sense. Instead, it transforms it to become something that has meaning only in a transposed mode of reading. That transposition causes the text to reflect principally metaphysical issues as embodied in the world of the Sephirot.

The mystical contacts which we have mentioned above sometimes culminate in what certain mystics call *unio mystica*, that is, moments of total fusion with a divine essence. There are many moments, however, in the religious life of certain people which have mystical potentials, but which do not entail an actual *unio mystica*.[48] Examples to that effect are many and varied. However, what should be of consequence for our discussion here is not so much the question of whether a certain text which elaborates upon the concept of mystical union, or even contains an actual description of such a union, can be taken as an evidence for the existence of a personal mystical experience, but the question, " Can texts be included in a mystical framework in spite of the fact that no specific mention is made in them of such a mystical union?" If a text can be included in the rubric of "mysticism" in spite of the fact that it does not report of an actual state of mystical union, what are the parameters by which such an inclusion is justified?

Evidently, the question touches upon the most central issues in the study of mysticism, and actually demands an answer that is tantamount to defining the genre of mystical literature. It goes without saying that any answer to that question should avoid stating matters in a closed, and dogmatic, manner. It should leave room for the inclusion of a reasonable variety of literary works that do not answer the strict requirements of a generic definition. In this respect, we would not refrain from including in that genre any kind of writing that consciously aims at accomplishing for people something that is equal to interiorizing and spiritualizing religious experiences. By interiorization and spiritualization we mean any process that turns experiences commonly connected with the material world and perceived by the physical senses into spiritual experiences that create an intensive realization of the divine.

---

[48] The question whether the concept of *Devequt*, spiritual proximity to God, entails mystical union, or not, has to be mentioned here. See, G. Scholem, *The Messianic Idea in Judaism*, Schocken Books: New York, 1971, pp. 203-227: "*Devekut*, or the Communion with God"; M. Idel, *Op. Cit.*, pp. 35-58: "Varieties of *Devekut* in Jewish Mysticism". We need not enter here a discussion of the differences in the positions Scholem and Idel take on this issue.

The Book of the *Song of Songs* can, once again, serve as a good example; it tells of the actual love affair between two young lovers. The erotic realism of the book is such that made many people raise their eyebrows. Its religious adequacy was often called into question, and some people expressed their doubts as to whether the book deserved inclusion in the Canon. The alleged name of its author, King Solomon, did the job of public relations for the book, and it was left in the place it now occupies. Its inclusion in the canonical scriptures was made possible, however, not before it was subjected to a process of allegorical interpretations, as a result of which that love story was viewed as actually, or ideally, unfolding between the People of Israel and their God. In later Christian and Jewish mystical traditions, the language and imagery of the *Song of Songs* played a prominent role in describing mystical relationships between humans and God. In Christian mysticism, the figure of Jesus could stand in place of God, and consequently the love-language of the *Song of Songs* was adjusted to the mystical realization of the Christ.

H

Before proceeding, we shall make a few more comments on the subject of Scripture and Mysticism. These are necessary not so much because of the Scripture-linked type of many phases of Jewish mysticism, but because of the fact that Scripture itself seems to contain important mystical features.[49] Although Qabbalah is professedly Scripture-linked by virtue of its multi-facetted interpretative stances, there are important phases of Jewish mysticism that are Scripture-linked only in a very general sense and in an indirect manner. In this respect, Merkavah mysticism and *Sefer Yezirah* are noteworthy cases in which no straightforward interpretation of Scripture is at hand. In one sense or another, however, Merkavah mysticism may still be said to relate Scripture, i.e. to the prophetic experiences of Ezekiel. But the scripture-oriented features of Merkavah mysticism are not more deeply marked than those of *Sefer Yezirah*. This small book, as indicated above, marks a turning point in the history and terminological essence of Jewish mysticism and contains a rather peculiar doctrine (rather: doctrines) of the creation of the world. Thus it may be said to lean on the scriptural

---

[49] The case for the mystical characteristics in Scripture are discussed in I. Gruenwald, "Reflections on the Origins and Essence of Jewish Mysticism", in: *Gershom Scholem's Major Trends in Jewish Mysticism 50 Years After*, ed. by P. Schäfer and J. Dan, J.C.B. Mohr: Tübingen, 1993, pp. 25-48.

passages in which the story of the creation of the world is told. Those elements in the book that are Scripture-oriented entail only the general subject matter and nothing that significantly contributes to the doctrine(s) contained in it.

As indicated above, it is one thing to admit that both Judaism and Christianity know of a long tradition of mystical interpretations of Scripture and, as we argue here, that there are mystical elements in Scripture itself. The assumption that Scripture itself contains certain mystical elements and passages is an often debated issue in modern scholarship. It so turns out that Christian scholars find it less difficult than do their Jewish colleagues to accept the view that the Hebrew scriptures are in one way or another mystically in-clined. For, in Christian scholarship—as also in Christian theol-ogy—a much wider definition of mysticism prevails than in its Jew-ish counterpart. Jewish scholars are used to working with a defini-tion of mysticism that has well-defined contours, and in this respect their definition is somewhat limited in scope and terms of reference. It can therefore be argued that in the case of Jewish mysticism, a more relaxed definition should preferably be suggested. If this hap-pens, new channels of discussion will be opened, and it is very likely that works which have hitherto been left out of consideration in the scholarly discussion of mysticism will be included in it. We have already referred to the fact that in the history of modern scholar-ship very few points of interaction between Jewish and Christian scholars have been achieved. This rather awkward situation is in urgent need of change. Hopefully, a new approach on the Jewish side of scholarship, which also entails a new orientation in the ques-tion of the definition of mysticism, will bring about that expected change.

Speaking of the mystical features of Scripture, it should be re-marked that their identification and characterization depends on a number of issues. We need not discuss them here, since they are the subject of a separate study that was published a short time ago. It generally makes sense, however, to say that all theophanies in Scripture can in one way or another be classified as mystical. There should be no substantial difference between scriptural modes of theophany and angelophany, and later, clearly mystically defined, forms of quests for unrestrained divine realizations. Otherwise, a conclusion can be reached to the effect that mysticism falls short of the scriptural forms of religiousness. This is a conclusion that mystics and their researchers would find difficult to accept as a matter of principle. For, such an acceptance paves the way to a delegitimatization of the mystical experience. Anything as radical as the mystical experience that declares itself to be less than its scriptural antecedents is clearly undermining its own relevance and validity. If, as suggested above, we modify our characterization of mysticism to allow for a greater variety of experiences to be included in it, then there should be no difficulty in "allowing" scriptural theophanies to hold the same status as their later mystical "imitations." In other words, from a phenomenological and experiential point of view, no lines of difference should be drawn between scriptural theophanies and later mystical realizations.

With this characterization of the relevant scriptural material there also goes a reorientation in regard to the hymns in Scripture that accompany theophanies. Rather than being treated as songs of praise said as thanksgiving hymns, they should be viewed as initially having an incantation-like function. It is conceivable to think that in saying them, people expected that a theophany could be realized. By and large, theophanies described in Scripture are linked to the redeeming acts of God. But there are also theophanies having other functions. For instance, there are clear indications to the fact that parts of the scriptural material relating to the sanctuary is somehow mystically aligned. The sanctuary is not only a place where the cult, particularly that connected to the bringing of offerings, is enacted; but, it also is a meeting place between God and Moses. At one point in the Book of Exodus we even hear that there actually were two separate Tents of Convening between God and Moses.[50] The Cloud of Glory which used to overhang the sanctuary is certainly another mode of theophany. If our interpretation is correct, then these elements also point in a mystical direction!

I

We have already mentioned the fact that in the comparative study of mysticism it is not uncommon to go to India or Japan for points of comparison with Christian mysticism. With all the interest that accompanies such comparative work, it would make more sense to center on comparisons with Jewish and Islamic mysticism. Intellectually speaking, Indian and Japanese mysticism are distant points of comparison. For a Western-oriented scholar, the Indian and Japanese types of mysticism are alien domains of spiritual activity, and should therefore be handled with caution in any comparative work. Speaking only for myself, I must confess that I find it extremely

---

[50] *Ex.* xxxiii: 6-11. There a vast scholarly literature on the subject, but it does not concern us here.

difficult to find the way into modes of mystical expression and thinking which come to my cognizance through translated source-material. As a matter of general rule and practice, mysticism is a highly and densely encoded domain. No justice can be done to it by simply translating mystical texts, actually selected terms, from one language into the other, particularly when those translations are made by people who know more about the language than about the "inner grammar" that is used in mystical formations.

By "inner grammar" we here mean those spiritual principles that constitute the internal dynamics of the experience and its literary expression. The inner grammar would explain the intentions behind the usage of this particular "subject" with that particular "predicate" in relation to that particular "object," and account for the special dynamics that hold the various components together. In regular speech we make our own choices about what we want to say and in which manner we want to say it. We are aware to a fair degree of self-consciousness of our motivations. However, when it comes to the utterances of other people, we may sometimes be at a loss in regard to their choice of words and overall intentions. This is particularly true when we try to decipher the codes of divine language, or the symbols used by mystics. For in decoding a message, or simply an utterance, we must account for the special choices of words, word-order and syntactical constructs used by the persons who builds a sentence out of these elements.

Reading the *Zohar*, which is mostly written in Aramaic, I find it a knowledge-thwarting experience when, to begin with, the text is translated into Hebrew. Hebrew and Aramaic share a cultural tradition, and, linguistically speaking, are very close to one another. Still, as anyone who has tried doing so knows, translating from the *Zohar*-Aramaic into Hebrew more often than not becomes a problematic task, and is certainly done at the expense of the translated text. People who know Aramaic, and are also knowledgeable in the Judaic religious tradition, are more or less able to make sense of at least the surface-meaning of the text. But people coming from outside of the Judaic tradition will meet many obstacles on their way. By the same token, I find it very unlikely that people who are not proficient in Sanskrit are able to approach Buddhist mystical texts in a satisfactory way. Reading those texts in any of the European languages can hardly do justice to their unique contents. Moreover, I find it rather strange that scholars deem to describe Buddhist mysticism by explaining a selective list of technical terms instead of presenting analyses of full quotes and passages. Outsiders, that is, non-initiated readers, should show more restraint in the handling of

mystical ideas and texts that are not fully and directly accessible to
them.

But the incommunicability and intranslatability of mystical ideas
and texts is not only a matter of the language used in each case. We
have already referred to the fact that mystical experiences and notions are often created as a result of ontological changes of human
consciousness. We repeat this observation at this point because it
has direct bearing on the way mystical language and other forms of
expression should be handled. In reading mystical texts one must
expect modes of expression that are characteristic of what may be
called a language within a language, or a "second language." Mystical language operates on a different level of meaning than does
language used for ordinary, day-to-day, purposes. Thus, when
reading the personal accounts of mystics, something more involved
than the simple sense of the words used must be taken into account.
This must have far-reaching consequences for the study of mysticism, and especially for the study of mystical texts that are written
in linguistic vernaculars with which one is only cursorily familiar.[51]

Speaking of the special qualities of mystical language, mention
should be made of the fact that it is common to treat it as esoteric
in nature. In its simple sense, esotericism means the concealing of
information in coded forms of expression. In most cases, this also
involves the complementary claim to the effect that the source of
the esoteric information is divine or angelic. Furthermore, it is assumed that it was granted in an exclusive manner to a small and
select group of people. It is indeed common practice in many religious societies to hold secret certain types of information.[52] The
reasons for doing so are many and varied. It stands to reason to
think that secret information is emblematic of class consciousness
and claims of social status. Only those initiated as the inner circle of
the group are in possession of that information. They enjoy special
social status and prerogatives, which may be used—and even ma-

---

[51] In this respect we move one step further than the usually maintained incommunicability of mystical experiences. In any event, the silence required on the part
of the initiated person in relation to his knowledge of the Gods is a frequently
discussed scholarly issue. See, K. Schneider, *Die Schweigenden Goetter*, Olms:
Hildesheim, 1966. See further G. Scholem, "Zehn unhistorische Saetze ueber
Kabbalah", in: *Judaica 3*, Suhrkamp: Frankfurt am Main, 1973, pp. 264-271.

[52] There is a vast scholarly literature on the subject. From the more recent
publications I would recommend W. Burkert, *Ancient Mystery Cults*, Harvard Univ.
Press: Cambridge (MASS.) and London, 1987; and Ch. Riedweg,
Mysterienterminilogie bei Platon, Philon und Klemens von Alexandrien, Walter de Gruyter:
Berlin and New York, 1987.

nipulated—for all kinds of purposes. As a rule, however, it must be admitted that mystics are humble-minded persons and have no special claims from their surrounding social environment. They live a secluded life, and in many cases their austere spiritual and physical practices draw them in the direction of severe monastic life.[53] Thus, it may be on the side of the overstatement to argue that mystical esotericism necessarily creates class consciousness. Although some mystics used to live in groups, in the case of Safed in the sixteenth century, for instance, it is safe to say that as a rule mystics are inclined to live on their own. Their monastic inclinations, if they take an active form, are more in the nature of hermiticism.

The mystic type of self-isolationism has more to do with the awareness of the fact that the ordinary forms of communication, paradoxically speaking, shut other people off from the social and intellectual company of mystics. Linguistic expression, in this respect, fails to accomplish what it generally does. Those who still want to approach mystics and read their writings must do so on the assumption that a different means of handling language should be applied. Thus, in order to do full justice to the mystical mind, a so-to-speak binary linguistics has to be invented. Words and phrases should be viewed as if operating on two different, though to some extent parallel, levels of signification and meaning.

Notwithstanding the above, there are on record cases in which mystical information was translated into terms of merits and privileges. This happened particularly when matters that concern liberation/redemption and intellectual or social integrity were lying at stake. However, in a more general sense, esotericism implies a unique interpretative approach to sacred texts/scriptures written in antiquity. The texts are read and interpreted in such a way as to facilitate the discovery of new truths in them. As we have indicated above, these truths are discovered on the assumption that the lexical meaning of the words used in the text is neither binding nor the only one possible.[54] In the case of the Qabbalah, for instance, the scriptural texts are read in such a way that renders almost every word in them as a potential symbol of the ten divine Sephiroth, or

---

[53] It should be pointed out, though, that Jewish mysticism in Talmudic and post-Talmudic times was not connected to any form of monastic life. However, the Qumran people, who definitely cultivated some kind of mysticism, were sectarian monastics! In one way or another, they contributed to the idea of Christian monasticism.

[54] The reader is once again referred to I. Gruenwald, *Apocalyptic and Merkavah Mysticism*, Chapter One.

emanations. Any phrase or sentence-construct reflects a certain configuration of those Sefiroth, including the special dynamics that holds
that configuration together. This is a highly complex technique, both
of reading the texts in question and of understanding their message.

The claim that a certain interpretation can substantially interfere
with the plain sense of the scriptural text, actually to the point of
radically changing the meaning of the text (as that meaning figures
in the minds of many a reader), deserves more than cursory attention. There is no exaggeration in claiming that this fact is tantamount to abandoning the commonly accepted rules and frameworks of what people consider to be the reasonable limits within
which scriptural texts are allowed to move in relative interpretative
freedom.

One last remark on the esoteric nature of mystical language:
Esotericism is no invention of medieval Qabbalah. Its first speci-
mens are found, on Jewish soil in Second-Temple Apocalypticism.
From there certain esoteric components entered Merkavah mysticism, although that kind of mysticism is, by-and-large, not esoteri-
cally oriented. In the Middle Ages, Jewish esotericism came under
the spell of the dual notion of *al-zahir* and *al-batin* as developed in
the framework of Islamic theology and philosophy. These terms
respectively designate the open exoteric, and closed esoteric, aspects of either God or a sacred text. In this respect, we return to the
binary nature of mystical language, with all the difficulties that it
entails for the reader and scholar. However, as we are going to see
in the examples discussed in the next section, the complication in
this case also means enrichment in terms of the linguistic potentials
and the conceptual layout.

We have made this last point about the history of esotericism for
a very specific reason; one of the major questions that arise in the
study of Jewish mysticism is that of the historical continuity. In
relation to that it is very common to find such arguments as those
that try to make it evident that even if no clear historical affiliations
can be found between one phase of Jewish mysticism and the other,
one is entitled to assume that a latent undercurrent links between
those two phases.[55] In principle that may well be the case. However,

---

[55] We did so ourselves, when different chiromantic texts were compared. It was
argued, and also accepted in the scholarly world, that since a certain chiromantic
terminology and practice is shared by the Qumran sectarians, the Merkavah mystics and later on among medieval Qabbalists, some kind of historical continuity has
to be assumed as linking between those three groups. However, literary similarity
may point to historical affiliation, but need no of necessity do so. See, I.
Gruenwald, *Op. Cit.*, pp. 218-224.

such assumptions cannot, and should not, replace serious historical study. In some cases, such assumptions are the best we can reach at, particularly when strong affinities make it almost self-evident that some kind of historical link has to be assumed. But, generally speaking, scholarly work has still a long way to go before a clear cut case can be made concerning the evidential historical-continuity between trends spread out over hundreds of years, and more.

J

When we come to the point at which examples from Qabbalah literature are introduced into the discussion, we should be reminded of the fact that Qabbalah does not cover the whole range of mystical possibilities in Judaism. There are still phases of mystical expression—such as those of the Hekhalot writings—that do not maintain the kind of coded attitude towards scriptural texts as we have just pointed out. The Hekhalot writings contain descriptions of experiences in the course of which the people concerned had angelic or divine visions and revelations. Evidently, these are different modes of mystical realization. This is not only a question of form but also of content and essence. These modes also involve different psychological positions. Mystical visions and auditions are certainly qualitatively different from intensive intellectual forms of contemplation, particularly those that are connected to, and also conditioned by, a given text. For it is one thing to use one's own language and individual forms of expression in a rather free manner, and another one to build one's own mystical perceptions in patterns of language that are, as in the case of Qabbalah, twice bound by pre-fixed patterns: the scriptural text itself and the allegorical-symbolical structure of the ten Sephirot that are said to be reflected in that text.

However, it is highly fascinating to see how the Qabbalists work with the scriptural texts and actually deem that they see in them a divine essence that can, theurgically speaking, be worked upon. The following is a good example to the way in which this is accomplished: In the so-called "Introduction" to the first book of the *Zohar*, we find an interesting elaboration on the word "ELOHIM", which in Biblical Hebrew is one of the more common [plural] names of God. In Qabbalah, "ELOHIM" is the name of the third Sephirah, also called BINAH (= Sagacity or Prudence). Accordingly, the "person" of God as embodied in His name becomes a mystically realized entity called "ELOHIM", and is not identical with the usual concept of God. God, that is

God in His ELOHIM-configuration, is part of the world of the Sephirot.[56]

The Sephirot are spiritual entities in which the essence of the supernal, hidden God (called "EN SOF", that is, the boundless) is manifested in modes that can be gleaned out of the scriptural text when appropriately read and interpreted in line with Qabbalistic principles. Almost every single word in the scriptural text can be understood as relating to one of those ten Sephirot and to their special modes of dynamic interaction. Every configuration of that interaction has a particular way of influencing the lower worlds. Evidently, if "ELOHIM" is not identical with God Himself, but with one of His so-to-speak lower manifestations, then the mystical realization of God is accomplished in a what may be referred to as a secondary divine essence, or better, manifestation. In other words, the mystics of the *Zohar* believe that only certain aspects of the Deity can be realized. His hidden essence is as unrealizable as any rationalistic philosopher in the Middle Ages could wish. There are other mystics, of course, who gave expression to other views; but what characterizes the mysticism of the *Zohar* is the depersonalized manner in which God is realized. This, by all standards, is a unique mystical position to take.

The first verse in *Genesis*, in its Hebrew word-order, reads: "In beginning (!) created Elohim the heaves(s) and the earth". A Qabbalistic reading of the text would be as follows: "BEGIN-NING" [2]/ created/ "ELOHIM" [3], "HEAVEN(S)" [6] and "EARTH" [10]. All nominals in the sentence (printed in a capitalized mode and followed by numbers in square brackets) correspond to four different Sephirot in a sequence of ten. They are, in their order of occurrence in the sentence: *Hokhmah* (Wisdom) [2], *Binah* (Sagacity or Prudence) [3], *Tif'eret* (Beauty) [6], and *Malkhut* (Kingdom) [10]. In other words, the fact that "BERESHIT" comes before "ELOHIM" not only in the scriptural word-order, but also in the very act of creation, establishes a radically new concept of God and the act of creation. All that is brought about in an interesting metamorphosis of the linguistic structures. The adverbial phrase commencing with the word (BE)RESHIT [in the beginning] is

---

[56] For a good overview of the Qabbalistic doctrine of the Sephirot, see. G. Scholem, *Major Trends in Jewish Mysticism*, Fifth and Sixth Lectures. I. Tishby's discussion of the subject is much more detailed and contains many passages in translation, organized according to subjects. All in all, Tishby's book, *The Wisdom of the Zohar*, already referred to above, is a treasure house of information. His notes to the various passages in translation are short and limited to technical explanations.

turned into a nominal sentence: "Beginning" [2] first created "Elohim" [3], then "Heaven(s)" [6], and finally "Earth"[10]. What we realize here is a radical re-writing of Scripture. In contradistinction to many other forms of re-writing Scripture known to us from biblical times onward, in Qabbalah a lot happens that may be characterized as transforming the very essence of our understanding the concepts of language and of God. Language as a conceptual essence is made into a form of revelation. It does not tell about revelation, but is the revelation of the divine essence itself. It becomes the medium in which revelation occurs. Since every word in Scripture is understood as relating to the Sephirotc world, almost every utterance in the *Zohar* entails a rule-breaking formulation in relation to God and that world.

In attempting once again to suggest a point of comparison between Qabbalah and Christian mysticism, it may not be just a word-play if we say that Qabbalah is logos(=word)-mysticism, while its Christian counterpart is the mysticism of the "Logos"(=Jesus, the Christ). Notwithstanding this word-play, it should by now be clear to the reader that when using the word "mysticism" in a Jewish and a Christian context, sometimes utterly different things are presupposed and meant.

Since the *Zohar* evolves in a completely new concept of God,[57] it will be interesting to go into the details of yet another example in which the Qabbalistic notion of ELOHIM is elaborated upon. In this example the author treats the word ELOHIM in a even more arbitrary and radical manner than in the previous case. He splits the name into two separate segments, and inverts the order of the letters. The passage once again comes from the so-called Introduction to the Book of Genesis (fol. 1/b). It begins by quoting *Isaiah* xl:26: "Lift up your eyes on high and see: who created these?" The Hebrew wording for the question reads: "*mi bara eleh?*" However, the *Zohar* drops the question mark, and turns the sentence from a question into a regular statement. Consequently, it reads "*MI*" created "*ELEH*", "Who" created "These"! For reasons that need not be specified here, "MI" is one of the symbols of the third Sephirah, Binah. In other words, Binah created "these," that is, the rest of the [lower] Sephirot. Thus the meaning of the whole statement is, "Those who in a contemplative manner lift up their eyes to the

---

[57] We cannot here enter a discussion of how that concept of God developed. Many factors here played an important role, not least among them being *Sefer Ha-Bahir*.

heavenly world of the Sephirot will realize that the lower Sephirot emanated from Binah."

In this connection it should be mentioned that the phrase "to lift up one's eyes" in scriptural Hebrew means "to have a visionary experience"! Examples of that effect are quite numerous, though the reasons for our interpretation will be given on another occasion. Having in mind our comments on the esoteric modes of interpretation, we can here say that there are cases in which the scriptural writers themselves create encoded forms of expression, or more simply, use a kind of technical language that is not easily deciphered by outsiders. However, the point made by the *Zohar* is clear even without that particular interpretation of the words in *Isaiah*. If our interpretation is correct, it only adds the contemplative aspect of the special way of reading the phrase, *mi bara eleh*. The word *eleh* is spelled in Hebrew with the first three letters of the word Elohim. The consonantal reading is the same, though the vocalization is different: "eleh" and "eloh...." In other words, the totality of the Sephirotic world is conceived only when the "MI" and the "ELEH" are fused together into one word, "ELOHIM." Notice that the "MI" is a backward reading, from right to left, of "elohIM." "ELOHIM," as we saw, is also one of the symbolic configurations of the third Sephirah, Binah, and it is thus expressive of the totality of the Sephirot-world as incorporated in, and emanated from, Binah. Those who will see in this way of treating the divine name a measure of downgrading the divine essence are not far from the truth. However, the price seemed worth paying for the Qabbalists, since it so-to-speak bought the ticket for conceptualizing "God" in a place in which he was as close to man as possible.

What we here have is an interesting linguistic and theological phenomenon. As a result of a process of fragmentation, or atomization, of the Hebrew lexicon, including for that matter the names of God too, new configurations of the divine essence suggest themselves to the mystical mind. In other words, mystics can work on the divine essence by, once again, so-to-speak playing around with words and scriptural phrases. This is not a simple word-play. It actually amounts to a radical change in the notions people have of God and the creation of the world. What the Qabbalists achieve is, according to their own conviction, a realization of the infinitely rich variety of configurations of the divine essence. Those configurations are like kaleidoscopic permutations of the same existing components. This is not something that a person who is not initiated into the secret methods of reading Scripture can easily understand and fully grasp.

The story, however, does not come to an end at this point. As has already been observed, the Qabbalistic way of reading Scripture rings about a disintegration, or even deconstruction, of the text of Scripture. It transforms every single unit in it into an utterance about God, including for that matter all the sayings about the scriptural laws. Obviously, such an interpretative position can have its clear anarchical potentials. We have already referred to this point above. Thus it is no wonder that this way of reading Scripture was not readily accepted by the greater part of the Jewish population educated on Halakhic norms.

Several Qabbalistic writings are actually written in the form of "Dictionaries." They are either alphabetically arranged or in the structure of the Ten Sephirot. The most conspicuous example is that of Joseph Chicatella *Sha`arei Orah* (The Gates of Light; or as the text was called by its Renaissance translator into Latin, *Portae Lucis*).[58] However, in spite of its Dictionary-like appearance *Sha`arei Orah* is not a dictionary or lexicon in the ordinary sense of the term. The book develops interesting Qabbalistic notions of its own. A quick reading of that book shows that even many of the principally halakhic notions in Judaism (such as Shabbat, Tephilin [= phylacteries], and the blowing of the Shofar) become Qabbalistic entities symbolically conceived as Sephirot.

The Qabbalisitc approach to language has many consequences, among which the cognitive ones occupy important place and role. By "cognitive" we here mean anything that relates to people's perceptions and consequent mental reactions. Different people perceive of reality in different ways. Different people, too, have wider and narrower horizons of perception. People also have different cognitive capacities: some can only see the material world around them; others believe that they can go, in spirit, beyond reality into unknown spiritual or supernatural domains. The Qabbalists conceive of the material world, as also of the history of Israel, as a reflection of celestial, or Sephirotic, domains. *Mutatis mutandis*, the material world and the history of the People of Israel as they unfolded in scriptural times were a reflection of divine realities as structured in and by the Sephirot. In other words, there were times in which people went, as an old rabbinic saying has it, in the ways of God. In Qabbalistic terms, walking in the ways of the Deity

---

[58] The story of the Christian adaptations and interpretations of the Qabbalah in Europe during the Renaissance is one of the most fascinating stories in the history of ideas. We can mention it here only in passing. For a general orientation the reader may consult G. Scholem, *Kabbalah*, Keter Publishing House: Jerusalem, 1974, pp.194-201, and the Bibliography [which requires updating] on p. 209/210.

means to participate in divine transactions. This in essence is the Qabbalistic version of a mystical *imitatio dei*. Those people who study Scripture in a mystical manner do the same, but on a more spiritual level than the ones whose life-stories are recorded in Scripture, and who walked in the ways of God, in the moral sense of the term. In one way or another, the mystical way of life brings about a close interaction between humans and the divine. There is a strong sense of interdependency between the two, in every respect possible.

We may even go one step further and argue that if the stories of Scripture are mostly realizable on a spiritual level, then material history as such has no meaning. Its significance lies in its realization as the "history" of the unfolding of the divine essence, in celestial as well as in terrestrial domains. Mystical cognition may, thus, be characterized by its transformative qualities. It transforms reality into, or onto, spiritual substances. We may even say that it shows that essence is spiritual, while all other phases of existence are, in Platonic terms, transient appearances. The transformative qualities of Qabbalah are also present in the above mentioned interaction between the divine and the human. Both are interlinked in a what may be described as a *perpetuum mobile* of give and take, add and substract. What lies at stake is the increasing or the decreasing of the divine power in itself and in its relation to the world.

The stories of the three Patriarchs—Abraham, Isaac and Jacob—reflect in the eyes of the Qabbalists the various interactions between three Sephirot which occupy a central position in the framework of the ten. Those three Sephirot respectively are: *HESED* ("Grace"), *GEVURAH* ("Power", also referred to as *DIN*, "[severe] Judgement"), and *RAHAMIM* ("Compassion", also referred to as *TIF'ERET*, "Beauty"). They are numbers four, five and six in the sequence of the ten Sephirot. Everything that happened to the Patriarchs did not only reflect the inner dynamics in which the corresponding Sephirot were involved, but was also conditioned by the rules and principles that regulate and govern that dynamics. In this respect the scriptural narrative moves on two parallel levels: the first—the earthly and historical level, and the second—the heavenly, or metaphysical, one. This brings us back to the point already made above, to the effect that the Qabbalah-mystics developed a method of reading Scripture in a bi-level, or binary, mode.

Thus we find that the name Abraham (pronounced in Hebrew as Avraham) is interpreted as combining the idea of creation ["*bara*", created] and sexual procreation ["*ever*", the male sex-organ]! The idea is developed in the *Zohar* (vol. I, fol. 3/b) in the following manner: "When Abraham came, as it is written (*Genesis* ii:4), "These are the generations of the heavens and the earth, when they were created" [in Hebrew: *be-hibar'am*; it is spelled with the same consonants as the name of the Patriarch]. And we have learned (in: *Genesis Rabbah*, parag. XII, 8): [Do not read *be-hibar'am* but] *be-Avraham* (=with, or in, Abraham). And because everything was concealed (!) by means of the word *bara*, the letters turned to intercourse, and the "Pillar" (=a midrashic metonym for Abraham, applied here with all its Freudian implications!) emerged and begot [all] the generations. [This is the meaning of the segment] *ever* (=penis) [in the name Avraham], [which is] the [Sacred] Foundation (in Hebrew: *YESOD*, which in Qabbalistic symbolism is the male sex organ; it functions as such in the sacred intercourse between the sixth Sephirah, *Tif'eret*, [a feminine name given to an entity that has masculine functions, and is also called "The holy and blessed One', *Ha-Qadosh Barukh hu]*, and the lowest of the Sephirot, *Malkhut*, "Kingdom" which also represents the Qabbalistic notion of the People of Israel) upon which the world rests. When the *ever* was inscribed by the word *bara* (in Hebrew both words are composed of the same consonants, though in reversed order), the Supernal Hidden One (=God) inscribed something else for the sake of His name and His glory. And this [also] is the mystery of [the above-quoted verse] *mi bara eleh*".

This is a highly involved specimen of *Zohar*-writing. It consists of a densely arranged series of images all of which are pointing in a number of directions: cosmological, historical and sexual. From a literary point of view, it creates another layer of midrashic-interpretation on top of the rabbinic one. Thus, in order to read the *Zohar* one has to be fairly well acquainted with the Hebrew of Scripture, the rabbinic midrashic material, Aramaic, as also with the nature of the symbolic exegesis of the Qabbalah. Out of them all the *Zohar* creates its own world of ideas. In the three cases which we have just studied we see that, when it comes to giving expression to the most outlandish notions about God and the function of the sephirot, actually nothing stands in the writer's way. Both "ELOHIM" and "AVRAHAM" become metaphysical notions which interact in a mystical manner. Mysticism in this case stands for a world that is newly conceived and created in the mind of the mystical reader.

K

Among other things, Jewish mysticism is closely connected to the world of magic and theurgy. This brings us to a point the discussion of which has wider implications than just in the area of Jewish

mysticism. Students of Jewish mysticism are familiar with the problem: the practices connected with the mystical experiences bear
strong resemblance to magical practices. This particularly holds
true of Merkavah mysticism and of the various aspects of what is
sometimes called practical Qabbalah. We have already referred to
the fact that there are experiential dimensions in Qabbalah, even
when they are not explicitly mentioned and described. However,
practical Qabbalah entails the use of magical together with
Qabbalistic elements. The purpose of those practices is to ask God
to do all kinds of special favours to the practicing person, to fulfil
his personal wishes and to provide protection against enemies and
evil spirits. In many cases, charms, incantations, and particularly
so-called magical names (technically referred to as "nomina
barbara," outlandish names) are applied in those practices. In this
connection amulets play an important role.

In studying those items of practical Qabbalah, one can hardly
distinguish between the "holy" Qabbalah and the idolatrous magic
and theurgy. The difference between magic and theurgy can be
described in the following manner: magic uses all kinds of spiritual
powers and energies to create favourable situations for the persons
who avail themselves of the right practices. The domains of magic
are usually those restricted to the immediate environment of the
practitioner. In theurgy, however, similar practices are applied, but
their "address" is the Deity itself. Theurgy may roughly be described as the "science" of coercing the Gods, and particularly of
bringing about changes in divine realms.

It goes without saying that both domains, magic and theurgy
(and to a considerable extent astrology, too) were looked upon by
non-mystics and uninitiated people as being tantamount to one sort
or another of idol-worship. We cannot enter here a full-scale discussion of the prevalence of magic, or magical components, in
Judaism. Scholarly work done over the last century has convincingly shown that, in spite of the scriptural prohibitions against the
various magical arts, Jews did not always follow those injunctions to
the small letters of the law.[59] On the contrary, magic had a strong
impact on people's beliefs and practices, and this over a long period
of time and in many places. It is important to note in this connection that magic was not the arcane art of the simple people. On the

---

[59] The most recent study of Jewish magic is that incorporated in J. Naveh and
Sh. Shaked, *Magic Spells and Formulae*, The Magnes Press: Jerusalem, 1993.

contrary, even the talmudic sages used to practice magic, and when more conscientious positions were sought, the sages said that they practiced magic so as "to know and understand".[60] In other words, when the worse came to the worst in these matters, there always was an emergency-escape that could be used. In our case, that emergency-escape was the practicing of magic for so-called theoretical purposes.

In short, the cultural climate of Judaism was such that did not complicate matters to such an extent that made the practice of magic an issue stimulating guilt-feelings. When people considered magic to be a useful means of handling difficult situations, they did so without revealing a flush of shame on their face. In this respect, Jews were always the people of their own times. Officially, they were expected to conduct a self-imposed segregated life-style. However, when there was something to learn from the non-Jewish neighbour next door, and this was the case when the cures and remedies of one's own household proved to be less expedient than expected, then cultural and ideological barriers easily became as leaky as the actual needs required them to be. Some people became real experts in the *res magicae*, while others—as is so often the case in life—resorted to their help or to unprofessional imitation.

If this picture is a true-to-life one, then the mystics' use of magical elements and materials in their practices and speculative activities should not surprise us. On the contrary, the mystics in question just carried on something that was already maintained, and accepted, among various parts of Jewish society. Since mysticism generally involved an intensification of religious sensibilities, magic found its reenforcement in it. In connection with this it must be observed that it is a question of a different order, Whether the chief characteristics of a certain type of mystical activity can be defined as principally magical in nature, as Schaefer argued in relation to the Hekhalot literature, or not.[61] For my own part, I would say that magic and mysticism were always inter-twined activities. There are cases, such as that of *Sefer Ha-Razim* (a magical treatise written in Hebrew to all likelihood between the third and fifth century C.E.),[62]

---

[60] A handy, but not altogether satisfactory, handling of the subject of Magic in Talmudic times is E.E. Urbach, *The Sages*, Harvard Univ. Press: Cambridge, MASS., 1987, pp.97-134.

[61] See, P. Schaefer, *Hekhalot-Studien*, Mohr: Tuebingen, 1988, pp. 277-295: "The Aim and Purpose of Early Jewish Mysticism".

[62] English translation by M.A. Morgan, Scholars Press: Chico, CA., 1983. See comments in I. Gruenwald, *Apocalyptic and Merkavah Mysticism*, pp. 225-234.

in which Merkavah elements were added upon the magical material; and there are cases, such as the Hekhalot treatises, in which the magical material was added onto the initially mystical drive. However, what matters most in our eyes is the fact that magic prevailed across the cultural board in ancient and medieval Judaism. It may be left, however, to scholarly speculation as to whether the mystical strain in Judaism contributed in any significant manner to the legitimization of magic in the Jewish world, or whether the initial prevalence of magic in one way or another helped mysticism to find its way into wider circles than could otherwise be the case. However, the convergence of mysticism and magic in Late-Antiquity can equally count as a simple and unpremeditated fact of life, which requires no special commenting.

L

We shall end our discussion with a few observations on the connection between mysticism and eschatology, including for that matter messianism. The most conspicuous example to that effect is the case of Sabbatai Zevi, to which we have already referred at the beginning of our study. Since the future redemption of the People of Israel was always an acute issue in Jewish life and thinking, it is conceivable that Qabbalah would make its case, *inter alia,* by suggesting key solutions to the problems involved in the materialization of the messianic expectations. However, what would characterize the Qabbalistic doctrines concerning the Messianic events is their preoccupation with the various processes in the divine world of the Sephirot that have to be accomplished before the actual inception of the messianic era. As can be expected, those processes are mainly connected with the inner dynamics of the Sephirot. Something must be accomplished in the very structure of the Sephirot prior to the coming of the Messiah and the final act of redemption. However, whatever happens in the world of the Sephirot was here as elsewhere dependent on what the Qabbalists do or abstain from doing. They believed that the key to the salvation of the People of Israel was largely in their hands. And that key was primarily applicable in metaphysical domains.

The so-called "classical" Qabbalists, that is the Qabbalists that were active and guided in the conceptual framework of the *Zohar,* believed that as a result of the sin of Adam and Eve in the Garden of Eden something devastating had happened in the realm of the Sephirot. To the best of their understanding, this was a sin that had so-to-speak cosmic repercussions. Lurianic Qabbalah in the sixteenth century, added another dimension to that catastrophe: At the beginning of the world the "Vessels" broke asunder, not being able to contain the amount and intensity of the divine lights.[63] Consequently the divine lights were scattered in the profane and material world. Any act of messianic redemption was from that moment onwards conceived as being dependent on the restoration of the divine lights to their divine source. In both cases a metaphysical process has to be brought to its termination before the process of the historical redemption can set in. Interestingly, however, the concept of the *Zohar* is formulated in a strong sexual language. It tells of the catastrophic rift within the world of the Sephirot. This is a story of the separation between the sixth Sephirah, "Tif'eret," and the tenth one, "Malkhut" (see above). Current symbols of those two Sephirot are God (*Ha-Qadosh Barukh Hu*) and the People of Israel. In other words, God was metaphysically separated from His People. Since yet another symbol of the tenth Sephirah is "Shekhinah," the Dwelling aspect of the Deity (originally, in the Sanctuary), that act of separation can also be described as occurring within divine realms, between one Sephirotic entity and the other.[64]

However we conceive of that event in the midst of the divine world, it is first of all a meta-historical event. Only secondarily does it have implications to matters happening in terrestrial and historical domains. Secondary-ness in this case is no token of triviality. One reason for that is that Evil came into being as a result of that separation. As a rule, Evil thrives in the realm of disturbed realities. It threats to destroy the divine and it waits for the sins of mankind to nourish upon and draw its strength from. Wherever it makes its appearance in Qabbalisitc writings and concepts, Evil crystallizes in mythical realms and forms of expression. In one way or another, the concepts of Evil in Qabbalah are one of the most profound conceptual manifestations of the doctrine of Evil in Judaism. This is explained not only by the strong mythical colours in which evil is painted in Qabbalah, but also by its omnipresence and omnipotence.[65]

---

[63] See, G. Scholem, *The Messianic Idea in Judaism*, Schocken Books:New York, 1971, pp. 1-48.

[64] On the feminine element in divinity as conceived in Qabbalah, see, G. Scholem, *On the Mystical Shape of the Godhead*, pp. 140-196.

[65] On the doctrine of Evil in Kabbalah in relation to its mythical ways of thinking, see, G. Scholem, *On the Mystical Shape of the Godhead*, pp. 56-87; *On the Kabbalah and Its Symbolism*, pp. 87-117.

In each case mentioned above, the sixth Sephirah is equivalent to the male principle, and the tenth is equivalent to the female principle. In other words, a separation which has clear sexual implications has set in, and both parties involved are in need of metaphysical reunion. As we have already indicated above, that metaphysical reunion is conceived of in strong erotic language. It induces the impression that in reality something physical is meant. In any event, as long as the metaphysical separation persists, there is no hope for redemption on earthly domains. The redemption of the People of Israel is intrinsically linked to a metaphysical process that has to come into effect in the realm of the Sephirot. As long as there is no final reunion achieved in those realms, there are constant fluctuations in the relationship between those two Sephirot and also in the fate of the People of Israel. When the People of Israel observe the Mitzwoth, that is: God's commandments in their rabbinic (and, for that matter, also Qabbalistic) interpretation are fulfilled, there prevails a state of metaphysical union in the world of the Sephirot. But, since in the present historical era, prior to the eschatological redemption, human behaviour is not as perfect as one could wish, and people are prone to return constantly to modes of disobedient behaviour, separation in that realm sets in time and again. In the Qabbalisitc view, this is the reason for the prolongation of the exilic conditions of the People of Israel.

From a religious point of view, this belief puts great responsibility on every one of the People of Israel. The divine is completely dependent in its fate on the acts of human beings. This is particularly true of the sages in every generation.[66] East European Hasidism, and its unique concept of the *Zaddiq* is only one example out of the many that can be given of this phenomenon. On the one hand, every individual has a chance of taking part in the process of bringing about the expected reunification in the divine world. On the other hand, the efficacy of the *Zaddiq* is such that transcends that of other individuals and the group. Thus, the universal, cosmic and metaphysical implications of every act of obedience and disobedience makes man an active participant in the cosmic and the divine order. This bestows special dimensions on the microcosmos-macrocosmos relationship. And it epitomizes the concept, as mentioned above, to the effect that redemption is in the hands of the People of Israel, as also is the continuation of the state of exile.

---

[66] On the role of the *Zaddiq*, "the righteous one", in Qabbalistic thinking, see, G. Scholem, *On the Mystical Shape of the Godhead*, pp. 88-139.

"Exile" here means not only a historical situation of which the People of Israel partake as a result of the destruction of the Temple, but also a metaphysical reality which conditions the fate of God in His Sephirotic existence.

Since, as we have noted, the whole process is also envisioned in sexual terms, there is an interesting link between historical events and sexual behaviour, both on the personal as also on the cosmic levels. In one sense or another, this is also what happens in Christian mysticism. The figure of the Redeemer, the Christ, becomes the object of the mystical quest, which more often than not is envisioned in strong sexual terms. For a Christian, then, consummation of the mystical experience is a participation in the redeeming activity of the Christ. Naturally, in one way or another all this means an upgrading of the sexual act. Taking into consideration the ascetic attitude towards sexual intercourse as generally professed in the Middle Ages, one may argue that the mystical attitude towards the sexual act spiritualizes it and transforms its essence into a theurgic event. One may even argue that by spiritualizing the sexual act it is divested of its basically carnal nature. This is certainly the case, when viewed in the religious context in which that position is adapted. However, there are clear indications to the fact that in certain mystical circles there was a significant intensification in the interest in sexuality.[67] This, in turn, was yet another fire that inflamed the suspicion of the omniscient outsiders.

It may be argued that in shifting the emphasis from earthly, historical, to heavenly, or spiritual, domains, the whole process of redemption is not only spiritualized but actually neutralized. One of the most interesting debates in modern scholarship that dealt with this issue turned about the question whether Qabbalah, and particularly its Hasidic offspring in East Europe contributed to the neutralization of the messianic element in Judaism, or not. Scholem thought that this was the case,[68] while I. Tishby thought he had ample historical evidence to prove the contrary.[69] We need not

---

[67] See the interesting discussions of this issue in M. Idel, "'We Have No Kabbalistic Tradition on This'", in: I. Twersky, Rabbi Moses Nahmanides (RAMBAN): Exploration in His Religious and Literary Virtuosity, Harvard Univ. Press: Cambridge [MASS], 1983, pp.52-73; and: "Maimonides and Kabbalah", in: I. Twersky (ed.), Studies in Maimonides, Harvard Univ. Press, Cambridge [MASS.] and London, 1990, pp. 31-80.

[68] See, G. Scholem, "The Neutralization of the Messianic Element in Early Hasidism", in: The Messianic Idea in Judaism, pp.176-202.

[69] See, I. Tishby, "The Messianic Idea and the Messianic Tendencies in the Rise of Hasidism", in: Studies in the Kabbalah and Its Branches, [in Hebrew], Magnes Press: Jerusalem, 1993, Vol. II, pp. 475-519.

enter the details of the debate here, neither are we obliged to make up our minds and decide in favour of one view or the other. However, it seems to us reasonable to argue in favour of the view that saw the potential of neutralization in the spiritual attitude of the Qabbalah, in general! In fact, there are plenty of quotes that can be brought in support of Scholem's view, but there are also historical examples, of no lesser interest, that point in the direction of Tishbi's claim.

M

This brings us to a point at which it is no longer possible to avoid discussing the various affinities between Qabbalah and Gnosticism. Scholem insistently argued in favour of viewing certain Qabbalisitc strains, and also important sections of Merkavah mysticism, in light of a gnostic Weltanschauung. In his studies of *Sefer Ha-Bahir* (an anonymous book that made its first appearance at the end of the twelfth century in Southern France), Scholem argued that a clear gnostic influence left its imprint in the book.[70] Since *Sefer Ha-Bahir* had an enormous influence on any future developments of the doctrine of the ten Sephirot, everything said about this book could with some justice be stretched to cover other books which were written in the same wake. In addition to that, Scholem saw in Merkavah mysticism "an inner Jewish concomitant to Gnosis".[71] In other words, the study of Jewish mysticism was in the eyes of Scholem inextricably linked to the realization of the place Gnosticism allegedly had in the building processes of that mysticism. Since, for instance, the Qabbalistic doctrine of evil has clear dualistic ingredients, it was reasonable to find points of correspondence between Qabbalah and Gnosticism. Gnosticism maintained a heavily-painted mythical orientation in its handling of the problem of evil. In this mythical orientation good and evil were as dualistically conceived as they were in Zoroastrianism. However, in dealing with gnostic forms of dualism and discussing their relevancy for the understanding and evaluation of Jewish mysticism, one should beware of being carried away by similarities that are no more than structural. Gnosticism, as we know it since the discovery, in 1945, of the Gnostic "library" in Nag Hammadi, basically—though not initially—was a form of Christian heresy. It has been shown that in itself

---

[70] See, G. Scholem, *Origins of the Kabbalah*, pp. 68-80.
[71] See, G. Scholem, *Kabbalah*, p. 13. See the response to that characterization in I. Gruenwald, *From Apocalypticism to Gnosticism*, pp. 191-205.

it was strongly dependent of Jewish texts and ideas! In other words, not only does it sound peculiar when argued that Jewish mysticism was influenced by Gnosticism, but the very subject of influences should in principle be viewed in the reverse direction.

When it comes to the discussion of structural affinities, however, those who argue that particularly in the doctrine of the Sephirot such affinities with Gnosticism are traceable have a better, though no perfect, case in their hands. There is a clearly-marked theosophical dimension in the Gnostic concept of the divine pleroma (=the metaphysical domain in which God conceptually, and mythically, unfolds). The theosophical dimension of Gnosticism is characterized by its emphasis on descriptions of events related to the development of the divine pleroma. Before the creation of the world certain events happened that brought about a split in the divine realms. The various beings inhabiting the pleroma, usually referred to as Archons, rebelled against the supreme God, called in the gnostic writings Incorruptibility or Imperishability. One of the major moves in that rebellion was the creation of the material world and of Man. The similarity in this case with Qabbalistic notions and doctrines is only of very evasive and structural nature. The Archons in the gnostic world view are evil, and whatever comes into being through their creative agency is basically evil and corrupt. This by no means can be said in relation to the Sephirot. One major figure among these Archons is no other than the God of Israel, or Sabaoth. We cannot enter here a detailed discussion of the various issues involved in this position. However, there is very little of it that can in reality be found in Qabbalah. It is simply inconceivable that such radical notions, which practically speaking caused a total inversion of Jewish concepts and values, could serve as a basis or model for any kind of mystical doctrine in Judaism.

We now come to the last point in our discussion: Scholem wanted to see in the mystic's ascent to heaven something that reflected a similar ascent in a gnostic context. But it has, once again, to be remarked that the heavenly ascents of the gnostics marked the termination of their life on earth. They were so-to-speak called back to their heavenly source of light. They escaped from their captivity in the material world to find eternal refuge in the realms of light. Those realms belong to the Imperishable God who dwells beyond and above the realms of the evil gods. On their way up to the heavenly realms of light, the gnostics (or better: their spiritual essence) had to show all kinds of secret passwords and amulets to the archons, who, because of their evil nature, attempted to block the way to the source of light. Although the Merkavah mystics had to produce similar passwords when moving from one heavenly palace to the other, their ascent was in no conceivable way an escape from earthly powers. After finishing their heavenly tour, they returned to earth to report of their experiences to their fellow mystics.

However, what is of even greater interest in connection with the allegedly gnostic components in Jewish mysticism is the question of the nature of the mystical knowledge, as such. The Greek word "gnosis" means "knowledge', and the question can be asked if there is some kind of special knowledge that the mystics wanted to gain in the course of their experiences. Clearly, it would sound redundant if mystical experiences are evaluated as information-seeking experiences. The intensity of the emotions and the extraordinary quality of the mystical type of spirituality cannot be reduced to information-centered characterizations. However, Jewish mystics in general would quite often praise themselves for the richness and depth of the knowledge gained in the course of their mystical undertakings. Secrets concerning cosmological matters, details of eschatological events, information about the nature of human beings and their alleged crimes committed clandestinely, not to mentions the secrets of the Torah and the essence of the divine realms—all create an impressive list of secret knowledge. In this respect, the mystics of Judaism continue the tradition of the apocalyptic visionaries of the Second Temple period.[72]

Evidently, there is in Jewish mysticism an atmosphere of acquiring universal knowledge; still, there stretches a vast distance between acknowledging this fact and assuming that the basic goals of the mystical experience is the gaining of secret information for its own sake. We believe that this conclusion is worth keeping in mind when reading the books and treatises written by, or attributed to, the Jewish mystics. By all standards, these books assume expert knowledge on the part of the reader. Without being well informed in the areas of rabbinic midrash, both on the technical-Halakhic and the aggadic-homiletic levels, as also in the history of Jewish thought and philosophy, there is no point in even attempting to approach those mystical writings. In this respect, Jewish mysticism is of a much more technical and learned nature than are many of the writings of its Christian counterpart. Christian mysticism is very often spontaneous in nature, that is, it gives expression to personal feelings and outbursts of emotions. This may also explain the fact

---

[72] See, M.E. Stone, "Lists of Revealed Things in Apocalyptic Literature", in: *Selected Studies in Pseudepigrapha and Apocrypha*, Brill: Leiden, Etc., 1991, pp.379-418.

that Christian mysticism is much more accessible to the average, moderately informed, reader than its Jewish kin.

Sharing the knowledge and expertise of the Qabbalah-mystic is a spiritual odyssey in itself. It takes years of contemplative wanderings to discover one's own spirituality, and many more to realize its comprehensive dimensions. The depth of one's own self can be discovered in its immeasurability, provided adequate maps of spiritual guidance are at hand. In learning to read mystical texts with care and attention, a few such maps can be discovered. However, some maps have to be drawn with intuition and imagination. For the trip sometimes takes us through unmarked ways and to uncharted territories. The study of mysticism can be a matter of intellectual curiosity; but curiosity easily turns into personal commitment. When this so happens, the mystical ladder of ascension helps us climb down into the deep recesses of our own being, where opposites lose their distinctive qualities. Then the end marks a new beginning.

JUDAIC SYSTEMS OTHER THAN RABBINIC

HELLENISTIC JUDAISM

Lester L. Grabbe
(University of Hull)

In the history of Judaism, or at least in the history of scholarship on Judaism, no subject has been more fascinating nor occasioned more controversy than the question of Judaism and Hellenization. How did the coming of the Greeks affect the Jews? Were the Jews Hellenized or did they resist it? Were Judaism and Hellenization irreconcilably opposed? Was there a "Hellenistic Judaism" in opposition to a "Palestinian Judaism"? Were the so-called "Hellenists" traitors to their religion? These questions only introduce a debate, acrimonious at best, while in the mind of some, almost a matter of religious life and death.

As will be clear in my discussion, nothing is simple. There are no simple definitions, and many of the historical questions cannot be answered with any certainty. The reader should expect little to be straightforward. What I shall provide is a path through the tangle of the terrain. It will be important to see not just the narrow subject of the Jews but the much broader one of Hellenization of the ancient Near East. The Jews and their situation cannot be understood apart from this context. Without the necessary breadth, the questions relating to Judaism may be give uninformed or misinformed answers by failing to recognize how similar the Jewish situation was to that of many other minority ethnic groups, as well as where essential differences lay.

1 THE HELLENISTIC WORLD

1.1 The Question of Definitions

Discussions about Hellenization and Hellenistic Judaism have been bedeviled by definitions. Much debate has been wasted because discussants were talking about different things under the same name or because they were using terms which meant one thing in one context and something rather different in another. Ideally, definitions would be best approached after digesting the background discussion to be found in 2.2. As that section will indicate,

Hellenization was a very complex affair, and "Hellenization" (and "Hellenist") can be used with a variety of senses, depending on what particular aspect or focus one has in mind.

First of all, Hellenization refers to the entire phenomenon created by the Greek conquest of the ancient Near East—the new Hellenistic world. When the Greeks established their rule, they imposed their overlordship on millennia-old civilizations with millions of inhabitants. Greek rule replaced that of the native monarchs, but it would have been impossible to replace the customs, religions, languages, practices, beliefs, and worldviews of the native populations—even if that had been the intent. The Hellenistic kingdoms set up after Alexander's death had certain Greek characteristics, but they were in many ways only the old Persian, Egyptian, Babylonian, Syrian, etc., kingdoms continuing in slightly modified form. The imperial court was Greek and some of the administrative structure had been modified, but much went on as it had for centuries.

"Hellenization" is used in a second sense to apply to a cultural phenomenon, with its complex set of elements derived from both Greek and Near Eastern sources. Hellenization was neither "Hellenism" nor "Orientalism"; it had characteristics of both but was a new entity—it was *sui generis*. Some regions and institutions were almost purely Greek while others remained unadulterately native, not to mention mixtures of various sorts. The balance of the different elements was not static, however, but constantly changing and developing. Thus, Hellenistic culture can be adequately described only as a process.

A third sense concerns the individual, focusing on the measure to which specific Greek practices were adopted or conformed to. From this point of view, one could speak of degrees of Hellenization, referring to the extent of the effort made to adhere to Greek ideals and customs. Thus, individuals might be viewed as if being on a spectrum of Hellenization, with the purely Greek at one end and the purely native at the other.

These definitions become even more complicated when one turns to Judaism. Not infrequently, a theological agenda (perhaps often unconscious) has skewed the direction of discussion and prevented a properly dispassionate consideration of the issues. "Hellenistic Judaism" has been used in two senses. It often refers to a literary phenomenon: Jewish writings in the Greek language. Of course, behind these writings were authors or, in some cases, translators. In the Septuagint version of the Bible and in some other writings, the Greek work is a literal translation of a Semitic original and still retains many of the characteristics of the original. In addition, we possess many works which were composed in Greek from the beginning, sometimes by writers who had Greek as their first and perhaps only language. The problem is what sort of Jew—or Judaism—is presupposed by a particular writing. A second aspect of Hellenistic Judaism is a geographical one. The vast majority of Greek-speaking Jews lived outside Palestine, and the vast majority of Jews living outside Palestine (except perhaps for those in Babylon) were Greek-speaking. "Hellenistic Judaism" is, then, often used to mean the Judaism outside Palestine.

Both these uses are potentially misleading. All Jews were a part of the Hellenistic world and thus in some sense "Hellenistic"; the fact that one used Hebrew or Aramaic does not negate this. Furthermore, many Jews in Palestine had some knowledge of Greek, and it seems certain that some important Jewish works in Greek were composed in Palestine. There is, therefore, a certain ambiguity about the term "Hellenistic Judaism". Taking a cue from the third point above, we can say that all Jews—Palestinian or Diasporan—were on the Hellenistic spectrum, with some being much nearer the native end and others rather closer to the Greek end.

1.2 Hellenization as a Phenomenon

Hellenization formally began when Alexander landed in Asia Minor in 334 BCE, yet in one sense Hellenization was underway long before this. Asia Minor had had a large Greek population, the Ionic Greeks, for many centuries. They saw themselves as kindred of the Greeks on the mainland and islands, but they were under the rule of the Persians from about 550 BCE. Greek influence had also spread to other parts of the Mediterranean world. Sicily and southern Italy had a number of Greek colonies and became known to the Romans as Magna Graeca ("Greater Greece"). The Phoenicians of Tyre, Sidon, Byblus, and other coastal cities had long established themselves as leading traders, spreading their colonies far to the west in the Mediterranean and even venturing out into the Atlantic. But the Phoenician cities on the eastern shores of the Mediterranean had a good deal of contact with the Aegean, absorbing much from Greek culture. They could be said to be Hellenized long before Alexander (Starr; Millar). Finally, Greek mercenaries were ubiquitous in the eastern Medterranean, used by everyone from Babylonians to Egyptians, including apparently even the last kings of Judah.

Alexander's precise aims for his empire can only be speculated on
since he did not live to carry them out. Perhaps his alleged idealistic
union of conqueror and conquered, Greeks and natives, into one
universal empire and culture is exaggerated. Whatever Alexander's
intent, things changed radically after his death. For forty years, his
generals (*diadochi* "successors") fought among themselves for control
of his empire or at least an ample slice of it. At the end of those
decades of continual fighting and constantly shifting boundaries
and alliances, the Hellenistic world was divided three ways: mainland Greece and Thrace under the Antigonids; the Seleucid empire
of Syria, much of Asia Minor, and Mesopotamia; and the
Ptolemaic empire of Egypt and southern Syria.

The successors of Alexander were pragmatists, not idealists.
They were interested in power, territory, wealth, and privilege. The
Greek soldiers who had fought under their banner were rewarded
with land and cities. Alexander and his successors built cities all
over the ancient Near East on the model of the city states back in
Greece, especially on the democratic model of Athens. These
Greek cities (*poleis*) were for the benefit of Greek settlers and their
descendants, not the natives. Although some natives might live in
them or work the land as serfs for the Greek overlords, they were
not citizens. There was no particular desire to share power or privilege with the natives. Any idea of a "melting pot" in which the
Greeks and Orientals merged was absent. It was not in the interest
of the immigrant Greeks to bring natives into their ranks. Nor were
they particularly interested in forcing their culture onto the natives.

Nevertheless, this ethnic apartheid could not be maintained forever, and the barriers began to break down as time progressed.
Indeed, the stark picture painted in the previous paragraph is too
black and white. Some important native cities continued to flourish,
sometimes incorporating themselves as *poleis*. Some cities had a
minority Greek population which did not control the administration. So intercourse of some sort was possible from the start. Even
at the beginning both the Ptolemies and Seleucids found it useful to
employ the local rulers and aristocrats. Much administration
(though not all, by any means) was carried on in the Greek language. It was in the interests of the native aristocrats to employ
Greek secretaries and to provide a Greek education for their sons.
For the upperclass and the wealthy the adoption of Greek ways was
often a useful move. They were in a position, and had the means, to
do so. For those on the bottom of society—the vast majority—little
changed. They continued to eke out a living by whatever means
their ancestors had done, and their way of life probably differed

little from that of hundreds of generations before under the Persians, Babylonians, Assyrians, and pharaohs.

The native cults flourished. The temples were in the vanguard of those preserving the native culture. The priesthoods of these had usually been accorded certain privileges under the native monarchs, and they saw no reason to give them up. Their own best interests lay in maintaining the resources and rights they had under previous administrations. Some Greek cults, especially associated with the ruler cult, might be incorporated into the temple routine, but they did not replace the pre-existing cults. When the Greek language was used, the native gods might be given Greek names and have their myths expressed in Greek terms, but the cult itself was unaffected. Being polytheists themselves, the Greeks could hardly object to the gods of the natives, and there is no indication they wanted to. Identification of Greek and Oriental gods was common, yet no "take over" by the Greeks was implied in this. The Greeks found this a useful way of understanding the indigenous cults; in their turn, some native writers translated their myths into Greek (e.g., Berossus in Babylon and Manetho in Egypt).

The essence of the Hellenistic world was the Oriental and the Hellenic existing side by side. Any idea of a general "melting" together (*Verschmelzung*) of the Greek and native cultures is generally mistaken. Much later, there is some evidence of a blending of cultural elements at various points, but more often it is merely the borrowing of some elements of one culture into the other. By far the major characteristic was the existence of the old and the new, the Greek and the Oriental, side by side. The native aristocracy may have found the adoption of some Greek ways useful and even attractive; this did not erase pride in the achievements of their culture which was often seen to be far older than and even superior to that of the Greeks. The Phoenicians may have put Greek motifs and inscriptions on their coins, but they continued to put Phoenician ones on as well. The Ptolemies found it useful to take on the trappings of the pharaohs; their court conduct, however, remained primarily Greek.

The form of the Greek empires was very much dominated by the characteristics of the ancient Near Eastern empires. The Greek city-states had been small territories with a core of citizens and a large number of slaves to do most of the work. The Greek empires were run by a small ruling class with a large bureaucracy at its beck and call, with many different ethnic, cultural, and linguistic groups under its control. The economy was not primarily based on slaves but rather on peasants bound to the land. Much of the fighting force was composed of mercenaries. All these elements were inherited from the old Near Eastern empires, not from the classical Greeks.

It is often claimed that Greek became the *lingua franca* of the Near East. In one sense that is true in that it became the major language of administration and the one common language spoken and understood from Macedonia to India. Yet it was hardly the language of most of the people (far greater numbers continued to speak one of the varieties of Aramaic until the Islamic conquest), nor was administration carried on exclusively in Greek. Recent studies have shown that documents in Mesopotamia continued to be written in Akkadian cuneiform, and much writing in Egypt was in Egyptian demotic. Aramaic continued to be used for inscriptions in many places, though little in the way of administrative documents has survived.

The process of Hellenization continued under the Romans. Once again, the ruler had changed but the culture continued. The civilization of the Roman empire was essentially Greek. Rome ruled, but the Greeks dominated culture: literature, aesthetics, even language over much of the Empire belonged to the Greek tradition. Hellenistic culture was the basic culture of the Mediterranean and western Asia from Alexander to the barbaric invasions in the West and the Islamic conquest in the East. This is not to say that the situation remained static or that the Romans did not make their contribution. Nevertheless, Greco-Roman culture was Hellenistic at its heart, as the Romans themselves acknowledged, even if grudgingly at times.

2 HELLENIZATION AMONG THE JEWS

2.1 *The Jews in the Greek Diaspora*

The Jews were like any other ethnic minority in the Greco-Roman world. Outside their own enclave of the small province of Judea, many Jews lived in the various cities in Egypt, Syria, Asia Minor, and even as far away as Rome. Jews in the Diaspora had much in common with their kindred in Judea, but inevitable differences existed, caused by their environment and a situation in which they were a definite minority. They could not take the views and religion of their neighbors for granted. There was the constant presence of pagan cults and shrines which might influence them or, more likely, their children.

Our knowledge of the communities in the Diaspora is episodic and incomplete, being based mainly on inscriptions and passing references in Greco-Roman literature. We do not have enough information to trace the history of any of the communities. Even for Alexandria, whose Jewish community we know best, enough is known for a continuous history of a few decades at most.

2.1.1 Geography of Jewish Communities

The Jewish community in Egypt is probably the best known because written material has been better preserved in its dry climate. From the Zenon papyri in the third century BCE to Roman documents of the second century CE, many references to Jews and to Jewish communities have come down to us. The Jewish community in Egypt has a long history. We know of a Jewish military colony at Elephantine which was most likely already there when the First Temple fell in 587 BCE. It is also alleged that Jews were taken to Alexandria in the time of Ptolemy I. It was in Alexandria, probably about 250 BCE in the reign of Ptolemy II, that the Pentateuch was first translated into Greek. This was important to the community which was now primarily Greek speaking. The rest of the Old Testament was translated over the next century or so (the so-called Septuagint or Old Greek). The significance of the Septuagint cannot be overestimated. It became the Bible as far as many thousands of Jews were concerned, and a significant amount of biblical interpretation extant from antiquity relies on the Septuagint as its base text. It was also an important vehicle for the process of Hellenization among the Jews.

With the Roman conquest, relations began to be strained between the Jewish and the Greek communities of Alexandria because the Jews of Palestine had aided the Romans in their takeover of Egypt. This came to a head in 38 CE when riots against the Jewish community erupted. The immediate cause seems to have been a desire on the part of some Jews to enter the ranks of the citizens, an act which the Greeks objected to. Delegations from both communities appealed to the emperor Caligula, but he was assassinated before any decision was made. His successor Claudius issued a decree asserting Jewish religious rights but requiring them to be happy with their current status and not to seek citizenship. In the revolt of 115-17 CE the Alexandrian community seems to have been decimated and the famous synagogue there destroyed.

The situation in Asia Minor and Syria is less well documented than in Egypt (but see the recent study of Trebilco at 3.11 below).

General statements about large numbers of Jews in these areas can be found in Josephus (*War* 2.18.2 §462-63) and Philo (*Gaium* 33 §245); the inscriptional and literary references confirm this, though it would be difficult to estimate numbers. Communities are attested by inscriptions and material remains at Antioch, Apamea, Sardis and Priene, Pergamum, Smyrna, Ephesus, Hierapolis, Miletus, Acmonia, and Aphrodiasias, while literary references put Jews at a variety of other sites, such as Damascus. Josephus quotes a decree of Antiochus III about the settlement of a Jewish colony of 2000 families in Lydia and Phrygia (*Ant.* 12.3.4 §§147-53). The community in Antioch is said to date from the time of Seleucus I, while the one is Sardis may well be as early as the Persian period.

The Jews in Rome date from at least as early as the Maccabean period, since they were allegedly expelled from the city in 139 BCE. After the fall of Jerusalem to Pompey in 63 BCE, many Jews were taken as slaves to Rome. With time, these or their descendents were manumitted and swelled the ranks of the Jewish community as freedmen. When Augustus banned the *collegia* (political associations), synagogues were specifically exempted. Several incidents in the first century CE are recorded by Josephus, including an expulsion of many Jews in 19 and another under Claudius (some think there were two expulsions under Claudius). In the next few centuries, the community is known from sporadic sources of information, one of the more important being the catacombs or underground cemeteries (Leon). An analysis of these and the tomb inscriptions is very instructive about the languages, names, and religion of the Roman Jews.

2.1.2 *Organization of the Communities*

The Jews were like other ethnic groups within the Greek cities, inhabitants of the city but outsiders to those who controlled and ran the *polis*. Even when born in the city they were not usually a part of the decision-making process or partipants in power. Subject to the laws of city and state, they could be at the mercy of arbitrary administrative decisions which might infringe both freedom and religion. The Greek cities and the old native cities usually had a small citizenship which ran the civic activities. The majority of inhabitants were not citizens, however, and had no political rights in government.

If Josephus were to be believed, the Jews also had the rights of citizenship in various of the Greek foundations (*War* 2.18.7 §§487-88; *Ant.* 12.1.1 §8; 19.5.2 §§280-85; *Ag. Apion* 2.4 §§35-41). Unfortunately, this is only Jewish propaganda. Although a few Jews are known to have possessed citizenship (such as Philo in Alexandria), they were the exception. Most Jews did not possess citizenship and did not have the rights which came with that status. This is hardly surprising since most ethnic groups in the cities were in the same position. The idea of citizenship must have been attractive since we have evidence that some Jews were seeking to enter those ranks. Our best information comes from Alexandria where original documents suggest that Jews were using various means to try to break through the social barriers and to have their children enrolled in the gymnasium and the ephebate, necessary steps to the acquisition of citizenship. It is for this reason that Claudius issued a decree in 41 CE which ordered the Jews not to exceed their station, though it asserted their general religious rights.

In sum, a few Jews in various Greek cities possessed citizenship. Most did not, however, having to make do with the same general conditions that most of their neighbors did.

It was common for Jews to live in a community, however, which would have given support to them in their ethnic and religious identity. In many cases, especially in the larger cities, they would gain permission to incorporate as a *politeuma*. This was a common form of formal association for ethnic groups in the cities of the Hellenistic world. A *politeuma* was officially recognized by the government and allowed the community to have certain rights to regulate its own affairs. The community would determine its own form of government, the laws by which it operated, and the judicial system by which they were enforced. We know of Jewish *politeumata* in several cities and can speculate that it was used in many others. Not all Jewish communities were so recognized, but even if not incorporated as a *politeuma*, they might make arrangements with the local city government about some sorts of religious and other rights.

This is not to suggest that there were not Jews, especially as time went on, who did not rise to prominent positions in their local cities or areas. Inscriptions and literary references show they did. Whenever this happened, it would have created certain tensions with their religious beliefs, as the next section will discuss.

2.1.3 Worship and Religious Practice

In both the Hellenistic kingdoms and under Roman rule, Jewish worship was not usually hindered. Religious tolerance was normal in a polytheistic society, as long as the state did not feel in some way threatened by the religion. We have many instances of formal recognition of Jews' rights to abide by their ancestral laws. The known cases where this was abridged usually had to do with a clash of interests, such as transporting money out of a region to Jerusalem. Sometimes local officials objected to this, for understandable reasons. Also, large assemblies at festival times could make administrators nervous, and special dispensation might be needed to allow traditional celebrations.

As in Palestine, the formal focus of religion was the temple. Writers such as Philo show in what high esteem it was held in the Diaspora, and the multitudes of pilgrims from far away regions who traveled to Jerusalem each fesitival confirmed this. Yet for day-to-day worship the temple was inaccessible; furthermore, a need was felt for some sort of institution to provide a community focus. The synagogue filled these needs. Evidence for the synagogue in Egypt already occurs from about 250 BCE.

The place of the synagogue in the Jewish community is often taken for granted (Grabbe; Flesher). This seems to be justified in the Diaspora communities. *Proseuchē* "prayer house" is the term most widely used in inscriptions and literary sources such as Philo. "Synagogue" is also a Greek term (*sunagogē*) meaning "assembly"; it does not occur for a building or place until about the middle of the first century CE, only for the congregation of people. The Diaspora synagogue seems to have been much more than just a place of prayer. Judging from inscriptions and passages in Philo, an important function was their frequent dedication to the king or ruler. Jews could then claim full loyalty to the temporal government while carrying on with their traditional religion uncompromised. Otherwise, their refusal to participate in pagan cults, including the emperor or ruler cult, might place them under suspicion of being enemies of the state. Other religious activities also took place, especially reading of the Law and its exposition. But little beyond this can be inferred since there are few data.

Inscriptions and literary references from a wide variety of periods indicate that some Jews became quite prominent in their local cities and expressed their loyalty formally by donations and public services. We have evidence that the legend of Noah was incorporated into a local flood legend at Apamea and even appears on coins. Names of Jewish young men are found on the ephebate lists of Sardis and Iasus, making them members of the gymnasium and candidates for citizenship. Tomb inscriptions record the status of individuals who were archons and members of the governing council. These and other data show that Jews did not always remain aloof or keep themselves in ghetto-like communities. On the contrary, in many cities the Jews—or at least some Jews—seem to have been very active in civic life.

Since civic activities often included dedications to pagan gods or ceremonies relating to the gods, how did the Jews in civic positions respond to this? In most cases we do not know. Imperial decrees around 200 CE allowed Jews to hold office but to be exempted from activities which conflicted with their religion. Before that, however, Jews still seem to have held office in some cases. One can suspect that they acquiesced passively to the pagan ceremonies; that is, they did not participate actively but were present and witnessed the rites when required. If so, we still should not assume that these Jews had abandoned their religion, considering the fierce attachment to the ancestral religion mentioned in all our literary sources. Indeed, in all our literature we know of only one or two individuals alleged to have left their religion altogether. This suggests that those who held office were willing to make certain compromises without feeling that it detracted from their loyalty to Judaism. Philo (discussed in the next section) demonstrates knowledge of shows and spectacles which could only have been those provided by the Greek civic authorities in Alexandria. To label such Jews as "unorthodox" or aberrant in some way is to ignore the historical data. Judaism in this period was characterized by diversity, and apart from the unifying symbolism of the Jerusalem temple, there was no overall religious authority.

2.1.4 To Be a Hellenistic Jew—the Example of Philo

No better example of a Hellenistic Jew can be found than Philo of Alexandria (c. 20 BCE to 50 CE). He was a member of a long-established wealthy family which possessed Alexandrian citizenship. He shows evidence of a good Greek education and seems to have known only Greek; all the evidence available indicates that he had little or no Hebrew. He had studied the Platonism and Stoicism current in his time. Contrary to many Jews, Philo was completely at home in the Greek culture and lifestyle of the Alexandrian community. If anyone was "Hellenized", Philo fell into this category.

Philo was, however, also a completely observant Jew who identified with the Jewish community and religion. It is not automatic that this would be so, judging from statements in his own writings. Some of his fellow Jews who allegorized the Scriptures, he tells us, argued that observance of the Law was unnecessary so long as its spiritual meaning was realized and appreciated. Philo did not agree with this. For example, with regard to the festivals or circumcision, his emphasis is on the "spiritual" meaning of the observance. Nevertheless, he regarded physical circumcision and actual festival celebrations as necessary for the correct practice of Judaism (*Migr.* 91-93). Philo could and did allegorize with the best of them—and regularly concentrated on the "deeper" significance of the text—but he did not let this diminish his careful observance of the traditional customs. Like the martyrs of 2 Maccabees 7, he regarded the Torah's requirements worth dying for.

2.2 Hellenistic Judaism in Palestine

Thanks primarily to the Zenon papyri, 1 and 2 Maccabees, and Josephus, the history of Judaism in Palestine is much better known than that in the Diapora. This history is extremely important for the subject of this chapter since the history of Judaism in the two centuries after Alexander is the history of the Hellenization process. Therefore, this history will be traced in some detail here.

Judea, with a high priest at its head, was one of many small states within the Greek empires. Later, this state was to do something very unusual, perhaps unique; it was to throw off the Seleucid yoke, become an autonomous, independent state, and expand its borders. Until that happened, though, the Jews were one more small subject state and one more ethnic group within the Ptolemaic and then the Seleucid kingdom.

2.2.1 Under Ptolemaic Rule

Little is known about the initial period of Greek rule over Palestine. The alleged meeting between Alexander and the Jerusalem high priest is no more than legend (*Ant.* 11.8.1-6 §§304-45). Jerusalem was apparently taken by Ptolemy I at least once during the wars of the Diadochi (*Ant.* 12.1.1 §§3-10; *Ag. Apion* 1.22 §§209-12). Apart from that, the picture is blank until about the middle of the third century BCE. There are one or two pieces of vital evidence, however: (a) a receipt in Aramaic from the middle of the third century BCE, found in Jerusalem, has two Greek words (Cross); (b) an Aramaic-Greek bilingual from Edom, is dated about 300-275 BCE (Geraty). These demonstrate how quickly the Greek language was already penetrating into the culture of Palestine.

Much of what we know about Ptolemaic Judea comes from the Zenon papyri. Zenon was an agent of the Egyptian finance minister Apollonius, one of the most powerful men in Egypt after Ptolemy II. In 259 BCE Zenon took a year-long journey through Palestine and southern Syria to take care of business interests for Apollonius. The correspondence from that time and later shows a Palestine administered like one of the nomes of Egypt, apparently without a governor of its own (though this is disputed). The main concern of the Ptolemaic government was to see that the revenues from the region were extracted at their maximum practical level. To ensure this, they had administrative and revenue agents at every level down to the individual local village. Some of these agents were natives used by the Ptolemies, but descendents of the Greek conquerors also functioned in the tax-collecting service, often at the higher levels. This careful supervision by Greeks meant that most Jews were to a lesser or greater extent exposed to Greek language and culture from the beginning of the Greek period.

The use of native administrators was not limited only to the lower levels. Local aristocrats and sheiks were used to govern at a very high level. A good example is Tobias, the head of a military colony across the Jordon. Zenon spent time with him and later corresponded with him. Whether Tobias himself spoke Greek is not certain, though he probably knew some, but he employed a Greek secretary. He shows himself at home in the Hellenistic world, fully able to entertain agents of the Egyptian administration. Surviving correspondence even shows Tobias sending gifts of slaves to Apollonius, and of exotic animals to Ptolemy II himself.

We also have knowledge of the activities of Tobias' descendents (*Ant.* 12.4.1-11 §§157-236). The source of the knowledge is a semi-legendary account and thus not always reliable, but the general picture fits well with the Palestine known from the Zenon papyri. Tobias' son or grandson Joseph managed to secure the tax-collecting rights for Palestine and Syria. Joseph's son Hyrcanus secured them in his turn. The story as told by Josephus illustrates several points: Judeans were at home in the Greek court of Alexandria, apparently speaking Greek and happy to participate in its activities. The Tobiads were aristocrats but they were also married into the high priestly family of the Oniads. As members of the ruling class, they are not representative of all Jews of the times, but they are a part of the overall picture. They are one stratum of the Jews and represent the aristocratic and priestly leadership.

2.2.2 The "Hellenistic Reform" in Jerusalem

Ptolemaic rule came to an end in 200 BCE when Antiochus III finally took back Palestine and southern Syria. The Jews were divided into factions, some supporting the Ptolemies and others the Seleucids, but the latter gained the upperhand and helped Antiochus to take Jerusalem. Antiochus rewarded the Jews by a special charter (given in detail by Josephus in *Ant.* 12.3.34 §§138-46) which allowed the traditional laws and customs to be observed and also granted certain financial privileges for a shorter or longer period. Such a charter was a standard practice for new conquerors of the time.

A quarter of a century later, in 175 BCE, Antiochus IV became emperor. Hardly was he on the throne than Jason, the brother of the Jerusalem high priest, came to him with a proposition. If Antiochus would grant Jason the priesthood in place of his brother Onias III, he would pay an extra amount of tribute. Jason was granted not only this but also another favor which he requested: for an additional payment he would be allowed to turn Jerusalem into a Greek city, a polis. Thus began the "Hellenistic reform", one of the most controversial and misunderstood episodes in Jewish history.

The main account of the Hellenistic reform is found in 2 Maccabees 4 which is clearly hostile to Jason. We have no source which takes the side of Jason and his colleagues. This has to be kept in mind in trying to reconstruct what happened. According to 2 Maccabees, Jason had abandoned the Law and traditional Judaism and was in general a thoroughly wicked man. This opinion cannot be taken at face value but must be tested by the rules of historical criticism: its particular bias is quite evident.

We are not told what Jason's motives were. The chances are that he was a "phil-Hellene", one who admired the Greeks and their culture. Perhaps he realized the advantages which might accrue to Jerusalem if it became a *polis*. What his aim clearly was not was to transform the Jewish religion. To do so would have gone against Jason's own best interests. The basis of his power was the temple and its cult. Anything which subverted the temple and its income would have damaged him and his supporters among the priests and aristocracy. Furthermore, 2 Maccabees is unable to give any examples of law-breaking on Jason's part. It can only speak in generalities, using such emotive words as "wicked" and "unlawful", but it actually lists no unlawful activities.

The Hellenistic reform of Jason was thus not a religious reform. Jerusalem was changed into a Greek polis. A group of individuals (most likely the upperclass inhabitants who were able to pay for the privilege) was enrolled as citizens, though the original form of government with a council of elders and the high priest at its head remained. The main change mentioned in the sources was the building of a gymnasium where the youth would be educated and trained for future citizenship. Apart from the gymnasium, little seems to have been different from previously. The essential form of government was apparently the same; the temple functioned as before; the priests offered the daily sacrifices; the cult continued; no pagan statues were set up in the temple or other pagan features introduced. Nor do we read of any objections or reactions on the part of the people. If there were those who did not like what Jason and his supporters did, we have no knowledge of it. From all that the sources tell us, the new constitution was implemented smoothly and efficiently, with the general agreement (or at least acquiescence) of the inhabitants of the city and the country.

The Hellenistic reform was ultimately aborted, but the cause was not objections of the people. Rather, another priest by the name of Menelaus played the same trick as Jason and attempted to buy the priesthood by offering a yet higher price, which Antiochus accepted. This was about the year 172, so Jason's experiment with a Greek *polis* came to an end after only about three years. There is no evidence that Menelaus kept up the Hellenistic reform. Now the people did finally react, not to Hellenization but to something else: rumors of religious sacrilege—that Menelaus had been selling some of the temple vessals. They rioted and killed Menelaus' brother. Then the council—the same council organized by Jason and supportive of his reforms—sent a delegation of some of their own members to Antiochus to ask for Menelaus' removal. They were unsuccessful. Menelaus, unlike Jason, violated the Law. About 170 BCE he not only gave over a large amount of the temple treasure to Antiochus but even conducted him through the inner parts of the temple itself, contrary to all Jewish law. A couple of years later when Judaism was suppressed, it is not certain what part Menelaus played in it. Most of our sources blame Antiochus, but there are suggestions that Menelaus was also involved (e.g., 2 Macc. 13:38).

In sum, the exact reconstruction of events is impossible from present knowledge, but all the available evidence suggests that Menelaus was completely different from Jason. Jason had ousted his brother from the high priesthood, which would no doubt have been regarded as an unlawful act under normal circumstances. How he explained this to the people is not known, but his assumption of the office and his introduction of a new constitution for Jerusalem went

unopposed as far as we know. His measures did turn Jerusalem into
a Greek city, but the religion and essential government continued
as before. With Menelaus, things changed. He seems to have dis-
continued the Hellenistic reform. His actions brought opposition
from the council and people; he desecrated the temple by bringing
Antiochus into it and giving him temple money; and eventually he
seems to have had a hand in the measures to suppress traditional
Jewish worship. Judaism suffered as a religion but it did not suffer
because of the Hellenistic reform.

2.2.3 Hasmonean and Roman Rule

The story of the brave fight of the Jews against the Seleucid empire
to restore their temple and worship is well known and recorded in
detail in 1 and 2 Maccabees. The Maccabean revolt was not,
though, a fight against Hellenization. Many of those who partici-
pated in the early stage (c. 168-164 BCE) were interested only in
the restoration of religious rights. Once the temple was retaken and
the decrees forbidding Jewish worship rescinded, they were content
to return to their previous place in the Seleucid empire. The
Maccabees and their supporters would be satisfied only with the
removal of the Syrian yoke from Judean shoulders, but the concern
was political domination, not cultural values. They continued to
fight. Having won independence, however, the Hasmoneans ruled
like other Hellenistic kings for the next century. Native Jewish literature and traditions continued to flourish in Hebrew and Aramaic but so did writing and translations into Greek. 1 Maccabees
was probably written originally in Hebrew but translated and survived only in Greek. Jason of Cyrene wrote a history of the revolt in
Greek, of which only the epitome in 2 Maccabees survived.
Eupolemus, one of the righthand men of the early Hasmonean
court (2.2.4), wrote a history of the Israelite kings, also in Greek.
The Hasmoneans negotiated and corresponded with the Seleucids,
the Romans, and others around them, employing Greek language
and literary methods. The Hasmonean nation and court was certainly not antiHellenistic but fully at home in the Hellenistic world.

The coming of Rome did not change this. Roman culture was
mainly Greek culture in its literature and values. Judea came under
direct Roman domination in 63 BCE when Pompey intervened in
the disputes of the final two rival Hasmonean brothers. Under direct Roman rule, under Herod the Greek, and under his descendants, nothing seems to have been any different as far as
Hellenization was concerned. Hebrew and Aramaic language and

literature continued as before. Most Palestinian Jews spoke one of these as their first language. Yet Greek was also known and used to lesser or greater extent by a significant number of Jews. Herod and his successors supported building projects using the best Greek architecture, both at home and elsewhere in the Mediterranean world. The Jerusalem temple was itself refurbished and expanded to become one of the most magnificent examples of Greco-Roman architecture of its time. Even the disastrous war with Rome in 66-70 did not alter this. Some of the leaders of the war—notably Josephus and Justus of Tiberius—had a Greek education and went on to write of their experiences in Greek.

Hellenization was a process which began with Alexander and did not cease when Judea ceased to be a nation. For a thousand years, Jewish history was a history of Jewish activities, literature, and culture as a part of the Hellenistic world. The native was not lost, but as time went on it was transformed by new methods of interpretation, by re-expression in new forms of literature, and by new developments in philosophy and thought. Much of this transformation came about by the influence of Greek literature and thought. The new did not drive out the old. Greek did not replace Semitic. The two existed and moved forward in a creative synthesis in which the native elements were not submerged but continued to vitalize Jewish culture even as it responded to new conditions and influences.

2.2.4 Josephus and Eupolemus—Two Hellenistic Palestinian Jews

As an educated Jew from a well-off family Josephus evidently had some Greek education while growing up. Although he emphasized the Jewish privileging of knowledge of the Law, he was already able to communicate in both spoken and written Greek before the war with Rome. For example, he was sent to Rome as part of an embassy to request the release of certain priests who were hostages. The choice of Josephus suggests that he had some knowledge of Greek and would be able to acquit himself satisfactorily in the capital of the Empire. He was later able to communicate with Romans, apparently without interpreters.

When Josephus put his experiences to paper, he claims that his first history of the 66-70 war was "in his native language" (probably Aramaic: *War* 1.Pref.1 §3). However, all the writings which have come down to us are in Greek. He admits to having used Greek assistants (*Ag. Apion* 1.9 §50), which helps to explain the good Greek style of the *War*, but he almost certainly had a good foundation in

the language on which to build. The later *Antiquities* is generally
admitted not to be as skilled in Greek usage, suggesting that
Josephus wrote it on his own. It would be hardly surprising that this
Palestinian did not fully master the intricacies of Greek literary
convention, but this could be true even of one who knew the language well. That Josephus gained a good foundation in Greek already in his youth is a justified inference.

Further evidence of Josephus' position in a Hellenistic culture
can be found in his literary works. Although he may have had some
literary models in Jewish writings, he shows knowledge of Greek
literary practise and of a number of Greek writers. It has been
persuasively argued that Josephus used Thucydides and Polybius as
a model for the *War*, and Dionysius of Halicarnassus, for the *Antiquities*. Many other evidences of Greek influences can be found in his
works: The Greek version (Septuagint) of certain books of the Bible,
rather than the Hebrew, was drawn on. Biblical history is presented
in a format that would be easily understood by an educated Greco-
Roman, with potentially embarrassing episodes such as that of the
golden calf omitted. Biblical figures such as Moses and David are
presented as models of the Hellenistic wiseman and statesman.
Abraham is the teacher of the Egyptians in astronomy (astrology)
and mathematics.

Less is known about Eupolemus, but much in his biography
parallels that of Josephus: he was a part of the ruling establishment;
he had a Greek education and used it in the service of his country;
he wrote a work which attempted to put Semitic Jewish tradition
into Greek dress. The son of an important Jewish official who negotiated with Antiochus III, he was high up in the Maccabean administration and sent on an embassy to Rome (1 Macc. 8:17-18; 2
Macc. 4:11). Most think he was also the writer of the Greek work,
On the Kings of Judah, which has been preserved only in fragments.
The extant portions show not just a bare translation of the traditions in Kings/Chronicles but an interpretation and adaptation,
drawing on Greek literary and cultural ideas.

In short, Josephus and Eupolemus had taken up the Hellenistic
genre of apologetic historiography (Sterling) and used it to present
Jewish history and culture. Although Palestinian Jews deeply rooted
in their own native culture and tradition, they fitted into the wider
Hellenistic world without any problem.

2.3 Summary and Conclusions

The desire to emphasize the uniqueness of the Jewish religion has sometimes led to an artificial separation of Judaism and Hellenization. In fact, the Jews were as much a part of the Hellenistic world as any native peoples. Much of our knowledge of Hellenistic Judaism comes from literature, primarily nonhistorical literature. One of the main problems is how to relate the literary phenomenon to the historical situation. How does a writing reveal a particular Jewish constituency—a Judaism? The idea of trying to reconstruct a community from a writing is hardly new, but past attempts have sometimes operated with a rather restrictive set of assumptions. The data available from literary and inscriptional sources has increased considerably in recent years, but new methods of looking at the data have been equally important in recognizing that the old picture has had to be altered rather drastically.

We now realize that Judaism in the Hellenistic world was characterized by diversity—there were many Judaisms. Jews had a fierce loyalty toward the religion of the fathers and clear willingness to die, if necessary, to adhere to it. Yet the precise way in which one showed loyalty varied tremendously. Some practices would no doubt have been considered beyond the pale by most Jews, such as those (few!) who removed the marks of circumcision in order to participate in Greek athletic contests (1 Macc. 1:15). But large numbers of Jews saw little or no problem with being a part of the Hellenistic world. It was not always easy to practice the dietary or purity laws, and many found the easiest path that of living inside a Jewish community which put up some sort of barrier to the Greco-Roman environment. But communication, influence, and intercourse were inevitable and not necessarily thought undesirable. Some Jews welcomed the more overt Hellenistic lifestyle, especially those who could afford it, and saw no conflict with being loyal Jews as well.

Because of the sparsity of data, it is often difficult to characterize the individual Judaisms at whose existence the sources give tantalizing hints. How did they worship? What did they believe? In most cases, we can only guess. If we conceive of Hellenization as a spectrum, ranging from the completely Greek to the completely native, Jews will be found at most points on the spectrum. The poor in Palestine itself lived much as their ancestors had done. They would have been near the native end of the scale. Their way of life would have been difficult for most Jews in the Diaspora—even the poor—for whom Greco-Roman culture and life was a daily reality. Isolation was neither possible nor desirable. The continual presence of pagan worship may have created difficulties, yet some Jews managed to live with it and even rise to high office without succumbing. Perhaps they made compromises that others would have frowned on, but we cannot say that they did not do what they did with a clear conscience. It only confuses matters to attempt to insert the modern concepts of orthodoxy and even orthopraxy into the discussion. Beyond certain basic concepts of the Law, being a Jew was what one made of it, and who was in a position to say otherwise?

We can now summarize briefly some of the main conclusions of the discussion:

1. Hellenization was a complex process, lasting centuries. It combined the Greek and the Near Eastern, and the native heritage is as much a part of the Hellenistic world as is the Greek.

2. There were a range of reactions to the presence of Greek culture. For the many poor at the bottom of society, little was likely to have been different. For merchants, crafts workers, petty officials, some knowledge of Greek language may have been important. For the few in the upper eschalons of society, a Greek education would have been a *sine qua non*. There is little evidence of cultural resistance (whether by the Jews or others). Most native peoples, though, had some pride in their own culture and some animosity toward the conquerors. A few overt aspects of Greek culture may have been resented as symbols of foreign overlordship and, in the event of a rebellion (of which there were a number), attacked as foreign. General cultural resistance seems to have been seldom, however, since the native culture was never displaced and the Greek borrowings generally assimilated with little question.

3. Jews were very much a part of this process, whether in Palestine or outside it. The situation and reaction was much like that of other minority ethnic groups within the Hellenistic empires. We have many examples of "Hellenistic Jews" who were fully loyal to their religion but saw no need to isolate themselves from the Hellenizing process.

4. The Maccabean revolt was primarily a matter of religious restoration at first, then later an independence movement. What it was not was a movement against the Greek aspects of Hellenistic culture. There was a range of attitude among the so-called "Hellenists", and they should not be lumped together as they often are. The so-called "Judaizers" similarly covered a specrum of views, but they were primarily concerned with the restoration of the temple cult and religious rights.

5. The one area where Jews did find themselves at odds with the rest of the Hellenistic world was in the area of religion. They alone of all ethnic groups refused to honor gods, shrines and cults other than their own. On the other hand, Jewish religious rights were generally respected by the Greek and Roman authorities. The single exception is the religious suppression under Antiochus IV about 168-165 BCE, an incident which has yet to be explained satisfactorily. The attempt by Caligula to place his statue in the Jerusalem seems to have had a more complex cause, possibly even a reaction against Jewish intolerance of a Roman cult in a non-Jewish area.

6. There was a wide variety of Judaisms in antiquity. The loyalty of Hellenistic Jews to their ancestral religion did not mean that they conformed to a rabbinic model. The idea that some were "orthodox" and others not (or even some "more orthodox" or others "less orthodox") represents a modern confessional position, not a scholarly description, and has no place in the discussion. Available evidence shows that most Jews known from antiquity were loyal to their religion in their own way, even if their particular form of Judaism differed considerably from the rabbinic or other later forms which became normative.

3 RECENT AND CLASSICAL STUDIES

3.1 E. Schürer

The classical text for Judaism during much of the Hellenistic period is Emil Schürer's *Geschichte des jüdischen Volkes im Zeitalter Jesu Christi*, which first appeared in 1874 and went through four editions. This has now been translated into English and updated by G. Vermes, F. Millar, and others as *The Jewish People in the Age of Jesus Christ*. Schürer's work was characterized by its thoroughness in collecting the data of the original sources from both the Jewish and the relevant Greco-Roman sources: archeological, epigraphic, literary. This has now all been updated in perhaps the most useful collection and handbook for Judaism from about 200 BCE to 135 CE.

Schürer's main contribution to the study of Hellenistic Judaism is its thorough collection of epigraphical and other data on Jews in areas outside Palestine and on important Greek cities in Palestine (mainly in §§22, 23, and 31). Information on individual Jewish communities is often scattered in separate studies and difficult of access. The new Schürer attempts to bring together all original material (whether in Greek or other languages) and consider it in the light of recent study. The text gives a synthetic treatment of each city, while the footnotes are an invaluable mine of data and references. This is the place to begin for anyone doing research on most Jewish communities outside Palestine and within. The discussion of questions of city organization, regional government, administration, taxation, and the like are very important, especially for those without a specialist knowledge of the Greco-Roman world.

Not to be overlooked is the thorough treatment of Jewish literature (especially in vol. 3, though also in vol. 1). Although Collins (3.10 below) is recommended as the initial study of the literature of Hellenistic Judaism, this is not because the new Schürer's survey of scholarship on individual books is not equally valuable. Anyone looking at scholarship on any individual Jewish writing in Greek would do well to consult Schürer as well as Collins.

The main weakness of Schürer lies in its volume 1 which appeared already in 1973. Since editorial policy developed as work progressed, the first volume was the least revised and remains the most unreliable. (Indeed, the footnotes of the later editors sometimes contradict the translated but unrevised text!). Volume 1 is probably less important for the subject of Hellenistic Judaism than vols. 2 and 3, but it covers such important subjects as the Ptolemaic period, the Hellenistic reform, and the Maccabean revolt. Here the treatment in Schürer needs thorough revision in the light of more recent work (see 2.2.2 above).

3.2 V. A. Tcherikover

Apart from Schürer, probably the most important single book on Hellenism and Judaism is Victor Tcherikover's *Hellenistic Civilization and the Jews*. Tcherikover possessed a formible knowledge of the scholarship and sources of the Hellenistic world and the Judaism in it. His earliest work was a study of Greek foundations in Syria during the Roman period. He produced a study of the Zenon papyri and went on to edit (with others) a collection of papyri relating to the Jews in Egypt (*CPJ*); this remains a major accessible source of original documents on the Jewish community in Egypt to the second century CE. Many other individual studies on Judaism of the period also appeared, unfortunately not yet collected together.

His very readable *Hellenistic Civilization and the Jews* is divided into two sections. The first part treats Hellenistic civilization in Palestine, with an overview of its history and institutions. This part of the study concentrates on the century or so from Tobias to the time of Simon Maccabee. Tcherikover's analysis of the sources is consistently illuminating even when one disagrees with his conclusions. One of the most controversial elements is his argument that the revolt against the Syrians was initiated by the Hasidim, a thesis he developed as an alternative to that of Bickerman with whom he disagreed. The problem is whether we really know anything about the Hasidim (Davies). The second part addresses the subject of Hellenistic civilization in the Diaspora. Here Tcherikover could draw on his extensive work on the Zenon papyri and other sources relating to Egypt. One important subject dealt with in skillful detail is the question of citizenship for Jews in the many Greek cities.

3.3 E. J. Bickerman

Perhaps no single scholar has been more important for the study of Hellenistic Judaism than E. J. Bickerman. Without his name no discussion of the subject could be complete. In several books and innumerable articles Bickerman addressed the whole period of Judaism in the Greek period, wrestling with many individual topics and problems in studies characterized not only by attention to details of philology, sources, and data in their historical context but also by common sense, thoroughness, and even genius at times. Like Tcherikover, Bickerman was at home in the Hellenistic sources as few can be today. His depth of knowledge and learning is an example to all subsequent researchers. The standard scholarly position on many issues today is that first laid out and defended by Bickerman.

The difficulty with discussing Bickereman in this context is to find a single work which can be pointed to as the one to read above others. I shall single out his *Gott der Makkabäer* (ET *God of the Maccabees*) for readers, though this is to some extent arbitrary. In this short book Bickerman attacked the problem of the causes of the Maccabean revolt and gave an answer which is still accepted by some and has made a permanent contribution to the debate. He put the religious changes at Jerusalem in the context of the Hellenistic world. Like Tcherikover he showed the complexities of the process of Hellenization. He demonstrated that the cult set up in Jerusalem under the aegis of Antiochus IV was not Greek but Syrian. He also showed that Antiochus was not religious enthusiast or reformer as often painted. This led him to a thesis which has remained controversial: he concluded that the initiative to change the cult came from the "Hellenists" among the Jews who wanted to create an "enlightened" religion on the analogy of the Reform Movement in Judaism in the nineteenth century.

Some of Bickerman's other important works should also be indicated. His *Institutions des Seleucides* is still an important reference on the Seleucid empire. Many of his articles relating to Second Temple Judaism have been collected into the three-volume *Studies in Jewish and Christian History*. He also wrote two histories of the Second Period period, but these are not as helpful as one one would like. The first was the publication of lectures in the book, *From Ezra to the Last of the Maccabees*. The second is the post-humous publication, *The Jews in the Greek Age*. Unfortunately, neither of these is very well documented, and it is difficult for any but the specialist to follow up his conclusions or to know the basis and sources on which they are arrived at.

3.4 A. Momigliano

As a classical historian and scholar, the breadth of Arnaldo Momigliano's knowledge and the number of articles published is astonishing. Beginning in 1955 his countless reviews and articles have been published in collections in the series *Storia et Letteratura*, reaching eight volumes so far. Only a portion of this work involved Judaism, yet he maintained a lifelong interest in Hellenistic Judaism and periodically wrote articles or reviewed books on some aspect of the subject.

As with Bickerman, it is difficult to single out one study on which to concentrate, especially since many of these are in individual articles. However, his book *Alien Wisdom: The Limits of Hellenization* is probably the one most important work for Hellenization and Hellenistic Judaism, especially in the two essays "The Hellenistic Discovery of Judaism" (pp. 74-96) and "Greeks, Jews and Romans from Antiochus III to Pompey" (pp. 97-122). In such a brief compass Momigliano establishes some of the essential points with regard to Hellenization. His main focus is on various native groups which came into contact with the Greeks, that is, the Greeks and their "neighbors": the Celts, the Jews, the Iranians, and others.

3.5 M. Hengel

In 1969 Martin Hengel produced a classical study in his *Judentum und Hellenismus*. It was revised in 1973 and translated into English (*Judaism and Hellenism: Studies in their Encounter in Palestine during the Early Hellenistic Period*) in 1974 and continues to be an influential book in any study of the question. Hengel carried forward the work of Tcherikover, Momigliano, and especially Bickerman. What he attempted to do was to cover the whole interaction between Judaism and Hellenism to the time of the Maccabean revolt. He divided his study into three parts: the political, administrative, and economical side of Hellenization; the linguistic, educational, and cultural side; and the specific encounter of Hellenization with Palestinian Judaism. (A fourth section looked at the Hellenistic reform in Jerusalem.) Hengel concluded that from "about the middle of the third century BC all Judaism must really be designated 'Hellenistic Judaism' in the strict sense," so that one cannot separate Palestinian Judaism from Hellenistic Judaism (1974: vol. 1, p. 103-6).

Hengel's study has met with widespread applause for its breadth of learning and the cogency of his basic arguments. He has also received some justified criticisms, though only one critic has rejected his thesis outright (Feldman). In the way that examples are selected and presented, Hengel did appear to exaggerate the place of Greek education and language in Palestine. Also, Bickerman's thesis about the cause of the Maccabean revolt (that the Jewish 'Hellenists' instituted the religious suppression themselves) is accepted rather uncritically. Partly in response to criticisms, Hengel went on to develop and expand his study of the question in two shorter works. One of these was his *Juden, Griechen und Barbaren* (ET *Jews, Greek, and Barbarians*) in 1976 and, most recently, *Zum Problem der "Hellenisierung" Judäas im 1. Jahrhundert nach Christus* (ET *The "Hellenization" of Judaea in the First Century after Christ*). Any study of Hellenization and Judaism must take full account of these works.

3.6 M. Stern

Over a lifetime of work, M. Stern devoted a good deal of his efforts to Judaism of the Second Temple period. These appeared in a variety of separate studies and articles. His greatest contribution lies in his three-volume collection, *Greek and Latin Authors on Jews and Judaism*. This is primarily an assemblage of quotations from "pagan authors", a useful source book but not a synthetic study. Nevertheless, there is more to Stern's collection than an extremely useful and thorough gathering of references. Stern's own contribution is found in the introductions and detailed notes to the texts. Here he makes his mark as an interpreter of Judaism and Jewish history.

3.7 E. R. Goodenough

Edwin Goodenough was one of the first important challengers to the idea of "normative Judaism" (Moore) which was based on rabbinic (and later) literature. His *magnum opus* was his 13-volume *Jewish Symbols in the Greco-Roman Period*. This was not just a collection of data about symbolism in Jewish art, as it has often been treated, but a powerful addressing of the question of the nature of Judaism in the Hellenistic period. The symbolism found in Jewish synagogues, cemeteries, and inscriptions, primarily of the first few centuries of the common era, shows a Judaism (or Judaisms) differing in many ways from the contemporary rabbinic Judaism. Similarly, Philo shows a type of Judaism which uses the traditional Jewish scriptures but differs from that known from the Hebrew Bible or rabbinic literature. Much of the Judaism in the Hellenistic period quite unashamedly borrowed pagan symbolism and used motifs eschewed and forbidden by the rabbis, yet its emphasis was on the traditional Jewish stories and law. Goodenough showed that Judaism could be "normative" without being rabbinic.

Goodenough had attacked a cherished view, and this was not popular. His work was known and used for the data, but his conclusions were generally ignored at the time. In the past two decades, though, the general truth of his arguments have been confirmed from other perspectives. His work deserves to be read for its primary aim and not just as a quarry for useful data. Especially important are his Part V "The Problem of Method" (in vol. 4) and Part XVI "Summary and Conclusions" (in vol 12). Many readers will find the abridged edition in one volume an extremely valuable resource, not least the introductory essay by the editor which provides an orientation to the work, its history, and its reception by the scholarly community.

Goodenough's work on Philo must also be briefly mentioned, especially since so much of his scholarly work was devoted to the Alexandrian. He wrote a number of studies on Philo, but the one most recommended to the non-specialist is his *Introduction to Philo Judaeus*. For one without any background in the subject, it would be better to begin with Sandmel, but Goodenough's work is more detailed and wider in coverage.

3.8 A. Kuhrt and S. Sherwin-White (ed.)

If one wants a general survey of Hellenistic history from Alexander to the beginning of the Roman empire, the two-volume history of

E. Will is unsurpassed. Equally valuable but from another angle is E. S. Gruen's work on Rome and the Hellenistic world. When it comes to a coverage of the process of Hellenization in all aspects, however, no other work does the job as well as the collection edited by A. Kuhrt and S. Sherwin-White, *Hellenism in the East*. It is almost entirely devoted to the situation in the Seleucid empire, with only occasional references to Ptolemaic Egypt. This is not a handicap, however, since the situation in Egypt is better documented and has been more intensively studied over the past century. There is so much new or overlooked information on the effect of Seleucid rule on the old areas of Persia, Babylonia, and Assyria that this collection breaks extensive new ground and seriously outdates previous overviews. A brief review of its contents is in order, though this cannot hope to do justice to its important data and discussions:

S. Sherwin-White ("Seleucid Babylonia") demonstrates that Greek rule in Babylonia did not mean the cessation of the traditional culture. Not only did it continue to thrive but did so with Seleucid encouragement. A. Kuhrt ("'Berossus' *Babyloniaka* and Seleucid Rule in Babylonia") looks at Berossus as a good example of a native who reacts to Greek rule. Although he follows the Babylonian Chronicle tradition faithfully, he introduces concepts known only from Greek literature. R. J. van der Speck ("The Babylonian City") concludes that the coming of Hellenization did not change the basic character of the Babylonian city despite some adaptation of Greek styles as time went by. J.-F. Salles ("The Arab-Persian Gulf under the Seleucids") argues that the main interest of the Seleucids in the Gulf region was one of economic control, not conquest or settlement. There is little evidence of major Greek influence in the area. F. Millar ("The Problem of Hellenistic Syria") continues previous studies on the process of Hellenization. One of his main points is how difficult it is to assess the question in Syria because of the sparseness of the sources. M. Colledge ("Greek and non-Greek Interaction in the Art and Architecture of the Hellenistic East") argues that Greek influence began already before Alexander, and native art flourished long after him. The two thrived side by side, but "hybrid" forms developed at an early time and became more dominant as time went on.

For a further development on many of these points, especially those brought up in Sherwin-White's essay, the recent book by Sherwin-White and Kuhrt is required reading.

3.9 S. J. D. Cohen

There are number of good introductions to Josephus which can be generally recommended (e.g., Bilde; Rajak; especially of value is the short treatment by H. Attridge). When it comes to a critical engagement with Josephus, however, no single work so far surpasses S. J. D. Cohen, *Josephus in Galilee and Rome*. Its aim is not primarily to give a full overview of Josephan scholarship but rather to focus on how Josephus worked as a historian, his aims and objectives, his biases, his value. Above all, Cohen provides an extended engagement with Josephus in action.

Cohen's focus is on a comparison of the *War* and the *Life*, but this study impinges on many of the issues about how Josephus worked and his trustworthiness as a historian. Any use of Josephus must consider his sources and their quality, his aims and goals, and his prejudices and biases. These all come out in Josephus' own experiences in the 66-70 war with Rome. He was not just an armchair historian—he also lived through history and made history. What he wrote about was often very personal to him Yet he had absorbed many of the conventions of Hellenistic historiography, as well, so that any use of Josephus as a source must take into account these various levels and pulls. Cohen does a superb job of showing how these operate in a significant part of Josephus' corpus.

3.10 J. J. Collins

It was noted under 1.1 that Hellenistic Judaism is to a considerable extent a literary phenomenon. Many useful treatments of the literature are available, including Schürer (3.1) and Nickelsburg. Probably the best overview of literary Hellenistic Judaism is J. J. Collins' *Between Athens and Jerusalem*. Collins focuses very much on a survey of the literature, with the expected literary critical data of authorship, dating, and provenance. He goes beyond this, however, to classify the literature according to genre and background. In Part One he deals with those writings which concern national and political identity: chroniclers and historians, poets, and those who wrote on religion and politics. Part Two looks at identity through ethics and piety: testaments, oracles, apocalyptic and mystical writings. Collins' can be criticized for his omissions. He leaves out such writings in Greek as 1 Maccabees (apparently because it probably had a Hebrew original). More important is the omission of two major writers in Greek, Josephus and Philo of Alexandria, which means that Collins' work is incomplete. Nevertheless, out of this survey emerges Hellenistic Judaism in much of its complexity.

3.11 P. Trebilco

One of the main lacks has been a comprehensive study of Judaism in the Diaspora, apart from Egypt. This has now been partly filled by Paul Trebilco's *Jewish Communities in Asia Minor*. He has been able to draw together a good deal of the scattered data to give us a picture of Judaism in Asia Minor. There is even sufficient information to paint a more comprehensive picture of a few communities: those at Sardis and Priene, Acmonia, and Apamea. Trebilco also addresses some other issues of concern to students of the period: the questions of women leaders and the prominence of women in general, of citizenship, and of "God-fearers". The charge that Jews of Asia Minor were syncretistic is handled with care and sensitivity but firmly rejected. Because of the accidents of preservation, most original material is from the second, third, and fourth centuries CE. This means that little is known of the communities before the first century of the Common Era, an unfortunately state of affairs since comparison with the earlier period would have been instructive.

BIBLIOGRAPHY

Attridge, H. W. "Josephus and his Works," in M. E. Stone (ed.), *Jewish Writings of the Second Temple Period* (CRINT 2/2; Assen: Van Gorcum, 1984) 185-232.

Bickerman, E. J. *Der Gott der Makkabäer: Untersuchungen über Sinn und Ursprung der makkabäischen Erhebung* (Berlin: Schocken, 1937); ET *The God of the Maccabees* (SJLA 32; Leiden: Brill, 1979).

— (Bikerman, E.) *Institutions des Seleucides* (Paris: Geuthner, 1938).

— *From Ezra to the Last of the Maccabees: Foundations of Post-biblical Judaism* (New York: Schocken, 1962).

— *Studies in Jewish and Christian History* (AGJU 9; Leiden: Brill, 1986).

— *The Jews in the Greek Age* (Cambridge, MA: Harvard, 1988).

Bilde, P. *Flavius Josephus between Jerusalem and Rome: His Life, his Works, and their Importance* (JSPSS 2; Sheffield: JSOT, 1988).

Cohen, S. J. D. *Josephus in Galilee and Rome: His Vita and Development as a Historian* (CSCT 8; Leiden: Brill, 1979).

Collins, J. J. *Between Athens and Jerusalem: Jewish Identity in the Hellenistic Diaspora* (New York: Crossroad, 1986).

Cross, F. L. "An Aramaic Ostracon of the Third Century B.C.E. from Excavations in Jerusalem," *Eretz Israel* 15 (1981) *67-*69.

Davies, P. R. "Hasidim in the Maccabean Period," *Journal of Jewish Studies* 28 (1977) 127-40.

Feldman, L. H. "Hengel's *Judaism and Hellenism* in Retrospect," *Journal of Biblical Literature* 96 (1977) 371-82.

Flesher, P. V. M. "Palestinian Synagogues before 70 CE: A Review of the Evidence," *Approaches to Ancient Judaism VI*: Studies in the Ethnography and Literature of Judaism (BJS 192; Atlanta: Scholars, 1989) 68-81.

Frerichs, E. S., and J. Neusner (ed.) *Goodenough on the History of Religion and on Judaism* (BJS 121; Atlanta: Scholars, 1986).

Geraty, L. T. "The Khirbet el-Kôm Bilingual Ostracon," *Bulletin of the American Schools of Oriental Research* 220 (Dec. 1975) 55-61.

Goodenough, E. R. *By Light, Light: The Mystic Gospel of Hellenistic Judaism* (New Haven, CT: Yale, 1935).

— (with H. L. Goodhart), *The Politics of Philo Judaeus, Practice and Theory: with a General Bibliography of Philo* (New Haven, CT: Yale, 1938).

— *Jewish Symbols in the Greco-Roman Period* (vols. 1-13; Bollingen Series 37; New York: Pantheon, 1953-65).

— *An Introduction to Philo Judaeus* (revised ed.; Oxford: Clarendon, 1962).

— *Jewish Symbols in the Greco-Roman Period* (abridged edition, ed. with Introduction by J. Neusner; Bollingen Series;Princeton, NJ: Princeton, 1988).

Grabbe, L. L. "Synagogues in Pre-70 Palestine: A Re-assessment," *Journal of Theological Studies* 39 (1988) 401-10.

Gruen, E. S. *The Hellenistic World and the Coming of Rome* (2 vols. Berkeley/ Los Angeles: University of California, 1984).

Hengel, M. *Judentum und Hellenismus: Studien zu ihrer Begegnung unter besonderer Berücksichtigung Palästinas bis zur Mitte des 2 Jh. v. Chr.* (WUNT 10; Tübinger: Mohr, 1969); ET *Judaism and Hellenism: Studies in their Encounter in Palestine during the Early Hellenistic Period* (2 vols.; London: SCM; Philadelphia: Fortress, 1974).

— *Juden, Griechen und Barbaren: Aspekte der Hellenisierung des Judentums in vorchristlicher Zeit* (Stuttgarter Bibel-Studen 76; Stuttgart: KBW Verlag, 1976); ET *Jews, Greeks and Barbarians: Aspects of the Hellenization of Judaism in the preChristian Period* (Philadelphia: Fortress; London: SCM, 1980).

— *Zum Problem der "Hellenisierung" Judäas im 1. Jahrhundert nach Christus* (1989); ET *The "Hellenization" of Judaea in the First Century after Christ* (London: SCM; Philadelphia: Trinity, 1989).

Kuhrt, A., and S. Sherwin-White (ed.) *Hellenism in the East* (London: Duckworth, 1987).

Leon, H. J. *The Jews of Ancient Rome* (Morris Loeb Series; Philadelphia: Jewish Publication Society of America, 1960).

Millar, F. "The Phoenician Cities: A Case-Study of Hellenisation," *Proceedings of the Cambridge Philological Association* 209 (1983) 55-71.

Momigliano, A. "Josephus as a Source for the History of Judaea," *Cambridge Ancient History* (Cambridge University Press, 1934) 10.884-87.

— "'Richerche sull' organizzazione della Giudea sotto il dominio romano (63 a. C.-70 d. C.)," *Annali della Scuola Normale Superiore di Pisa*, Classe di Lettere 3 (1934) 183-221, 347-96.

— *Contributo alla storia degli studi classici* (Storia e Letteratura 47- ; Rome: Edizione di Storia e Letteratura,1955-).

— *Alien Wisdom: The Limits of Hellenization* (Cambridge: Cambridge University, 1975).

— "Greek Culture and the Jews," *The Legacy of Greece: A New Appraisal* (ed. M. I. Finley; Oxford: Clarendon, 1981) 325-46.

Moore, G. F. *Judaism in the First Three Centuries of the Christian Era* (3 vols.; Cambridge, MA: Harvard, 1927-30).

Nickelsburg, G. W. E. *Jewish Literature between the Bible and the Mishnah* (Philadelphia: Fortress, 1981).

Rajak, T. *Josephus: The Historian and his Society* (London: Duckworth, 1983).

Sandmel, S. *Philo of Alexandria: An Introduction* (Oxford/New York: OUP, 1979).

Schürer, E. *The Jewish People in the Age of Jesus Christ* (revised G. Vermes, et al.; 3 vols. in 4; Edinburgh: T & T Clarke, 1973-87).

Sherwin-White, S., and A. Kuhrt. *From Samarkhand to Sardis. A New Approach to the Seleucid Empire* (London: Duckworth, 1993)

Starr, C. G. "Greeks and Persians in the Fourth Century B.C.: A Study in Cultural Contacts before Alexander," *Iranica Antiqua* 11 (1975) 39-99; 12 (1977) 49-115.

Sterling, G. E., *Historiography and Self-Definition. Josephos, Luke-Acts and Apologetic Historiography* (Supplements to Novum Testamentum 64; Leiden-New York-Köln: Brill, 1992).

Stern, M. *Greek and Latin Authors on Jews and Judaism* (3 vols.; Jerusalem: Israel Academy of Arts and Sciences, 1974-84).

Tcherikover(Tscherikower), V. A. "Palestine under the Ptolemies (A Contribution to the Study of the Zenon Papyri)," *Mizraim* 4-5 (1937) 9-90.

— *Hellenistic Civilization and the Jews* (New York: Jewish Publication Society, 1959).

Tcherikover, V. A., A. Fuks, and M. Stern (ed.) *Corpus Papyrorum Judaicarum* (3 vols.; Cambridge, MA: Harvard; Jerusalem: Magnes, 1957-64).

Trebilco, P. R. *Jewish Communities in Asia Minor* (SNTSMS 69; Cambridge University Press, 1991).

Will, E. *Histoire politique du monde hellénistique* (323-30 av. J.-C. (2 vols.; Annales de l-Est, Mémoire 30; Nancy: Publications de l'Université, 19792, 1982).

ABBREVIATIONS

Ag. Apion	Josephus, Against Apion
Ant.	Josephus, Antiquities of the Jews
CPJ	Tcherikover, V. A., A. Fuks, and M. Stern (ed.), Corpus Papyrorum Judaicarum
War	Josephus, The War of the Jews

THE JUDAIC SYSTEM OF THE DEAD SEA SCROLLS

Johann Maier
(University of Cologne)

1 INTRODUCTION

Many of the principal characteristics of Judaism emerged during the exilic and early post-exilic periods when older traditions received their final shape according to the ideals of the exiled elites of Jerusalem and Judah. While the Hebrew Scriptures of the later "Bible" experienced their decisive stages of redaction, the oldest texts of the so-called "intertestamental" literature emerged. It is beyond question that some contents and components of the latter are of older origin than the last redactional stages of some Biblical books. Concerning the Hellenistic-Roman period of Palestinian Judaism, three important groups of source material are available:[1] (1) The texts from Qumran, the only original documents from this period, (2) the so-called "Pseudepigraphs and/or Apocrypha of the Old Testament," with the exception of some Hebrew/Aramaic fragments among the Qumran texts only extant in ancient translations, (3) the "New Testament", and (4) the writings of the Jewish historian Flavius Josephus. On his work rests our knowledge about the Jewish groups of the era before the destruction of the second temple: Sadducees, Pharisees, Essenes, and Zealots.[2] His discussion of the first three is rather stereotypical in character in so far as they are described as philosophical schools; and the longer passages concerning the Essenes are particularly puzzling. Some of their contents have parallels in the works of some non-Jewish authors speaking about Essenoi or Essaioi,[3] and it is not quite clear whether the two variants of the name indicate originally different groups. Josephus portrayed the Essenes as a very important group subdivided into two groups, the first with most members living in communities throughout the country, and the second as a more elitist

[1] E. Schürer, The History of the Jewish People in the Age of Jesus Christ, vol. I-III (Edinburgh: 1973/872); shorter treatments of recent date: B. Otzen, Judaism in Antiquity (Sheffield: 1990; J. Maier, Zwischen den Testamenten (Würzburg: 1990).

[2] G. Stemberger, Pharisäer, Sadduzäer, Essener (Stuttgart 1990).

[3] G. Vermes—M. D. Goodman, The Essenes. The Greek and Latin Evidence (Sheffield: 1989).

group living apart in a community of "celibates" very similar to or even identical with the Qumran community. This constellation reminds one, of course, of the relationship between "camp"-communities in CD (the "Zadokite Document" or "Damascus Document") and the yahad-community of Qumran.[4]

A number of parallel details seems to justify the identification of Essenes and Qumran people.[5] Despite this prevalent view, it seems strange that Essenes are not mentioned in the NT, more so as Josephus described in a few sentences the Sadducees and Pharisees, according to him the politically most influential groups, while dedicating to the Essenes comparatively detailed and long descriptions in War 2:119-161; Antiquities 15:371-379, and 18:18-22. Josephus had evidently been led by a special interest to present the Essenes in such a detailed manner. Some assume that he felt compelled to proceed in this manner because of their real socio-political significance.[6] Others suppose an anti-Christian motivation.[7] A third and perhaps more probable explanation is that the Essenes never existed in this sense as an important third group, and that Josephus, out of apologetic reasons constructed for his public a third large party whose pacifistic attitude exceeded even that of the moderate Pharisees and elitist Sadducees, and which with its Hellenistic characteristics could arouse sympathies among the non-Jewish readers. In this respect the Qumran texts provide significant evidence: the Qumran people were not pacifistic at all and not hellenized in the manner described by Josephus. There are other contradictions too, and in sum they lead to the conclusion that the Essenes of Josephus represent only an apologetical construct and that, in spite of all the similarities in details, they cannot be regarded as clearly identical with the Qumran community, more so considering the literary character of the passages in Josephus. Josephus himself had scarcely any personal knowledge about the Qumran community or the

---

[4] J. Maier, "Zum Begriff JChD in den Texten vom Toten Meer", in: Zeitschrift für die alttestamentliche Wissenschaft 72,1960,148-166. For a comparision with organizational patterns of Hellenistic cultic associations see M. Weinfeld, The Organizational Pattern and the Penal Code of the Qumran Sect (Fribourg/Göttingen: 1986).

[5] Beall T. S., Josephus' Description of the Essenes Illustrated by the Dead Sea Scrolls (Cambridge: 1988).

[6] H. Stegemann, "The Qumran Essenes—Local Members of the Main Jewish Union in Late Second Temple Times" in The Madrid Qumran Congress, ed. J. Trebolle Barreras—L. Vegas Montaner, vol. I (Leiden: 1993) 83-166.

[7] A. Paul, "Flavius Josèphe et les Esséniens", in The Dead Sea Scrolls, ed. D. Dimant—U. Rappaport (Leiden: 1992) 126-138.

"Essenes."[8] He had to rely on sources and, indeed, used four of them:[9] (1) originally non-Jewish anecdotes, perhaps already collected in the work of Nicolaus of Damascus depicting "Essaiaoi" as mantics; (2) a doxographical source about the three philosophical schools adapted to a Jewish ambience with the Zealots as "fourth school;" (3) a Hellenistic-Jewish source about "Essaiaoi", also used by Philo and others with a number of parallels in Qumran texts; (4) a source portraying "Essenoi" as a kind of Pythagoreans. Already these sources disclose apologetic tendencies, in particular by presenting the members of an alleged or real Jewish group as ascetics of the high moral standards accorded to a Hellenistic predilection for sages of this kind. In view of these facts, Josephus cannot serve as the point of departure for a reliable description of the Qumran community. On the contrary, it is necessary to treat Josephus' alleged Essaioi and Essenoi and the Qumran texts apart from each other. Only secondary comparisions and conclusions concerning their relationship can methodologically be legitimated.

The Qumran texts are the only available documents from this time that explain the self-understanding of a concrete Jewish group before 70 A.D. Comparable sources of Sadducean or Pharisaic origin are not extant and the use of later Rabbinic traditions implies an anachronistic approach.[10] In order to facilitate by comparison and contrast the access to an historically based view of early Rabbinic Judaism as it emerged after 70 C.E.,[11] it seems reasonable to sketch the ethos and belief of this relatively well documented kind of Judaism.

2 THE FINDS AND THEIR CHARACTER

The remnants of a library as discovered since 1948 in caves 1-11 near Chirbet Qumran represent only a small part of the original treasure which consisted of more than 800 scrolls and documents with texts in Hebrew and Aramaic; in addition some texts were

---

[8] The eremite Banus with whom Josephus as a youth allegedly spent some time in the desert is scarcely to be regarded as an "Essene".

[9] See: R. Bergmeier, Die Essenerberichte des Flavius Josephus. Quellenstudien zu den Essenertexten im Werk des jüdischen Historiographen (Kampen: 1993).

[10] See J. Neusner, The Rabbinic Traditions about the Pharisees, 3 vols. (Leiden: 1971), and cf. the shorter version: The Pharisees. Rabbinic Perspectives (Hoboken/NJ: 1985).

[11] J. Neusner, First Century Judaism in Crisis (Nashville; 1975); further references in: J. Maier, Geschichte der jüdischen Religion (Freiburg/Br.: 1992).

written in Greek.[12] Only very few of the scrolls survived the centuries more or less undamaged, and all of them are already published. The bulk of the material consists of fragments, much of them too small to be taken into account and many of the others are difficult to read or to identify. Most of the fragments were found during the excavations directed by P. de Vaux 1951/56 and were brought to the Rockefeller Museum in Jerusalem.[13] Other fragments and all of the more or less intact scrolls are now in the "Shrine of the Book" of the Israel Museum. The whole of the material has been photographed and in 1993 was reproduced and published in form of microfiches.[14] This microfiche edition includes a complete and revised list of all the texts with detailed bibliographies. Several circumstances render the exploitation of fragments more difficult than that of scrolls: (1) Most of the remaining fragments are of very small size, (2) their identification as parts of the same scroll or the same text was and to some extent still remains a difficult task, (3) the original position of the fragments within the scrolls must be reconstructed in order to understand them properly.[15] It is clearly evident that theories and hypotheses based on readings of single isolated fragments or on texts supplemented in lacunae are only of rather restricted value.

Not all of the extant scrolls and fragments are writings from the Qumran community itself. Some of the materials are of older origin, such as the biblical texts, and non-biblical ones such as the Book of Jubilees and the Books of Enoch, in their original Hebrew/ Aramaic form attested to by Qumran fragments. They were brought to Qumran and were copied there. Other texts reflect the thinking and situation of the community itself. These are to be regarded as Qumran literature proper, even if some contents may be of older origin, for the use and working up of sources was for authors at that time a matter of course. They wrote according to the requirements of their community. The difference between author and redactor, therefore, seemed insignificant in comparison to the functional significance of the texts composed.

The bulk of the extant material was copied during the first century B.C., a smaller part during the (late) second century B.C., and

---

[12] For introduction se J. A. Fitzmyer, The Dead Sea Scrolls (Missoula 19772); id., Responses to 101 Questions on the Dead Sea Scrolls (Atlanta: 1993).

[13] E.-M. Laperrousaz, Qoumrân (Paris: 1976).

[14] E. Tov etc., The Dead Sea Scrolls on Microfiche (Leiden 1993).

[15] H. Stegemann, "Methods for the Reconstruction of Scrolls from Scattered Fragments" in Archaeology and History in the Dead Sea Scrolls ed. L. H. Schiffman (Sheffield: 1989) 189-220.

in certain cases even earlier. The smallest portion was written during the first century C.E. through 66 C.E. when Qumran was destroyed by the Zealots or the Romans. The datings are based on
highly reliable palaeographic evidence as well as on a number of
Carbon-14 tests.[16] The best preserved texts are on scrolls and fragments written during the first Century B.C., a span of time which
seems to have been the most important period in the history of the
group. This explains to a certain extent the lack of evidence for the
Qumran community in (the considerably later) NT writings.

3 History and "Historical" Self-definition of the Group

A closer reading of Josephus reveals, however, that he ascribed to
the Essenes a concrete socio-political relevance only for the times of
the Hasmonean rulers Jonathan, John Hyrcanus, and Alexander
Yannai. This fits the archaeological evidence according to which
the Qumran settlement was founded towards the end of the second
century B.C. The few clear hints of historical circumstances in
Qumran texts (4QpNah = 4Q169; 1QpPs 37 = 4Q171) point to
the time of Alexander Jannai (104/3-76 B.C.) as a decisive stage of
the community's history. Until now, research has concentrated on
the problem of the pre-history and early history of the Qumran
community, trying to identify certain persons mentioned in the
Scrolls by enigmatic polemical attributes such as the "Teacher of
Righteousness", his counterpart, the "Priest of Iniquity" ("Wicked
Priest"), and the "Man (or Preacher) of Lies"; or to identify groups
labelled as "Jehudah", "Ephraim and Manasse", and "House of
Absalom".[17] Several hypotheses and contradicting datings have
been proposed, however, which are not the subject of this paper.[18]

---

[16] G. Bonani, M. Broshi etc., "Radiocarbon Dating of the dead Sea Scrolls",
Atiqot 20 (1991) 27-32.
[17] For an overview see F. García Martínez, "Judas Maccabeo Sacerdote
Impio?", Mélanges bibliques et orienteaux en honneur de M. Mathias Delcor, ed.
A. Chaquot etc. (Kevelaer: 1986) 164-181; Ph. R. Davis, Behind the Essenes
(Atlanta: 1987) 15-32.
[18] See P. R. Callaway, The History of the Qumran Community (Sheffield:
1987). In addition see P. R. Davies, Behind the Essenes (Atlanta: 1987). For the
"Groningen hypothesis", essentially also presupposed in this paper, see: F. García
Martínez, "Qumran Origins and Early History: A Groningen Hypothesis", in The
First International Colloquium on the Dead Sea Scrolls Mogilany May 31—June
2,1987 ed. Z. J. Kapera (Wroclaw: 1989 (= Folia Orientalia vol. XXV, 1988) 113-
136.
F. García Martínez, "Orígenes del movimiento Esenio y qumranico", in Il
Simposio Biblico Espagnol (Valencia-Córdoba: 1987) 527-556.

For a description of the "Judaic system" of the Qumran community counts in first place its own view of history and its own definition of its place and role in it.

Instructive points of departure for an analysis of this kind are some passages in the Zadokite Documents (CD).

(a) CD 6:5ss. applies in a typological manner Num 21:16-18 to an early period of the group in question, when they went to "the Land of Damascus." Usually interpreted as a metaphor for Qumran, which is possible but meets difficulties in chronological respect, or for Mesopotamia,[19] which is unlikely, "Damascus" may refer to a real sojourn in Syrian territories, perhaps during the "reform" in Jerusalem after 175 B.C. when the Zadokites had lost their position, forming with their supporters an oppositional movement, or during the early Maccabean campaigns. They defined themselves, anyway, as the true representatives of Israel who are ready to stick to the Covenant with God and to renew it as "the new covenant in the Land of Damascus."

(b) An apparently more precise chronological statement is given in CD 1,5-12 according to which, 390 years after the deportation into exile under Nebuchadnezzar, a "root of the planting" sprouted out of the remnant of Israel which were ready for repentance.[20] They acknowledged their sinfulness, but remained without guidance for twenty years, until God "raised for them an Enactor of Justice (the Teacher of Righteousness) to guide them on the way of His heart. And he made known for latter generations what he did to a latter generation, to a community of traitors, those who departed from the way." Unfortunately, we cannot establish the exact chronology which the writer of this passage had in mind. This means that we cannot take the date of 597 or 587/6 B.C. for a sure point of departure from which to count forward the 390 years. This 20 years of uncertainty, however, could be located in the first half or in the middle of the 2nd century B.C.

(c) CD 5:2-5 states that between the time of Joshua and Zadok no reliable knowledge of the Torah existed and that Israel, at the

---

[19] J. Murphy O'Connor in a series of articles; see "The Damascus—Document Revisited", Revue Biblique 92 (1985) 223-246.

[20] For "planting" as a metaphor for the community see also 1QS 7:5; 11:8; 1QH 6:15-17; 8:4ss. It is like the metaphors "fundament", "house", building" very common in prophetic-apocalyptic traditions, each of them related to temple/paradise symbolism; cf. H. Muszinsky, Fundament, Bild und Metapher in den Handschriften von Qumran (Rom: 1976).

author's times, lives in an analogous situation. The reasons given
are: (1) the Torah exemplar in the Ark of the Covenant remained
sealed up and unaccessible until Zadok (from the line Eleazar-
Pinchas), the first of the "Zadokites", entered service at the Temple
of Solomon; (2) the published exemplar (nigleh) of the Torah had
been hidden by Joshua (and the elders) because of the Ashtarot cult
of the people; (3) CD sees this period without Torah in typological
analogy to the time after 175 B.C., when the Zadokites (Oniades)
lost their traditional hold of the high priest's office; (4) the catastrophic end of the kingdom of Judah, the destruction of the First
Temple, the exile, and the new deplorable situation were the consequences of God's wrath toward the Israelites, who ignored the correct Torah regulations, i.e. following the Zadokites who regarded
themselves as guardians of the Covenant.[21]

The passages cited refer to a critical stage in the history of the
broader movement in the aftermath of which certain secessionist
tendencies took place. Zadokites may have played in this earlier
stage a leading role, for it is not impossible that a Zadokite opposition already existed before 175 B.C. Differing political and religious
orientations were rather common among the Judaean establishment in the Persian period and during the Seleucide-Ptolemaic
conflicts over Palestine. The Zadokites contributed thanks to their
traditions and to their systematic way of thinking (see the Biblical
P—traditions)[22] much to the development of theological ideas particularly as attested to in the Book of Jubilees or in the Books of
Enoch.

Other Zadokites went with Onias IV to Egypt into exile. The
majority of the priests, however, chose the way of compromise and
made their peace with the Hasmoneans, forming the priestly aristocracy within the group of the "Sadducees." Qumran Zadokites
and Sadducees, therefore, had many older traditions in common
but should not be regarded as identical, as the latter rejected
eschatological tendencies, consequently restricting the written revelation to the Pentateuch. To a certain extent, this is also true for the
priesthood of Samaria, of Zadokite origin too, a fact which explains
some of the similarities of this group with Qumran traditions.

---

[21] On this passage see J. Maier, "Von Eleazar bis Zadok", Revue de Qumran
15 (1991) 231-241, referring to B.-Z. Wacholder, "The «Sealed» Torah Versus the
«Revealed» Torah", Revue de Qumran 12 (1986) 351-368.
[22] About such priestly traditions and their bearings on Second Temple Judaism
see now: I. Knohl, Miqdash ha-demamah (Jerusalem: 1993).

It was the appearance of a so-called Môreh ha-çedeq ("Teacher of Righteousness", more precisely: "Enactor of Justice") with clear cut authoritative claims that led to profound controversies and finally to a splitting of the pre-Qumranic oppositional movement. He was a priest, apparently a Zadokite, but the exact time of his activities remains uncertain, in part due to difficulties in identifying his opponents, the "Man (or: Preacher) of Lie" and the "Priest of Iniquity." The latter was perhaps, in the first place, a polemical designation corresponding to the title of the Highpriest, and was eventually used for two or more of the Hasmonean rulers.[23] The Title "Teacher (Môreh) of Righteousness" points to priestly prerogatives, for le-hôrôt means to enact law, to proclaim a regulation or a sentence, a terminus technicus for authoritative legal advising and deciding, particularly by priests. It is significant that Rabbinic Judaism retained this sense of hôrôt while conferring the function of Môreh (halakhah) to the Sage. A more appropriate translation of this title would be "Enactor" or "Advisor of Justice." Indeed, the primary claim of the "Teacher of Righteousness" concerned Torah authority. In addition, this claim was connected with a definition of "the time" in its relationship to the end of the days.

4 THE QUEST FOR AUTHORITY

4.1 Authoritative Sources

For a description of a social-religious entity like the Qumran community, it is first of all necessary to define the authoritative basis on which it based its decisions, and to identify the authoritative institutions and functionaries entitled to make such decisions. The second task is a rather simple one: except for the "Teacher of Righteousness" as a authoritative figure sui generis, it is clear that, within the Communities of CD and 1QS/1QSa, the priests or more precisely, the Zadokites, played the decisive part.

Qumran research has been, from its very beginning, predominantly the domain of biblical scholars; and, they presupposed as a matter of fact for Qumran what they were used to presupposing as exegetes of the Bible. They spoke about "the Bible" and Qumran without much critical consideration, happy to have in their hands biblical manuscripts about a thousand years older than the mediae-

---

[23] Woude A. S. van der, "Wicked Priest or Wicked Priests?" Journal of Jewish Studies 33 (1982) 349-359.

val ones. Consequently, the principal question concerning the non-
Biblical materials seemed to be their relationship to "the Bible."
Already a glimpse into the text list of the microfiche edition of 1993
edited by E. Tov illustrates this state of affairs: non-biblical texts
figure regularly as "apocryphal" and "pseudepigraphical," as "ex-
panded Biblical texts" or as "paraphrases." Only in rare cases did
Qumran scholars realize the fundamental difference between the
Christian "Bible" and the Jewish Scriptures. Unfortunately, Jewish
Qumran scholars contributed little toward putting this fact into the
right place, for they too were used to speaking of "the Bible and
Qumran" instead of differentiating carefully between Torah,
Prophets and other Scriptures.[24] Most Qumran scholars had no
knowledge whatever about post-biblical Judaism, and particularly
not about the essence and history of Jewish law and cult. The situation changed considerably when some experts in the history of
Jewish law began to concern themselves with the scrolls. The
"biblizistic" orientation, however, remained dominant in so far as
most of them tried to prove that almost all of the legal traditions in
Qumran resulted from exegesis of Biblical texts.[25] This method has
been criticised concerning some details but never on principle.[26]
Some hermeneutic devices ascribed to the Qumran community due
to these biblizistic presuppositions, in fact, do not fit its own concept of revelation and authority, but correspond rather to Christian
and Jewish biblical canon theology and hermeneutics.

4.2 The Zadokite Claim to enact the Torah

Considering the community's own historical outlook as described
above, a more complicated situation emerges.
A traditional priestly and institutionalized Torah authority bound
to the Zadokites was in charge of Torah.[27] Their prominent position has already been stated in the Book of Ezekiel (Ez 40:46;
44:15; 48,11). In Qumran, however, their exclusive right to enact
Torah is stressed in an unequivocal way, as in 1QS 5: 1-4:

> This is the rule for the men of the yahad who are ready to turn back
> from all evil and to stick to everything which He had commanded
> according to His will, to separate themselves from the community of
> the men of evil, to form a yahad in Torah and goods, obedient to the

---

[24] For the basic differences mentioned see J. Neusner, Judaism and Its Social
Metaphors (Cambridge 1989), index p. 253s. s.v. "Essenes at Qumran"; Foundations of Judaism, Atlanta (Scholars Press) 19932,7-9.82-86.
[25] See particularly the publications of L. H. Schiffman (see bibliography).
[26] See J. M. Baumgarten, Studies in Qumran Law (Leiden: 1977).
[27] For the priestly privilege to be in charge of the central court of appeal cf. Dt
17:8-13 and the formulation of the issue in 11Q19 56: 1-12).

Sons of Zadok, the priests, the keepers of the Covenant, and to the majority of the men of the yahad, who stick to the Covenant. On their authority passes the decision about the rank of status (of everyone) concerning Torah, goods, and jurisdiction, to perform faithfulness, yahad, humility, justice and law, charity and regardful behaviour in all their ways.

And ibd. 7-9:

Everybody who enters the corporation of the yahad shall enter the Covenant in the presence of all the willfuls and impose upon himself by a binding oath to return to the Torah of Moses according to everything which He had commanded, with all his heart and with all his soul, according to all which is revealed from it to the Sons of Zadok, the priests, the keepers of the Covenant and enactors of His will, and to the majority of the men of their (!) Covenant ...

1QS IX:12-15 illustrates the practical significance for the community's particular organization:

These are the commandments for the Maskil to proceed according to them with every living according to the order of precedence of every time and the reputation of each person, to do the will of God according to all the revealed for every time, and the learning of all the knowledge, which results according to the times, and the prescription of the time, to distinguish and weigh the sons of justice according to their spirit and the elect of the time to ... etc.

1QS VIII:15 formulates as a resumé: "This is the record (midrash) of the Torah, which He has commanded by Moses to do according to all the revealed from time to time, and as the prophets revealed by His holy spirit." This sentence contains both aspects, the Torah of Moses and its application to the respective "time" which must be defined by the interpretation of the prophetic oracles.

The relationship between Torah and "time" concerns not only the community but every individual member because of its consequences for his rank and prestige within the community connected with the order of precedence as indicated in 1QS V:21ss., a text which emphasizes that priests are the decisive factor in the process of evaluating the "spirit" and rank of each member.

This oppositional movement and its Qumranic offspring claimed that the actually effective Torah was to be found only by Zadokite mediation and enactment. This was not due to mere transmission of laws or by exegesis of written laws (like Rabbinic midrash), but like an oracle attained by DRSh, meaning both the application and response procedures as well.[28] It is a process of continuous revela-

---

[28] The semantic scale includes the meanings: "To keep (step by step) close to", "to seek and find"; "to be concerned with", "to care for"; "to summon", "to demand", "to proclaim", "to enact".

tion, a legislative advising procedure based on the belief in an essentially already given Torah (of Moses), which in its entirety is
only accessible for priests/Zadokites, who are able to decide what
of this "hidden" Torah has to be practiced at each "time" and who,
together with the members of the council of the yahad, determine
the actual prescriptions in force. The result is an official record
called midrash ha-Torah. Thus, "the hidden" becomes "the revealed," not primarily through exegesis, but by acts of proclamation of the binding norms, eventually becoming grouped according
to subject in serakhim. But there is another aspect.[29] The "revealed" laws are to be treated as arcane and remain thus "hidden"
for outsiders, as explicitly stated in 1QS 8:10-12:

> When they remain firm in the "fundament" of the yahad for two years
> in perfect conduct (11) they shall {separate themselves} as a holy insti-
> tution/sanctuary within the Council of the men of the yahad. And if
> anything (of the Torah) is hidden to Israel, and they present them-
> selves[30] before the man (12) who is advising (dôresh), he shall not con-
> ceal it (the "hidden" prescription) out of fear of a disloyal spirit

The usual translation presupposes a meaning like "studying" or
"interpreting" for dôresh, but the situation is that of 1QS 6:3-4:

> In the place where these ten (members) are (living) must not be missing
> a man (dôresh ba-tôrah) concerned with (or: in charge of) advising the
> Torah, day and night,[31] concerning the good conduct ('al ypwt) of each
> one with his companion.

In this instance, most translators also prefer "studying" or "interpreting," but what the group of ten members mentioned previously
needs, first of all, is an expert in Torah matters, precisely as in the
case of a camp of ten in CD 13:2-6. In this example, the expert
must be a priest well versed in the Book HHGJ which seemes to
have been one of the fundamental Scriptures of the yahad community.[32]

The Torah, as revealed to the community by its institutions,
remains "hidden" to Israel outside the yahad community. It can,
therefore, be said that Israel went astray concerning the "hidden"
(CD 3:13-14). They would have been able to know it as "revealed"

---

[29] L. H. Schiffman, Law ... 45ss., treats only one aspect of both.
[30] nmç'w: usually translated as: "has been found by him" (or similar); but "they"
refers to the men already mentioned before.
[31] Refers probably to "not be missing".
[32] This priest must not be confused with the priest whose presence is indispen-
sable out of the ritual reasons mentioned in both contexts.

by submitting to the priestly/Zadokite authority, and in the times of Qumran, to the discipline of the yahad community.

Analogy and difference in relation to later Rabbinical "Halakhah (from Sinai)" are evident: Rabbinic Judaism replaced the functional position of the priests by that of the Sages; the Rabbinical schools replaced the priestly institution. Their method to define the Halakhah, however, was also an authoritative and creative one, although restricted to the "Oral Torah," and likewise not necessarily derived by exegesis (like late Rabbinic Midrash).[33] Furthermore, it is not by mere chance but due to traditional terminology that Rabbinical Judaism used the verb le-horot and the designation moreh with Halakhah as subject as a terminus technicus for the authoritative function of the Sage.

4.3 "The Teacher of Righteousness" and "The Torah of the Time"

During the initial stages of the Qumran community, the Moreh ha-çedeq, usually translated as "Teacher of Righteousness," played a decisive role. In view of the fact that his principal opponent is called "Priest of Iniquity" (or: "Wicked Priest") a designation like "Priest of Righteousness" would seem more suitable, if it was the office of the High priesthood which was at stake—as is usually assumed. The designation Moreh, however, points to a different issue, although within the priestly frame, with the verb horot being a term for Torah advising given by priests.[34] It may be that the Judaean constitution of the Persian and Early Hellenistic periods provided, beside the High Priest, a special position for a priestly prophet in charge of Torah matters. A corresponding prophetic office, besides the High Priest and the Judge (king), is attested to in Josephus (Antiquities 4:218) in his interesting account of Dt 17 (Antiquities 4:216-218) regarding the supreme court of appeal. Another hint is perhaps the future prophet who, according to 2 Macc 4:46, is expected to decide how to treat the defiled stones of the altar of the temple. In any case, the translation "Adviser of Justice" matches the claims implicated in Moreh ha-çedeq more precisely. If the title Moreh ha-çedeq really corresponded to an office as assumed, this office was not that of an exegete but that of a Torah

---

[33] J. Neusner, Torah. From Scroll to Symbol in Formative Judaism (Philadelphia 1985).

[34] Cf. also J. C. Treeves, "The Meaning of Moreh Sedeq in the Light of 11QTorah", Revue de Qumran 13 (1988) 287-398.

adviser or Torah enactor and that of a prophet. Consequently, the claim expressed by the title primarily regards Torah authority.[35]

The Qumran community attributed Torah monopoly and the eventual claim to a specific office as Torah enactor as well as an extraordinary kind of prophetic authority to their Moreh ha-çedeq on the basis of the priestly/Zadokite line of authority. According to 1QpHab 7:1ss., God revealed to this "Teacher" by his holy spirit the actual meaning of the prophetic texts that serve to define the "time" for a Torah in force to be practiced in view of the immanent end of the days. The text explicitly presupposes that the prophet Habakkuk himself did not know the real meaning of his words. They are, consequently, a kind of riddle to be solved or a dream to be interpreted. Furthermore, it is the term for dream interpretation, PShR/PTR, which (with the noun pesher) served as a term for this kind of actualizing, expounding and eschatologization of prophetic texts. Pesher never appears in a context concerning Torah (legal) contents, for they are subject to derosh and hôrôt. So, the "Teacher of Righteousness" and those following after him claimed for themselves direct Torah enacting (lidrosh and le-horot Torah) and inspired interpretation (pesher) of prophetic texts. This combination led to the provocative claim that the Teacher and his followers were able to determine the appropriate time for each midrash ha-Torah or the Torah for each time in relation to the end of the days. While for an eschatological interpretation and the actualizing application of prophetic texts parallels may be found in Rabbinic (and, of course, Christian) literature, presents pesher as a specific Qumran term that eventually developed in the context of these combined functions, of Torah enacting and interpretation of prophets (and psalms). The very climax of Qumranic claims, however, parallels later Christian tradition but not Rabbinic Judaism.

This climax, that of Qumranic claims to authority, consisted of the designation of the "Teacher of Righteousness" as "a prophet like Moses" (Dt 18:18).[36] To call someone "a prophet like Moses" means nothing less than to claim for him the same unique relationship to God and to the Torah. The Christians claimed it for Jesus Christ and consequently spoke of a "new law."[37] In Rabbinic and

[35] Cf. Greek nomothetês in LXX Ps 9:21.

[36] See G. J. Brooke, Exegesis at Qumran, Sheffield 1985, 309-319 on 4Q175 (4QTest), citing Dt 5:28s.; 18:18s.; Num 24:15-17 (eschatological prophecy; Dt 33:8-11 (privileges of "Levi"), Josh 6:26 (against Jericho, priestly city with Hasmonean palace). Cf. also 4Q158,6.

[37] For a long time research has been focussed on parallels and differences between the figures of Jesus Christ and the "Teacher", see: G. Jeremias, Der Lehrer der Gerechtigkeit (Göttingen: 1963).

later Judaism, such a claim rarely happened. But it was towards the end of the second century B.C., however, that Hasmonean propaganda ascribed to John Hyrcanus the three qualities of Moses: that of a military leader, that of a statesman, and that of a prophet (Josephus, De Bello Iudaico 1:68). All of this points to the fact that during the last third of the second century B.C. the issue of Torah authority was subject to intensive disputes connected with the question of concrete political power.

4.4 Results

"Torah" texts form components of whole books like 11Q19/11Q20 (Temple Scroll). Many fragments are remains of scrolls with legal contents or components, such as 2Q25; 4Q159; 4Q185; 4Q229; 4Q251; 4Q256-265; 4Q274-283; 4Q294-298; 4Q394-399(4QMMT); 4Q512-514(4QOrd); 4Q523-524; 5Q11-13. There is enough reason to assume that the legal contents of the Book of Jubilees had the reputation of "Torah." Other scriptures may be added, especially the Book HHGJ/W which is mentioned several times in addition to the Torah or alone as a book containing regulations which the members, particularly a Maskil (instructor), should know very well. Much legal material is included in texts like CD, 1QS, and 1QSa, in part collected in specific Serakhim.[38] Such collections seem to have been the result of institutionalized legislative procedures like midrash ha-Torah, a term which was also used to denote the product, the record.[39] DRSh and midrash (originally demanding and mediating an oracle) denote enacting and proclaiming, not exegesis and interpretation. This does not exclude occasional interpreting processes in the course of the midrash procedures, but these are not called midrash. This usage appears not only in the Greek translations; for, even the Targumim used it for DRSh, consequently TB' (to summon, demand), and never applied one of the verbs for interpretation.[40]

The Zadokites in Qumran were, of course, not interested in a concluding definition of a "canon" as the basis open for interpreta-

---

[38] See L. H. Schiffman, Law ... 75ss.
[39] See also 2 Chr 13:22; 24:17 (LXX: biblion!).; "record" is also the correct translation of 4Q174 (Flor) 1:14: A mi[d]rash min/from (of): Blessed [the] man ... etc. In 4QS "midrash" replaces twice "serek".
[40] The best lexicographical analysis is still that of I. Heinemann in his article "Midrash" in: Enzyclopedia miqra'it 4,1962,695-701. Almost all later publications tried to introduce Rabbinic connotations.

tion, as long as the priestly privilege secured their right to decree the concrete contents of the Midrash ha-Torah in the sense of an institutionalized actual revelatio continua on the basis of the concept of a universal and, as a whole, essentially undefined Torah of Moses.

5 THE CULTIC THEOLOGY OF THE YAHAD COMMUNITY

5.1 Cosmic Order and Cultic Calendar

Zadokite cultic theology had its roots in basic convictions shared throughout the ancient world; the sanctuary and the ritual order represent the order of the cosmos (in Israel: of the creation), and the performance of the cult sustains cosmic order and provides natural prosperity. Natural processes as well as conditions for human life are exposed to the influence of cosmic, angelic or demonic powers.[41] Astrological determinism was a logical consequence of this world view, in addition to the ethical dualism which characterizes the Qumran view of man.[42] It was due to its cultic components that the Torah gained the significance of a cosmic law and a plan of God's creation.

Consequently, the cult was of public interest with the priests performing functions in the service of the society. At the same time, their ritual corresponded to functions performed by superhuman beings in charge of cosmic processes in the heavenly realms. The priests in service saw the performance of their duties not only in analogy but also in a relationship of mutual influence to the liturgic performances in heaven. Consequently, priests could also be called "angels." It was particularly a Qumran text extant in fragments of about ten exemplars which gives full insight into this priestly self-definition, the Shîrê `ôlat hash-shabbat.[43] This text represents a kind of "agenda" for staging the Sabbath liturgy of a quarter of the year (13 sabbaths), in heaven as well as on earth.[44] It is obvious that,

---

[41] M. J. Davidson, Angels at Qumran. A Comparative Study of 1 Enoch 1-36, 72-108 and Sectarian Writings from Qumran (Sheffield: 1992); P. von der Osten-Sacken, Gott und Belial (Göttingen: 1969).

[42] H. Lichtenberger, Studien zum Menschenbild in Texten aus Qumran (Göttingen: 1980).

[43] C. Newsom, Songs of the Sabbath Sacrifice: A Critical Edition (Atlanta: 1985); id., "«He has established for himself priests». Human and Angelic Priesthood in the Qumran Sabbath Shirot", in Archaeology and History in the Dead Sea Scrolls ed. L. H. Schiffman (Sheffield 1990) 101-120.

[44] It is not the normal liturgy of every Sabbath but that for the the additional service for the Sabbaths 1-13 of one "tequfah" as a calendric unit within the cycle

in the face of such presuppositions, every deviation from the cultic order had to be regarded as disastrous for both the cosmic and human realms.[45] This fact explains the bitter disputes about the correct cult calendar during the period of the Second Temple. We don't know the pre-history of this dispute; but, its seems plausible that, at some time during the Persian or early Hellenistic period, older calendric traditions were replaced by "modern" ones and some priests, even in the Zadokite clan, resented this change and defended the old practice as part of the Torah. In any case, there is ample evidence from the Books of Enoch and the Book of Jubilees that the Qumran Community defended this calendric tradition and regarded the question of the correct cult calendar as a central part of its dispute with Jerusalem (cf. 4QMMT). According to cultic thinking, the observation of an incorrect calendar implied the invalidity of all cultic performances. Consequently, no valid atonement could be attained at the Sanctuary of Jerusalem. Therefore, the land as well as the people remained defiled and laden with guilt, a situation with dire consequences for the natural environment as well as for society and its members.[46] In a community with a belief which is organized according to such cultic concepts, rules about ritual purity and impurity played an important role.[47] This is particularly true in view of the claim of the yahad to be a substitute for the expiatory functions of the defiled sanctuary of Jerusalem. The holy men of the yahad apparently lived as if they were priests in service, a state of being which required special ritual measures, such as avoidance of alcohol[48] and sexual intercourse.[49]

As society in Israel constituted a people chosen by God for the performance of His will (the Torah), both aspects merged into one, the cultic/cosmological aspect and the concept of election, the

---

of the year according to the solar calendar. See J. Maier, "Shîrê ʿôlat hash-shabbat: Some observations on their Calendric Implications and on their Style" in The Madrid Qumran Congress ed. J. Trebolle Berrara—J. Vegas Montaner, vol. II (Leiden 1993) 5543-560.

[45] Cf. D. W. Suter, "Fallen Angel, Fallen Priest: The Problem of Family Purity in 1 Enoch 6-16", The Hebrew Union College Annual 50 (1979) 115-135.

[46] P. Garnet, Salvation and Atonement in the Qumran Scrolls (Tübingen: 1977).

[47] W. Paschen, Rein und Unrein (München 1970); M. Newton, The Concept of Purity at Qumran and in the Letters of Paul (Cambridge 1985); J. Neusner, The Idea of Purity in Ancient Judaism (Leiden: 1973).

[48] This does not exlude ritual drinking of "new wine" (tîrôsh as reshît wine) at certain cultic occasions.

[49] In the literature about Qumran frequently misinterpreted as celibacy. But sexual intercourse was according to this rigid tradition fordidden for everybody in the whole "City of the Sanctuary" (11Q19 45:11s.; CD 12:1-2).

question for the correct ritual practice and the question for the identity of Israel, each connected by the one Torah for both realms of life. It was due to this combination that the dispute received its implacable character. Dualistic thinking characterized the concept of election from its very inception as expressed already in biblical texts. Mankind is divided as Israel and as "the nations," this theme corresponding to the antagonism between God and the idols; Torah obedience is the way of life, and disobedience leads to death. God's realm is the world of light; his enemies abide in darkness. In Qumran it was the cosmic aspect, in particular, which deepened the gap between followers and enemies, conferring to human antagonism a supernatural significance. This led in systematic consequence to the dualism of the confrontation between a group and its enemies appearing as a confrontation between the powers of light and darkness, between "sons of light" and "sons of darkness," between the "lot of God" and the "lot of Belial," the Satan. There was no need of direct Persian influence to create such convictions although it might have stimulated their evolution in forming part of an already hellenized world view of the time.[50] It may also be that some dualistic concepts found their way into priestly traditions, particularly in cosmological contexts.[51]

5.2 Eschatology

The Zadokite members of the oppositional movement regarded their own days as the critical transition from history to the Eschaton and amalgamated in a systematic manner priestly traditionalism and revolutionary eschatological expectations.[52] Consequently, the Qumran texts exhibit the whole range of eschatological expectations of each tradition, the priestly/cultic prerogatives remaining always preserved.[53] Like 1QM, a text which describes the last wars of the sons of light against the sons of darkness, 1QSa contains an organizational pattern for Israel at the end of the days which resembles the organization of the yahad community of Qumran. The position of the ruler, the "Anointed one of Israel" (or "Sprout of

---

[50] For dualism in the Hellenistic era see now P. F. M. Fontaine, The Light and the Dark, I-III (Leiden: 1986/88); for Qumran: P. von der Osten-Sacken, Gott und Belial (Göttingen: 1969).

[51] A. Hultgård, "Prêtres Juifs et Mages Zoroastriens—influences religieuses à l'époque hellénistique", Revue d'histoire et de philosophie religieuse 68 (1988) 415-428.

[52] J. Neusner, The Formation of the Jewish Intellect (Atlanta 1988) 77ss.

[53] Laperrousaz M., L'attente du messie (Paris: 1982) 39ss.

David"), corresponds to that in the law of the king in 11Q19 56:12ss. This position provides, in contrast to Dt 20:14-20, a con- :olling function for the priests, particularly for the High Priest when in charge of the Urim-Tummim oracle. As in 1QS 5:3-8 where a priest must be present and must take precedence in each group of ten within the yahad community, the Anointed one of Araon takes precedence in 1QSa (1QS28a), a text concerning Israel at the end of the days.[54] In the War Scroll (1QM) it is not actually the Davidic ruler who leads the wars; the priests, with their prayers and signals, play the decisive part in these campaigns. The wars seem staged in a liturgical manner similar to the heavenly liturgy in the Shîrê ʿôlat hash-Shabbat. It is only by the help of the hosts of heaven that Israel prevails in these last wars against its earthly and demonic enemies.

The priestly privileges concerning the administration of Torah and justice also form part of the eschatological order, and accord- ing to 4Q174 a Torah enactor (doresh ha-Torah) is expected to appear together with the Davidic ruler. It may be that his function is identical with that of the prophet mentioned with the two Anoint- ed ones in 1QS 9:11.[55]

A very special priestly figure in the eschatological scenery of Qumran is Melchizedek (s. 11QMelch), the prototype of the priest- hood of Jerusalem being, at the same time, its heavenly representa- tive with eschatological functions. The relationship of his functions to those of the two Anointed ones is not clear. It seems that eschatological speculation focused on different subjects: the fate of the cosmos as a whole and the fate of the individual in relationship to the fulfilment of duties as a member of Israel, represented by the yahad community. In so far as priestly thinking determined this community, the question of historical development was of second- ary importance compared with the central theme of priestly self- understanding, to join in service the angels in the functions of wor- ship, thereby sustaining the order of creation. It is probably due to this point of view that the resurrection of the dead has only a marginal place in Qumran writings and that eschatological motifs of cosmological significance appear by far more often than the tra- ditional motifs in poetic Qumran texts as 1QH. At this point, the systematic force of this kind of Zadokite theology becomes once more apparent. In spite of the uncontested significance of tradition-

---

[54] See L- H. Schiffman, The Eschatological Community of the Dead Sea Scrolls. A study of the Rule of the Congregation (Atlanta: 1989); id., Law, Custom .... (Jerusalem 1993) 268-311.
[55] Usually conceived as a kind of Eliah redivivus.

al eschatological expectations, there emerges a universalistic device of the drama at the end of the days, determined primarily by cosmological, angelological, and demonological data. This appears in the imagery of Hymns (cf. 1QH col. 3 etc.) without any connection with the concept of election—except, of course, the elected speaking "I," which is to be understood as a representative "I."[56] The original "Sitz im Leben" of such concepts of cosmic catastrophes seems to have been the same as that of the creation and chaos traditions. It is due to systematic thinking that they became part of an eschatological system as developed in 1QS 3:13—4:26, where the universal catastrophe corresponds to the creational determinism of God, thus resolving finally the tension of theodicy implicated in the particularistic concept of election.

5.3 Functional Replacement of the Sanctuary by the Community

The self-definiton of this group played both aspects, the cultic one and the "historical"/eschatological one. We do not know whether or not the settlement at Qumran had been established as a center for a broader movement. It seems plausible, however, that in an early stage the yahad community defined itself as a surrogate cultic center, not as an alternative Temple in a topographical sense, but in a functional sense as expiating institution in place of the invalid atonement of the Jerusalem cult. Several passages, particularly in 1QS, contain definitions of this kind formulated in a catechetical style (1QS 7:25—8:10; 9:3-6). Again, the priestly precedence is obvious. In 1QS 7:5-7 and similarly in 1QS 9:5-6, for instance, priests form a kind of "Holy of Holies," the laics the "house" or the "Holy" of the sanctuary, together understanding their task in attaining atonement for the land in terms of their separation from the people and by their special way of jahad-life. This implied a way of living like that of officiating priests at the Sanctuary with concrete ritual obligations. Not the last among them were regulations concerning holiness and ritual purities secured by an internal communal economy and thoroughly supervised organization.

Considering the archaeological evidence and the diminishing number of scrolls written during first century A.D., it is not very likely that this community, when in its last stages, still served as a center of a broader movement. Erosive and divisive effects of internal differences determined the development of the group, inducing

---

[56] Sometimes interpreted as indicating personal (biographical) "confessions" and experiences of the Teacher of Righteousness.

the emergence of a speculative, exclusive, and extremistic theology
with negative consequences for its relations with the environment
(see below ch. 7).

6 STARTING POINTS FOR SPECULATIVE THEOLOGY

The priestly traditions and the intellectual expertise which
Zadokites contributed to the basic convictions of their "apocalypt-
ical" allies were fundamental presuppositions for the development
of a characteristic theological speculation. A number of so-called
"sapiental" works[57] and "mystery" texts,[58] unfortunately extant only
in fragments, contain examples of a theological re-working of older
sapiental materials used as a medium of expression in the Qumranic world view. Only one longer passage of a strictly systematic
doctrinal character is preserved, the peculiar composition 1QS
3:13—4:26. It represents a fully developed yahad-theology, disclos-
ing the two afore-mentioned aspects of cultic and eschatological
components with their consequences for the view of creation as a
whole, for the fate of humanity, Israel, and the individual members
of the community.[59] Many passages in other Qumran texts, particularly in the Hymns (1QH), can be read and understood more adequately, thanks to this tractate. It emphasizes God's function as
creator as well as Good and Evil. God created both forces, that of
light and that of darkness, each acting coexistently in the cosmos
and inside the individual. This is represented by a Prince of Light
and a Prince of Darkness (Belial) with their respective angelic or
demonic hosts. Since everything must follow God's determining
norms, however, there emerged a polar anthropological concept.
One side represents the principle of dualistic determination; the
other represents the option for justice or iniquity, truth and false-
hood, life and death. It is a kind of universalization of the choice
between obedience according to the Torah and transgression as
expressed in Dt 30:15.19. The text, however, only mentions the
Torah explicitly in 1QS 4:22 where a reference to the covenant and
the election places the whole device in a traditional frame. The
consequences, as found in Dt 28-29 (referred to in a description of
a covenantal ceremony 1QS 1:16—3:13) are those of curse and

---

[57] 1Q26; 4Q423; 4Q184; 4Q185; 4Q302- 4Q308; 4Q410-421; 4Q423+423a-
426; 4Q463; 4Q 472-477; 4Q485-487; 4Q498; 4Q521; 4Q525.
[58] 1Q27; 4Q299-301.
[59] H. Stegemann, "Zu Textbestand und Grundgedanken von 1QS III,13 -
IV,26", Revue de Qumran 13 (1988) 95-131.

blessing as eschatological consequences in the cosmic as well as in
the individual realms. This seems to indicate that some basic ideas
of the passage are not specifically Jewish. The authors, however,
were surely convinced enough to express no foreign (Zoroastric)
ideas. It is obvious that the sectarian drive in the development of
the community's theological thinking was a dynamic and innovative one and that in the course of time the importance and significance of such "dogmatic" concepts increased. Due to psychological
and physical reasons, it was not possible to practice this kind of
lifestyle in the yahad for a long time without an explanation for the
continuous delay of the allegedly near time of salvation. Throughout Jewish history, to stress the concrete differences of practice in
legal and ritual questions was a common method of self-definition;
but, it provided insufficient motivation for such a rigid lifestyle
throughout the centuries. It is significant that the passages, where in
4QMMT such practical differences are listed, formed part of a
larger composition with theological/eschatological components.
The systematical tractate in 1QS 3:13—4:26 also contains an explanation for the disappointing delay of the last end; the
eschatological processes are called "mysteries" which are firmly
embedded in God's universal device. This device cannot be realized except by the Torah, the "Torah of the time" enacted by the
Zadokites in the institutions of the yahad community.

7 THE RELATIONSHIP WITH THE WORLD OUTSIDE

During first century B.C., the men of the Qumran jahad community claimed to dispose of the only way of life which all repentants of
Israel were forced to share under the penalty of being regarded as
"traitors to the Covenant" and counted among the "sons of darkness." One of the consequences was that their concept for the organization of Israel in the end of the days, as attested in 1Q28a,
exhibits fundamental traits of the yahad community. This presupposes that the group regarded itself no longer as a preliminary stage
in an eschatological drama aiming at the restoration of Israel in
accordance with its traditional constitution; it claimed that its sectarian institution was identical with Israel. It is comprehensible that
from this time forward the center risked the abandonment of its
"diaspora" which was scarcely able or willing to live according to
such extreme standards as the "men of holiness" in 1QS.

The radicalization which presumably took place in the yahad
community had not only severe consequences regarding the rela-

tionship to other Jews but to mankind in general. Jews who were not willing to see through membership in the yahad community the only true way of repentance and Torah fulfillment were called "wicked ones" or "traitors," and were regarded as "sons of darkness" together with all the foreign enemies of Israel. They were typologically represented by the traditional hostile peoples of Amalek, Edom, Moab, the Philistines, etc. The confrontation, therefore, was an absolute one inwardly as well as outwardly. There is no single hint that the exhortations to repent and to return to the Torah presuppose a kind of religious propaganda as was the later case in Rabbinic Judaism which endeavoured to convert at least the majority of the people to its kind of Judaic system and way of life by restricting absolute internal confrontation to the minimum. On the contrary, 1QS 9:12-24 states explicitly that the members are not entitled to tell outsiders anything of the group's "revealed" Torah. These tactics of arcane discipline and self isolation were certainly no basis for the emergence or maintenance of a broader movement.

Josephus attests to a characteristic attitude of the Sadduceans: they behaved as an elitist group without interest for the concerns of the majority.[60] This attitude is understandable from the priestly point of view, for priests were convinced to do the best for all by doing their duty, performing their ritual duties while certain to share the company of their heavenly colleagues. The sectarian inner development of the Qumran community was the logical consequence of an elitist priestly self-definition combined with extremist eschatological expectations which resulted in a dualistic evaluation of everything and everyone, particularly effective in the frame of such a rigid and exclusive type of organization as the yahad.

One group whose secession from the earlier broader movement that the Qumran community evidently resented seems to have been the Pharisees, called dôrshê halaqôt, "advisors of smooth rulings." They apparently shared the eschatologically revised deuteronomistic view and hopes of Israel's history; but, they tried to find a way to live according to a Torah not restricted to an elitist and extremist group as a way for as many as possible of all of the people of Israel. It may be that the Pharisaic-Rabbinic principle not to impose on the public unbearable burdens had one of its roots in a reaction to such extremist tendencies as attested to in the Qumran scrolls.

---

[60] Flavius Josephus, De Bello Iudaico 2:166.

TEXT EDITIONS (AND TRANSLATIONS)

1) M. Burrows, The Dead Sea Scrolls of St. Mark's Monastery, fasc. I (New Haven: 1950): 1QIsa, 1QpHab; fasc. II (New Haven: 1951): 1QS.
2) E. L. Sukenik, The Dead Sea Scrolls of the Hebrew University (Jerusalem: 1956): 1QSb, 1QM, 1QH.
3) N. Avigad—Y. Yadin, A Genesis Apocryphon (Jerusalem: 1956); R. T. J. A. Fitzmyer, The Genesis Apocryphon of Qumran Cave I. A Commentary (Roma: 1971²).
4) E. Lohse, Die Texte von Qumran. Hebräisch und deutsch (Darmstadt: 1986⁴).
5) DJD: Discoveries in the Judean Desert (Oxford: 1955-1982): vol. I: D. Barthélemy—J.T. Milik, Qumran Cave 1 (1955 1964²); vol. II: P. Benoit—J. T. Milik—R. de Vaux, Les grottes de Murabba'at, i-ii (1960/61); vol. III: M. Baillet—J. T. Milik—R. de Vaux, Les "Petites grottes" de Qumran. Exploration de la falaise, les grottes 2Q, 3Q, 5Q, 6Q, 7Q à 10Q,le rouleau de cuivre I-II (1962); vol. IV: J. A. Sanders, The Psalm Scroll of Qumran Cave XI(11QPsa) (1965); vol. V: J. M. Allegro, Qumran Cave IV.1 (4Q 158—4Q 186) (1968); vol. VI: R. de Vaux—J. T. Milik, Qumran grotte IV.2 (4Q 128—4Q 157) (1977); vol. VII: M. Baillet, Qumran grotte IV.3 (4Q 482—4Q 520) (1982).
6) Aramaic Texts: J. A. Fitzmyer—D. J. Harrington, A Manual of Palestinian Aramaic Texts (Roma: 1978); K. Beyer, Die aramäischen Texte vom Toten Meer (Göttingen: 1984).
7) English translation: G. Vermes, The Dead Sea Scrolls in English (London: 1987³).
8) German: J. Maier, Die Qumran-Essener, vol. I: Die Texte vom Toten Meer in deutscher Übersetzung (München: 1994).
Spanish: F. García Martínez, Textos de Qumran (Madrid: 1992).
9) C. Newsom, Songs of the Sabbath Sacrifice: A Critical Edition (Atlanta: 1985).
10) Y. Yadin, The Temple Scroll, vol. I-III (Jerusalem: 1977; Hebrew text and English translation: 1983; J. Maier, The Temple Scroll (Sheffield: 1985); G. J. Brooke (ed.), Temple Scroll Studies (JSP Suppl. Series 7, Sheffield: 1989); St. O. Wise, A Critical Study of the Temple Scroll from Qumran Cave 11 (Studies in Ancient Oriental Civilization 49, Chicago: 1990).
11) M. Broshi (ed.), The Damascus Document Reconsidered (Jerusalem: 1992. Contains pp. 51-62: J. Baumgarten, "The Laws of the Damascus Document in Current Research").
12) J. H. Charlesworth—J. Milgrom etc. (eds.), The Dead Sea Scrolls. vol. I: The Rules. 1: Rule of the Community and Related Documents (Tübingen: 1993).
13) G. Vermes—M. D. Goodman, The Essenes. The Greek and Latin Evidence (Sheffield: 1989).

SELECTED BIBLIOGRAPHY:

For Introduction:

P. R. Callaway, The History of the Qumran Community (Sheffield: 1987).
J. A. Fitzmyer, The Dead Sea Scrolls (Missoula: 19772); id., Responses to 101 Questions on the Dead Sea Scrolls (New York: 1993).
E.-M. Laperrousaz, Qoumrân (Paris: 1976).
J. Maier, Zwischen den Testamenten. Geschichte und Religion in der Zeit des Zweiten Tempels (Würzburg: 1990); id., Geschichte der jüdischen Religion (Freiburg/Br.: 1992).
G. Stemberger, Pharisäer, Sadduzäer, Essener (Stuttgart: 1990).
Stone M. E. (ed.), Jewish Writings of the Second Temple Period (Assen: 1984).

Collections and Important Contributions:

J. M. Baumgarten, Studies in Qumran Law (Leiden: 1977); id., "The Laws of the Damascus Document in Current Research", in: M. Broshi (ed.), The Damascus Document Reconsidered (Jerusalem: 1992) 51-62.
M. Delcor (ed.), Qumran. Sa piété, sa théologie et son milieu (Leuven 1978).
D. Dimant—U. Rappoport, The Dead Sea Scrolls. Forty Years of Research (Jerusalem: 1989).
M. Fishbane—I. Tov (ed.), Sha'arei Talmon (Winona Lake: 1992).
F. García Martínez et al. (eds.), The Scriptures and the Scrolls. Studies in Honour of A. S. van der Woude on the Occasion of his 65th Birthday (Leiden: 1992).
F. García Martínez, Qumran and Apocalpytic. Studies on the Aramaic Texts from Qumran (Leiden: 1992).
I. Heinemann, "Midrash", in: Enzyclopedia miqra'it 4 (1962) 695-701.
Z. J. Kapera (ed.), The First International Colloquium on the Dead Sea Scrolls Mogilany May 31—June 2,1987 (Folia Orientalia vol. XXV, 1988, Wroclaw: 1989)
G. Klinzing, Die Umdeutung des Kultes in der Qumrangemeinde und im Neuen Testament (Göttingen: 1971).
H. Lichtenberger, Studien zum Menschenbild in Texten aus Qumran (Göttingen: 1980).
J. Neusner, Torah. From Scroll to Symbol in Formative Judaism (Philadelphia: 1985); id., J. Neusner, The Formation of the Jewish Intellect (Atlanta: 1988); id., Foundations of Judaism (Atlanta 19932).
L. H. Schiffman, The Halakhah at Qumran (Leiden: 1975); id., Sectarian Law in the Dead Sea Scrolls (Brown Judaic Studies 33, Chico: 1983); id., The Eschatological Community of the Dead Sea Scrolls (Atlanta: 1989); id., Law, Custom and Messianism in the Dead Sea Scrolls (Jerusalem: 1993, in Hebrew);
L. H. Schiffman, (ed.), Archaeology and History in the Dead Sea Scrolls (JSP Suppl. Series 8, Sheffield: 1989).
H. Shanks, Understanding the Dead Sea Scrolls. A Reader from the Biblical Archaeology Review (New York: 1992).

S. Talmon, Collected Essays III: Qumran Studies (Leiden: 1989).
J. Trebolle Barreras—L. Vegas Montaner (eds.), The Madrid Qumran Congress, I-II (Leiden: 1993).
Van der Woude A. S. (ed.), The Book of Daniel in the Light of New Findings (Leuven: 1993).
M. Weinfeld, The Organizational Pattern and the Penal Code of the Qumran Sect (Fribourg/Göttingen: 1986).

THE JUDAISM OF THE SYNAGOGUES
(FOCUSING ON THE SYNAGOGUE OF DURA-EUROPOS)

Jonathan A. Goldstein
(University of Iowa)

1 INTRODUCTION

There is a penalty for sharing my discoveries with the readers of this chapter: if I am to be honest, I must also inform them of the depths of our ignorance. Although the rabbinic and patristic literatures are vast, and although archaeological discoveries multiply, there are huge gaps in our knowledge. Thus, there is, in general, no reason to assume that in their synagogues the widely scattered Jews of antiquity, in the Roman, Parthian, and Persian empires and elsewhere, either followed or rejected the beliefs and practices described in the Mishnah, the Talmudim, and the rest of rabbinic literature.

Few texts tell us what those scattered Jews believed and did. Archaeology can uncover and identify synagogues, but only rarely can it tell us how they were used. For example, the overwhelming majority of the known ancient synagogue buildings contain no unequivocal evidence of a separate section for women.[1] Should we infer that women were excluded from all such structures? Or that there were no restrictions on the presence of women? Only one known ancient synagogue has rather good evidence for a separate section for women.[2] The variety of the buildings is such as to lead to the conclusion that local customs and local tastes determined the architecture of the synagogues and, probably, also the practices of the congregations.[3]

---

[1] See Andrew Seager, "The Architecture of the Dura and Sardis Synagogues," in *The Synagogue*, edited by Joseph Gutmann (New York, 1975), 156-58. In a letter to me of January 29, 1993, Joseph Gutmann wrote, "In my opinion Seager's judgment that there is no convincing evidence of a women's section in ancient synagogues still holds."

[2] See Tsvi 'Uri Ma'oz, "*Bet ha-keneset bi-tequphat ha-bayit ha-sheni*," *Eretz-Israel* 23 (1992), 340-41.

[3] See, e.g., Marilyn J. Chiat, "First Century Synagogue Architecture: Methodological Problems," in *Ancient Synagogues: The State of Research*, edited by Joseph Gutmann ("Brown Judaic Studies," 22; Chico, 1981), 56, and Gideon Foerster, "The Art and Architecture of the Synagogue in its Late Roman Setting in Palestine," in *The Synagogue in Late Antiquity*, edited by Lee I. Levine (Philadelphia, 1987), 144.

The Judaism of every ancient synagogue should be inferred as far as possible from the local evidence. Usually, that evidence, beyond the architecture of the building, is extremely sparse. In so many cases, nothing tells us when the synagogue was built, what officials presided, what rituals were performed, what prayers were said.

One ancient synagogue, the one at ancient Dura in Syria, stands as something of an exception to this rule (the local name of the town was "Dura"; when Alexander the Great conquered the area, the town received the Graeco-Macedonian name "Europos"). Even for that synagogue we do not know, for example, what regulations governed the presence of women. Inscriptions tell us that the *structure* in its final form (presumably without its paintings) was completed in the year 556 of the Seleucid era, in the second year of the Roman emperor Philippus, that is, in 245 C.E., after the vernal equinox.[4]

The inscriptions give the names and titles of officials at Dura, but we have to guess at their functions. A tiny parchment fragment gives us a piece of a grace after meals.[5] An elaborate set of surviving wall-paintings lets us see something of the local practices with clothing and something of the community's beliefs and hopes.

Although the paintings, now in the Damascus Museum, have deteriorated, early photographs and drawings and especially the copies made by the competent artist, Herbert Gute, let us know much of what originally stood on the walls.[6] Some of the paintings

---

[4] Joseph Gutmann (editor), (*The Dura-Europos Synagogue: a Re-evaluation [1932-1992]* ["South Florida Studies in the History of Judaism," edited by Jacob Neusner et al., Number 25; Atlanta, 1992], x-xi with xxxiii, n .1) condemns my dating and adheres to the 244/45 proposed by Carl H. Kraeling (*The Synagogue*, Final Report VIII, Part I of *The Excavations at Dura-Europos* [New Haven, 1956], 6, 223), but Kraeling stated his date without argument, and other scholars simply copied it. Mine has the following basis. The year 1 of the Babylonian Seleucid era used by the peoples of the Euphrates valley began in the early spring of 311 B.C.E. See Elias Bickerman, *Chronology of the Ancient World* (Ithaca, NY, 1968), 71; Richard A. Parker and Waldo H. Dubberstein, *Babylonian Chronology, 626 B.C.-A.D. 75* (Providence, 1956), 37. Consequently, early spring, 1 C.E., is equivalent to the beginning of the year 312, and early spring, 245, is equivalent to the beginning of the year 556 of the Seleucid era. Furthermore, the second regnal year of the emperor Philippus began December 10, 244 (Ernst Stein, "Iulius 386," *Realencyclopaedie der klassischen Altertumswissenschaft*, ed. by Pauly, Wissowa, et al., X [1919], 758), so that the completion of the synagogue came in 245 C.E., sometime after the beginning of spring.

[5] *The Parchments and Papyri*, edited by C. Bradford Welles, Robert O. Fink, and J. Frank Gilliam, Final Report V, Part I, of *The Excavations at Dura-Europos* (New Haven, 1959), no. 11, to be corrected by my review, *Journal of the American Oriental Society* 81 (1961), 431.

[6] Cf. my *Semites, Iranians, Greeks and Romans: Studies in Their Interactions* (Atlanta, 1990), 68-75.

contain labels in Aramaic or Greek. The content of some others seems obvious. A large proportion of the surviving paintings clearly depicts scenes from the Hebrew Bible. One is tempted to assume that they all do. Yet many of the details do not fit what the Bible says!

2 KEYS TO SOLVING THE PUZZLES

I believe that the following can serve as keys to the enigmatic aspects of the paintings of the Dura synagogue.

A. The Jews of Dura, like the rabbis of the Babylonian Talmud lived in the valley of the Euphrates river between the two superpowers of their time: in the west, for the time being ruling Dura, was the Roman empire; in the east until 224 C.E. was the Parthian empire, and thereafter was the Sassanian Persian. Like the rabbis and like most peoples living under foreign masters, the Jews of Dura in all probability yearned for liberation. As mortals, they were naturally grieved by the fact of death. At least from the second century B.C.E. on, Jewish sects (including the Christians) believed in immortality or resurrection. Biblical prophecies indeed predicted both a resurrection of the dead and the liberation of the Jews from foreign domination.[7]

Furthermore, several prophets predicted a last great war pitting the gentile powers against each other and/or the Chosen People.[8] That conflict would be a part of the great age of liberation: it would follow soon after the exodus from the exile (Ezekiel 38:8, 12, 16). By the first century C.E., this war came to be called the "War of Gog and Magog," a name derived from a popular misreading of Ezekiel 38.2. For some Jews it could imply that Gog and Magog were separate powers.[9] The superpowers of the period of the Dura synagogue were Rome and the Iranian empires, first that of the Parthians and then, after 224, that of the Sassanian Persian dynasty. The repeated clashes of the rival superpowers gave rise in the minds of the Jews to the belief that the War of Gog and Magog would be a war between Rome and Parthia or Sassanian Persia.[10]

---

[7] See especially Daniel 2, 7-12; resurrection: Dan 12:2-3.

[8] In this paragraph, I repeat material from my *Semites*, 78. Great war predicted: Ezekiel 38-39, Joel 4(3):9-14, Haggai 2.22, Zechariah 12:1-9, 14:2, 13.

[9] Revelation 20:8, *Sibylline Oracles* iii. 319-22, and the statement of Rabbi Elᶜazar bar Abina at *Genesis Rabbah* 42:4; see also Joseph Klausner, *The Messianic Idea in Israel* (New York, 1955), 375-76, 398, 401, 422, 450, 464, 496-501.

[10] See Jacob Neusner, *A History of the Jews in Babylonia*, Volume I (2nd printing, revised: Leiden, 1969), 31 (n. 1), 84-85; cf. III (Leiden, 1968), 182, and IV (Leiden, 1969), 35, 53-54, 68, 319, 375; *Genesis Rabbah* 42:4.

All Mesopotamian Jewry lived near the theater of those wars, and Dura was a strategic Roman border post facing the rival power throughout the time that the Jews there could look at the paintings on the walls of their synagogue. Some of those predictions about the "last days" set time-limits within which the great events would occur[11] and those time limits appeared to be past.[12]

Consequently, the Jews of Dura believed that fulfilment of those prophecies was imminent. How could God violate the promises he had revealed through His prophets? Accordingly, we may expect that the Jews of Dura wanted to see depictions of the future fulfilments of those prophecies. An artist could also cater to their fervent hopes by depicting past events which resembled and fore-shadowed the predicted fulfilments. Our expectations will prove to be justified.

B. The paintings of the synagogue are separated from each other by a framing vine-pattern. Within one frame, time and space can often be telescoped, so that more than one moment or one place is shown, as when Elijah brings to life the son of the widow from Zarephath (WC1 from I Kings 17:17-24; the woman brings the dead child; Elijah takes him; the woman holds her living child) or as in the painting from the book of Esther: on the left, Mordechai in royal attire rides in triumph through the streets of Shushan, led by humiliated Haman (Esther 6:1-12), whereas, on the right, King Ahasuerus on his throne, accompanied by Queen Esther and Mordechai, later receives a record of the number of the enemies of the Jews slain in Fortress Shushan (Esther 9:11). Some of the anom-alies in the paintings can be solved by taking note of this telescop-ing.

C. No other ancient synagogue with wall-paintings has been dis-covered (despite a Talmudic reference to such synagogues). But other evidence can be used. The ancient synagogue of Gaza has a floor mosaic useful for interpreting the Central Composition.[13] Early Christian churches contain mosaics and paintings strikingly parallel to the iconography of the Dura synagogue, so much so, that the resemblances cannot be coincidental. The designers for the synagogue and the churches must have drawn on shared traditions. A Christian picture can contain labels or can be better preserved or

---

[11] Notably, the predictions in Daniel 7-12.

[12] In the third century C.E., the great Babylonian Jewish sage, Abba Arikha (usually called simply "Rabh"), a contemporary of the synagogue, is reported to have said, "All the time limits [set by the prophecies for the coming of the Mes-siah] have passed . . . " (Babylonian Talmud, *Sanhedrin* 97b).

[13] Talmudic reference: Palestinian Talmud, 'Abodah Zarah 3:3, p. 42d. Syna-gogue of Gaza: see my *Semites*, 81-85.

clearer than the one at Dura and thus can be used to explain its enigmas. On the other hand, the artists who worked for ancient Near-Eastern kings were astonishingly conservative in the motifs they chose to portray (though *styles* of portrayal could vary widely). These motifs can be found long before the time of the synagogue, in Sumer, Assyria, and elsewhere. They can also be found after the time of the synagogue, in Sassanian and Muslim Persia. The Sassanians were ruling at the time of the synagogue, and one can show that its artists drew upon Sassanian patterns. Thus, early Christian remains and pieces of Near-Eastern royal art can be used to interpret the paintings of the synagogue.[14]

D. Despite wide agreement among scholars, some scenes in the paintings have been wrongly identified. Careful attention to details can supply a correct interpretation.

E. There has been a prevalent misconception in interpreting the clothing shown in the paintings. Some male figures wear the trousered garb known from ancient literature and art objects to have been characteristic of the Iranians. Other male figures wear the two-striped tunic (*chiton*) and rectangular cloak draped over the shoulders (*himation*) well known from Greek literature and art. However, the garments worn by non-priestly Israelites and Jews of the Holy Land (and by many other populations of eastern Mediterranean lands) may well have long been similar to those of Greek civilians. The Greek word *chiton* is Semitic in origin, cognate to the the Hebrew *kuttonet* or *ketonet*. The outer garment or cloak, called *'adderet* in the Hebrew Bible, in the Greek versions is frequently called *himation*. In the times of the Mishnah and the Talmudim, the rectangular outer cloak which bore the fringes commanded by Numbers 15:37-41 was called *tallit*, a loan word from the Greek *stole*. Thus there is nothing peculiarly Greek in the chiton and himation worn by prophets and angels in my interpretation of the Dura paintings.[15] Those costumes were not felt to be foreign, and neither were the supposedly Iranian trousers.

---

[14] See my *Semites*, 81-113. Joseph Gutmann (*Re-evaluation*, xi with xxxiii, n.1; xii-xiii with xxxiv, n. 8; xviii-xix with xxxviii, n.27) in my judgment has failed to appreciate the striking character of the parallels between the Dura paintings and some pieces of early Christian art and has also failed to appreciate the astonishing conservatism of the motifs of ancient Near Eastern royal art. At xxxviii, n. 27, Gutmann correctly noted that in my earlier studies I did not use the fundamental work on Justinian's artistic programs, F. W. Deichmann, *Ravenna, Hauptstadt des spätantiken Abendlandes* (3 volumes in 5: Wiesbaden, 1969-76). I have now studied Deichmann's work and find that it gives excellent support to my theories.

[15] See *Genesis Rabbah* 36:6 (*tallit*) and Douglas R. Edwards, "Dress and Ornamentation," *The Anchor Bible Dictionary*, II (1992) 232-33, 235-36.

F. The painter or painters (from now on, I shall use the singular) of the Dura synagogue was a person of limited skill, as one would expect in that small provincial outpost. It could hardly be a great artistic or intellectual center. Nevertheless, the intellectual content of the paintings is highly sophisticated and elaborate and has those striking later parallels in Christian art. We are driven to assume that the *painter* with his small talent was a local person, whereas the *designer* worked in a Jewish community more favorable to intellectual developments. It is likely that the painter received instructions in words, not sketches to copy. These assumptions will enable us to explain some strange aspects of the paintings.

G. If we can show that there is a coherent scheme giving rise to the general arrangement of the paintings, that scheme may serve as a clue to the meaning of one or more of them.

H. Joseph Gutmann demands that the paintings be linked to the ceremonies and prayers of the congregation and to their life and thought, and on that ground finds fault with my interpretations.[16] For both Jews and Christians, scripture-reading was a part of the service. Thus, *any* artistic representation of a passage in scripture would be connected with the ceremonies and prayers of a church or synagogue. Naturally, Jews or Christians would tend to choose to have illustrated those passages which reflected their dearest beliefs and hopes.

I have special names for the contents of the central portion of the west wall. To designate the rest of the paintings of the synagogue, I use the system of Kraeling.[17] Framed compositions survive from the four walls of the building. The first letter of a designation (W, N, E, S) signifies the wall, west, north, east, or south. Three parallel bands of paintings originally stood on each wall, designated from top to bottom as A, B, and C. The framed panels in each band are numbered from left to right. Thus, WC1 is the leftmost framed composition in the bottom band of the west wall.

3 Paintings which present Few Problems

Let us first discuss briefly the paintings on which other scholars and I are in general agreement[18] or on which I can add little or nothing.

---

[16] *Re-evaluation*, xix-xx.

[17] *Synagogue*, 66-67, and Plans IX-XII.

[18] On this general agreement, see Gutmann, *Sacred Images:* Studies in Jewish Art from Antiquity to the Middle Ages (Northampton, 1989), Chap. VII, 1317-18.

SC1 is too fragmentary to identify. SC2 shows Elijah and the widow of Zarephath (I Kings 17:8-16). SC3 shows the failure of the prophets of Baal after they accepted Elijah's challenge and tried to have their god send down fire from heaven to consume the offering on the altar at Mount Carmel (I Kings 18:20-29). The Israelite plotter, Hiel, hides in or under the altar, intending to light a fraudulent fire for Baal, if necessary, but is about to be killed by a snake sent by God. The legend of Hiel is not in the text of the Bible, but rabbis told of it, and the Christian Fathers, Ephrem Syrus and John Chrysostom, knew the story.[19]

SC4 shows the next event, Elijah's successful sacrifice on Mount Carmel (I Kings 18:30-39). In WC1, Elijah restores to life the son of the widow from Zarephath (I Kings 17:17-24). Thus, there is a continuous strip of paintings from the career of Elijah, extending from SC2 through WC1; but, according to the biblical narrative, the scene of WC1 should follow SC2 and precede SC3. We shall have to inquire as to why the designer departed from the biblical order.

We have noticed how WC2 telescopes two obvious scenes.[20] On the left, Haman, dressed as a slave, leads Mordechai, dressed in royal attire and mounted on the king's horse, through the city (Esther 6:6-11). On the right, a report of the number of the slain enemies of the Jews is brought to the king (Esther 9:12), as Queen Esther sits with him, enthroned even higher than he, and Mordechai, the viceroy, stands at his side (Esther 9:12).

Scholars have disagreed on the meaning of the four very large male figures in chiton and himation standing in the middle of WC2.[21] Elsewhere in the paintings, that combination of apparel and size belongs to prophets. Here it belongs to angels (in the Hebrew Bible, both prophets and angels are called "messengers of the LORD"). Rabbi Yohanan was an important Palestinian authority who was a contemporary of the Dura synagogue (he died in 279 C.E.). At Babylonian Talmud, *Megillah 15b*, he is quoted as saying that *three* angels helped Esther become queen. A distinguished pupil of Rabbi Yohanan was Rabbi Abbahu. At Babylonian Talmud, *Megillah* 16b, Rabbi Abbahu is quoted as saying that when King

---

[19] Louis Ginzberg, *The Legends of the Jews* (7 vols.; Philadelphia, 1928), IV, 198; VI, 319, n. 15.

[20] General agreement on their content: Gutmann, *Sacred Images*, Chap. VII, 1317.

[21] See Erwin R. Goodenough, *Jewish Symbols in the Greco-Roman Period* (13 vols.; "Bollingen Series," XXXVII; New York, 1953-68), IX, 182-83.

Ahasuerus was about to react angrily to the report of the number of the slain (Esther 9:12), *one* angel slapped him (and turned his anger to favor).

Can our four angels be the result of combining the two legends? The scene of Rabbi Yohanan's legend is not depicted in the painting! However, angels are conspicuously numerous in the rabbinic elaborations on Esther.[22] Jews told how the angel Gabriel brought about Mordechai's triumphant ride.[23] The number of four angels need not have been derived by adding those of R. Yohanan's legend to those of Rabbi Abbahu's.

Scholars have disagreed about some other paintings, but they do not require close analysis here. Let us consider them next. Fragmentary, SB1 portrays a triumphant procession with the ark.[24] For our purposes, it does not matter whether the occasion is David's transferral of the ark to Jerusalem (II Sam 6:12-19) or Solomon's bringing of it into the temple (I Kings 8:1-4). The account of the dedication of the Tabernacle has Moses doing everything (Exodus 39:17-33), so that event is not what is depicted.

WA1 is too fragmentary to identify positively. Only portrayals of legs or feet survive. At the right there is a male figure in chiton and himation and, near him, another, in the attire which kings wear in the synagogue paintings.[25] Perhaps the picture portrayed an event from David's or Solomon's reign. WA2 is also fragmentary. One can see that it contained (from left two right), two elegantly clad women, a man in royal attire, an elaborate chair bearing a man in chiton and himation (below his chair is a Greek label, *synkathedros*, "seated counselor"), a very elaborate throne bearing the Greek label "Slemon" (evidently the local pronunciation of Solomon's name), another man in chiton and himation, and, at the right edge, another "counselor's chair." Solomon's divine power and wisdom were demonstrated by two events involving women: his judgment between the two harlots[26] and his reception of the Queen of Sheba.[27]

---

[22] See Ludwig Blau, "Angelology.—Biblical, Talmudical, and Post-Talmudical," *Jewish Encyclopaedia*, I (1901), 585.

[23] Ibid. and Second Targum to Esther 6:1; Ginzberg, *Legends*, IV, 433-34, and VI, 476, n. 168.

[24] See Gutmann, *Sacred Images*, Chap. VII, 1319.

[25] Aaron wears it in WB2. See below, section 4c.

[26] Story: I Kings 3:16-27; aftereffects: ibid., 3:28-5:14.

[27] Story: I Kings 10:1-13; events which followed testifying to Solomon's wisdom, wealth, and power: 10:14-25.

Two women are shown, but their dresses are approximately equal in elegance. Can they be the queen and her attending lady? It is hard to view them as harlots. Furthermore, Scripture tells of Solomon's throne in I Kings 10, the chapter which tells of the Queen of Sheba, not in I Kings 3-5. EC2 is too fragmentary to identify. EC1 presents, at the right, the events of I Samuel 26: fugitive David and Abishai enter the camp of King Saul, who is dressed in the attire worn by kings in WC1, WC4, and the Central Composition, and by the high priest in WB2. Like the kings and unlike Aaron, Saul lacks the *chlamys*. From the sleeping king, David and Abishai take his spear and water jar. At the left, EC1 shows another person in the attire worn by kings and by the high priest. Like the high priest, this person wears the *chlamys*. Mounted on a white horse and armed, he leads an armed cavalry army on white horses, accompanied by two dogs. The horsemen, too, wear royal attire, but not the *chlamys*. The dogs, useful for tracking fugitives, would suggest that the army is Saul's and he is its leader. On the other hand, Saul is not reported to have had horses, whereas the LORD's angelic forces in the time of Elisha were seen to have possessed them (II Kings 6:17). Persian and other ancient Near-Eastern armies did use dogs.[28] Hence, the picture probably shows how God's heavenly army under an angelic chief protected the ancestor (or first incarnation) of the Messiah.[29] We infer that militant angels wore the costume of kings.[30]

Enough survives of NA1 to make it easy to recognize Jacob's dream of a ladder placed upon the earth and reaching heavenward, with angels ascending it (Genesis 28:12-17). The text speaks also of angels descending the ladder. I do not know whether the painter's failure to show the descenders is significant. They may have been omitted merely for lack of space.

The clothing of the ascenders requires explanation. Angels in WB4 and WC2 wear chiton and himation. The angels of Jacob's dream wear royal apparel, including the *chlamys*. We have inferred that is the costume for militant angels. Even though the angels of NA1, unlike those of EC1, are not armed, the designer has probably identified those of Jacob's dream (Genesis 28:12-17) with those of "God's army" (Genesis 32:1-2), and hence the ascenders wear the royal costume.

---

[28] Will Richter, "Hund," *Der Kleine Pauly*, II (1967), 1247.
[29] Cf. Goodenough, *Jewish Symbols*, X, 162-65.
[30] Cf. Kraeling, *Synagogue*, 72, n. 198.

At the close of the dream, God predicted for Jacob and his descendants glories which were not realities in the time of the synagogue. Jewish legends go farther in telling of God's revelations then to Jacob,[31] but the biblical text gave reason enough to put a depiction of the episode on the wall of the synagogue.

4 Scenes Partly or Wholly Misidentified

4a Those on the Torah Shrine

At the bottom center of the west wall of the synagogue of Dura stood a small structure (aedicula). That structure has been called the "Torah shrine." It contained a niche into which a scroll of the Pentateuch was placed. Jews followed the practice of Daniel (6:11) to pray facing Jerusalem, and the Torah shrine at Dura (as in modern synagogues) served to mark that direction.

Most of what is painted on the Torah shrine consists of symbols of immortality or resurrection. Some of these the Jews shared with ancient pagans and with the Christians of Dura. Such are the fruits on the soffit of the arch of the niche.[32]

On the vertical panel of the aedicula over the arch of the niche are painted (1) a seven-branched candelabrum (*menorah*), (2) a citron (*ethrog*), (3) a palm-branch, (4) a temple façade, and (5) a depiction of Abraham's attempt to sacrifice his son, Isaac. Items (1)-(4) belonged to the apparatus of Jewish worship in biblical times. Pictorial representations of them became symbols for Jews of hope for the afterlife.[33] The temple façade is *not* a depiction of a Torah shrine.[34] Two "round objects" occupy the space between the three columns at the center of the of the façade. They closely resemble the ends of a woman's breasts. Babylonian rabbinic tradition said the same of the poles for carrying the ark, viewed from outside, as they protruded into the fabric of the curtain of the Holy of Holies in Solomon's temple (I Kings 8:8 with Babylonian Talmud, *Menaḥoth* 98a-b).

---

[31] Ginzberg, *Legends*, I, 351-52.

[32] Erwin R. Goodenough demonstrated the existence of what he called a "lingua franca" of symbols of the afterlife in his *Jewish Symbols*, I-VIII. His views (ibid., IX, 66-67) about the fruits on the soffit are largely correct. So are his views about the fruits on the ceiling-tiles of the synagogue (ibid., IX, 48-55).

[33] Goodenough, *Jewish Symbols*, IX, 67-68. Jews could call the temple *bet hayyenu*, "the house of our life" (see, e.g., *Leviticus Rabbah* 19:5; *Sopherim* 13:12; cf. *Mekhilta*, *'Amalek* 2, p. 198 in the edition of H. S. Horovitz and I. A. Rabin [Jerusalem, 1960]).

[34] Goodenough, *Jewish Symbols*, IX, 69, argued that it was.

There is no reason to assume that the "breasts" in the painting are on rigid doors rather than in a curtain.

Scholars have agreed that the painting at the right of the vertical panel over the arch of the Torah niche depicts Abraham's attempted sacrifice of Isaac. With the help of a labeled early Christian parallel, E. R. Goodenough correctly argued that the small figure at the top of that painting is Sarah.[35] Sarah was not present at the attempted sacrifice. However, according to Jewish legend, on hearing of the episode, she was so shocked she died.[36] Sarah's presence in the picture is a good example of the telescoping of space in the paintings of the Dura synagogue, and helps display how the entire family suffered from God's testing command and thus earned God's blessing for their descendants (Genesis 22:17-18): "I shall surely bless you and shall surely make your descendants as numerous as the stars of the heaven and as the sand which is upon the seashore, and your descendants shall capture the gates of their enemies; and by your descendants shall all the nations of the earth bless themselves, because you have obeyed my command." The scene thus gave Jews hope of liberation and prosperity.

4b The Central Composition

One of the most puzzling groups among the synagogue paintings has been what I call the "Central Composition of the West Wall." It consists of four conspicuous figures, each of a standing man, and everything between them.[37] Erwin R. Goodenough called the area between the four standing figures the "reredos," a name useful for its brevity.[38]

In the synagogue of Dura the Central Composition occupied a place similar to the mural decoration of the apse in the Christian churches of the fourth century and later. Jews were taught that the foundation of their beliefs was the Torah revealed by God to Moses and embodied in the Pentateuch. Indeed, Jewish teaching and ritual and the content of the rest of the paintings of the west wall all directed the eyes of the worshipers toward the Torah shrine and toward the Central Composition above it. Thus, where movement

---

[35] Ibid., IX, 72-73.

[36] *Leviticus Rabbah* 16:2; see also Louis Ginzberg, *Legends*, I, 286-87; V, 255, n. 256.

[37] See figure 1, p. 156 (reproduced with the permission of the Princeton University Press from Goodenough, *Jewish Symbols*, XI, Plate I).

[38] *Jewish Symbols*, IX, 78.

is portrayed in the surviving paintings of the west wall, the action in the scenes on the left half of the wall moves toward the right, toward the center, whereas the action in the scenes on the right half of the wall moves toward the left, again toward the center.

The Central Composition is not the best preserved of the paintings of the synagogue. Parts of it certainly were obliterated in antiquity by the addition of more paint. Can a coherent interpretation be supplied from such unsatisfactory evidence? I believe that the answer is yes! I have used the keys (listed above) to unlock the secrets of the Central Composition and have been highly pleased with the results. My article on the topic has been published twice.[39] Nevertheless, Joseph Gutmann, the distinguished historian of Jewish art has reacted to it with skepticism. In the notes to this chapter I present my reply to the points raised by Gutmann.

Let us first describe what can be seen of the Central Composition. The painter drew a tree, spreading outward and upward from the base and vertical midline of the central space destined to be framed above the Torah shrine (the framing border-pattern was added later). The tree has vine leaves, so that it has been called a "tree-vine." It is drawn as if it grew out of the Torah shrine. At both sides of the foot of the tree-vine, the painter drew an impressive person on a royal couch-throne, with an ornate table in front of it; under the left table was perhaps a severed human head.

All these are stock motifs from ancient Near-Eastern royal art for depicting a victorious king, with which the artist (who quite possibly was a non-Jew) must have been familiar. The Jewish designer was pleased to take advantage of the procedure of ordering the artist to paint customary motifs, but the designer wanted to have Jacob's deathbed blessings portrayed, not the feast of a victorious king. The painter was ordered to obliterate the tables and the possible severed head. Over the obliterated material, the artist drew footstools. To the scene on the left, he added, by the couch, the twelve sons of Jacob; to that on the right, Joseph with his two small sons.[40]

Just above the blessing scenes and amid the foliage of the tree, the artist drew a king on a throne, playing a stringed instrument to assembled peaceful wild beasts. Except for portraying the musician

---

[39] "The Central Composition of the West Wall of the Synagogue of Dura-Europos," *Journal of the Ancient Near Eastern Society* 16-17 (1984-85), 99-141, and my *Semites*, 67-114.

[40] See my *Semites*, 70, 108-12.

as royal, the composition unmistakably follows the pattern of pagan depictions of Orpheus.[41]

The branches and foliage of the tree-vine spread still higher, into the space which was to be the center of Band B. There, right amid the foliage, the artist put an enthroned king, surrounded by 12 or 13 male figures in trousers. In front of the king, to his right and to his left, stand two male figures in chiton and himation.

The tree-vine symbolizes Israel and her destiny.[42] It seems to sprout from the Torah-niche. Did the designer think of it as sprouting only from the Torah, or also from the depiction of the attempted sacrifice of Isaac? He could indeed have thought of it as coming from both sources, but the logic of the painting argues against that. The attempted sacrifice is portrayed as coordinate with the menorah, citron, palm branch, and temple, none of which can be viewed as the source of Israel or of her destiny. At the end of the first book of the Torah, in Jacob's deathbed benedictions, the vine appears in a part of his blessing to Judah (Genesis 49:10-11) that was taken as a Messianic prophecy, very likely already by the writer of Zechariah 9:9. The ancient synagogue of Gaza has a floor mosaic on which a similar royal Orpheus is labeled as "David." There are also Christian portrayals of an Orpheus-Messiah. With the help of those parallels, I have been able to prove that the "Orpheus" of the Dura Synagogue is the Messiah of the Jews, as predicted in Isaiah 11:1-9.[43]

Scholars have disagreed on the meaning of the king with the 12 or 13 figures in trousers and the 2 figures in chiton and himation. However, Christian parallels (labeling the 2 who wear chiton and himation) and ancient Near-Eastern patterns of royal art have enabled me to show that the king is again the Messiah of the Jews, ruling over a united and harmonious Israel (as predicted in Isaiah 11:11-13). Assisting him are the two great prophets, Moses and Elijah, as predicted by Jewish and Christian texts.[44] The tree-vine seems to have no fruits. That would be an ill-omened symbol. But the Orpheus-Messiah and the king and his subjects are drawn amid the foliage. Surely the designer intended the worshipers to view, as fruits of of the tree-vine, the Messiah and the tamed beasts and the liberated tribes of Israel and the immortal or resurrected prophets. The idea could well have come from Isaiah 27:6.

---

[41] Ibid., 70. When the border pattern was added, the blessing scenes and the "Orpheus" figure both fit into Band C.

[42] See my *Semites*, 79.

[43] Ibid., 81-87.

[44] See my *Semites*, 87-99.

Christian parallels have also enabled me to show that the four conspicuous standing men surrounding the reredos each represent Moses at an important stage of his life. Moses' revelations made possible Israel's destiny, and pictures of Moses may have served to Judaize securely the many motifs borrowed from pagan royal art, even when the origin of those motifs was obvious to the worshipers.[45]

So interpreted, the Central Composition is an excellent example of successful application of our keys. It confirms our expectation, derived from history and from rabbinic sources, that God's final Messianic victory and the Jews' own liberation should be a major concern of the designer and his audience. It also probably contains allusions to the other major concern of the worshipers, the afterlife: Moses and Elijah are either resurrected or immortal as they stand with the Messiah, and the Messiah may be the resurrected David. All the more does the Central Composition contain both major concerns, if the designer thought that with the paintings on the Torah shrine it constituted a single unit. The composition contains telescoping of time and place. Early Christian artistic monuments and the patterns of ancient Near-Eastern royal propaganda art have contributed mightily to our explanation of the Central Composition, and though other scholars in some respects came close to my solution, they all have wrongly identified parts of it. Let us now examine other misidentified pieces.

4c WB2: Aaron and the Earthly Sanctuary

Panel WB2 contains a labeled male figure identified as Aaron (Moses' brother, the first high priest). From the several pictures of kings in the Dura synagogue, it is easy to see that except for his cape and headdress, Aaron wears royal attire. But pieces of Iranian royal art demonstrate that the headdress and cape (*chlamys*), too, are royal![46]

In WB2 Aaron stands by a shrine built like a Greek stone temple. The painter intended to show its front and one side, plus the roof, but he botched the perspective. Nevertheless, he showed the front entrance, four Corinthian columns along the left side of the temple, and another Corinthian column to the right of the front entrance. At each of the three visible corners of the temple roof is perched a winged female bearing a wreath. Figures so placed on a

---

[45] *Semites*, 87-89, 99.
[46] See Kraeling, *Synagogue*, 127-28, and nn. 449, 451.

temple are called "acroteria." Within the entrance, one can see the ark, standing in front of a curtain.

In front of the entrance to the temple are a set of cult-objects. Let us list them from left to right. First, there is a single-stalked vessel on a four-legged base. In a hollow at its top it contains material that is on fire. Then, there is a seven-branched candelabrum (*menorah*), its lamps all lit. Then, there is a second single-stalked vessel containing burning material. Finally, no longer directly in front of the entrance but rather a little to the right, is an altar with a sacrificed animal upon it.

In front of Aaron (indeed, concealing his feet) is a crenellated stone wall containing three doors. Over the middle door is a curtain flapping in the wind.[47] The tabernacle and the later Jewish temples consisted of an inner shrine surrounded by one or more enclosed courts. Accordingly, though only one face of the wall is shown, we may infer that the designer intended the viewers to perceive the wall as enclosing all the painted figures and structures except any which stand in front of it.[48]

A curtain occupies the left top corner and two more are portrayed at the right top of the picture, and they may represent the partitions enclosing the other side of the court and may indicate that the designer wanted to leave a hint that the tabernacle and its surrounding enclosure were made of cloth. The presence of curtains at the tops of WC2 and WC3, which cannot be so explained, renders unlikely that explanation of those in WB2. It is best to admit our ignorance in all three cases.

In any case, the court is to be viewed as completely enclosed. Standing within it, on the left, are the two trousered male figures (smaller than Aaron) bearing wind-instruments longer than their forearms, and, on the right, the two similar male figures with similar instruments and a bull and a ram. At least two of the wind-instruments have their tubes strengthened with rings. In front of the wall (and therefore outside it) is another trousered man carrying an axe and leading a bovine which has no visible genitals. Because the animal is to be slaughtered outside the walls,[49] and because it is apparently female and is reddish in color, we recognize the beginning of the ritual of the red heifer, the ashes of which were used in the procedure for removing the uncleanness incurred by contact with a dead body (Numbers 19).

---

[47] See Exodus 27:16; Mishnah, *Sheqalim*, 6:3.
[48] Cf. Goodenough, *Jewish Symbols*, X, 45.
[49] See Numbers 19:3.

If the designer had wanted to depict in the wrongest possible way events from the career of Aaron, he could hardly have made more "mistakes" than are contained in WB2. The sanctuary in Aaron's time was a portable tabernacle with walls of cloth and leather, not a temple of stone in the Greek style. Can anyone believe that images of the pagan goddess of victory stood as acroteria on the temple presided over by the pious Aaron?

Aaron was high priest, not king. His vestments are carefully described in Exodus 28. Why does he wear royal apparel in WB2? Surely the plate engraved with the words "Holy to the LORD" should be on Aaron's headdress (Exodus 28:36; Leviticus 8:9). Are the five smaller trousered figures priests? Are they Aaron's sons? Aaron had only four sons (Exodus 6:23), of whom Nadab and Abihu perished early (Leviticus 10:1-2, 12). Are the wind-instruments the silver trumpets of Numbers 10:1-10? To some observers, they look more like animal horns. Furthermore, the commandment in Numbers calls for only two, not four.

Exodus 40:17-23 gives a detailed description of the furnishings of the tabernacle and its enclosed court. Within the tabernacle, there should be the ark, the table, the candelabrum, and the single incense altar. The ark should be *behind* a "veil" or "curtain." On top of it should be its cover (the "mercy-seat") with the two cherubim. The altar of burnt-offering should stand *directly* in front of the entrance to the tabernacle. WB2 displays no table. The ark is *in front* of a curtain. The candelabrum is *outside* the tabernacle. Nothing resembles the incense-altar described in Exodus 30:1-6. We can, indeed, interpret the single-stalked vessels as incense-burners so as to have something corresponding to an incense altar in WB2,[50] but even then there are two burners, not one, and they stand outside the tabernacle. The altar of burnt-offering stands *to the right* of the entrance.

---

[50] Goodenough, *Jewish Symbols*, X, 11, says the single-stalked vessels of WB2 are incense altars, but at X, 29, he says the similar vessels in WB1 are censers (but the biblical Jewish censer [*maḥtah*] was shovel-shaped). Kraeling, *Synagogue*, 126, says the implements of WB2 are *thymiateria* ("incense vessels"), but ibid., 119, he says the similar vessels of WB1 are altars of incense, and ibid., 101-2 and figure 30, he identifies similar implements in WA1 variously as (single-lamp) candelabra and *thymiateria*. Clark Hopkins, *The Discovery of Dura-Europos* (New Haven and London, 1979), 156, calls the stalked implements of WB2 "incense-burners"; he says nothing about those of WB1 and WB3. In fact, candelabra and *thymiateria* could look very much alike, and *thymiateria* could have the size and function of altars. See Maurice Besnier, "Turibulum," *Dictionnaire des antiquités grecques et romaines*, edited by Ch. Daremberg and Edmond Saglio, V (no date), 542-44; E. Saglio, "Candelabrum," ibid., I, Part II (1908), 869-75; Walter Hatto Gross, "Turibulum," *Der kleine Pauly*, V (1975), 1006.

Using our keys and other information, we can "unlock" most of the puzzles of WB2. The picture is an extreme example of telescoping. No single event in Aaron's career is depicted. Indeed, the composition includes periods beyond Aaron's lifetime, for the designer intended to depict some fundamental Jewish institutions of the past which were connected with the priests and with any of the legitimate historical Jewish sanctuaries. The stone structures symbolize the first and second temples (and also Herod's). The presence of Aaron allows the stone structures to symbolize also the tabernacle. The use of the architectural patterns of pagan temples is again ascribable to the designer's preference, to let the painter draw what was familiar to him.[51]

Not all pagan temples had Victories as acroteria. The Jews of Dura clearly viewed the commandment prohibiting images (Exodus 20:4-5, Deuteronomy 5:8-9) as banning only those which were intended to be worshiped. Here, the winged females are not objects to be worshiped, but symbols of victory. Since they are on the temple where Aaron presides, the victory should belong to Aaron's God. One might think of the future Messianic victory over Israel's enemies, but that is difficult to connect with the tabernacle and the temples of the past. Most likely, here, as in the paintings on the front of the Torah shrine, the temple is viewed as a means of gaining the afterlife, and the winged Victories symbolize Isaiah 25:8 as read by Theodotion and Paul (I Corinthians 15:54), "Death has been swallowed up in victory."

Two considerations can explain Aaron's royal apparel. First, although I can find no biblical or ancient rabbinic text calling attention to the fact,[52] the high priestly vestments described in the bible strongly resemble royal clothing, as medieval[53] and modern[54] commentators have noticed. Second, an accurate reconstruction of the vestments prescribed in Exodus 28 is difficult even for a talented artist, and again we should bear in mind the way in which the designer tried to make things easy for the painter by telling him to paint using the familiar patterns of royal propaganda art. The plate engraved with the words "Holy to the LORD" may be absent from

---

[51] See section 4b, paragraph 5.

[52] But the Greek Bible and Josephus regularly call the high priest's headdress *kidaris*, the word for that of the Persian kings. See Goodenough, *Jewish Symbols*, X, 17.

[53] Moses ben Nahman (=Nahmanides), *Commentary to the Torah*, on Exodus 28:31-37.

[54] Menahem Haran, "Malbushim," *Entsiqlopediah miqra'it*, IV (1962), 1047; "K^chunnah," ibid., 19.

Aaron's headdress because the Jews of Dura avoided writing the LORD's name.[55]

The wind-instruments are indeed intended to be the ones Moses was commanded to make at Numbers 10:1-10. If their color is wrong for depicting silver, we might ascribe that to the failure of the designer to instruct the painter. Or we might take note of a fact, attested by Rabh Hisda, a Babylonian scholar who was a contemporary of the synagogue: Jews of the third century C.E. confused the meanings of the two terms *haṣoṣerah* ("trumpet") and *shofar* ("ram's horn").[56] The reinforcement of the tubes of trumpets by rings is found on Jewish coins[57] and is typical of Roman metal trumpets.[58]

When confronted by a drought or other disaster, Jews would implore the aid of God by using the ritual of a communal fast (*taʿanit*).[59] The ritual included the sounding of two ram's horns and two trumpets.[60] One might suggest that the designer has chosen to display that ritual, although no source connects it with Aaron. I think, however, that in the four priests and their instruments the designer has telescoped Numbers 10:9 with Numbers 10:10. On the right, two priests fulfil Numbers 10:9 by sounding trumpets on a festival, as is indicated by the sacrificial bull and ram standing beneath them.[61] On the left, two priests fulfil Num 10:10 by sounding trumpets in time of war or trouble. I did not include the axe held by the priest who leads the red heifer among the "mistakes" in WB2, although the usual slaughtering implement in rabbinic Judaism was a knife. Acceptable slaughter could also be accomplished by cutting the animal's throat with an axe, provided its blade was sharp and smooth.[62] In fact, we do not know what rules governed Jewish slaughter at Dura.

As for the depiction of two incense-burners instead of a single incense-altar, we may suppose that the designer, in his verbal instructions did not stress that the implement was single. The painter

---

[55] As is shown by the fragmentary grace, *The Parchments and Papyri*, no. 11.

[56] Babylonian Talmud, *Shabbath* 36a.

[57] See A. Reifenberg, *Ancient Jewish Coins* (second and revised edition; Jerusalem, 1947), Plate XIII, nos. 174 and 186.

[58] A. Reinach, "Tuba," *Dictionnaire des antiquités grecques et romaines*, edited by Daremberg and Saglio, V, 524-26.

[59] Mishnah, *Taʿanith* 2:1-3:9.

[60] Mishnah, *Rosh Ha-Shanah* 3:3-4

[61] Bulls and rams required for festival offerings: Numbers 28:11-12, 19, 27, 29:2, 8, 13, 17, 20, 23, 26, 29, 32, 35.

[62] Cf. Babylonian Talmud, *Pesaḥim* 70a, where the word *qophis*, rendered "chopper" or "knife for cutting bones," is a loan word from Greek *kopis* ("hatchet").

certainly knew of plural incense-burners in pagan sanctuaries, for he depicts them in WB4.[63]

Comte Robert du Mesnil du Buisson (followed by Goodenough) solved the problem of the ark which in WB2 stands in front of the curtain instead of behind it. An ancient artistic convention so reversed the order when the artist wished to portray simultaneously a curtain and what was behind it.[64]

A similar piece of artistic license probably explains the presence of the candelabrum and the incense-burners outside the "tabernacle." The ark was only 1 1/2 cubits high (Exodus 25:10, 37:1), whereas the incense altar was 3 cubits high (Exodus 27:1); if placed in front of the curtain as commanded in Exodus 40:26, the incense altar would have concealed the ark. The Bible does not specify the height of the candelabrum and places it on the left (south) side of the tabernacle, but it, too, could well have been tall enough to hide the ark. In order to present a clear view of the ark, the designer moved the candelabrum and the incense altar (interpreted by the painter as two incense-burners) toward the foreground. Care was taken, however, to place the implements in the space directly in front of the entrance to the "Tabernacle."

I do not know why the table does not appear in WB2. Perhaps the omission is accidental, or perhaps the painter thought that another implement would clutter the space in front of the entrance to the "tabernacle." I also do not know why the cherubim are not in the painting. Indeed, they are not shown with the ark anywhere in the synagogue. Perhaps the designer thought that it was forbidden to draw them.[65]

4d Moses' Inspiration Flows to Eldad and Medad

Panel WB1 shows a bearded man of heroic stature, wearing chiton and himation. He greatly resembles the figure of Moses reading the Torah at the lower right of the Central Composition. Surely he is Moses. His right hand holds a rod which touches a large round bowl on a square base, from which twelve streams of fluid are emerging. They flow toward twelve tents. Corresponding to each tent is a small male figure wearing kaftan and trousers. Ten of the small figures stand within the entrances of their tents. The other two, at the lower right, are outside theirs, one being about a step away from the entrance, the other several steps away from it.

---

[63] See also Kraeling, *Synagogue*, 101-2.
[64] See Goodenough, *Jewish Symbols*, X, 11.
[65] Cf. Babylonian Talmud, *'Abodah Zarah* 43a-b.

At the top center, there is a shrine with a triangular pediment supported by two Corinthian columns. Having discussed WB2, we may be sure that the shrine represents the Tabernacle. In front of the shrine are items of cultic furniture: a lit seven-branched candelabrum between two unlit incense-burners.[66] In front of the candelabrum is a three-legged table.[67] The reason here for the position of this furniture outside the tabernacle would be the same as in WB2. There is no trace of the ark. The interiors of ten of the tents are dark, but two interiors are bright: one is just to the left of the Tabernacle; the other is the second to the right.

The tents are surely intended to be seen as arranged in a circle around the Tabernacle, as in Numbers 2. If they had been drawn realistically so, one would not have been able to see the entrances and interiors of some of the tents, for they would have faced away from the observer. The artist worked to solve the problem: he distorted the circle and placed the Tabernacle at the top center. He showed the entrances to all the tents and placed outside the entrances the occupants of the two last tents on the right.

The water-miracles in the text of the Torah can account for features of this painting, but not for the complete composition. Thus, the Israelites found *twelve* springs at Elim (Exodus 15:27, Numbers 33:9) but neither Moses nor his rod did anything to bring them into existence. At Rephidim (alias Massah-and-Meribah) Moses with his rod turned a rock into a *single* source of water (Exodus 17:1-7). Moses sinned grievously (Numbers 21:16-18) in bringing forth water from a rock by striking it with his rod instead of speaking to it, at Qadesh (alias the Waters of Meribah), but nothing is said there of multiple streams, and one would be surprised to see Moses' grievous sin portrayed. The Israelites sang a song to a (single) well in the wilderness; however, not Moses but the princes of the people dug it "with the scepter and with their staves" (Numbers 21:16-18).

More details of the painting fit Jewish legends of a marvelous well which followed the chosen people on their desert journey, gushed forth in multiple streams, and gave drink to every Israelite at the entrance to his own tent.[68] The surviving Jewish sources

---

[66] Incense was burned daily, in the early morning and in the early evening (Exodus 30:7-8). The unlit burners show that the time is neither of those two.

[67] I do not know why the table has only three legs instead of the four required by Exodus 38:13.

[68] Gutmann, *Sacred Images*, Chapter VIII, 98-100. However, contrary to Gutmann's assertion (ibid., 99), *Deuteronomy Rabbah* 19:26 and *Targum Pseudo-Jonathan* to Numbers 21:17 do not say that the well set itself up in front of the Tabernacle.

ascribe the existence of the well to the merit of Miriam, not to Moses. Only the Koran and Byzantine Christian texts connect Moses and his rod with that well.[69] In so doing, they surely transmit a Jewish legend. Sura 7:160 of the Koran says, "We inspired Moses, when his people asked for water, saying, 'Smite the rock with your staff!' And there gushed forth therefrom twelve springs, so that each tribe knew their drinking-place." Though one may doubt that the heroic figure is *smiting* a rock, unquestionably the painting reflects narratives of water-miracles in the text of the Torah and in parabiblical legends told by Jews. However, even the Jewish legend transmitted by non-Jews does not account for the ten dark tents and the two illuminated ones.

Only one narrative in the Torah tells of illumination flowing only to two Israelites (other than Moses), while the rest of the people are not illuminated: the story of Eldad and Medad at Numbers 11:11-29. When the labor of leading the unruly Israelites became too arduous for Moses, God told him to assemble 70 leading elders at the Tent of Meeting, and He would transfer to them some of Moses' inspiration, so that they could share with him the burdens of leadership. Moses assembled the elders. God transferred inspiration to them. On receiving the inspiration, the elders prophesied briefly and then ceased to do so.

However, Eldad and Medad, two elders, had remained in the camp. They had been among those listed as leaders but had not gone to the Tent of Meeting with the 70. Even so, the inspiration came upon them, and they prophesied in the camp. Nothing in the text says they ceased to do so. Indeed, a youth ran and told Moses what they were doing, and when Joshua urged Moses to restrain them, Moses replied, "Are you jealous on my account? Would that all the LORD's people were prophets, that the LORD would put His spirit upon them!"

The story implies that God could transfer inspiration from Moses to the 70 elders, but also that those elders were not capable of retaining the gift of prophecy. If Eldad and Medad, who were not at the Tent but in the camp, received inspiration, it must have been flowing outward into the camp, and the two men must have had a special capability of receiving it. Jewish legend says that Eldad belonged to the tribe of Benjamin, and Medad, to that of Ephraim.[70] In the regulations for the encampment of the Israelites at Numbers

---

[69] See the references cited by Gutmann, *Sacred Images*, chap. VIII, 99, n.20.

[70] *Numbers Rabbah* 15:19, *Midrash Tanḥuma* (Eshkol edition, Jerusalem, no date), *Behaʿaloteka* 12; *Midrash Tanḥuma*, ed. by Solomon Buber (Vilna, 1885), IV, 57.

2:1-25, the twelve tribes surround the Tent of Meeting, three on each side. Ephraim and Benjamin are situated to the west, but between them encamps Manasseh. The illuminated tents in the painting do have a dark tent located between them! If Eldad and Medad had a special ability to receive the inspiration flowing into the camp, any member of any tribe there who possessed that same capability, would have received the same lasting gift. Thus we are led to assume that after the 70 elders ceased to prophecy, 12 streams of inspiration were flowing into the camp, but only Eldad of Benjamin and Medad of Ephraim were capable of receiving the lasting gift. And so we have the streams flowing to all 12 tribal tents, but only the tents of Eldad and Medad are illuminated. The use of water in a Jewish or Christian text as a figurative representation for divine inspiration is well-attested.[71] In connection with such use in WB1, one should look especially at Paul's I Corinthians 10:4 (which surely here reflects contemporary Jewish usage).

Jewish Bible readers knew that God later promised (at Joel 3:1) to fulfil Moses' wish (Numbers 29), that He would inspire *all* His people to be prophets. Seeing the illumination of only two tribes, and remembering Moses' wish, the worshipers at Dura would view the event portrayed in the painting as a foreshadowing of that great fulfilment.

Jewish legend went on to guess what prophecies were uttered by Eldad and Medad. One source says the two predicted both the war of Gog and Magog and the resurrection of the Jewish dead.[72] Other sources say the two predicted the war of Gog and Magog and say nothing about the resurrection.[73]

It is probably no coincidence that another painting of Band B (SB1), in my interpretation, depicts the war of Gog and Magog.[74]

On the other hand, the view,[75] that the history of the ark is the subject of Band B, is untenable. The ark is absent from WB1 and

---

[71] Jewish examples: Amos 8:11-12, Isaiah 44:3; Isaiah 55:1 with Babylonian Talmud, *Baba Qamma* 17a.

[72] *Targum Pseudo-Jonathan* to Numbers 11:26.

[73] *The Fragment Targums of the Pentateuch*, edited by Michael L. Klein (Rome, 1980), I, to Numbers 11:26, and *Neophyti 1*, edited by Alejandro Diez Macho (Madrid, 1974), Tomo IV, to Numbers 11:26, and the references cited in n. 28. Babylonian Talmud, *Sanhedrin* 17a, ascribes to Rab Nahman, an important Babylonian Jewish scholar of the third and early fourth centuries, the view, that Eldad and Medad prophesied about the matters connected with Gog and Magog. See David Joseph Bornstein, "Nahman ben Jacob," *Encyclopedia Judaica* XII [1971], 773-74.

[74] See below, section 6b.

[75] Gutmann, *Re-evaluation*, XX-XXII.

WB2. Its absence from WB1 is explainable: the ark was then a three days' journey away from the camp (Numbers 10:33)[76] and had nothing to do with the water miracles or with the flow of inspiration to Eldad and Medad. Why did the painter draw a stone temple in WB1, when the designer surely intended to portray an event from Moses' lifetime? Perhaps the designer was not sufficiently careful in formulating the instructions.

5 WHAT DO THE PICTURES ON THE SOUTH WALL AND THE LEFT SIDE OF THE WEST WALL HAVE IN COMMON? IS THERE ANY CONTRAST BETWEEN THEM?

The paintings on the south wall and on the left side of the west wall all present events and institutions of the past that constitute peacemeal foreshadowings of the expected general fulfilments that belong to the "end of days." Thus, Elijah once defeated Baal on Mount Carmel, but idol-worship continues in the world until God will destroy it. Elijah revived one dead child; he will return, and there will be a general resurrection. Mordechai was "king for a day," and Solomon reigned and prospered for one lifetime, whereas the Messiah's rule will be lasting. Aaron and the priests carried on the vital rituals in the tabernacle and the temple, and the ark entered Jerusalem or the temple in the time of David or Solomon, but the city and the successive temples were later destroyed, and the tabernacle disappeared, though Jews believed God would eventually restore them.

Several of the paintings of the south wall are lost or unrecognizable, so that we cannot be sure that a coherent scheme was involved. Nevertheless, we know that WB1, the scene of Elijah resurrecting the widow's son, appears out of biblical sequence. Though we would expect it to stand on the south wall, it stands on the west one. We may infer that the foreshadowings of the great miracles of liberation and resurrection belong on the west wall, not on the south.

The paintings on the Torah shrine and in the Central Composition allude to promise (God's blessing to Abraham and Jacob's blessings to his descendants) and eschatological fulfilment (the Messiah and the resurrection). Does this scheme extend to the right side of the west wall and to the north wall? How does the sole recognizable scene on the east wall fit in?

---

[76] See the rabbinic stories in Ginzberg, *Legends*, III, 243, and VI, 85, n. 456.

6 The Right Side of the West Wall:
More Scenes that have been Partly
or Wholly Misidentified

6a WA3: Moses leads the Exodus from the Exile

WA3 would seem to be overidentified. At first sight, it is easy to see
in it the exodus from Egypt. At the right side of the picture, a large
group of men-at-arms and civilians marches out of a walled city.
Several times in the biblical exodus story a city is mentioned as the
location (Exodus 1:11; 9:29, 33; 12:37) so the walled city is an
appropriate representation of Egypt. Two Corinthian columns, one
red, one black, stand by the open doors of the walled city. If they
represent the pillar of fire and the pillar of cloud (Exodus 13:21-22),
their position in the picture *behind* the people who have marched
out, fits Exodus 14:19, provided that the designer identified the
angel of that verse with one or both pillars. Above the city and
especially over the drowning men is a black cloud. Over the city
there are also narrower strips of gray and pink, and beyond the
drowning men the black strip disappears and stripes of light gray
and pink appear below a band of darker gray and two hands of
God. This configuration would fit the somewhat awkward verses
Exodus 14:19-20 and also the rabbinic tradition (based on an interpretation of Leviticus 23:43) that God sheltered the Israelites under
clouds of glory after the exodus.[77]

Ahead (to the left) of the marching people, a figure of heroic size
in chiton and himation raises a massive staff above his head, and in
front of him large numbers of men drown in a body of water. On
the other side of that water, a similar figure of heroic size holds his
staff at waist level. Farther left, a third similar figure points his staff
downwards, as a group of soldiers and civilians to the left of him
stand, lined up beside a body of water.

How can the soldiers and civilians be other than the Israelites
departing from Egypt?[78] How can the figure of heroic size be other
than Moses? How can the drowning men be other than the Egyptians in the Red Sea? How can the body of water at the left, by the
people in formation, be anything but one of the pools that served

---

[77] See Ginzberg, *Legends*, II, 374-75.
[78] *hamushim* at Exodus 13:1 can mean "armed," and *ṣiv'ot* at Exodus 6:26, 7:4,
12:17, and 12:41 means "hosts [of men-at-arms]," while Exodus 10:9-11 and
12:31-32, 37, imply that Israelite non-combatants, too, marched out. See also
Goodenough, *Jewish Symbols*, X, 118.

Moses' flock in the desert? Yet each representation of Moses is labeled in Aramaic: the one on the right, as "Moses when he went out from Egypt and cleft the sea"; the one in the middle, simply as "Moses"; and the one on the left, as "Moses when he cleft the sea." Who needed any of those labels?

There are other strange aspects to this painting, if it represents the first exodus, the one from Egypt. Falling upon the walled city are flecks of red and balls of brown or gray.[79] Lightning can flash during a hailstorm, but lightning is not red. Hail is not brown though it may be gray. In the biblical narrative, the plague of hail (Exodus 9:18-34) comes well before the exodus (Exodus 12:37-42) and still farther before the crossing of the Red Sea (Exodus 14:15-15:21). Though one might suggest that the designer has telescoped the plague with the exodus, why should he have singled out hail from the *ten* plagues? Jewish legends have fire and hail falling upon the *Egyptians* at the Red Sea, but not upon their "home city." One or two lizards appear on the city wall.[80] Nothing in the biblical text on the exodus and the crossing of the Red Sea suggests one or more lizards.

As Goodenough recognized,[81] on the outer curve of the arch over the gateway, at the keystone, is the Graeco-Roman image of Ares (Mars), with a winged Victory in the wedge-shaped spaces at each end of the curve. If the walled city represents Egypt, it is pagan. But why portray its paganness by putting *Graeco-Roman* deities over its gateway—and that, on a painting in a synagogue?

The story in the Bible emphasizes repeatedly (Exodus 14:4, 6-7, 9, 17-18, 23, 25-26, 28, 15:2, 4-5, 19-20) that the Egyptians were armed when they drowned. In the painting, those who drown are unarmed; in fact, most of them are naked.[82]

Behind the figures of the middle and left Moseses runs a series of bands, in which bluish or lavender stripes alternate with white ones. There is wide agreement that the colored bands represents heaps of water between twelve white paths in the Red Sea, in accordance with a rabbinic tradition that Moses cut strips in the sea like twelve

---

[79] The color is brown in Goodenough, *Jewish Symbols*, XI, Plate XIV; gray in Kraeling, *Synagogue*, Plate LII.

[80] Goodenough, *Jewish Symbols*, X, 107; Kraeling, *Synagogue*, 76.

[81] *Jewish Symbols*, X, 107-8.

[82] Goodenough, *Jewish Symbols*, p. 126. There is, indeed, a midrash attributed to Rabbi Nathan (a sage of Babylonian origin!), that the Egyptians when they sank in the Red Sea were stripped naked (cited by both Goodenough and Kraeling).

slices in a loaf of bread, one for each of the twelve tribes.[83] But the bands suggest anything but *heaps* of water, that stood like walls to the left and right of the crossing Israelites (Exodus 14:22). Furthermore, as Goodenough noticed,[84] the artist has taken all pains to distinguish the "paths" and the water between them from the sea at the right and from the fishy pool at the left.[85] Thus it is difficult to view the stripes as parts of the Red Sea or of its bottom.

However, let us grant for the moment that the white "paths" between the colored stripes are the routes used by the Israelites to cross the sea. There are still strange facts about WA3. The "Egyptians" are shown drowning *before* the paths for the escape of the Israelites appear, in contrast to Exodus 14:15-29! At the far left of WA3, the Israelite tribe-princes (holding tribal banners) and men-at-arms and civilians stand by a pool containing leaping fish. The leftmost Moses' staff points down into the pool. The attributes of the pool fit none of the water-miracles of the Pentateuch and have yet to be explained.[86]

Two hands of God appear in WA3, one over the bluish bands and one over the fishy pool. Why should the fishy pool be given the same rank among miracles as the crossing of the Red Sea and the drowning of the Egyptians? And why should Moses, standing by the fishy pool, be identified as "Moses when he cleft the sea." If the details of WA3 do not fit the first exodus, what do they fit? What did Jews believe about the second exodus, their miraculous redemption from their captivities? Though there had been a return from the Babylonian Exile, the glorious prophecies about miraculous liberation from the hands of Assyria and later conquerors had not been fulfilled. Believers held that if those prophecies had not been fulfilled in the past, they must become reality in the future, and hence came the belief in the second exodus.

Believers knew that the hand of God would be active in the second exodus as in the first (Isaiah 51:9-11). Indeed, the second would be more miraculous than the first (Jeremiah 16:14-15, 23:7-8). One could thus expect it to duplicate everything in the first exodus and to add more wonders. Prophetic texts specify some of the miracles. Jews would be liberated not only from Egypt but also

---

[83] See Kraeling, *Synagogue*, 85, nn. 257-58; Ginzberg, *Legends*, II, 22, and VI, 6, n. 36.

[84] *Jewish Symbols*, X, 128.

[85] I do not know what Kraeling means by "horizontal and vertical perspective" (*Synagogue*, 85).

[86] See Goodenough, *Jewish Symbols*, X, 129.

from Mesopotamia and elsewhere and would return to Jerusalem (Isaiah 11:11-12, 27:12-13).

The fortified walls of the oppressor city would be unable to keep the Chosen People in captivity because God himself would break open the bars of the gates (Isaiah 43:14, Jeremiah 51:3). The oppressor *city* would be destroyed like Sodom (Isaiah 13:29, Jeremiah 50:40) by fire and brimstone from heaven. The ruined capital would become a haunt of reptiles.[87]

Israelites by a timely exit from the doomed capital would escape the fire and the brimstone (Jeremiah 51:6, 45).

The oppressor army would become unfit to bear arms (Jeremiah 51:30). One could infer from the prospect of the duplication of the wonders of the first exodus that the oppressor army would drown. Jews looking for explicit prophetic confirmation of that drowning may have found it at Isaiah 43:17[88] or at Zechariah 10:11.[89] They might have found further confirmation in the flooding of the oppressor city, predicted at Jeremiah 51:42, 55.

At the same time, God would turn many of the Israelites into mighty warriors (*gibborim*), who would return to promised lands from their exile (Zechariah 10:5-12), though the redeemed Chosen People would still have many non-combatants (Zechariah 8:4-5).

Moses would lead the liberated Israelites, as numerous rabbinic traditions assert.[90] Jewish Bible readers at Dura and elsewhere in Babylonia could have inferred, from the questions at Isaiah 63:11-14, the possibility of a second Moses to lead the second exodus. The context suggested that only sin was standing in the way (ibid., verse 10).

God would also make rivers spring up in the desert to supply His liberated people with water.[91] As soon as the darkness of the captivity has been left in the past, God's own radiance will shine upon the Israelites.[92]

---

[87] So says the Hexaplar Greek of Jeremiah 51(Greek 28):37(39). It may be significant that the animal at ruined Babylon in Isaiah 14:23 is the *qippod*; the animals in ruined Edom at closely parallel Isaiah 34:11 are *qa'at weqippod*; and at ruined Nineveh in closely parallel Zephaniah 2:14 they are also *qa'at weqippod*, and the "Septuagint" Greek there renders *qa'at* as "chameleons."

[88] By taking as future the participles and verbs in the imperfect.

[89] By taking "The pride of Assyria shall be driven down" to mean drowning, as the context could suggest.

[90] See Ginzberg, *Legends*, II, 302, 316, 373; III, 35, 312-313, 481; VI, 157 (n. 930), 167 (n. 966).

[91] Isaiah 35:6-7, 41:17-18, 43:19-20, 44:3, 48:21.

[92] Isaiah 42:16, 49:9, 60:1-2; Ezekiel 34:12. Targum Isaiah 35:10 says a cloud of glory will be over them.

According to Ezekiel 47:1-12 (cf. Zechariah 14:8), from under the "threshold" or "podium" (*miphtan*) of the temple would emerge a stream of water, and it would gush out eastward from under the south wall, growing deeper and deeper as it flowed. It would go into the desert of the Jordan rift and into the Dead Sea, sweetening its waters, which will be filled with abundant *fish*. The next subject treated by Ezekiel is the allotment of land to the restored Chosen People, so it is easy to infer that the shores of the sweetened Dead Sea, full of fish, will be a destination for the returning exiles.

If we interpret WA3 to make it depict the second exodus, we find that the designer has included the walled city (called "Babylon" by the prophet: Jer 51:12, 44, 58), her gates unbarred; she is destroyed like Sodom, as fire and brimstone fall upon her. Red flecks easily represent fire. Some observers may have difficulty seeing the brown or gray balls as brimstone, but the color visible today may have faded or may have been distorted by the preservative varnish.

Reptiles are on the city walls. Armed and unarmed Israelites have marched out from the doomed city. Her warriors have been disarmed and drowned *before* rivers spring up in the desert. The bluish stripes more naturally represent rivers in the desert than they do walls of water. WA3 at its left end presents the Israelites as having crossed the desert with the help of the rivers. They stand by the sweetened Dead Sea, ready to ascend the valley of the wonderful stream to reach Jerusalem and the site of the temple. Did the designer merely telescope the time for traversing the distance from Babylonia to Palestine? Or did he believe that the redeemed would experience the miracle of the "contraction of the road," the miraculous shortening of distance?[93]

We may also note that Moses' rod perhaps "draws waters joyfully from the fountains of salvation" (Isaiah 12:3), while the Israelites in formation may be singing Isaiah 12:1-2, 4-6. Over them floats a pink cloud of glory.

Other details in the painting confirm that WA3 portrays a latter-day exodus. Ares and the Victories over the curve of an arch are characteristic of the Roman commemorative monuments called "arches of triumph."[94] At Dura there was a commemorative arch

---

[93] See Ginzberg, *Legends*, V, 287, n. 287. Isaiah 14:1 could imply miraculously rapid transport over the distance.

[94] Kähler, "Triumphbogen, *Realencyclopaedie*, VII^A (1939), 464-65; Almut von Gladiss, "Triumphbogen," *Der kleine Pauly*, V (1975), 971. For example, Mars is on the keystone of the central "archlet" of the arch of Septimius Severus in the Roman Forum, with Victories in the wedge-shaped spaces at each end of the curve (Kähler, *Realencyclopaedie*, VII^A, 393); and Mars is on the keystone of the south face of the east archlet of the arch of Constantine near the Roman Forum, and in the wedge-shaped spaces at each end of the curve of the central archlet are Victories.

honoring the Roman emperor Trajan (98-117). Nothing survives of its sculptures.[95]

Arches of triumph are free-standing structures, unconnected with any wall, but they clearly are patterned after city gates, and probably originated as imitations of the gate (*Porta Triumphalis*) through which a victorious Roman commander led his army, with the spoils and the captives, across the sacred boundary (*pomoerium*) of Rome and through the streets of the city in a "triumph." Though originally the *pomoerium* ran on or near the line of the walls, under the Roman republic the walls were built farther out, leaving the *pomoerium* and the *Porta Triumphalis* well inside the city.[96]

There is insufficient information to tell us what the *Porta Triumphalis* looked like at the time of the triumph in 70 C.E. of the emperor Vespasian and his son Titus after their conquest of Judaea. A part of that triumph is portrayed in the sculptures on the Arch of Titus at Rome. There, the soldiers marching with the spoils turn and enter an elaborately carved archway, which has a Victory at the one end shown of the curve of the arch.[97] Is the pictured archway on the arch of Titus the *Porta Triumphalis?* There are strong arguments against the hypothesis.[98]

By the mid-third century C.E., generations of Jews could have remembered how their forebears had been humiliated by being led captive into Rome through the *Porta Triumphalis*.[99] The painting shows the coming reversal of that humiliation. The artist did not need to have accurate knowledge of the *Porta Triumphalis* at Rome. He knew that arches of triumph were peculiarly Roman. He could easily recognize that they looked like city gates with Victories and keystone figures added. We may assume that he merely patterned the gateway in WA3 after the free-standing commemorative arches he had seen.

Thus, one meaning of the doomed walled city is surely Rome. In the prophecies of Jeremiah and Isaiah, the doomed city is Babylon. In the times of the Dura synagogue, Jews and Christians frequently

[95] See the accounts of Maurice Pillet, S. Gould, and A. B. Hatch in *The Excavations at Dura-Europos: Preliminary Report of Fourth Season of Work, October 1930—March 1931*, edited by P. L. V. C. Baur et al. (New Haven, 1933), 3-4, 56-68.

[96] Filippo Coarelli, *Il Foro boario dalle origini alla fine della repubblica* (Roma, 1988), 371-72 and notes 33-35. Warren G. Moon identified the arch in WA3 as the *Porta Triumphalis* ("Nudity and Narrative: Observations on the Frescoes from the Dura Synagogue," *Journal of the American Academy of Religion* 60 [1992], 598-99).

[97] Kähler, *Realencyclopaedie*, VII^A, 386.

[98] Michael Pfanner, *Der Titusbogen* (Mainz am Rhein, 1983), 71-72. See Coarelli, *Foro boario*, 363-414, for a treatment of the *Porta Triumphalis* from early Rome down past the time of the Dura synagogue.

[99] Perhaps they read of it in Josephus' Aramaic or Greek (*War* vii.5.4-6.129-57).

interpreted biblical prophecies about Babylon as prophecies about Rome.[100]

But the walled city may have simultaneously another identity. There was a commemorative arch, of Trajan, at Dura. The crenellated walls and the arched gateway in WA3 strikingly resemble even the configurations at the great west (or "Palmyrene") gate of Dura.[101] Even closer was the resemblance of the configurations at the northeast or "river" gate of the city.[102] The main roads westward from Dura probably ran along the south shore of the Euphrates, so an exodus of Jews from the city would probably go out through the river gate.[103]

If our argument is correct, notice how profound—and how audacious—was the faith of the designer (and of whatever Jews at Dura understood his designs) in the imminent fulfilment of the Messianic prophecies. Dura was an important Roman military base. Certainly the painting displays the belief that there will be an exodus from Rome; possibly it shows an exodus from Dura. The soldiers who are drowning are the garrison of one or both cities; they belong to the Roman army!

Can this be? Or is it not rather excluded by the labels in the picture? The rightmost Moses is identified as "Moses when he left Egypt and cleft the sea." Surely the walled city must represent Egypt! There is reason to believe that in portraying Messianic topics that were subversive to the empire ruling them, Jewish artists protected themselves by using ambiguous labels. At the synagogue of Gaza, built in the sixth century C.E., there is a mosaic of a king dressed like a Roman emperor, playing a lyre to docile wild beasts. A label identifies the person as David. The historical David did not tame wild beasts; he killed them. The person portrayed must be the Messiah of the Jews, who could indeed bear the name David or even be the resurrected David (Jeremiah 30:9, Ezekiel 34:23-24). But to have identified him as the Messiah of the Jews, who would

---

[100] E.g., II Baruch 67:7, Ginzberg, *Legends*, VI, 280; Revelation 14:8, 16:19, 17:5, 18:2, 10, 21.

[101] See Clark Hopkins in *The Excavations at Dura-Europos: Preliminary Report of Fifth Season of Work, October 1932—March 1932*, edited by M. I. Rostovtzeff (New Haven, 1934), 4-5, 7-8; Hopkins, *The Discovery of Dura-Europos* (New Haven and London, 1979), 28; Maurice Pillet in *The Excavations at Dura-Europos: Preliminary Report of First Season of Work, Spring 1928*, edited by P. V. C. Baur and M. I. Rostovtzeff (New Haven, 1929), 10-16 and Plate II.

[102] See M. Pillet in *The Excavations at Dura Europos: Preliminary Report of Second Season of Work, October 1928—April 1929*, edited by P. V. C. Baur and M. I. Rostovtzeff (New Haven, 1931), 6.

[103] *Preliminary Report of First Season*, 6; *Preliminary Report of Second Season*, 5; Hopkins, *Discovery*, 253.

bring the Roman Empire to its end, would have been regarded subversive, especially in the Christian Roman Empire. The ambiguous label, "David," was safer.[104]

The case of WA3 may well have been similar. There was a Jewish diaspora in Egypt. The second exodus would liberate those Jews, too (Isaiah 11:11, 27:12-13), and perhaps Moses himself would be their leader. But the portrayal of Roman triumphal structures and the illustration of prophetic texts on the second exodus and on the doom of tyrannical Babylon—all that cannot be made to fit the first exodus. However, if a case could be made for interpreting WA3 as an innocuous depiction of a past event, the subversive intent could be concealed.

When Jews of Dura boldly had the coming fall of the Roman empire portrayed in their synagogue, they were not unusual. The Palestinian and Babylonian rabbis were glad to contemplate the same prospect; and as long as the Roman empire remained pagan, Christians preached of its fall.[105] The members of these groups waited for God to act in his own time and did not rise in revolt, and that is why most of them survived unmolested.

In contrast to the paintings of the left side of the west wall, WA3 presents a scene that is eschatological and permanent. The Jews will be restored forever from exile (Joel 4:20; Isaiah 60:15-22). Let us see whether this contrast is true of other paintings of the right side of the west wall.

6b NB1, WB4, and WB3

Scholars have been badly misled into thinking that NB1, WB4, and WB3 depict portions of the story of the ark in I Samuel 4:1-7:1 and II Samuel 6.[106]

Though the ark is present in NB1 and WB3, the battle of Eben-ezer (I Samuel 4:10-17) was a total defeat for the Israelites, and no cavalry took part (certainly none on the Israelite side!). NB1 depicts an evenly-matched conflict of two sides consisting of both infantry and cavalry and cannot represent the battle of Eben-ezer.

---

[104] See my *Semites*, 81-83.
[105] Revelation 14:8, 16:19, 17, 18:2-24, 19:2-3; II Baruch 67:7; *Genesis Rabbah* 88:6 (where Rome is not called "Edom" but is identified with the doomed "fourth kingdom" of Daniel 7:7); *Genesis Rabbah* 44:17 and *Leviticus Rabbah* 13:5 (where Rome is identified with the "fourth kingdom" and is called "Edom," but the meaning is clear from the context); Babylonian Talmud, *Yoma* 10a. On "Edom" as a name for Rome, see Ginzberg, *Legends*, V, 272, n. 19.
[106] See Gutmann, *Sacred Images*, Chap. VII, 1317-18.

WB4 cannot represent the humiliation of Dagon (I Samuel 5:1-5). Though the ark is present, not one, but two idols have been toppled and damaged. Neither has lost both hands, and only one of them has lost its head. The bovines look like bulls or steers, not like lactating cows, and are not tied to the "cart." Two men goad them to move. On the "cart" there is no trace of the 5 golden tumors and the 5 golden mice or of a container for them. All these facts are contrary to I Samuel 5:1-5, 7:5, 8, 17-18.

The "Closed Temple" of WB3 has Victories for acroteria and symbols connected with the Last Days on its doors (as I hope to argue elsewhere). With ten columns visible, it doubles the splendor of the Israelite sanctuary in WB2 (the counterpart of WB3, on the left side of the west wall). In being closed and having no signs of activity, WB3 also contrasts with WB2. The "Closed Temple" is surrounded by seven walls. Beth-Shemesh was a humble border town (I Samuel 6:9-15, 18-20); it could hardly have been the subject of WB3. Nor could Solomon's temple, because it did not fit any of the facts we have just cited; I can think of no reason for the designer to portray the first or second temple as closed.

I have published correct identifications of these three pictures.[107] I restate them here. NB1 depicts the war of Gog and Magog.[108] The forces of Gog and Magog, consisting both of cavalry and infantry (Ezekiel 38:4, 15; Zechariah 12:4) slay one another (Ezekiel 38:21, Haggai 2:22, Zechariah 14:13). The battle is a draw which will continue until both sides have been annihilated.[109] The Israelites, liberated from exile (Ezekiel 38:8, 12), lack horses but are armed (Joel 4[3]:11, Zechariah 12:6-7; nothing shows that the soldiers around the ark are hostile gentiles or that the ark has been captured).[110]

Trusting in their God, they stand by fearlessly (Ezekiel 38:8, 11, 14, 39:26; Joel 4[3]:16-20, Zechariah 12:6-7). None of the biblical texts on the war mentions the ark. The Bible says nothing about what happened to that object when the first temple was destroyed. Legends grew up, long before the time of the Dura synagogue,

---

[107] NB1: *Semites*, 78, n. 49 (first published in 1985); WB4 and WB3: ibid., 64-66 (first published in 1969).

[108] See section 2, paragraph 3.

[109] The scene is influenced by, and contrasts with, the common motif of a *victory* in battle, much used by the Sassanian Persians. See my *Semites*, 107, n. 172, and especially the cameo depicting the victory only a few years after the painting was made, of Shapur I over the Roman emperor Valerian (Roman Ghirshman, *Persian Art: the Parthian and Sassanian Dynasties* [New York, 1962], Plate 195).

[110] Cf. Goodenough, *Jewish Symbols*, X, 175-76.

about disappearance of the ark and its future reemergence at the time of God's promised restoration of Israel.[111]

In NB1, a rider on a white horse and a rider on a black horse charge at one another. The contrast is probably meaningful. White ordinarily symbolizes good, and black, evil.[112] At the time of the Dura synagogue, the two rival powers in what was thought to be the war of Gog and Magog were Rome and Persia. Can the designer and the Jews of Dura have favored one over the other? The Babylonian Talmud leaves no doubt that Babylonian rabbis favored Persia over Rome, though they could find good reasons why God would destroy both empires.[113] Thus, even in Roman Dura, Jews may have looked more favorably on Persia than on Rome! The subversive implications of the painting would not have been perceptible to Romans unless explained to them.

WB4 presents a midrash on Isaiah 46:1-2, 52:11-12, and perhaps 48:20. In a grammatically and etymologically correct translation, the Targum and the "Septuagint" of Isaiah 46:1-2 say that the idols of Bel and Nebo have been smashed and have been transformed into cattle struggling under a heavy load.[114] The "bull whackers," dressed like the ordinary priests of WB2, are probably the "bearers of the vessels of the Lord" of Isaiah 52:11, though they conduct and do not bear and though the only vessel shown is the ark. The three heroic figures behind them, wearing chiton and himation, are the angelic escort one could expect for the ark and its "bearers" on the basis of Isaiah 52:12. We treated (in connection with NB1) the belief in the reappearance of the lost ark. One would expect the ark to be the burden of the cattle, except that nothing connects it with the beasts or even with the axle under it. The ark here is portrayed as an ancient Near-Eastern throne, even to having cushions![115]

---

[111] See my *II Maccabees* ("Anchor Bible," volume 41A; Garden City, New York, 1983), 182-83. Reports that the ark was taken to Babylon: Ginzberg, *Legends*, VI, 380, n. 134, and 410, n. 62.

[112] See Goodenough, *Jewish Symbols*, X, 172-75.

[113] See especially Babylonian Talmud, *Yoma* 10a, *Sanhedrin* 98 (Jewish hopes placed in Persian and Median horses).

[114] Cf. Babylonian Talmud, *Megillah* 25b, *Sanhedrin* 63b; *Song of Songs Rabbah* 7:9. Bel as bull: L. Malten, "Der Stier in Kult und mythischem Bild," *Jahrbuch des Deutschen archäologischen Instituts*, XLII (1928), 106. Bel and Nabu (=Nebo) were widely worshiped in Syria and Mesopotamia; see Franz Cumont, *Fouilles de Doura-Europos (1922-23)* (Paris, 1926) 199-201; Susan B. Downey, *The Stone and Plaster Sculpture*, Final Report III, Part I, Fascicle 2, of *The Excavations at Dura-Europos* ("Monumenta Archaeologica," Volume V; Los Angeles, 1977) , 226. Bel in trousers: ibid., 278 and 354.

[115] See Stanley A. Cook, *The Religion of Ancient Palestine in the Light of Archaeology* (London, 1930), 22.

When one considers this throne with the other thrones portrayed in the Dura paintings and with the relevant rabbinic texts, one immediately recognizes that the ark is being portrayed, suspended above wheels, like the Heavenly Merkabhah (chariot-throne of God) in Ezekiel 1, not as a mere box on a clumsily drawn cart with a misdrawn axle. Early Jewish mystics indeed so viewed the ark, as the Earthly Merkabhah, and interpreted I Samuel 6 on that basis.[116] Accordingly, the three angels escorting the ark may also be the three archangels who attend the throne of God.[117] As the ark departs from exile, its power destroys the idols of the pagan gods and turns those deities into mere cattle. Indeed, we may be sure that for the designer and for the Jewish Bible readers of the time, Bel and Nebo were *examples*. God would destroy *all* pagan deities.[118]

Despite the discrepancies of WB4 from the story of the ark in the books of Samuel, there is good reason to see the influence of that narrative in the picture.[119] The designer's faith that the pagan gods would be destroyed was as bold as his faith in the fall of Rome. The broken idols in WB4 look exactly like the image of Adonis in his temple adjacent to the synagogue![120] Bel had a temple not very far away, by the northwest corner of the walls![121] By the use of slightly misleading labels in WA3, the designer seems to have disguised the prospect of the fall of Rome during the second exodus. Similarly, he may have disguised his bold expectation of the fall of the gods of the pagan neighbors of the synagogue by making it look like a past event, the humiliation of Dagon, though careful observers would perceive the discrepancies.

The Closed Temple of WB3 is the Heavenly Temple. At the End of Days, it will descend to earth.[122] Until then its doors are

---

[116] See Gershom Scholem, *Jewish Gnosticism, Merkabah Mysticism, and Talmudic Tradition* (New York, 1960), 20-30. See also A. Aptowitzer, "*Bet-hamiqdash shel ma'alah 'al pi ha-aggadah*," *Tarbiz* II (5691=1930-31), 146; there is a somewhat imperfect English translation by Aryeh Rubinstein, "The Celestial Temple as Viewed in the Aggadah," in *Binah: Studies in Jewish History, Thought, and Culture*, edited by Joseph Dan (Volume II of "Binah: Studies in Jewish Thought"; New York, Westport, and London, 1989), chapter 1 , 7.

[117] See Ginsberg, *Legends*, V, 71-72, n. 13.

[118] See Isaiah 2:18, 20; 21:9; Jeremiah 10:12, 51:47, 52.

[119] Hellenistic Jews connected Isaiah 46:1-2 with I Samuel 6; two important manuscripts, the *Sinaiticus* and the *Alexandrinus*, at Isaiah 46:1 have "Dagon" instead of "Nebo."

[120] Goodenough, *Jewish Symbols*, X, 75.

[121] The map at Hopkins, *Discovery*, xx, shows the locations of the two temples and the synagogue.

[122] See the thorough study of A. Aptowitzer, "*Bet-hamiqdash*," *Tarbiz* II (5691=1930-31), 137-53, 257-77; English translation, "The Celestial Temple," in *Binah*, edited by Joseph Dan, chapter 1.

shut.[123] Its splendor is greater than that of the earlier, earthly temples (in fact double), in fulfilment of Isaiah 61:6-7, Jeremiah 17:12, Haggai 2:9, and I Enoch 90:29. The seven walls shown with the Heavenly Temple represent the seven heavens. Most of the relevant Jewish texts have the Heavenly Temple, before its transfer to earth, residing in the fourth heaven (*Zebhul*), as does WB3.

Bands A and B of the surviving paintings of the right side of the west wall thus portray permanent achievements of God and His people at the End of Days: the second exodus, the Heavenly Temple (destined to descend to earth), and the destruction of paganism. We may add NA1 and NB1, from the north wall, also on the right side of the Synagogue. The promises God made to Jacob at the time of his dream of the ladder (Genesis 28:13-15) are permanent. Furthermore, according to Jewish legend, Jacob in the course of his dream saw visions of permanent importance and great eschatological content: the angels of the four kingdoms of Daniel 7, the revelation at Mount Sinai, the raising of Elijah into heaven, and the heavenly temple.[124] The War of Gog and Magog will be the Last War and is an event of the Last Days.

Do the paintings of Band C of the right side of the synagogue fit into this scheme?

6c WC3: The Anointing of the First David, or the Second?

WC3 is labeled in Aramaic, "Samuel when he anointed David." If the label is correct, the picture should depict I Samuel 16:10-13. In the painting, a supernaturally tall person in chiton and himation (a prophet's garb) pours oil over the head of a person, also in chiton and himation, but the latter's himation is dark and is peculiarly draped (in the same manner as on the lower left Moses of the Central Composition) so as to cover the hands. Alongside the anointed man stand six others in chiton and himation; three of those himations are pink, two are yellow, and one is white.

In Jewish belief, Samuel's anointment of David is permanent. It constitutes the foundation of an eternal dynasty, of which the Messiah will be a member (II Samuel 7:8-16, 22:51-23:5). Thus, even if the label is absolutely correct, the picture fits the scheme that we have hypothesized, that the right side of the west wall displays the permanent and the eschatological. But WC3 has strange aspects.

---

[123] See Revelation 11:15-19, 15:5; cf. Ezekiel 44:1-3.
[124] Ginzberg, *Legends*, I, 351; Aptowitzer, "*Bet-hamiqdash*," 152 and 268 (Hebrew), 13 and 21 (English).

According to I Samuel 16:10 and 13, Samuel anointed David in the midst of his *seven* brothers. Yet the painting shows only six spectators! One might try to solve the difficulty by noting that in the list at I Chronicles 2:13-16 David has only six brothers. But there still may be a problem. The narrative of I Samuel 16 is not explicit on whether Jesse stood with his sons when David was anointed, though the designer, like Christian artists, may have assumed Jesse did.[125] If so, only five "brothers" are shown! Jesse is a somewhat distinguished figure in Jewish legend,[126] but David's brothers are mere names. Why are they clothed like prophets or angels?

These questionable aspects of WA3 give us good reason to look at the Jews' traditions concerning the second David, their Messiah. A midrash on Micah 5:4-5 identifies the "eight princes of men" who will defend Judah against "Assyria" (i.e., against any future invading power);[127] the princes will be Jesse, Saul, Samuel, Zephaniah, Amos, Hezekiah, Elijah, and the Messiah.[128] Of these, Samuel, Zephaniah, Amos, and Elijah obviously deserve the prophet's chiton and himation. So does Saul (I Samuel 10:6-10, 18:10, 19:23-24). The inspiration possessed by the Messiah (according to Isaiah 11:2-3) should qualify him for membership among the prophets. Rabbinic legends tell that Hezekiah was clairvoyant through the aid of the Holy Spirit,[129] and God at first intended him to be the Messiah.[130] Perhaps the mention of Jesse in Isaiah 11.1 and 10 might confer prophetic status on Jesse, too. If not, perhaps the designer's list of "princes" was different from that preserved in rabbinic literature, at least in having one of the eight be a prophetic figure and not Jesse.

One way or another, we have accounted for the number and the clothing of the figures in the painting. Moreover, the eight "princes," according to Micah 5:4-5, would ravage the invading power, named "Assyria" in oracular language, but "Rome" and perhaps "Persia" in reality. Thus, there was good reason for concealing the full meaning under a label that was only partly truthful.

---

[125] Cf. Goodenough, *Jewish Symbols*, X, 166.
[126] Ginzberg, *Legends*, II, 260; IV, 81, 82, 86; VI, 264, n. 88.
[127] See *Genesis Rabbah* 16:4.
[128] See Ginzberg, *Legends*, V, 130, n. 142.
[129] Ginzberg, *Legends*, IV, 273.
[130] Ibid., 272; VI, 366, n. 70.

6d WC4: The Preservation of the First Moses or the Second? Or of the Messiah?

At first sight, it seems clear that depicted, at the right of WC4, is Pharaoh decreeing the casting of male Israelite infants into the Nile (Exodus 1:22); in the middle, Moses' mother, having placed him in an ark of bulrushes, lays it in the reeds at the river's edge (Exodus 2:3); and at the left, Pharaoh's daughter, bathing nude, rescues the infant (Exodus 2:5-6). Goodenough, however, noticed strange aspects of the picture, if it shows the infancy of the first Moses. The nude bather is drawn according to the iconography of the Iranian goddess Anahita, and in the background, standing with the two females who should be Moses' mother and his sister, are three more females, drawn according to the iconography of the Greek nymphs.[131] Goodenough had too strong a tendency to look for Iranian influence. The nude goddess could at least equally well be Ishtar, goddess of Babylonia,[132] especially in view of Isaiah 47:1-3, "Come down . . . O virgin daughter of Babylon; Sit on the ground without a throne . . . . Take the millstones and grind meal; . . . Pass through the rivers. Thy nakedness shall be uncovered, Yea, thy shame shall be seen . . . ." "Virgin daughter of Babylon" in the prophecy is a personification of the city, Babylon. The goddess, Ishtar, despite her promiscuity, could have been given the epithet "virgin"[133] and is equally good as a personification of Babylon.[134] The prophet tells the personified city to become a slave. Jewish readers of Isaiah 14:2 would know that the personified tyrant city would become a slave to the Jews.

As for the nymphs, in Greek legend they are the nurses of infant gods, heroes, and kings. The infant first Moses needed only his own mother as his nurse (Exodus 2:7-9). A common pattern in literature is the theme of the endangered infant savior or king, well known from the Gospel according to Matthew (2:13-21), which is surely based on the stories of Moses.[135]

---

[131] *Jewish Symbols*, IX, 200-224.

[132] See Jeremy Black and Anthony Green, *Gods, Demons and Symbols of Ancient Mesopotamia: An Illustrated Dictionary* (London, 1992) , 108-9.

[133] The equally promiscuous Ugaritic goddess ʿAnat receives the epithet "virgin" (*btlt*; Elia S. Artom and Yaʿaqov Yohanan Rabinovitz, *Entsiqlopediah miqra'it*, II [1954], 383).

[134] See Morris Jastrow, *The Religion of Babylonia and Assyria* (Boston, 1898), 82-85.

[135] On the pattern and on its presence in Matthew, see W. D. Davies and Dale C. Allison, jr., *A Critical and Exegetical Commentary on the Gospel according to Saint Matthew* ("The International Critical Commentary"; Edinburgh, 1988), I, 190-95, 257-72, 558.

In Matthew, the endangered savior is the Christian Messiah. At
Dura, the endangered infant could indeed be the second Moses.
But with a goddess as his slave and the nymphs as his nurses (cf.
Isaiah 49:23, 60:16, 66:11-12), he is more likely a king, the Jewish
Messiah. The painting outdoes Isaiah 49:23, 60:16, 66:11-12: not
merely the kings and queens of the pagans will serve the Chosen
People; the deities of the pagans will do so. Rabbinic literature
preserves no such legend of the endangerment and rescue of the
second Moses or of the Messiah and none of the subservience of
pagan deities. The sole evidence for such tales would be our painting. But if Christians could tell a story of their endangered infant
Christ, Jews could do so, too, of their Messiah.

6e NC1. Scenes from Ezekiel's Prophetic Career

There can be no doubt that NC1 is based on scenes from Ezekiel's
prophetic career. Nevertheless, I have been unable to find a complete solution for the difficulties of NC1. When the picture is compared with the biblical text of Ezekiel, with ancient Jewish and
Christian literature in Greek and Latin, and with rabbinic midrash,
many possible interpretations of individual features of the composition suggest themselves, but it is difficult to assemble them into a
coherent whole, and we know that the designer liked coherent
schemes.

Let us begin with a description of NC1. At the left edge of of the
painting is evidently an olive tree.[136] To the right of the tree are
three figures of heroic stature. To judge by their faces, builds, and
clothing, all three represent the same person. They stand in three
different poses, dressed in white soft boots, a reddish-brown elaborately embroidered smock, and green trousers. At their feet are
scattered three right arms with hands, three right legs with feet, and
four heads with short hair.

A hand from heaven holds the first figure by the hair of his head,
a clear clue that at least the first trousered figure is the prophet
Ezekiel (Ezekiel 8:3). To the right of him is the second trousered
figure. His right hand is open, gesturing toward the body parts. His
left hand is raised, pointing upward and to the right, and thus not

---

[136] See figure 2, p. 157 (reproduced with the permission of the Yale University
Art Museum from Goodenough, *Jewish Symbols*, XI, figures 348 and 349). For
convenience, the very long NC1 has been divided into two halves. Olive tree: cf.
H. Riesenfeld, "The Resurrection in Ezekiel XXXVII and in the Dura-Europos
Paintings," in *No Graven Images: Studies in Art and the Hebrew Bible*, edited by Joseph
Gutmann (New York, 1971) , 147-49.

directly at an open right hand of God above his head. The gestures
can easily be interpreted as oratorical. The third trousered figure
also has his left hand raised, perhaps toward a third right hand of
God, which stands over the cleft in a mountain which has split in
half. At the summit of each of the two halves is an olive tree, and
from the rift between the two fragments tumble more heads and
body parts. An overturned building lies upon the right fragment of
the mountain. At its foot lie three lifeless whole corpses, and above
it is another hand of God. A fourth trousered figure stands to the
right of the split mountain, with his right hand raised above shoul-
der level and his left hand stretched out and downward, possibly in
an oratorical posture.

From the olive tree at the left edge and up to the right edge of
the right half of the split mountain and the extended right forearm
of the fourth trousered figure, the background of the painting is a
very pale green (perhaps intended to be colorless). From that point
on, in the middle portion of NC1, the background becomes a deep
pink or red.[137] Even the right elbow of the fourth trousered figure
has the reddish background. To the right of him again lie three
lifeless whole corpses.

Three female persons with butterfly wings fly in and approach
the dead bodies. A fourth such female is on the ground and striding
toward the three corpses. To the right of her, another male figure
of heroic stature, with the same facial features and build as the
trousered persons, but wearing chiton and himation, raises his right
hand to head level in a peculiar gesture: the thumb, ring finger and
little finger are folded over the palm, and the index and middle
fingers are extended.

To the right of the person in chiton and himation stand, in close
formation under a hand of God, ten smaller figures, also in chiton
and himation. To the right of them are two more hands, three
more feet, and a head. Yet another heroic figure in chiton and
himation extends his right arm at waist level over the body parts,
holding his open palm outward, as if presenting the ten smaller
figures. To the right of him is an unriven mountain with an olive
tree on top. At this point, the reddish background ends.

Let us pause here, and attempt to explain what is being shown in
the left two thirds of the composition. The first details of the picture
can be shown to be based on Ezekiel 8:2-11:24. A supernatural

---

[137] Kraeling noticed the change in the color of the background (*Synagogue*, 183,
185, 189) without appreciating its significance.

hand carried Ezekiel, by his hair, away from his place of exile in Babylonia to Jerusalem, where he beheld the atrocious wicked acts being perpetrated there and God's punishment of them, heard God promise a restoration of the exiles, and saw how the cherubim carried "the glory of the Lord" and how "the glory of the LORD rose out of the city and stood upon the mountain to the east [the Mount of Olives]." Thereupon, a spirit of God picked Ezekiel up and returned him to his place of exile in Babylonia.

The olive tree at the left edge probably is meant to stand at least for the Promised Land, "a land of olives" (Deuteronomy 8:8), and, more likely, for the Mount of Olives, so as to signify the starting point from which the supernatural hand has carried Ezekiel back to Babylonia. In a departure from the chronology of the book of Ezekiel, the designer next presented 6:1-7, *not* 37:1-14 with its valley of dry bones; there are no dry bones in the picture, and the dry bones were in a valley, not on or by a mountain. In 6:1-7, the LORD tells Ezekiel to prophesy to the mountains of Israel: the idolatrous furniture upon them shall be destroyed in war, and they shall be covered with the corpses of the inhabitants, and the bones on the mountains will be scattered around the (ruined) altars, though fugitives will survive, scattered in the countries of the gentiles. Ezekiel addresses the prophecy to the "mountains of Israel," but predicts destruction only for the people and structures. Clearly, he assumes that the mountains suffer when such desolation is inflicted (33:28, 35:12, 36:1-12). But 6:1-7 says nothing of the riving of a mountain. Something of the sort can be inferred from 38:20, in a prophecy of the downfall of Gog, but the Jews of Dura surely believed that event would occur during the Last Days, not in Ezekiel's lifetime. Indeed, we find the splitting of the Mount of Olives in Zechariah 14:4, taken as a prophecy of the Last Days by Jews at the time of the synagogue. Did the designer believe that the (still future) splitting of the Mount of Olives was a part of the punishment of the mountains of Israel for the sins committed in the time of Ezekiel? Perhaps. A Jewish tradition says that in the time to come, when the Mount of Olives will split, the bodies of all Israelites will travel through the earth and emerge through the cleft to be resurrected.[138] I do not know how to fit these eschatological traditions about the Mount of Olives into NC1.

In any case, the second Ezekiel, standing under the hand of God, prophesies to the mountain. The third Ezekiel points to the havoc

---

[138] See Riesenfeld, "Resurrection," in *No Graven Images*, edited by Joseph Gutmann, 147-49.

wrought by the third hand of God as he stands by the split mountain which is littered with dismembered corpses and with an overturned building. In the context of Ezekiel 6:1-7, the dismembered corpses are those of the idolaters of his time. Ezekiel 6:5 mentions only scattered *bones*; nowhere in the passage are dismembered corpses mentioned. In the vision of the dry bones, the bones are reassembled *before* they are covered with sinews and flesh and skin (37:7-8). Why, then, do the picture and Christian parallels to it[139] contain severed heads and body parts instead of bare bones? I have no solution to the problem. The scene of NC1 characterized by the greenish background is unrelievedly one of the punishment of sin. To judge by the background of the right hand of the fourth Ezekiel, he, too, belongs to that part of the composition.

A different fate from that of the dismembered corpses seems to await the three bodies shown as whole, lying on the the right side of the split mountain. They seem to be repeated in the section with the reddish background. In classical Greek and Roman art, females with butterfly wings are Psyches, personifications of souls.[140] The heroic figure in chiton and himation, in the context of the synagogue paintings, should be a prophet or an angel. His face and build are those of the first four Ezekiels. His gesture in ancient pagan and Christian art may well be connected with ideas of immortality or resurrection.[141]

So we have Ezekiel assisting at an act of resurrecting the dead, as at 37:1-14. Rabbinic traditions, probably based on the "valley of Dura" at Daniel 3:1 (the only named Babylonian valley in the Bible), located the vision of the dry bones at Dura![142] The designer may have done so, too. Again, I can find no reason why in this part of the painting only whole corpses are shown and no dry bones.

Why do Ezekiel's clothes change? The first four Ezekiels are clad very like the ordinary priests in WB2 (Ezekiel was a priest), and belong to the part of the picture which has the greenish background and treats punishment of sin. Prophets who bring benefit and consolation, like Moses and Elijah, wear the chiton and himation. Moses in the exodus leads the people into the region over which hangs the pink cloud. Ezekiel wears the chiton and himation for the resurrection, in the region with the reddish background.

The Psyches came, and the corpses returned to life, more bodies than were shown in death! No fewer than ten resurrected figures,

---

[139] Goodenough, X, 181-82.
[140] See Otto Waser, "Psyche," *Ausführliches Lexikon der griechischen und römischen Mythologie,* edited by W.H. Roscher, III (Leibzig, 1897-1909), 3234-56.
[141] See Goodenough, *Jewish Symbols,* X, 184.
[142] See Ginzberg, *Legends* IV, 330, VI, 418-19, n. 90.

with hands raised in reverence for the miracle, stand under the fifth hand of god, and another Ezekiel in chiton and himation stands to the right, gesturing as if to present the ten. Parts of dismembered bodies still lie directly under the extended arm of the Ezekiel. Who are the resurrected ten? Who are the dismembered? In 6:3, the prophet predicts that *war* will bring about the coming destruction. In war, the relatively innocent often perish along with the guilty. Resurrection can compensate them for their undeserved suffering. That may be part of what is symbolized, but why are there *ten* figures? In Ezekiel, "Israel" often means "Judah" or all twelve tribes. But careful reading of 37:1-28 makes it probable that "Israel" in 37:1-14 means the "lost ten tribes." Enough persons from those tribes will be deserving, so that ten figures can represent them. The still dismembered corpses symbolize the guilty and undeserving, in accordance with Isaiah 66:24 and Daniel 12:3.

Why are the resurrected shown in chiton and himation? According to Ezekiel 36:27, in the time to come, God will confer His spirit upon all members of the Chosen People. Thus, they all will be prophets! The unriven mountain is a restored mountain in the Age of Restoration (Ezekiel 34:13, 36:1-15).

The Jews of Dura lived near the regions said to have been the places of exile of the ten tribes (II Kings 17:6) and eagerly looked forward to fulfilment of the prophecies of the restoration of those tribes, an event which they regarded as part of the Last Days. The designer may have taken the vision of Ezekiel 37 as merely symbolic of that restoration; he may have also have seen in it a foreshadowing of the final resurrection. The scenes with the reddish background are placed in conformity with the position in the book of Ezekiel of the vision of the valley of dry bones, but what they show is at least in part the fulfilment of that vision, during the Last Days! We may infer from the picture, that Ezekiel received the vision during his career, but will be resurrected during the Last Days to participate in its fulfilment. His chiton and himation, too, may belong the the Last Days, rather than to his mortal career.

To the right of the restored mountain, the background changes to a pale color, rather like what it had in the left third of NA1. A man with features, build, and clothes like those of the first four Ezekiels (except that he is wearing a sword) kneels and clings to the side of a large altar. Behind the altar is a tent, and within its black interior are a set of objects, Comparison with WB1 and WB4 makes it certain that they are cultic utensils, including an incense burner atop a small table, in front of which are two unidentifiable round implements. An armored person wearing a diadem grasps the "Ezekiel" from behind. To the right of the altar, a trousered figure raises a sword, preparing to decapitate a person who is probably the same as the kneeling "Ezekiel," while four armored figures in the background look on.

Goodenough correctly identified the scene as based upon a legend of the execution of Ezekiel. Pieces of such a legend survive in the apocryphal *Lives of the Prophets*. According to their editor, Charles Cutler Torrey, the *Lives* go back to a Jewish original of the first century C.E.[143]

The relevant part of the account in the *Lives* is as follows. Ezekiel . . . was slain by the chief (*hegoumenos*) of the Israelite exiles who had been rebuked by him for his worship of idols . . . . He pronounced judgement in Babylon on the tribes of Dan and Gad, because they dealt wickedly against the Lord, persecuting those who were keeping the law . . . . He also foretold, that because of their sin Israel would not return to its land but would remain in Media, until the end of this evildoing. One of their number was the man who slew Ezekiel, for they opposed him all the days of his life.

The data in the *Lives* are not sufficient to explain the tent, the altar, and the armored figures. We can, however, use clues in the painting and in the book of Ezekiel to reconstruct a narrative which could have led to what we have in NC1. How did Ezekiel most infuriate the Judaean exiles in Babylonia and the Israelite exiles in Mesopotamia? His own prophecies give strong hints.

Elders of Israel, surely repentant "sinners" who believed in Ezekiel's prophetic authority, came to consult him, probably in the sixth year of the exile (14:1; for the date, cf. 8:1 and 20:1). Ezekiel (14:1-11) replied with a message from God which accused them of idolatry and added dire threats. In the seventh year of the exile, to a similar group of elders, Ezekiel replied with a still more hostile message from God (20:1-44); though it promised restoration to a nation which He would purge of rebels, even those who would be restored would remember their former ways and loathe themselves (21:33-44). Such revelations could easily have infuriated a delegation which at first was repentant and had come reverently to consult Ezekiel. We can imagine them turning murderously hostile to the prophet.

The tent in NC1 has an altar directly in front and contains furniture that is surely cultic. If we compare that assemblage with

---

[143] Torrey, *The Lives of the Prophets* ("Journal of Biblical Literature, Monograph Series," Volume I; Philadelphia, 1946), 3-12.

the sanctuaries in WB1 and WB2, we find ample justification for calling it a "tabernacle sanctuary." We should take note of a remarkable fact: though Ezekiel (14:3-5, 20:30-32) accuses the elders and their followers of idolatry and worse, there is no idol in the tent and no sacrifice upon the altar (contrast the altars in SC3 and SC4).

On the other hand, the prophet at 20:27-29 lays stress upon the sin of worshiping at a "high place" (bamah). A "high place" was an Israelite sanctuary for offering sacrifices at any other location than that of the temple in Jerusalem, forbidden by Deuteronomy 12:2-14 and regarded as sinful throughout I and II Kings. In the very next chapter, Ezekiel makes the plural sanctuaries of the land of Israel a target for reproof and says that the LORD's *sword* will cut off there both the righteous and the wicked (21:6-10)!

We know that Ezekiel delivered all his prophecies in Babylonia. There is no report that he died in the Promised Land. The account in the *Lives* locates his execution in Babylonia. Surely the tent and the altar, too, are in Babylonia. Together they constitute an Israelite sanctuary outside the site of the temple in Jerusalem. Are they a "high place"? The absence of a sacrifice upon the altar (whereas there was to be a daily offering upon the altar of the legitimate sanctuary) suggests that the designer imagined the exiles as copying the procedure of the Transjordanian tribes (Joshua 22:10-29) and as setting up a "sanctuary not for sacrifice."

Ezekiel, however, would not have accepted this expedient. It, too, was sinful. He predicted instead a return to Jerusalem (20:33-42, 40:1-48:35). But there was no sign of any such return in the near future. What were the exiles to do in the meantime? Ezekiel had nothing to offer them. He may have roused the murderous wrath of the exiles by going around wearing the "LORD's sword" as a demonstration against the "illicit" sanctuary . He may have sought refuge at the altar he regarded as illicit (though illicit, it was not idolatrous). Even so, the chief of the exiles, wearing his diadem, arrested him and had him executed. Such would have been the story portrayed in the right third of NC1.

To judge by the account in the *Lives of the Prophets*, the person responsible for ordering the execution of Ezekiel was the chief of the *Israelite* exiles, evidently backed by the tribes of *Dan* and *Gad* and the *Israelites* who had been exiled to *Media* (II Kings 17:6). All these names and descriptions refer to members of the lost ten tribes. The designer may well have seen the still-separated heads and body-parts at the right of the resurrection scene as those of the *Israelites* responsible for Ezekiel's execution. By precise retribution, dismemberment is the punishment for decapitation. The resurrection-scene stands to the left of the execution because the chronology is that of Ezekiel's life: he saw the vision of the resurrection long before he was executed.

Details of the painting may reflect historical reality. In the time of the synagogue, under the Parthian and Persian kings, the exilarchs, rulers of the Jewish community of Babylonia, enjoyed quasi-royal authority, such as is indicated by the diadem of the armored man who arrests Ezekiel.[144] Beginning with the Assyrians, the empires of the ancient Near East raised troops from the conquered peoples, and exiled and fugitive Israelites are known to have served as mercenaries.[145] In a community of persons recently exiled, the soldiers could well have been the most most prosperous and prominent.

NC1 can be viewed as fitting the scheme we have hypothesized for the synagogue, with past and temporary wonders on the left and eschatological and permanent ones on the right. The predicted restoration of the ten tribes will be permanent. If there really is an allusion in the painting to the final resurrection, that, too, will be a permanent achievement of God. Ezekiel through his martyrdom permanently made the point that Jews must not have a temple unless it is on the site chosen by God. Though the Dura synagogue is decorated as a palace for God and the Messiah,[146] the painting thus emphasizes that it is a synagogue, not a temple.

Does the left-right scheme that we have found apply to the east wall, too? The sole recognizable picture there is EC1, on the right half of the wall. Like WC3, EC1 can be viewed as depicting a permanent achievement of the LORD, for the events in I Samuel 26 proved the right of David to be king, and his dynasty is to be permanent. Thus, the left-right scheme certainly applies to the west wall and possibly to the east wall. The surviving paintings of the south wall, according to that scheme, belong where they are, on the left. The surviving paintings of the north wall, correspondingly, belong where they are, on the right.

---

[144] See Jacob Neusner, "Exilarch until the Arab Conquest," *Encylopaedia Judaica*, VI (1971), 1023-27.

[145] Notably in the case of the community at Elephantine in upper Egypt (see Bezalel Porten, *Archives from Elephantine* [Berkeley, 1968]). For traces of Jews as mercenaries in Babylonia, see II Maccabees 8:20 and my *II Maccabees*, 331.

[146] See my *Semites*, 113.

7 What can we know about the Religion
of the Jews of Dura

The many contacts between the paintings and rabbinic midrash strongly suggest that the Jews of Dura were connected at least in some way with that tradition. The representation of the ark in WB4 as the earthly throne of God shows that the designer had contact with *Merkabhah* mysticism. The fringed himation worn by prophets and angels lets us see how they treated one point of ritual law: the fringes consist of three threads, as required by the view of the School of Hillel.[147] The parchment fragment of a grace after meals, too, shows that the practice of the Jews of Dura in that ritual was close, if not identical, to that of Babylonian rabbis. The composer of the prayer used poetic techniques similar to those of the school of Rabh.[148]

The Jews of Dura certainly did not agree with the interpretation of Exodus 20:4 and Deuteronomy 5:8 that forbade all artistic imagery. They probably deduced, from Exodus 20:5 and Deuteronomy 5:9, that the intention of the artists and the worshipers made a difference: if there was no intention to use the images as objects of worship, artistic imagery, at least in two dimensions, was permitted.

The Jews of Dura were vitally interested in eschatology. They passionately believed in the coming destruction of the oppressive empires that ruled over them, in the destruction of pagan religion, in the liberation of the Jews and their restoration to their homeland, in the coming of the Messiah, in the resurrection of the dead, in God's bestowing of the gift of prophecy upon all Israel. Until God in His own time brought about their restoration (and that time would be soon), they could worship only in a synagogue, not in a temple. Great as was their discretion in concealing the full import of the paintings by labels and by other means, we can be astonished by the audacity they showed in displaying such perilous topics.

---

[147] Connections with rabbinic tradition and *Merkabhah* mysticism: See Jacob Neusner, "Judaism at Dura-Europos," in *Re-evaluation*, edited by Joseph Gutmann, 179-81. For rabbinic views concerning fringes, see *Siphre* Deuteronomy 234 (to Deuteronomy 22:12), in *Sifre on Deuteronomy*, edited by Louis Finkelstein (New York, 5729=1969).

[148] See my *Semites*, 63; Morton Smith, "On the Yoṣer and Related Texts," in *The Synagogue in Late Antiquity*, edited by Lee Levine, 86-94, and J. Yahalom, "Piyyut as Poetry," ibid., 113-18.

SELECTED BIBLIOGRAPHY

Aptowitzer, A., *"Bet-hamiqdash shel ma'alah 'al pi ha-aggadah," Tarbiẓ* II
(5691=1930-31), 137-53. 257-77. English translation by Aryeh
Rubinstein, "The Celestial Temple as Viewed in the Aggadah," in
Binah: Studies in Jewish History, Thought, and Culture, edited by Joseph
Dan (Volume II of "Binah: Studies in Jewish Thought"; New York,
Westport, and London, 1989), chapter 1
Black, Jeremy, and Green, Anthony, *Gods, Demons and Symbols of Ancient
Mesopotamia: An Illustrated Dictionary* (London, 1992)
Coarelli, Filippo, *Il Foro boario dalle origini alla fine della repubblica* (Roma,
1988)
Deichmann, F. W., *Ravenna, Hauptstadt des spätantiken Abendlandes* (3 vols in
5: Wiesbaden, 1969-76)
Downey, Susan B., *The Stone and Plaster Sculpture,* Final Report III, Part I,
Fascicle 2, of *The Excavations at Dura-Europos* ("Monumenta
Archaeologica," Volume V; Los Angeles, 1977)
Ghirshman, Roman, *Persian Art: the Parthian and Sassanian Dynasties* (New
York, 1962)
Ginzberg, Louis, *The Legends of the Jews* (7 vols.; Philadelphia, 1928)
Goldstein, Jonathan A., *Semites, Iranians, Greeks, and Romans: Studies in Their
Interactions* (Atlanta, 1990)
Gutmann, Joseph (editor), *Ancient Synagogues: The State of Research,* ("Brown
Judaic Studies," 22; Chico, 1981)
Gutmann, Joseph (editor), *The Dura-Europos Synagogue: a Re-evaluation (1932-
1992)* ("South Florida Studies in the History of Judaism," edited by
Jacob Neusner et al., Number 25; Atlanta, 1992)
Gutmann, Joseph (editor), *No Graven Images: Studies in Art and the Hebrew
Bible* (New York, 1971)
Gutmann, Joseph, *Sacred Images: Studies in Jewish Art from Antiquity to the
Middle Ages* (Northampton, 1989)
Gutmann, Joseph, (editor), *The Synagogue* (New York, 1975)
Hopkins, Clark, *The Discovery of Dura-Europos* (New Haven and London,
1979)
Kraeling, Carl H., *The Synagogue,* Final Report VIII, Part I of *The Excava-
tions at Dura-Europos* [New Haven, 1956]
Levine, Lee I, (editor), *The Synagogue in Late Antiquity* (Philadelphia, 1987)
Ma'oz, Tsvi 'Uri, *"Bet ha-keneset bi-tequphat ha-bayit ha-sheni," Eretz-Israel* 23
(1992), 340-41
Moon, Warren G., "Nudity and Narrative: Observations on the Frescoes
from the Dura Synagogue," *Journal of the American Academy of Religion* 60
(1992), 587-658.
Neusner, Jacob, *A History of the Jews in Babylonia,* Volumes I (2nd printing,
revised: Leiden, 1969), III (Leiden, 1968), and IV (Leiden, 1969)
Neusner, Jacob, "Judaism at Dura-Europos," in *Re-evaluation,* edited by
Joseph Gutmann, 155-92
Rostovtzeff, M. I., Bellinger, A. R., Hopkins, C. and Welles, C. B. (edi-
tors), *The Excavations at Dura-Europos: Preliminary Report of the Sixth Season
of Work, October 1932—March 1933* (New Haven, 1936)
Scholem, Gershom, *Jewish Gnosticism, Merkabah Mysticism, and Talmudic Tra-
dition* (New York, 1960)
Welles, C. Bradford, Fink, Robert O. and Gilliam, J. Frank (editors), *The
Parchments and Papyri,* Final Report *V,* Part *I,* of *The Excavations at Dura-
Europos* (New Haven, 1959)

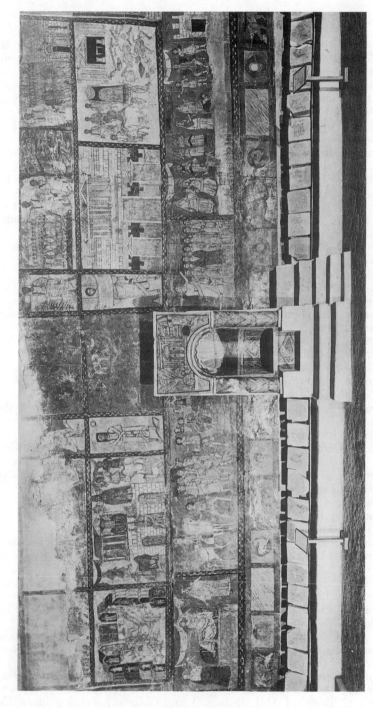

Fig. 1. The west wall of the Synagogue of Dura-Europos.
(Reproduced from Goodenough, *Jewish Symbols*, XI, Plate I; credit: Princeton University Press.)

Fig. 2a. Left half of the Ezekiel cycle of the Synagogue of Dura-Europos (NC1), as copied by Alexander Gute. (Credit: Yale University Art Gallery Dura-Europos Collection.)

Fig. 2b. Right half of the Ezekiel cycle of the Synagogue of Dura-Europos (NC1), as copied by Alexander Gute. (Credit: Yale University Art Gallery Dura-Europos Collection.)

RABBINIC JUDAISM

RABBINIC JUDAISM
ITS HISTORY AND HERMENEUTICS

Jacob Neusner
(University of South Florida)

1 THE FORMATION OF RABBINIC JUDAISM

The history of the formation of Judaism tells the story of how [1] philosophy became [2] religion, which was then re-presented as [3] theology. The medium of theological re-presentation was hermeneutics, so that, when we know how the Torah is properly read, we discern the theology of Judaism. Before proceeding, I hasten to give a simple definition of hermeneutics, that of Wilhelm Dilthey, since the rest of this chapter depends upon my claim that in its hermeneutics, the Talmud re-presents the Torah: "The methodological understanding of permanently fixed life-expressions we call explication...explication culminates in the interpretation of the written records of human existence...The science of this art is hermeneutics."[1] When we know the rules of explication that instruct us on how to interpret the Torah, we gain access to the theology that governs the presentation of the religion, Judaism.

The priority of hermeneutics in the theological venture is not difficult to explain. We deal with a Judaism that affords religious experience—knowledge of God, meeting with God—in particular in books. While that same Judaism, like any other religious system, also meets God in prayer, obedience to the covenant, and right conduct, and expresses the sense of the knowledge of God in music and in art, in pilgrimage and in dance, in rite and in cult, and in most of the ways that religions in general celebrate God, what makes this Judaic system distinctive is its insistence that God is made manifest in, and therefore known through, documents, which preserve and contain the encounter with God that in secular language we call "religious experience." Just as, if the principal medium for meeting God were theater or music, we should search for theology in aesthetics, so since the principal meeting of encounter with God is the Torah, and the Torah is given in writing and oral formulation as well, this Judaism promises knowledge of God

---

[1] Cited by K. M. Newton, *Interpreting the Text*, p. 42.

through the documents of the Torah, and its theological medium will be hermeneutics (as much as philosophy).

The character of the evidence therefore governs. Because the formation of (this particular) Judaism as a religious system is fully exposed in its successive documents, the history of that Judaism's formative age—the first six centuries of the Common Era—comes to us in the right reading of the Torah. In this Judaism, the Torah comprises the holy documents and persons—written and oral documents, and the person of "our sages of blessed memory;" the deeds and teachings of sages take the form of stories and statements preserved in the same documents. Not only so, but because the medium for theology in a religious system is fully exposed in its successive documents, the history of that Judaism's formative age—the first six centuries of the Common Era—comes to us in the right reading of the Torah.

Stated in documentary terms, the formative history of Judaism tells a story in three sentences. It shows, first, how the Judaic system emerged in the Mishnah, ca. 200 C.E., and its associated Midrash-compilations, ca. 200-300 C.E., as [1] a philosophical structure comprising a politics, philosophy, economics. These categories were defined as philosophers in general understood them: a theory of legitimate violence, an account of knowledge gained through the methods of natural history, and a theory of the rational disposition (and increase) of scarce resources.

This philosophical system then was turned by the Talmud of the Land of Israel and related Midrash-compilations, ca. 400-500 C.E., into [2] a religious system. The system was effected through the formation of counterpart categories: an anti-politics of weakness, an anti-economics of the rational utilization of an infinitely renewable resource, a philosophy of truth revealed rather than rules discovered.[2]

Then, finally, the religious system was restated by the Talmud of Babylonia and its companions of Midrash-collection, ca. 500-600 C.E. In those writings it was given [3] theological re-presentation

---

[2] The characterization of the first two stages in the formation of Judaism is contained within these books of mine: *The Economics of the Mishnah*. Chicago, 1989: The University of Chicago Press; *Rabbinic Political Theory: Religion and Politics in the Mishnah*. Chicago, 1991: The University of Chicago Press; *Judaism as Philosophy. The Method and Message of the Mishnah*. Columbia, 1991: University of South Carolina Press; and *The Transformation of Judaism. From Philosophy to Religion*. Champaign, 1992: University of Illinois Press.

through the recovery of philosophical method for the formulation of religious conceptions. In the great tradition, we may say, the formation of Judaism took place through [3] the final synthesis of [1] the initial thesis and [2] the consequent antithesis. That Hegelian pattern helps make sense of the history of religious expression and idea that the canonical books of Judaism expose.

Theology is the science of the reasoned knowledge of God, in the case of a Judaism made possible by God's self-manifestation in the Torah. Seen in its whole re-presentation in the Talmud of Babylonia, the theology of Judaism sets forth knowledge of God. This is in two ways. The first (as I just said) is to know God through God's self-revelation in the Torah. This requires that we know what the Torah is, or what torah is (in a generic sense, which can pertain to either message or media or modes of thought). Then knowing how to define and understand the Torah affords access to God's self-revelation. The second is to know through that same self-revelation what God wants of Israel and how God responds to Israel and humanity at large.[3] That specific, propositional knowledge comes through reasoned reading of the Torah, oral and written, the Mishnah and Scripture, represented by the Talmuds and Midrash-compilations, respectively.[4] The hermeneutics governing these documents encapsulate that knowledge of reasoned explication.

The priority of hermeneutics in the theological inquiry in a religion expressed through documents (more than, e.g., through creeds, institutions, persons, dancing, singing, acting, or laughing, crying, eating, starving, and the like, all of which, as a matter of fact, convey the systemic statement of this Judaism too) is then self-evident. Through defining the hermeneutics of the Torah, we learn how the theology of Judaism explains what it means to reason

---

[3] I paraphrase Ingolf Dalferth, "The Stuff of Revelation: Austin Farrer's Doctrine of Inspired Images," in Ann Loades and Michael McLain, eds., *Hermeneutics, the Bible and literary Criticism* (London, 1992: MacMillan), p. 71. Dalferth was my colleague when I was Buber Professor of Judaic Studies at the University of Frankfurt, and it was in reading his writing that I began to think along the lines that come to fruition in this theory. Other definitions and premises will yield other ways of reading the theology of the Judaism of the dual Torah.

[4] And that explains why we still will have to undertake a separate account of the theology yielded by the hermeneutics of the Midrash-compilations (not only, or mainly, specific words or phrases or sentences found hither and yon in "The Midrash," as the ignorant conduct the inquiry). The characterization of the hermeneutics of Midrash-compilations, early, middle, and late, will stand side-by-side with the theory set forth here.

about the Torah, showing how this is to be done in quest of truth
about Israel's right action and conviction. The explanation is set
forth in the hermeneutics of the Torah, spelled out in the two
Talmuds to the Mishnah, and the several Midrash-compilations to
Scripture. All together, these writings expound the Torah and exemplify the correct hermeneutics for understanding the Torah. The
task of describing the theology of Judaism therefore is to identify
the correct hermeneutics; and the work of framing statements of
normative theology requires proper hermeneutics in the analysis of
the Talmud's re-presentation of the Torah: the rules of explication,
in Dilthey's definition.

The schematic classifications of the successive, related Judaic systems as philosophical, religious, and theological, therefore derive
from the character of the successive documents, the Mishnah,
Yerushalmi, and Bavli.[5] What makes all the difference in the second
Talmud's re-presentation of the Judaic religious system therefore is
the character of that Talmud itself. Through analysis of the
hermeneutics that conveys the intellectual program of that medium,
a religion rich in miscellaneous but generally congruent norms of
behavior and endowed with a vast store of varied and episodic but
occasionally contradictory ideas was turned into a proportioned
and harmonious theology.[6]

Having laid heavy emphasis on the priority of the Bavli, I hasten
to qualify matters. As a matter of fact, the process of theological re-
presentation went forward in two stages. In the first, in the Talmud
of the Land of Israel, the philosophical document that stated that
system gained both a vast amplification, in which the categories
and methods of the original statement were amplified and instanti-
ated, but also in which took place a remarkable reformulation in
counterpart-categories. Of the three traits of "tradition," e.g. as
defined in the tractate Avot in its apologia for the Mishnah— harmony, linearity, and unity,—the first of the two Talmuds systematically demonstrated the presence of two: harmony and linearity.

---

[5] That is within the qualification that the Yerushalmi did part of the work of
theologizing the Mishnah, the work of showing its proportion, composition, harmony, and coherence. The second Talmud did this work, but it also accomplished
the far more sophisticated intellectual tasks.

[6] But I maintain that an important part of the theological work was undertaken
by the first of the two Talmuds, which means the differentiation between the two
Talmuds provides the key, in literary analysis, to the hermeneutical priority of the
second of the two.

The second undertook to demonstrate all three, all together and all at once and everywhere, that is to say, the law behind the laws, meaning, the unity, the integrity of truth. That shown, we know the mind of God, the character of truth.

Viewed as a whole, the result is then to be classified as not philosophical but religious in character and theological in re-presentation. Alongside, earlier Midrash-compilations undertook the task of showing the relationship between the two media of the Torah, the oral and the written, by insisting that the Mishnah rested on Scripture. The goal was to show linearity and, of course, harmony. They furthermore began the definition of the Torah—in our terms, the reading of Scripture—by systematizing and generalizing the episodic cases of Scripture. The goal was to demonstrate the comprehensiveness of the Torah: its cases were meant to yield governing rules. The later Midrash-compilations continued that reading of Scripture by formulating syllogistic propositions out of the occasional data of Scripture.

The religious writings that formed the second stage in the unfolding of Judaism—Talmud of the Land of Israel, Sifra and the two Sifrés somewhat before, Genesis Rabbah and Leviticus Rabbah somewhat afterward, finally were succeeded—and replaced—by the Talmud of Babylonia and related Midrash-compilations, particularly Song of Songs Rabbah, Lamentations Rabbah, and Ruth Rabbah. These were documents that restated in rigorous, theological ways the same religious convictions, so providing that Judaism or Judaic system with its theological statement. In these writings, the religious system was restated in a rigorous and philosophical way. The associated midrash-compilations succeeded in making a single, encompassing statement out of the data of the several books of Scripture they presented.

The re-presentation of the religious system in the disciplined thought of theology took the form of rules of reading the Torah—oral and written—and through those rules exposing the character of the intellectual activity of thinking like God, that is, thinking about the world in the way God thinks. The theology of Judaism—reasoned knowledge of God[7] and God's will afforded by God's self-manifestation in the Torah[8]—affords access in particular to the

---

[7] That is a standard definition of theology.

[8] That is my restatement of a standard definition of theology to state what I mean by, theology of Judaism.

mind of God, revealed in God's words and wording of the Torah. Through the Torah, oral and written, we work out way back to the intellect of God who gives the Torah. Thus through learning in the Torah in accord with the lessons of the Talmuds and associated Midrash-compilations, humanity knows what God personally has made manifest about mind, that intellect in particular in which "in our image, after our likeness" we too are made. That defines the theology of the Judaism of the dual Torah and in particular forms the upshot of the Talmud's re-presentation of that theology.

Reading the Mishnah together with one or the other of its Talmudic amplifications, the Talmud of the Land of Israel or the Talmud of Babylonia, or Scripture together with any of the Midrash-compilations, on the surface does not convey such an account. The canonical writings—the Mishnah and Talmud of the Land of Israel or the Mishnah and Talmud of Babylonia and their associated Midrash-collections—portray not successive stages of the formation of a system but rather a single, continuous Judaism, which everywhere is read as unitary and uniform. Not only so, but in the persons and teachings of sages that same Torah makes part of its statement. But, when examined as single documents, one by one, in the sequence of their closure, to the contrary, matters look otherwise. Each writing then may be characterized on its own, rather than in the continuous context defined by the canon of which it forms a principal part.

Then the formation of Judaism, correctly described, may be stated in a single sentence. [1] The Mishnah, then [2] the first Talmud, then [3] the second Talmud, together with their respective sets of associated Midrash-compilations, yield the history of a three-stage formation.

The first tells how the document that set forth first Judaic system formed a philosophy, utilizing philosophical categories and philosophical modes of thought (philosophy, politics, economics, for categories, Aristotelian methods of hierarchical classification).

The second explains how the categorical formation was recast into religious classifications, from philosophy to Torah, from a politics of legitimate power to an anti-politics of weakness, from an economics of scarce resources to an anti-politics of the abundant resource of Torah-learning.

The third then spells out how the received categorical system and structure was restated in its main points in such a way as to hold together the philosophical method and the religious message through a hermeneutical medium. Here I specify the character of that medium and its content. As I have already indicated, I once more stress, less I be misunderstood, that this division between the second and the third should be shaded somewhat, since, as I shall show, by the operative definition of theology here, part of the theological work was carried on in the second—the Yerushalmi's—stage, part in the third. But, withal, the Bavli formed the summa, holding the whole together and making its own supreme and unique statement.

I have used the terms "philosophy" and "religion" and suggested they be treated as distinct categories of thought. Let me now spell out what I mean by "philosophy" and "religion." By "philosophy" I refer to the category-formation, inclusive of categorical definitions, put forth by philosophy in ancient times. By "religion" I refer to the category-formation put forth on a wholly-other-than philosophical basis in that same period. The one is secular and worldly in its data, utilizing the methods of natural history for its analytical work; the other is transcendental, finding its data in revelation, utilizing the methods of the exegesis of revelation for its systematic work. Both are exercises of sustained rationality, in the case of this Judaism, of applied reason and practical logic. But the one begins in this world and its facts, which are analyzed and categorized through the traits inherent in them, and the other commences in the world above and its truths, which are analyzed and categorized by the categories of revelation. The one yields philosophy of religion, the other, religious statements, attitudes, convictions, rules of life; the one represents one way of knowing God, specifically, the way through the data of this world, the other, a different way to God altogether, the way opened by God's revelation and self-manifestation, whether through nature or beyond. Let me now spell this distinction out with reference to the systemic results of a reading of the Mishnah and the Yerushalmi.

The Mishnah set forth in the form of a law code a highly philosophical account of the world ("world view"), a pattern for everyday and material activities and relationships ("way of life"), and a definition of the social entity ("nation," "people," "us" as against "outsiders," "Israel") that realized that way of life and explained it by appeal to that world view. We have no difficulty in calling this account of a way of life an economics, because the account of material reality provided by the Mishnah corresponds, point for point, with that given in Aristotle's counterpart. The Mishnah moreover sets forth a politics by dealing with the same questions, about the permanent and legitimate institutions that inflict sanctions, that occupy Greek and Roman political thinkers. There is no economics of another-than-this-worldly character, no politics of an inner "kingdom of God." All is straight-forward, worldly, material, and consequential for the everyday world. Then the successor-documents, closed roughly two centuries later, addressed the Mishnah's system and recast its categories into a connected, but also quite revised, one. The character of their reception of the received categories and of their own category-formation, emerging in the contrast between one set of documents and another, justifies invoking the term, "transformation," that is, of one thing into something else. That something else was a religious, as distinct from a philosophical, category-formation.

The first Talmud and associated Midrash-compilations attest to a system that did more than merely extend and recast the categorical structure of the system for which the Mishnah stands. They took over the way of life, world view, and social entity, defined in the Mishnah's system. And while they rather systematically amplified details, framed a program of exegesis around the requirements of clerks engaged in enforcing the rules of the Mishnah, they built their own system. For at the same time they formed categories corresponding to those of the Mishnah, a politics, a philosophy, an economics. But these categories proved so utterly contrary in their structure and definition to those of the Mishnah that they presented mirror-images of the received categories.

The politics, philosophy, and economics of the Mishnah were joined by the Yerushalmi to an anti-politics, an anti-economics, and an utterly-transformed mode of learning. In the hands of the later sages, the new mode of Torah-study —the definition of what was at stake in studying the Torah—redefined altogether the issues of the intellect. Natural history as the method of classification gave way to a different mode of thought altogether. As a matter of fact the successor-system recast not the issues so much as the very stakes of philosophy or science. The reception of the Mishnah's category-formations and their transformation therefore stands for the movement from a philosophical to a religious mode of thinking. For the system to which the Mishnah as a document attests is essentially philosophical in its rhetorical, logical, and topical program; the successor system, fundamental religious in these same principal and indicative traits of medium of intellect and mentality.

Given the definitions with which I began, how do I know whether a system is philosophical or religious? The answer is not subjective, nor the criteria, private or idiosyncratic. The indicative traits in both instances, to begin with, derive from and are displayed by documents, for—I take it as axiomatic—the mode of the writing down of any system attests to both the method and the message that sustain that system. From how people express themselves, we work our way backward to their modes of thought: the classification of perceived data, the making of connections between fact and fact, the drawing of conclusions from those connections, and, finally, the representation of conclusions in cogent compositions. All of these traits of mind are to be discerned in the character of those compositions, in the rhetoric that conveys messages in proportion and appropriate aesthetics, in the logic that imparts self-evidence to the making of connections, the drawing of conclusions, and in the representation of sets of conclusions as cogent and intelligible, characteristic of writing and expressed in writing.

In the Yerushalmi (and the Bavli later on) scarce resources, so far as these are of a material order of being, e.g., wealth as defined by the Mishnah and Aristotle, are systemically neutral. A definition of scarce resources emerges that explicitly involves a symbolic transformation, with the material definition of scarce resources set into contradiction with an other-than-material one. So we find side by side clarification of the details of the received category and adumbration of a symbolic revision and hence a categorical transformation in the successor-writings. The representation of the political structure of the Mishnah undergoes clarification, but alongside, a quite separate and very different structure also is portrayed. The received structure presents three political classes, ordered in a hierarchy; the successor-structure, a single political class, corresponding on earth to a counterpart in Heaven. Here too a symbolic transaction has taken place, in which one set of symbols is replicated but also reversed, and a second set of symbols given instead.

The Mishnah's structure comprising a hierarchical composition undergoes clarification, but alongside, a quite separate and very different structure also is portrayed. The received structure presents three political classes, ordered in a hierarchy; the successor-structure, a single political class, corresponding onass of persons (institution), rather than by a proportionate and balanced set of classes of persons in hierarchical order, and, moreover, that same theory recognizes and defines both legitimate and also illegitimate violence, something beyond the ken of the initial system. So, it is clear, another system is adumbrated and attested in the successor-writings.

The categorical transformation that was underway in the Yerushalmi, signaling the movement from philosophy to religion, comes to the surface when we ask a simple question. Precisely what do the authorships of the successor-documents speaking not about the Mishnah but on their own account, mean by economics, politics, and philosophy? That is to say, to what kinds of data do they refer when they speak of scarce resources and legitimate violence, and exactly how—as to the received philosophical method—do they define correct modes of thought and expression, logic and rhetoric, and even the topical program worthy of sustained inquiry? The components of the initial formation of categories were examined thoughtfully and carefully, paraphrased and augmented and clarified. But the received categories were not continued, not expanded, and not renewed. Preserved merely intact, as they had been handed on, the received categories hardly serve to encompass all of the points of emphasis and sustained development that characterize the successor-documents—or, as a matter of fact, any of them. On the contrary, when the framers of the Yerushalmi, for one example, moved out from the exegesis of Mishnah-passages, they also left behind the topics of paramount interest in the Mishnah and developed other categories altogether. Here the framers of the successor- system defined theiir own counterparts.

These counterpart-categories, moreover, redefined matters, following the main outlines of the structure of the social order manifest in the initial system. The counterpart-categories set forth an account of the social order just as did the ones of the Mishnah's framers. But they defined the social order in very different terms altogether. In that redefinition we discern the transformation of the received system, and the traits of the new one fall into the classification of not philosophy but religion. For what the successor-thinkers did was not continue and expand the categorical repertoire but set forth a categorically-fresh vision of the social order—a way of life, world view, and definition of the social entity—with appropriate counterpart-categories. And what is decisive is that these served as did the initial categories within the generative categorical structure definitive for all Judaic systems. So there was a category corresponding to the generative component of worldview, but it was not philosophical; another corresponding to the required component setting forth a way of life, but in the conventional and accepted definition of economics it was not an economics; and, finally, a category to define the social entity, "Israel," that any Judaic system must explain, but in the accepted sense of a politics it was not politics.

What is the difference between philosophical and the religious systems? What philosophy kept distinct, religion joined together:

that defines the transformation of Judaism from philosophy to religion. The received system was a religious system of a philosophical character; this worldly-data are classified according to rules that apply consistently throughout, so that we may always predict with a fair degree of accuracy what will happen and why. And a philosophical system of religion then systematically demonstrates out of the data of the world order of nature and society the governance of God in nature and supernature: this world's data pointing toward God above and beyond. The God of the philosophical Judaism then sat enthroned at the apex of all things, all being hierarchically classified. Just as philosophy seeks the explanation of things, so a philosophy of religion (in the context at hand) will propose orderly explanations in accord with prevailing and cogent rules. The profoundly philosophical character of the Mishnah has already provided ample evidence of the shape, structure, and character of that philosophical system in the Judaic context. The rule-seeking character of Mishnaic discourse marks it as a philosophical system of religion. But, we shall now see, the successor-system saw the world differently. It follows that a philosophical system forms its learning inductively and syllogistically, by appeal to the neutral evidence of the rules shown to apply to all things by the observation of the order of universally accessible nature and society.

A religious system frames its propositions deductively and exegetically by appeal to the privileged evidence of a corpus of truths deemed revealed by God. The difference pertains not to detail but to the fundamental facts deemed to matter. Some of those facts lie at the very surface, in the nature of the writings that express the system. These writings were not free-standing but contingent, and that in two ways. First, they served as commentaries to prior documents, the Mishnah and Scripture, for the Talmud and Midrash-compilations, respectively. Second, and more consequential, the authorships insisted upon citing Scripture-passages or Mishnah-sentences as the centerpiece of proof, on the one side, and program of discourse, on the other. But the differences that prove indicative are not merely formal. More to the point, while the Mishnah's system is steady-state and ahistorical, admitting no movement or change, the successor-system of the Yerushalmi and Midrash-compilations tells tales, speaks of change, accommodates and responds to historical moments. It formulates a theory of continuity within change, of the moral connections between generations, of the way in which one's deeds shape one's destiny—and that of the future as well. If what the framers of the Mishnah want more than anything else is to explain the order and structure of being, then their successors have rejected their generative concern. For what they, for their part, intensely desire to sort out is the currents and streams of time and change, as these flow toward an unknown ocean.

The shift from the philosophical to the religious modes of thought and media of expression—logical and rhetorical indicators, respectively—come to realization in the recasting of the generative categories of the system as well. These categories are transformed, and the transformation proved so thorough-going as to validate the characterization of the change as "counterpart-categories." The result of the formation of such counterpart-categories in the aggregate was to encompass not only the natural but also the supernatural realms of the social order. That is how philosophical thinking gave way to religious. The religious system of the Yerushalmi and associated documents sets forth the category-formation that produced in place of an economics based on prime value assigned to real wealth one that now encompassed wealth of an intangible, impalpable, and supernatural order, but valued resource nonetheless. It points toward the replacement of a politics formerly serving to legitimate and hierarchize power and differentiate among sanctions by appeal to fixed principles by one that now introduced the variable of God's valuation of the victim and the anti-political conception of the illegitimacy of worldly power.

This counterpart-politics then formed the opposite of the Mishnah's this-worldly political system altogether. In all three ways the upshot is the same: the social system, in the theory of its framers, now extends its boundaries upward to Heaven, drawing into a whole the formerly distinct, if counterpoised, realms of Israel on earth and the Heavenly court above. So if I had to specify the fundamental difference between the philosophical and the religious versions of the social order, it would fall, quite specifically,—to state with emphasis—*upon the broadening of the systemic boundaries to encompass Heaven*. The formation of counterpart-categories therefore signals not a reformation of the received system but the formation of an essentially new one.

The first fundamental point of reversal, uniting what had been divided, is the joining of economics and politics into a political economy, through the conception of *zekhut*, a term defined presently. The other point at which what the one system treated as distinct the next and connected system chose to address as one and whole is less easily discerned, since to do so we have to ask a question the framers of the Mishnah did not raise in the Mishnah at all. That concerns the character and source of virtue, specifically, the affect, upon the individual, of knowledge, specifically, knowledge of the Torah or Torah-study. To frame the question very simply, if we ask ourselves, what happens to me if I study the Torah, the answer, for the Mishnah, predictably is, my standing and status change. Torah-study and its effects form a principal systemic indicator in matters of hierarchical classification, joining the *mamzer*-disciple of sages in a mixture of opposites, for one self-evident example.

But am I changed within? In vain we look in the hundreds of chapters of the Mishnah for an answer to that question. Virtue and learning form distinct categories, a point I shall underline in the pertinent chapter, which follows, and, overall, I am not changed as to my virtue, my character and conscience, by my mastery of the Torah. And still more strikingly, if we ask, does my Torah-study affect my fate in this world and in the life to come, the Mishnah's authorship is strikingly silent about that matter too. Specifically, we find in the pages of that document no claim that studying the Torah either changes me or assures my salvation. But the separation of knowledge and the human condition is set aside, and studying the Torah deemed the source of salvation, in the successor-system. The philosophical system, with its interest in *homo hierarchicus*, proved remarkably silent about the affect of the Torah upon the inner man. The upshot is at the critical points of bonding, the received system proved flawed, in its separation of learning from virtue and legitimate power from valued resources. Why virtue joins knowledge (I call this "the gnostic Torah"), politics links to economics, in the religious system but not in the philosophical one is of course obvious. Philosophy differentiates, seeking the rules that join diverse data; religion integrates, proposing to see the whole all together and all at once, thus (for an anthropology, for example) seeing humanity whole: "in our image, after our likeness." Religion by its nature asks the questions of integration, such as the theory intended to hold together within a single boundary earth and Heaven, this world and the other, should lead us to anticipate.

The second systemic innovation is the formation of an integrated category of political economy, framed in such a way that at stake in politics and economics alike were value and resource in no way subject to order and rule, but in all ways formed out of the unpredictable resource of *zekhut*, sometimes translated as "merit," but, being a matter of not obligation but supererogatory free will, should be portrayed, I think, as "the heritage of virtue and its consequent entitlements." Between those two conceptions—the Torah as a medium of transformation, the heritage of virtue and its consequent entitlements, which can be gained for oneself and also received from one's ancestors—the received system's this-worldly boundaries were transcended, and the new system encompassed within its framework a supernatural life on earth. And appealing to these two statements of world view, way of life, and social entity, we may as a matter of fact compose a complete description of the definitive traits and indicative systemic concerns of the successor-Judaism. It remains to observe very simply: the Bavli in no way innovated in the category-formation set forth by the Yerushalmi, and, it follows, no important component of the Bavli's theological statement will have surprised the framers of the Yerushalmi's compositions and compilers of its composites.

My account of the formation of Judaism therefore may be stated in these simple stages, involving method, message, and medium:

1. THE METHOD OF PHILOSOPHY: the initial statement of the Judaism of the dual Torah took the form of a philosophical law code and set forth a philosophical system of monotheism, providing an economics, politics, and philosophy that philosophers in the Aristotelian and Middle- or Neo-Platonic traditions can have understood as philosophical (if they grasped the idiom in which the philosophical system was expressed). That is the point of my *The Economics of the Mishnah*;[9] *Rabbinic Political Theory: Religion and Politics in the Mishnah*;[10] and *Judaism as Philosophy. The Method and Message of the Mishnah*.[11]

2. THE MESSAGE OF RELIGION: through the formation of counterpart-categories to economics, politics, and philosophy, the successor-system, which came to expression in the Talmud of the Land of Israel and associated Midrash-compilations, set forth a religious system and statement of the same Judaism of the dual Torah. That

---

[9] Chicago, 1989: The University of Chicago Press.
[10] Chicago, 1991: The University of Chicago Press.
[11] Columbia, 1991: University of South Carolina Press. See also *The Making of the Mind of Judaism*. Atlanta, 1987: Scholars Press for Brown Judaic Studies, and also *The Formation of the Jewish Intellect. Making Connections and Drawing Conclusions in the Traditional System of Judaism*. Atlanta, 1988: Scholars Press for Brown Judaic Studies; and *The Philosophical Mishnah*. Atlanta, 1989: Scholars Press for Brown Judaic Studies. Volume I. *The Initial Probe;* Volume II. *The Tractates' Agenda. From Abodah Zarah to Moed Qatan;* Volume III. *The Tractates' Agenda. From Nazir to Zebahim;* and Volume IV. *The Repertoire.*

is the point of my *The Transformation of Judaism. From Philosophy to Religion.*[12]

3. THE MEDIUM OF THEOLOGY, MELDING METHOD AND MESSAGE: taking over that system and reviewing its main points, the final Talmud then restated the received body of religion as theology. That then is the point of this book, which explains how Judaism came to completion in its definitive statement when [1] the disciplines of philosophy were used to set forth the message of [2] religion so that Judaism stated [3] its theology. The Talmud that represented the Judaism of the dual Torah by joining the method of philosophy to the message of religion. In the context of Ideengeschichte, that accounts for the formation of normative Judaism.

2 THE HERMENEUTICS OF RABBINIC JUDAISM

Since the history of this Judaism is conveyed in documents, it is through the hermeneutics of those documents that the history of the formation of Judaism is best examined. That hermeneutics, as it unfolds, makes a highly coherent statement, one through which we are able to hold together and comprehend the massive corpus of documents with their facts, details about one thing and another, that all together comprise that Judaism. The hermeneutics of Rabbinic Judaism governs the explication of the two components of the Torah, the written ("the Old Testament") and the oral, which is written down in the Mishnah and other documents. To understand how Rabbinic Judaism reads any text, we have to commence with its reading of its initial text beyond Scripture, which is the Mishnah, and follow the unfolding of the hermeneutics of the oral Torah, encompassing the Mishnah and a successor-document, of Midrash, Sifra, as well as the two principal commentaries to the Mishnah, the Talmud of the Land of Israel ("Yerushalmi"), ca. 400, and the Talmud of Babylonia ("Bavli"), ca. 600.

Precisely what is at stake in an account of the hermeneutics of this Judaism—and therefore its historical formation—begins in a reliable definition of hermeneutics, that of K. M. Newton:

> The central concern of hermeneutics as it relates to the study of literature is the problem created by the fact that texts written in the past continue to exist and to be read while their authors and the historical context which produced them have passed away in time. Reading such

---

12 Champaign-Urbana, 1992: University of Illinois Press.

texts, therefore, becomes inseparable from the question of interpretation. Before the modern period hermeneutics was concerned primarily
with how scriptural texts such as the Bible should be read. Should the
Bible, for example, be seen as a text which exists in its own terms and
read accordingly or should any understanding of it be mediated by an
acceptance of the doctrines of the church?[13]

It follows that, by hermeneutics is meant "the rules of reading a text
and interpreting it." Then precisely what constitutes the understanding of a text, which is what I mean by, the rules for defining
and reading a document—text, context, matrix of meaning? Newton cites Wilhelm Dilthey's dictum, "an act of understanding constitutes what he called a 'lived experience.'" Dilthey states:

> The methodological understanding of permanently fixed life-expres-
> sions we call explication. As the life of the mind only finds its complete,
> exhaustive, and therefore, objectively comprehensible expression in
> language, explication culminates in the interpretation of the written
> records of human existence. This art is the basis of philology. The
> science of this art is hermeneutics.[14]

The hermeneutics that conveyed the rules of proper reading of the
Talmud formed out of occasional rules and conceptions a single,
demonstrably cogent statement, one of entire integrity. The
hermeneutics of all texts of Rabbinic Judaism commences with the
document, seen whole, and works backward to the components that
comprise the document, downward and backward to the individual
sentences. Any other approach takes sentences out of context or
treats them as having no context, yielding only philology; but philology is not hermeneutics, only the basis for the initial reading of
the text. We have of course to distinguish between text- and literary
criticism of the text, one of entire integrity. The agendum of
hermeneutics encompasses the issue of the author's—in theological
context, God's—original meaning in revealing the Torah and yields
the secular question, what do we think the original writer or com-
piler of a given document meant by saying things in one way,
rather than in some other, and how does a single program of
thought and expression govern the document as a whole. Setting
forth the explication of how the patterned language of successive,
connected documents instructs us on the meaning of those docu-

---

[13] K. M. Newton, *Interpreting the Text. A Critical Introduction to the Theory and Practice
of Literary Interpretation* (N.Y., 1990:Harvester/Wheatsheaf), pp. 40-41.
[14] Cited by K. M. Newton, *Interpreting the Text*, p. 42.

ments provides the methodological understanding that comprises the hermeneutics of the writing.

3 THE MISHNAH'S HERMENEUTICS

The explication of the Mishnah, as a whole and then passage by passage, depends upon the recognition that the Mishnah is made up of lists; these lists are composed of things that exhibit shared traits of an intrinsic order, e.g., they follow a common rule. They are then formed into sets of lists so as to yield the contrast with things that exhibit other traits and so follow a different rule from the one of the initial list; in the contrast between the one list and the other, we grasp the point of the lists, and the explication then takes the form of identifying lists and contrasting them; then articulating the lesson that is to be learned from the character and organization of lists. The governing hermeneutics throughout is the same: the hierarchical classification of all things, attained through showing through the comparison and contrast of lists how one thing relates to some other. That description of how the document is to be read takes account, also, of the highly formalized rhetoric of the document.[15]

List-making places on display the data of the like and the unlike and through the consequent contrast explicitly conveys the rule governing both; the necessarily-consequent hierarchization of the lists will be implicit in the contrast between the rule governing the one and that defining the other. The Mishnah therefore is set forth as a book of lists, with the implicit order, the nomothetic traits, dictating the ordinarily unstated general and encompassing rule of hierarchization.

The inner structure set forth by the hermeneutics of a logic of classification sustains the system of ordering all things in proper place and under the proper rule. The like belongs with the like and conforms to the rule governing the like, the unlike goes over to the opposite and conforms to the opposite rule. When we make lists of the like, we also know the rule governing all the items on those lists, respectively. We know that and one other thing, namely, the oppo-

---

[15] I spell out the form-critical rules of Mishnah-hermeneutics and summarize them in *A History of the Mishnaic Law of Purities*. Leiden, 1977: Brill. XXI. *The Redaction and Formulation of the Order of Purities in the Mishnah and Tosefta.*

site rule, governing all items sufficiently like to belong on those lists, but sufficiently unlike to be placed on other lists. That rigorously philosophical logic of analysis, comparison and contrast, served because it was the only logic that could serve a system that proposed to make the statement concerning order and right array that the Mishnah's authorship wished to set forth.

The hermeneutics I have described is illustrated in the following passage, drawn from Mishnah-tractate Sanhedrin Chapter Two, in which the authorship wishes to say that Israel has two heads, one of state, the other of church (cult), the king and the high priest, respectively, and that these two offices are nearly wholly congruent with one another, with a few differences based on the particular traits of each. Broadly speaking, therefore, our exercise is one of setting forth the genus and the species. This will permit us to hierarchize the two species and tell us which is the more important. The genus is head of holy Israel. The species are king and high priest. Here are the traits in common and those not shared, and the exercise is fully exposed for what it is, an inquiry into the rules that govern, the points of regularity and order, in this minor matter, of political structure. My outline makes the point important in this setting; I abbreviate the passage and give only the operative elements.

Mishnah-tractate Sanhedrin Chapter Two

1. The rules of the high priest: subject to the law, marital rites, conduct in bereavement

   2:1 A. A high priest judges, and [others] judge him;
        B. gives testimony, and [others] give testimony about him;
        C. performs the rite of removing the shoe [Deut. 25:7-9], and [others] perform the rite of removing the shoe with his wife.
        D. [Others] enter levirate marriage with his wife, but he does not enter into levirate marriage,
        E. because he is prohibited to marry a widow....

2. The rules of the king: not subject to the law, marital rites, conduct in bereavement

   2:2 A. The king does not judge, and [others] do not judge him;
        B. does not give testimony, and [others] do not give testimony about him;
        C. does not perform the rite of removing the shoe, and others do not perform the rite of removing the shoe with his wife;
        D. does not enter into levirate marriage, nor [do his brother] enter levirate marriage with his wife.

E. R. Judah says, "If he wanted to perform the rite of removing the shoe or to enter into levirate marriage, his memory is a blessing."

F. They said to him, "They pay no attention to him [if he expressed the wish to do so]."

G. [Others] do not marry his widow.

H. R. Judah says, "A king may marry the widow of a king.

I. "For so we find in the case of David, that he married the widow of Saul,

J. "For it is said, '*And I gave you your master's house and your master's wives into your embrace*' (II Sam. 12:8)"...

3. Special rules pertinent to the king because of his calling

2:4 A. [The king] calls out [the army to wage] a war fought by choice on the instructions of a court of seventy-one....

This truncated abstract shows the facts of the case. The hermeneutics requires the explication of the text through recognizing the taxonomy, that is, a study of the genus, national leader, and its two species, [1] king, [2] high priest: how are they alike, how are they not alike, and what accounts for the differences.

The premise is that the two classes of national leaders are alike and follow the same rule, except where they differ and follow the opposite rule from one another. But that premise also is subject to the proof effected by the survey of the data consisting of concrete rules, those systemically inert facts that here come to life for the purposes of establishing a proposition. By itself, the fact that, e.g., others may not ride on his horse, bears the burden of no systemic proposition. In the context of an argument constructed for nomothetic, taxonomic purposes, the same fact is active and weighty.

The Mishnah's hermeneutics, directing our attention to the traits of things and their classification and the hierarchical relationship between classifications of things, underscored the autonomy of the document. The original intent of its authors clear was to set forth a statement of monotheism in the form of a demonstration through natural history: all things rise to the One, above; all things derive and descend from the One, above. When, in ca. A. D. 200, the Mishnah reached closure and was received and adopted as law by the state-sanctioned Jewish governments in both the Roman empire, in the land of Israel, and Iran, in Babylonia, respectively, the function and character of the document precipitated a considerable crisis. Politically and theologically presented as the foundation for the everyday administration of the affairs of Jewry, the Mishnah ignored the politics of the sponsoring regimes. Since Jews generally accepted the authority of Moses at Sinai, failure to claim for the document a clear and explicit relationship to the Torah of Moses defined that acute issue. Why should people accept as authoritative the rulings of this piece of writing? Omitting reference to a a theological, as much as to a political myth, the authorship of the Mishnah also failed to signal the relationship between their document and Scripture. Since, for all Judaisms, Hebrew Scriptures in general, and the Pentateuch, in particular, represented God's will for Israel, silence on that matter provoked considerable response. Several successor-documents, exemplified by Sifra, formulated in response to the Mishnah, and the two Talmuds, set forth as commentaries to the Mishnah, then formulated their hermeneutics around the problem represented by the Mishnah's free-standing character.

Laws issued to define what people were supposed to do could not stand by themselves; they had to receive the imprimatur of Heaven, that is, they had to be given the status of revelation. That theological premise dictated the problematic addressed by the hermeneutics formulated for each of the legal documents of Rabbinic Judaism. Until the Mishnah, that had ordinarily meant, documents had to be set into relationship to Scripture. Accordingly, to make its way in Israelite life, the Mishnah as a constitution and code demanded for itself a theory of beginnings at (or in relation to) Sinai, with Moses, from God. The solution to the problem was ultimately set forth in the myth of the dual Torah, oral in addition to the written, of which the Mishnah formed the initial writing down.

But when it came forth, the character of the Mishnah itself hardly won confidence that, on the face of it, the document formed part of, or derived from, the revelation to Moses at Sinai. It was originally published through oral formulation and oral transmission, that is, in the medium of memorization. It is formulated in mnemonic patterns. But it had been in the medium of writing that, in the view of all of Israel until about A.D. 200, God had been understood to reveal the divine word and will. The Torah was a written book. People who claimed to receive further messages from God usually wrote them down. They had three choices in securing acceptance of their account. All three involved linking the new to the old.

In claiming to hand on revelation, they could, first, sign their books with the names of biblical heroes. Second, they could imitate the style of biblical Hebrew. Third, they could present an exegesis of existing written verses, validating their ideas by supplying proof texts for them. From the closure of the Torah literature in the time of Ezra, circa 450 B.C. to the time of the Mishnah, nearly seven hundred years later, we do not have a single book alleged to be holy and at the same time standing wholly out of relationship to the Holy Scriptures of ancient Israel. The Pseudepigraphic writings fall into the first category, the Essene writings at Qumran into the second and third. We may point also to the Gospels, which take as a principal problem demonstrating how Jesus had fulfilled the prophetic promises of the Old Testament and in other ways carried forward and even embodied Israel's Scripture.

Insofar as a piece of Jewish writing did not situate itself in relationship to Scripture, its author laid no claim to present a holy book to holy Israel. The contrast between Jubilees and the Testaments of the Patriarchs, with their constant and close harping on biblical matters, and the several books of Maccabees, shows the differences. The former claim to present God's revealed truth, the latter, history. So a book was holy because in style, in authorship, or in (alleged) origin it continued Scripture, finding a place therefore (at least in the author's mind) within the canon, or because it provided an exposition on Scripture's meaning. But the Mishnah made no such claim. It entirely ignored the style of biblical Hebrew, speaking in a quite different kind of Hebrew altogether. It is silent on its authorship through its sixty-two tractates (the claims of Abot, ca. 250, of course are post facto). In any event, nowhere does the Mishnah contain the claim that God had inspired the authors of the document. These are not given biblical names and certainly are not alleged to have been biblical saints. Most of the book's named authorities flourished within the same century as its anonymous arrangers and redactors, not in remote antiquity. Above all, the Mishnah contains scarcely a handful of exegeses of Scripture. These, where they occur, play a trivial and tangential role. So here is the problem of the Mishnah: different from Scripture in language and style, indifferent to the claim of authorship by a biblical hero or divine inspiration, stunningly aloof from allusion to verses of Scripture for nearly the whole of its discourse—yet authoritative for Israel.

4 SIFRA'S CRITIQUE OF THE MISHNAH'S HERMENEUTICS

The authorship of Sifra, ca. 300, undertook a vast polemic against the logic of classification that forms the foundation of the system of the Mishnah. This they did two ways. The first, and less important, was to demonstrate that the Mishnah's rules required exegetical foundations. That solved the formal problem of the Mishnah's failure to link its statements in a systematic way to verses of Scripture. The second, and paramount way was to attack the very logic by which the Mishnah's authorship developed its points. The recurrent principle of the reading of the Mishnah set forth by the authorship of Sifra insisted that the Mishnah's hermeneutics—systematic classification—does not work, because there is no genus, but only species. Therefore the Mishnah's Listenwissenschaft, its insistence that things are either like one another, therefore follow the same rule, or opposite to one another, therefore follow the opposite rule—these fundamental building blocks of Mishnaic thought prove deeply flawed. For if nothing is ever really like something else, then we cannot classify different things together, as the same thing. And, it follows, we also can make no lists of things that, whether in a polythetic or a monothetic framework, follow the same rule and therefore generate a generalization. Since, as we shall now see, the logic of the Mishnah begins with the premise that diverse species form a single genus, so can be subjected to comparison and contrast, that dogged insistence, time and again, upon the incomparability of species, forms a fundamental critique of the practical reason of the Mishnah.

The authors of Sifra mount a two-pronged polemic against the Mishnah, one a mere feint, the other the main attack.

[1] The authorship of Sifra commonly invokes the exact language of the Mishnah or the Tosefta, asks whether the position presented in that language, lacking all proof-texts drawn from Scripture, is not a matter of mere logic, and proves that it is not. That shows that what is required is law resting on scriptural proof.

[2] The authorship of Sifra systematically demonstrates the futility of the logic of *Listenwissenschaft*, classification or taxonomy, comparison and contrast, and consequent hierarchization. This it does in a very simple way. It shows that species that look as though they form a common genus do not in fact form such a genus. Therefore it is not possible to compare and contrast two species to find the law common to the two of them, if they compare, or the law that differentiates one from the other, if they contrast.

To see how this second principle of explicating the Mishnah accomplishes its program, we examine Sifra XVIII:II.1,[16] a hand-

---

[16] For the translation and interpretation of the document, see my *Sifra. An Analytical Translation*. Atlanta, 1988: Scholars Press for Brown Judaic Studies. I. *Introduction* and *Vayyiqra Dibura Denedabah* and *Vayiqqra Dibura Dehobah*. II. *Sav, Shemini, Tazria, Negaim, Mesora*, and *Zabim*. III. *Aharé Mot, Qedoshim, Emor, Behar*, and

some demonstration, with numerous counterparts throughout Sifra, of the impossibility of relying upon the intrinsic traits of things; these yield ambiguous results; only Scripture provides indubitable taxa:

XVIII:II.1

A. "The priest shall scoop out of it a handful:"
B. Is the rule that a single handful suffices not only for a single tenth ephah of the offering, but a single handful also suffices for sixty tenth ephahs?
C. Or is the rule that a single handful serves only a single tenth ephah, while there must be sixty handfuls taken up out of sixty tenth ephahs?
D. Lo, I reason as follows:

We have now to find out which classification covers our case; then the rule governing that classification obviously will pertain. The solution is to invoke the rules governing the classification of a given action, in the theory that the like follows the like, the unlike, the opposite. Hence if we establish that a given taxon encompasses both actions, we also know the rule governing them both. Everything therefore depends on proving that both actions fall into the same classification. But if we cannot show that fact, then we have no rule at all.

E. The meal offering requires the taking up of a handful, and it also requires frankincense. Just as in the case of frankincense, a single handful serves for a single tenth ephah, and a single handful serves also for sixty tenth-ephahs, so in the case of the taking up of the handful, a single handful serves for one tenth ephah, and a single handful serves for sixty tenth ephahs.
F. Or try taking this route:
G. The meal offering requires the taking up of a handful, an it also requires oil. Just as in the case of the oil, a single log of oil serves for a single tenth ephah, while sixty logs of oil are required for sixty tenth ephahs, so in the case of a handful, the taking up of a handful serves a single tenth ephah, while for sixty tenth ephahs, there must be sixty taking ups of handfuls.
H. Let us then see to the correct analogy:
I. We should establish an analogy from something which is wholly offered up on the altar fire to something that is wholly offered up on the altar fire, but oil should not then enter the picture, since it is not wholly burned up on the altar fire.

Behuqotai; Uniting the Dual Torah: Sifra and the Problem of the Mishnah. Cambridge and New York, 1989: Cambridge University Press; and *Sifra in Perspective: The Documentary Comparison of the Midrashim of Ancient Judaism* Atlanta, 1988: Scholars Press for Brown Judaic Studies.

J.   Or take this route:
K.   We should establish an analogy from something in which the
     smaller portion is indispensable to the validity of the entire portion
     [for instance, if any of the required fine flour or oil is lacking, the
     entire meal offering is null], but let us not propose proof from the
     example of frankincense, in which the lack of a smaller portion of
     the whole is not indispensable to the validity of the entire portion.
L.   [Accordingly, we appeal to Scripture to settle matters, as it does
     when it says:] "The priest shall scoop out of it a handful:"
M.   It is the rule that a single handful suffices not only for a single
     tenth ephah of the offering, but a single handful also suffices for
     sixty tenth ephahs.

This elegant exercise once more proves the falsity of appealing to
classification on the sole basis of the intrinsic traits of things for
settling a moot point, because taxonomy resting solely on the classification of the traits of things, and ignoring the Torah's classifications, yields contradictory results. Natural history is not possible;
only the Torah's classification, brought into relationship with natural history, yields reliable philosophy. That is the power of L, which
yields M; the hermeneutics of Sifra then is formed on the principle
of the critique of the taxonomy of natural history, insisting on the
taxonomy of the Torah as the corrective.

Conducting a sustained and brilliant polemic against the
Mishnah, the authorship of Sifra presents, in a systemic and orderly
way, an amazing, subtle demonstration that there is no such thing
as a genus, but only species. Then, it follows for our authorship,
Scripture serves as the sole source for rules governing otherwise
incomprehensible, because incomparable, species. A critical corollary is that the Mishnah not only rests upon false logic, but in
failing to tie its propositions to Scripture, its authorship has set the
law of the Torah upon unreliable foundations. The framers of Sifra
then correct the errors of logic, on the one side, and set forth solid
foundations in revelation, there alone, on the other. All of this they
do while working their way through what will seem, on the surface,
somewhat remote facts indeed.

Sifra's authorship proceeds to set forth the dual Torah as a single, cogent statement, doing so by reading the Mishnah into Scripture not merely for proposition but for expression of proposition.
On the surface that decision represented a literary and hermeneutical, not merely a theological, judgment. But within the deep
structure of thought, it was far more than a matter of merely how to
select and organize propositions. Presenting the two Torahs in a
single statement constituted an experiment in logic. It was a study
of that logic, in particular, that made cogent thought possible, and

that transformed facts into propositions, and propositions into judgments concerning the more, or the less, consequential. While the
Mishnah's other apologists wrote the written Torah into the
Mishnah, Sifra's authorship formed a hermeneutics that made it
possible for them to write the oral Torah—the Mishnah—into
Scripture. They took the position that the Mishnah is wholly dependent upon Scripture and authoritative, in the status (*but not the
classification!*) of the Torah, because of that dependency. Whatever is
of worth in the Mishnah can be shown to derive directly from
Scripture. So the Mishnah was represented as deemed distinct
from, and subordinate to, Scripture. This position is expressed in
an obvious way.

That is why, for its hermeneutical principle, which explains the
formation of most of the document's compositions, Sifra's authorship conducts a sustained polemic against the failure of the
Mishnah to cite Scripture very much or systematically to link its
ideas to Scripture through the medium of formal demonstration by
exegesis. Sifra's rhetorical exegesis follows a standard redactional
form. Scripture will be cited. Then a statement will be made about
its meaning, or a statement of law correlative to that Scripture will
be given. That statement sometimes cites the Mishnah, often verba-
tim. Finally, the author of Sifra invariably states, "Now is that not
(merely) logical?" And the point of that statement will be, Can this
position not be gained through the working of mere logic, based
upon facts supplied (to be sure) by Scripture?

The thrust of Sifra's authorship's attack on the Mishnah's taxonomic logic is readily discerned. Time and again, we can easily
demonstrate, things have so many and such diverse and contradictory indicative traits that, comparing one thing to something else,
we can always distinguish one species from another. Even though
we find something in common, we also can discern some other trait
characteristic of one thing but not the other. Consequently, we also
can show that the hierarchical logic on which we rely, the argument
a fortiori or *qol vehomer*, will not serve. For if on the basis of one set of
traits which yield a given classification, we place into hierarchical
order two or more items, on the basis of a different set of traits, we
have either a different classification altogether, or, much more
commonly, simply a different hierarchy. The attack on the way in
which the Mishnah's authorship has done its work appeals to not
merely the limitations of classification solely on the basis of traits of
things. The more telling argument addresses what is, to *Listenwissenschaft*, the source of power and compelling proof: hierarchization.
That is why, throughout, we must designate the Mishnah's mode of

Listenwissenschaft a logic of hierarchical classification. Things are not merely like or unlike, therefore following one rule or its opposite. Things also are weightier or less weighty, and that particular point of likeness of difference generates the logical force of *Listenwissenschaft*.

Because of Scripture's provision of taxa, we are able properly to undertake the science of *Listenwissenschaft*, including hierarchical classification. What can we do because we appeal to Scripture, which we cannot do if we do not rely on Scripture? It is to establish the possibility of polythetic classification. We can appeal to shared traits of otherwise distinct taxa and so transform species into a common genus for a given purpose. Only Scripture makes that initiative feasible, so our authorship maintains. What is at stake? It is the possibility of doing precisely what the framers of the Mishnah wish to do. That is to join together masses of diverse data into a single, encompassing statement, to show the rule that inheres in diverse cases. In what follows, we shall see an enormous, coherent, and beautifully articulated exercise in the comparison and contrast of many things of a single genus. The whole holds together, because Scripture makes possible the statement of all things within a single rule. That is, as we have noted, precisely what the framers of the Mishnah proposed to accomplish. Our authorship maintains that only by appeal to The Torah is this fete of learning possible. If, then, we wish to understand all things all together and all at once under a single encompassing rule, we had best revert to the (written) Torah, with its account of the rightful names, positions, and order, imputed to all things. The premise of hermeneutics—explication of the document whole, then in its parts—is the priority of the written over the oral Torah.

5 THE TALMUD OF THE LAND OF ISRAEL AND THE HERMENEUTICS OF THE MISHNAH

The next stage in the unfolding of the hermeneutics of rabbinic literature is marked by the provision, for the Mishnah, of a systematic commentary. This is the contribution of the authors of the compositions and the compilers of the composites that form the Talmud of the Land of Israel.[17] What the framers of the first Tal-

---

[17] For the distinction between composition and composite and how it explains the character of both Talmuds (and most Midrash-compilations, only Sifra being nearly wholly a composition), see my *The Rules of Composition of the Talmud of Babylonia. The Cogency of the Bavli's Composite.* Atlanta, 1991: Scholars Press for South Florida Studies in the History of Judaism.

mud accomplished was not the invention of the conception of a talmud, meaning, a sustained, systemic amplification of passages of the Mishnah and other teachings accorded the status of Tannaite authority. That had already been accomplished by whoever compiled the Tosefta, ca. 200-300, which laid out the Mishnah alongside supplementary teachings that amplified or enlarged its rules.[18] The notion of a talmud as a source of information was thus established; but information was left inert. What the first Talmud contributed was the definition of a talmud in which received facts ("traditions") were treated as active and consequential, requiring analysis and deep thought.

In first Talmud's primary point of interest is the demonstration that the oral Torah, the Mishnah, rests upon the written Torah; the two components of the Torah form a single revelation, with the oral part inextricably bound to the written, and that demonstration marks the work of Mishnah-commentary as not only theological in general—defining the Torah— but doctrinal in a very particular way. That polemic will define the both Talmuds' hermeneutics: how they interpret the received text, and what they choose for the center of their own statement as well. A second hermeneutical principle concerns the perfection of the Mishnah and the laws of the Torah contained therein, both Talmuds' writers concurring that inconsistency and disharmony would flaw the Torah and must be shown not to occur therein.

Before proceeding, let me give a single example of the character of Mishnah-exegesis found in both Talmuds. In this way we see how both Talmuds frame a hermeneutics centered upon the interpretation of paragraphs of the Mishnah, line by line. The intent of the hermeneutics—again formed out of a theology of the dual Torah—is to prove that the Mishnah depends upon Scripture and that it is flawless. The only narrowly-literary critical component of the Talmuds' commentary to the Mishnah concerns the correct wording of passages, but that rapidly shades over into an inquiry into principles of law. So the hermeneutics that forms the commentary-program finds its generative problematic in the myth of the dual Torah.

My illustration derives from both Talmud's reading of a brief passage of Mishnah-tractate Makkot. The unity of purpose— Mishnah-commentary— and the identity of proposition—the unity

---

[18] See *The Bavli That Might Have Been: The Tosefta's Theory of Mishnah-Commentary Compared with that of the Babylonian Talmud*. Atlanta, 1990: Scholars Press for South Florida Studies in the History of Judaism.

of the Torah, its perfection—should not obscure the simple fact that the two Talmuds do not intersect except at the Mishnah and at Scripture. The Talmuds bear each its own message, but both ask the same questions. Mishnah- and Tosefta-passages in both Talmuds are in bold face, Bavli's use of Aramaic in italics, Hebrew in regular type. Bavli page references are in square brackets; Yerushalmi-references accord with the system of my *Talmud of the Land of Israel. A Preliminary Translation and Explanation* (Chicago, 1983-1993: University of Chicago Press, I-XXXV.We begin with the Yerushalmi:

Yerushalmi to Makkot 1:8=B. to Makkot 1:10
[A] He whose trial ended and who fled and was brought back before the same court—
[B] they do not reverse the judgment concerning him [and retry him].
[C] In any situation in which two ger up and say, "We testify concerning Mr. So-and-so that his trial ended in the court of such-and-such, with Mr. So-and-so and Mr. So-and-so as the witnesses against him,"
[D] lo, this one is put to death.
[E] [Trial before] a Sanhedrin applies both in the Land and abroad.
[F] A Sanhedrin which imposes the death penalty once in seven years is called murderous.
[G] R. Eleazar b. Azariah says, "Once in seventy years. "
[H] R. Tarfon and R. Aqiba say, "If we were on a Sanhedrin, no one would ever be put to death. "
[I] Rabban Simeon b. Gamaliel says, "So they would multiply the number of murderers in Israel. "
[I.A] [Trial before a] Sanhedrin applies both in the Land and abroad [M. 1:8E],
[B] as it is written, "And these things shall be for a statute and ordinance to you throughout your generations in all your dwellings" (Num. 35:29).
[C] And why does Scripture say, "You shall appoint judges and officers in all your towns [which the Lord your God gives you]" (Deut. 16:18) In the towns of the Land of Israel.
[D] The meaning is that in the towns of Israel they set up judges in every town, but abroad they do so only by districts.
[E] It was taught: R. Dosetai b. R. Yannai says, "It is a religious requirement for each tribe to judge its own tribe, as it is said, 'You shall appoint *judges* and officers in all your towns which the Lord your God gives you, according to your tribes' " (Deut. 16:18).
[II.A] Rabban Simeon b. Gamaliel taught, "Those declared liable to the death penalty who fled from the Land abroad—they put them to death forthwith [upon recapture].
[B] "If they fled from abroad to the Land, they do not put them to death forthwith, but they undertake a trial *de novo.* "

The Yerushalmi wants the scriptural proof for the Mishnah's allegation; it then harmonizes the implications at hand. Since the proof text, I.B, yields results contrary to the assumed implications of that at C, D must indicate otherwise. Unit II is an independent saying, generally relevant to M. 1:8E. It is a simple paraphrase and clarification.

Since both Talmuds' read the Mishnah in much the same way, let us first examine their common hermeneutics, and then distinguish the second Talmud from the first. The two Talmuds resemble one another, since both to begin with comment on the same prior text, the Mishnah. Both take up a few sentences of that prior text and paraphrase and analyze them. Both ask the same questions, e.g., clarifying the language of the Mishnah, identifying the scriptural foundations of the Mishnah's rules, comparing the Mishnah's rules with those of the Tosefta or other Tannaite status. They furthermore compare because they organize their materials in the same way. They moreover take up pretty much the same topical agenda, in common selecting some divisions of the Mishnah and ignoring others, agreeing in particular to treat the Mishnah's divisions of Appointed Times, Women, and Damages. Both documents moreover are made up of already-available compositions and composites, which we may identify, in each document, by reference to the same literary traits or indications of completion prior to inclusion in the Talmuds.[19] So they exhibit traits of shared literary policy.

In both, moreover, we find not only the same received document, the Mishnah, but also citations of, and allusions to, the same supplementary collection to the Mishnah, the Tosefta, and also a further kind of saying, one bearing the marks of formalization and memorization that serve to classify it as authoritative ("Tannaite') but external to the composition of the Mishnah and the compilation of the Tosefta. The points of coincidence are more than formal, therefore, since both Talmuds cite the same Mishnah-tractates, at some points the same Tosefta-passages, and also, from time to time, the same external Tannaite formulations. When, therefore, we come to their points of difference, beginning

---

[19] But I hasten to add, my sustained comparison of the two Talmuds reveals remarkably little evidence that the framers of the two documents drew upon a common core of available, already-formulated compositions, that is, a counterpart to "Q"; and there is no evidence whatsoever that they shared a common core of completed composites. Where there is a corpus of shared materials, it is in the Mishnah and other sayings given Tannaite status and also in some, very few, statements of authorities who flourished in the third century; these sayings, when occurring in both Talmuds, tend to be utilized in the second Talmud in a manner unlike their use in the first. This is spelled out in *The Bavli's Unique Voice*.

with the fact that the second Talmud scarcely intersects with the first except at the formal points of juncture just now listed, we shall find all the more striking the fact that the second Talmud goes its own way and forms a writing that, while formally like the first Talmud, substantively differs from it, beginning, middle, and end.

What is talmudic about the two Talmuds is their unique hermeneutics, which is a critical, systematic application of applied reason and practical logic, moving from a point starting with a proposition through argument and evidence, met head-on by contrary proposition, with its argument and evidence, exchanging balanced responses, each to the position, argument, and evidence of the other, onward and for so long as it takes fully to expose every possibility of proposition, argument, and evidence—(ordinarily) ending with a firm (and occasionally even an articulated) conclusion.

To develop a taxonomy of the units of discourse contained equally within either of the two Talmuds, I answer the question, what kinds of units of discourse do the documents exhibit in common and how are they arranged? Both Talmuds invariably do to the Mishnah one of these four things:

(1) text criticism;
(2) exegesis of the meaning of the Mishnah, including glosses and amplifications;
(3) addition of Scriptural proof texts of the Mishnah's central propositions; and
(4) harmonization of one Mishnah passage with another such passage or with a statement of Tosefta.

The first two of these four procedures remain wholly within the narrow frame of the Mishnah passage subject to discussion. Therefore, in the natural order of things, what the two Talmuds will find interesting in a given Mishnah-passage will respond to the same facts and commonly will do so in much the same way. The second pair take an essentially independent stance vis-a-vis the Mishnah pericope at hand. That is where the Talmuds, engaged in a theological enterprise within the definition offered here, will take, each its own path. And that is precisely the point at which theological, as distinct from literary-critical, considerations enter in. Where the Talmuds are talmudic, it is in the theological program of systematic recapitulation of cases, formulation of propositions of an abstract character, expression of theology through a prevailing hermeneutics, not merely exposition of a passage through a constant exegetical plan.

The Talmuds do not merely clarify the Mishnah; both of them in point of fact re-present the Torah—a very different thing. We understand that fact when we remember what the Mishnah looks like as it stands on its own.[20] The writers of the Mishnah created a coherent document, with a topical program formed in accord with the logical order dictated by the characteristics of a given topic, and with a set of highly distinctive formulary and formal traits as well. But these are obscured when the document is taken apart into bits and pieces and reconstituted in the way in which the Talmuds do. The re-definition of the Torah accomplished by the Talmuds therefore represented a vast revision of the initial writing down of the oral component of the Torah—a point at which the hermeneutics shaded over into a profoundly theological activity.

For now the Mishnah is read by the Talmuds as a composite of discrete and essentially autonomous rules, a set of atoms, not an integrated molecule, so to speak. In so doing, the most striking formal traits of the Mishnah are obliterated. More important, the Mishnah as a whole and complete statement of a viewpoint no longer exists. Its propositions are reduced to details. But what is offered in stead? The answer is, a statement that, on occasion, recasts details in generalizations encompassing a wide variety of other details across the gaps between one tractate and another. This immensely creative and imaginative approach to the Mishnah vastly expands the range of discourse. But the consequence is to deny to the Mishnah both its own mode of speech and its distinctive and coherent message. So the two Talmuds formulate their own hermeneutics, to convey their theological system: [1] defining the Torah and [2] demonstrating its perfection and comprehensive character: unity, harmony, lineal origin from Sinai.

Both authorships take an independent stance when facing the Mishnah, making choices, reaching decisions of their own. Both Talmuds' framers deal with Mishnah-tractates of their own choice, and neither provides a Talmud to the entirety of the Mishnah. What the Mishnah therefore contributed to the Talmuds was not received in a spirit of humble acceptance by the sages who produced either of the two Talmuds. Important choices were made about what to treat, hence what to ignore. The exegetical mode of reception did not have to obscure the main lines of the Mishnah's

---

[20] My account of the Mishnah in its own terms is in my *History of the Mishnaic Law* (Leiden, 1974-1986: E. J. Brill), in forty-three volumes, and in *Judaism. The Evidence of the Mishnah*. Chicago, 1981: University of Chicago Press. Second printing, 1985. Third printing, 1986. Second edition, augmented: Atlanta, 1987: Scholars Press for Brown Judaic Studies.

system. But it surely did so. The discrete reading of sentences, or, at most, paragraphs, denying all context, avoiding all larger generalizations except for those transcending the specific lines of tractates this approach need not have involved the utter reversal of the paramount and definitive elements of the Mishnah's whole and integrated world view (its "Judaism"). But doing these things did facilitate the revision of the whole into a quite different pattern.

The undifferentiated effort to associate diverse Mishnah laws with Scripture is to be viewed together with the systematic breakup of the Mishnah into its diverse laws. The two quite separate activities produce a single effect in both Talmuds. They permit the Talmuds to represent the state of affairs pretty much as the framers of the Talmuds wish to do. Theology as a creative venture here determines to (re)define the Torah. And how is this done? Everything is shown to be continuous: Scripture, Mishnah, the Tosefta where cited, the authoritative sayings labeled Tannaite where used, ending in—the Talmud itself (whichever Talmud we examine, the effect being the same)! Then all things, as now shaped by the rabbis of the Talmud(s), have the standing of Scripture and represent the authority of Moses (now called "our rabbi"). Accordingly, once the Mishnah enters either of the two Talmuds it nowhere emerges intact. It is wholly preserved, but in bits and pieces, shaped and twisted in whatever ways the Talmuds wish. The Torah now forms a single, continuous statement. And that is the work of the first Talmud, not only of the second.

The question has now to be asked, when do the Talmuds speak for themselves not for the Mishnah? Second, what sorts of units of discourse contain such passages that bear what is "Talmudic" in the two Talmuds? These two questions produce the same answers for both Talmuds, which once more validates comparing and therefore also contrasting them.

1. THEORETICAL QUESTIONS OF LAW NOT ASSOCIATED WITH A PARTICULAR PASSAGE OF THE MISHNAH. In the first of the two Talmuds there is some tendency, and in the second, a very marked tendency, to move beyond the legal boundaries set by the Mishnah's rules themselves. More general inquiries are taken up. These of course remain within the framework of the topic of one tractate or another, although there are some larger modes of thought characteristic of more than a single tractate.

2. EXEGESIS OF SCRIPTURE SEPARATE FROM THE MISHNAH. It is under this rubric that we find the most important instances in which the Talmuds present materials essentially independent of the Mishnah.

3. Historical statements. The Talmud contains a fair number of statements that something happened, or narratives about how something happened. While many of these are replete with biblical quotations, in general they do not provide exegesis of Scripture, which serves merely as illustration or reference point.

4. Stories about, and rules for, sages and disciples, separate from discussion of a passage of the Mishnah. The Mishnah contains a tiny number of tales about rabbis. These serve principally as precedents for, or illustrations of, rules.

The Talmuds by contrast contain a sizable number of stories about sages and their relationships to other people. When the Talmuds present us with ideas or expressions of a world related to, but fundamentally separate from, that of the Mishnah, that is, when the Talmuds wish to say something other than what the Mishnah says and means, they will take up one of two modes of discourse. Either we find exegesis of biblical passages, with the value system of the rabbis read into the Scriptural tales; or we are told stories about holy men and paradigmatic events, once again through tales told in such a way that a didactic and paranaetic purpose is served.

The Talmuds are composites of three kinds of materials: [1] exegeses of the Mishnah (and other materials classified as authoritative, that is, Tannäite), [2] exegeses of Scripture, and [3] accounts of the men who provide both.[21] That classification corresponds to the media by which the Torah of Sinai is transmitted, in writing, orally, and in the persons of disciples of sages. Both Talmuds then constitute elaborate reworkings of the two antecedent documents: the Mishnah, lacking much reference to Scripture, and the Scripture itself. The Talmuds bring the two together into a synthesis of their compilers' own making, both in reading Scripture into Mishnah, and in reading Scripture alongside of, and separate from, Mishnah.

The hermeneutics of the two Talmuds exhibits integrity to the rules of the language of the Mishnah; that is, I cannot point to a single instance in which the Talmudic exegetes in either Talmud appear to twist and turn the language and message of a passage, attempting to make the words mean something other than what they appear to say anyhow. While the Talmuds follow a coherent hermeneutics that is very much their own, there is no exegetical

---

[21] I have dwelt on the stories about sages, where and how they figure and form part of the larger canon and the medium for its systemic statement, in, among other works, *Judaism and Story: The Evidence of The Fathers According to Rabbi Nathan.* Chicago, 1992: University of Chicago Press; and Why *No Gospels in Talmudic Judaism?* Atlanta, 1988: Scholars Press for Brown Judaic Studies.

program revealed in the Talmuds' reading of the Mishnah other than that defined, to begin with, by the language and conceptions of one Mishnah passage or another.[22] Nonetheless, the Talmuds do follow a hermeneutics quite distinct from the Mishnah's.

First, the Mishnah was set forth by Rabbi (that is, Judah the Patriarch, whose name stands for the people who wrote up the Mishnah) whole and complete, a profoundly unified, harmonious document. The Talmud insists upon obliterating the marks of coherence. It treats in bits and pieces what was originally meant to speak whole. That simple fact constitutes what is original, stunningly new and, by definition, Talmudic.

Second, the Mishnah, also by definition, delivered its message in the way chosen by Rabbi. That is to say, by producing the document as he did, Rabbi left no space for the very enterprises of episodic exegesis undertaken so brilliantly by his immediate continuators and heirs.

True, a rather limited process of explanation and gloss of words and phrases, accompanied by a systematic inquiry into the wording of one passage or another, got underway, probably at the very moment, and within the very process, of the Mishnah's closure. But insofar as the larger messages and meanings of the document are conveyed in the ways Rabbi chose through formalization of language, through contrasts, through successive instances of the same~ normally unspecified, general proposition, e.g.the need for exegesis was surely not generated by Rabbi's own program for the Mishnah. Quite to the contrary, Rabbi chose for his Mishnah a mode of expression and defined for the document a large-scale structure and organization, which, by definition, were meant to stand firm and autonomous. Rabbi's Mishnah speaks clearly and for itself.

For the Mishnah did not merely come to closure. At the very moment at which it was completed, the Mishnah also formed a closed system, that is, a whole, complete statement that did not require facts outside of its language and formulation, so made no provision for commentary and amplification of brief allusions, as the Talmuds' style assuredly does. The Mishnah refers to nothing beyond itself except, episodically, Scripture. That is to say, it raises no questions for on-going discussion beyond its decisive, final, descriptive statements of enduring realities and fixed relationships.

---

[22] That the second Talmud has its own hermeneutical program, as distinct from an exegetical one, of course is also the fact. I spell it out in the next section. But that the second Talmud has its own distinctive hermeneutics does not affect my contention that, in the ways specified here, the two Talmuds are identical.

The one thing that will have surprised the Mishnah's framers is the Talmuds.

The Talmuds' single irrevocable judgment is precisely opposite: this text needs a commentary. The Talmuds' first initiative is to reopen the Mishnah's closed system, almost at the moment of its completion and perfection. That at the foundations is what is Talmudic about the Talmuds: their daring assertion that the concluded and completed demanded clarification and continuation. Once that assertion was made to stick, nothing else mattered very much. The two Talmuds' message was conveyed in the very medium of the Talmud: a new language, focused upon a new grid of discourse to re-view a received writing.

If we stand back and reflect on the Mishnah's program, we recognize how different is that of the Talmuds. The Mishnah covers a broad variety of topics. The Talmuds contribute none of their own, but trawl across the entire surface of the Mishnah. The Mishnah is organized topically. The Talmuds may be broken down into discrete compositions and neatly-joined composites, none of them framed as free-standing, topical formations, all of them in one way or another depending upon the Mishnah for order and coherence. The Mishnah lays out rules and facts about a world beyond itself. The Talmuds negotiate rules and recast facts into propositions that concern the Mishnah—a different focus of discourse and perspective altogether. Continuous with the Mishnah, the two Talmuds in point of fact redirect the Mishnah not only by destroying its integrity and picking and choosing with its topical (and propositional) program, but also by forming of the detritus of the receiving writing a statement of their own. But it was not a statement that, in the end, concerned the Mishnah at all, rather, a statement about the Torah, and a statement of the Torah.

In accepting authority, in centering discourse upon the ideas of other men, in patiently listing even the names behind authoritative laws from olden times to their own day, the sages and framers of the Talmud accomplished exactly the opposite of what they apparently wished to do. They made a commentary. But they obliterated the text. They loyally explained the Mishnah. But they turned the Mishnah into something else than what it had been. They patiently hammered out chains of tradition, binding themselves to the authority of the remote and holy past. But it was, in the end, a tradition of their own design and choosing. That is, it was not tradition but a new creation. And so these Talmuds of ours, so loyal and subservient to the Mishnah of Rabbi, turn out to be less reworkings of received materials than works—each one of them—of remarkably independent judgment. The Talmuds speak humbly and sub-

serviently about received truth, always in the name only of Moses
and of sages of times past. But in the end it is truth not discovered
and demonstrated, but determined and invented and declared.

The redactional program of the men responsible for laying out
the materials of Talmuds may now be described. There is a pronounced tendency in both Talmuds to move from close reading of
the Mishnah and then Tosefta outward to more general inquiry
into the principles of a Mishnah passage and their interplay with
those of some other, superficially unrelated passage, and, finally, to
more general reflections on law not self-evidently related to the
Mishnah passage at hand or to anthologies intersecting only at a
general topic. Unlike the Mishnah, the Talmuds reveal no effort to
systematize sayings in larger constructions, or to impose a pattern
upon all individual sayings. If the Mishnah is framed to facilitate
memorization, then we must say that the Talmuds' materials are
not framed with mnemonics in mind. If the Mishnah focuses upon
subsurface relationships in syntax, the Talmud in the main looks
like notes of a discussion. These notes may serve to recreate the
larger patterns of argument and reasoning, a summary of what was
thought and perhaps also said. The Talmud preserves and expresses concrete ideas, reducing them to brief but usually accessible
and obvious statements. The Mishnah speaks of concrete things in
order to hint at abstract relationships, which rarely are brought to
the surface and fully exposed.

The Mishnah hides. The Talmuds spell out. The Mishnah hints.
The Talmuds repeat *ad nauseam*. The Mishnah is subtle, the
Talmuds obvious; the one restrained and tentative, the others
aimed at full and exhaustive expression of what is already clear.
The sages of the Mishnah rarely represent themselves as deciding
cases. Only on unusual occasions do they declare the decided law,
at best reticently spelling out what underlies their positions. The
rabbis of the Talmuds harp on who holds which opinion and how a
case is actually decided, presenting a rich corpus of precedents.
They seek to make explicit what is implicit in the law. The Mishnah
is immaterial and spiritual, the Talmud earthy and social. The
Mishnah deals in the gossamer threads of philosophical principle,
the Talmud in the coarse rope that binds this one and that one into
a social construction. The first of the two Talmuds moreover sets
aside the philosophical category-formation of the Mishnah in favor
of a deeply religious formation of counterpart-categories.[23]

---

[23] This is explained and fully spelled out in my *The Transformation of Judaism.
From Philosophy to Religion*. Champaign, 1992: University of Illinois Press. The sec-
ond Talmud then re-presents the religious system of the Yerushalmi as theology, as
I show in *Judaism States its Theology: The Talmudic Re-Presentation.*. I do not see a

The Mishnah speaks of a world in stasis, an unchanging, eternal present tense where all the tensions of chaos are resolved. The Talmuds address the real Israel in the here and now of ever-changing times, the gross matter of disorder and history. Clearly, the central traits of the Mishnah, revealed in the document at its time of closure in ca. A.D. 200, were revised and transformed into those definitive of the Talmud at its time of closure in ca. A.D. 400 for the earlier Talmud, 600 for the later. We know only that when we compare the Mishnah to the Talmuds we find in each case two intertwined documents, quite different from one another both in style and in values. Yet they are so tightly joined that the Talmud appears in the main to provide mere commentary and amplification for the Mishnah. So the two Talmuds are indistinguishable in form. But hermeneutics sets the second Talmud apart from the first.

6 THE TALMUD OF BABYLONIA: HERMENEUTICS AS THE MEDIUM OF THEOLOGY

While, as we have seen, the Bavli is like the prior Talmud in important ways, the second Talmud differs from the first because speaks in one, unique voice and takes shape out of a unique singular and economical hermeneutics; there is no other like it.[24] Quite how that

---

single important category in the Bavli that the Yerushalmi's category-formation does not encompass and set forth, and even in the setting of specific ideas, e.g., the theory of who, and what, is Israel, or the Messiah-theme, the Bavli forms a restatement of the Yerushalmi's basic notions.

[24] Claims of uniqueness of course can never be satisfactorily shown to be valid because we should have first to have examined all possible candidates of comparability. Having completed the comparison of the Bavli to the Yerushalmi (not to mention Scripture, the Mishnah, the Tosefta, and the prior Midrash-compilations, which required no sustained inquiry), I did compare the Talmud with some counterpart writings of Zoroastrianism in *Judaism and Zoroastrianism at the Dusk of Late Antiquity. How Two Ancient Faiths Wrote Down Their Great Traditions* (Atlanta, 1993; Scholars Press). For the Bavli in canonical context, see the seven-volume monograph, *The Bavli's Unique Voice. A Systematic Comparison of the Talmud of Babylonia and the Talmud of the Land of Israel*. Atlanta, 1993: Scholars Press for South Florida Studies in the History of Judaism. Volume One. *Bavli and Yerushalmi Qiddushin Chapter One Compared and Contrasted;* Volume Two. *Yerushalmi's, Bavli's, and Other Canonical Documents' Treatment of the Program of Mishnah-Tractate Sukkah Chapters One, Two, and Four Compared and Contrasted. A Reprise and Revision of The Bavli and its Sources;* Volume Three. *Bavli and Yerushalmi to Selected Mishnah-Chapters in the Division of Moed. Erubin Chapter One, and Moed Qatan Chapter Three;* Volume Four. *Bavli and Yerushalmi to Selected Mishnah-Chapters in the Division of Nashim. Gittin Chapter Five and Nedarim Chapter One. And Niddah Chapter One;* Volume Five. *Bavli and Yerushalmi to Selected Mishnah-Chapters in the Division of Neziqin. Baba Mesia Chapter One and Makkot Chapters One and Two;* Volume Six. *Bavli and Yerushalmi to a Miscellany of Mishnah-Chapters. Gittin Chapter One, Qiddushin Chapter Two, and Hagigah Chapter Three.;* and Volume Seven. *What Is Unique about the Bavli in Context? An Answer Based on Inductive Description, Analysis, and Comparison.* These remarks summarize the conclusions of that monograph in seven parts.

vast prolix (sometimes tedious) and dense writing turns out to say some few things, and to say them with such power as to impose its judgment upon an entire prior writing and also on the intellect of an entire religious world to come requires attention.

The writers of the Bavli's compositions and compilers of its composites rarely made original statements of doctrine or law. Commonly, they went over the ground of received ideas in their established formulation. What makes the Bavli unique—and definitive of the Judaism for which it speaks—is its identification of the proper medium of thought and discourse, which is the dialectical argument. It was rather through the public display of right reasoning, the exposition of argument that they made an original, and governing, statement of their own; that is why the hermeneutics provides the key to the Bavli's priority in the history of Judaism. Specifically, exposing the traits of rationality again and again in concrete exercises, the framers of the document said one thing about many things, much as, we have seen, the framers of Sifra did. But what they said gained heights of abstraction, aimed at transcendent truths formed in a lofty perspective; Sifra's hermeneutics conveyed a judgment about the proper ordering of the world, the right source of taxonomy. The Bavli's hermeneutics conveyed judgments of a considerably weightier character. By showing people how to think, then, in the context of a revealed Torah, the Bavli's framers maintained, one can also guide them to what to think: by reason of right reasoning formed into right attitudes, right thoughts lead to right deeds. In the "how" of thought, the "what" found form and substance. Hermeneutics is what contained the rationality that translated inchoate religion—rite, belief, attitude, symbol, myth, proposition and emotion alike, even in its initial theological formation—into a cogent and compelling statement about the nature of mind itself.

The demonstration is feasible because of one characteristic of the document. The Bavli is uniform, beginning to end. Different from, much more than, a haphazard compilation of episodic traditions, upon examination this Talmud shows itself to be a cogent and purposive writing. Through a single, determinate set of rhetoric devices, which themselves signal the definition of the writing and the rules of reading that writing, a single program of inquiry is brought to bear on many and diverse passages of two inherited documents, the Mishnah and Scripture. The voice is one and single because it is a voice that everywhere expresses the same limited set of sounds. It is singular because these notes are arranged in one and the same way throughout. The words ever-changing, the music forms a singular chant. Even the very study of the Bavli for ages to come conveyed that remarkable fact: it is a sung writing, never read, always recited in its own chant and song. The hermeneutics of the Bavli is aptly compared to musical notes in more than a metaphorical sense. Their writing therefore required not reading but response. That explains, also, the reason that the form of "reading" their document was singing: knowing the music, one could supply the right words; obviously, I identify the hermeneutics with that music. Right knowledge of how to decipher the script—musical notes, really—afforded access to the melody and its meaning, the music and the words. So the words written down form keys, signals to the modes of analysis.

The Talmud's statement of the Torah—oral and written, method and message alike—took a form unique in its context. All other Judaic writings (with the sole exception of the prior Talmud) made their statements whole and complete; what we see is what there is. No Midrash-compilation of antiquity requires knowledge extrinsic to that text or some other text (Scripture for instance) to yield its sense. By its distinctive formalization of speech, the Mishnah forms its own best commentary. When we know how it sends out its signals, we also can receive its messages. Other writings—The Fathers and the Fathers According to Rabbi Nathan, the Tosefta read in relationship to the Mishnah,—all contain a complete and wholly accessible (the facts being known) statement. The framers of the Bavli took a different route, one that required readers to participate in the writing of the statement that was to be made. It was a path, therefore, that would close doors of meaning to the lonely reader reading a fully exposed writing, opening them only to a conversation between master and disciple, a community of meaning formed out of the chorus, singing the text. The master sang the melody, the disciples the contrapuntal statement; the music then bore the message of the text.

For in that document the framers of the Bavli wrote down not fully exposed statements but only notes toward the formulation of a complete thought. They set down the annotated but abbreviated script—by which future masters and disciples might reconstruct for themselves the drama of inquiry and argument. I am inclined to think part of the Bavli's remarkable success lay in the space it left open for the reader to join in the writing—the recreation—of the book. What is conveyed through the instrument of sing-song—more really, the readers' sing-along—is the rhetoric, and, the rhetoric being everywhere uniform, what is opened by a protocol of rhetoric is not the case but the principle on which the case is to be decided; from principle we descend to underlying premise.

The character of the writing, not only its contents, therefore, set forth the systemic statement. The Bavli's one voice, sounding through all tractates, is the voice of exegetes of the Mishnah. The document is organized around the Mishnah, and that order is not a merely formal, but substantive. At *every* point, if the framers have chosen a passage of Mishnah-exegesis, that passage will stand at the head of all further discussion. *Every* turning point in every sustained composition and even in a large composite of compositions brings the editors back to the Mishnah, *always* read in its own order and *invariably* arranged in its own sequence. So the Bavli's authors and future readers sing together in a single way about some few things.

It follows that well-crafted and orderly rules governed the character of the sustained discourse that the writing in the Bavli sets forth. All framers of composites and editors of sequences of composites found guidance in the same limited repertoire of rules of analytical rhetoric: some few questions or procedures, directed always toward one and the same prior writing. Not only so, but a fixed order of discourse dictated that a composition of one sort, A, always come prior to a composite of another type, B. A simple logic instructed framers of composites, who sometimes also were authors of compositions, and who other times drew upon available compositions in the making of their cogent composites. So we have now to see the Bavli as entirely of a piece, cogent and coherent, made up of well-composed large-scale constructions.

The Bavli's one voice speaks in only a few, well-modulated tones: a scale of not many notes at all, comparable to our eight tone scale. But the tonal scale of the Bavli cannot sustain comparison with our musical scale, because while with our eight tones, we can produce an infinity of melodies, the Bavli's signals yielded only a few, rather monotonous ones; and that is the very success of the document in holding together a vast range of subjects within a determinate and limited hermeneutics. True, these few, monotonous melodies sometimes continue for so long a time as to produce the effect of tedium; but they do echo in the mind. In a probe I made,[25] I found that nearly 90% of the whole comprises Mishnah-commentary of various kinds. Not only so, but the variety of the types of Mishnah-commentary is limited. Cogent composites—a sequence of well-linked comments—are further devoted to Scrip-

---

[25] *The Bavli's One Voice: Types and Forms of Analytical Discourse and their Fixed Order of Appearance*. Atlanta, 1991: Scholars Press for South Florida Studies in the History of Judaism.

ture or to topics of a moral or theological character not closely tied
to the exegesis of verses of Scripture; these form in the aggregate
approximately 10% of the whole number of composites. So the
Bavli has one voice, and it is the voice of a person or persons who
propose to speak about one document and to do so in some few
ways. Let me spell out what this means.

First, we are able to classify *all* composites (among the more than
three thousand that I examined for the purpose of this description
of the document) in three principal categories: [1] exegesis and
amplification of the law of the Mishnah; [2] exegesis and exposition
of verses of, or topics in, Scripture; [3] free-standing composites
devoted to topics other than those defined by the Mishnah or Scripture. These classifications were not forced or subtle; the grounds for
making them were consistent; appeal throughout was to gross and
merely formal characteristics, not to subjective judgments of what
unstipulated consideration might underlie, or define the intention
of the framer of, a passage.

Second, with that classification in place, it is a matter of simple
fact that much more than four-fifths of all composites of the Bavli
address the Mishnah and systematically expound that document.
These composites are subject to sub-classification in two ways:
Mishnah-exegesis and speculation and abstract theorizing about the
implications of the Mishnah's statements. The former type of composite, further, is to be classified in a few and simple taxa, for
example, composites organized around [1] clarification of the statements of the Mishnah, [2] identification of the authority behind an
anonymous statement in the Mishnah, [3] scriptural foundation for
the Mishnah's rules; [4] citation and not seldom systematic exposition of the Tosefta's amplification of the Mishnah. That means that
most of the Bavli is a systematic exposition of the Mishnah. The
abstract that you read will conform to this description in the proportion and order of its comments on the Mishnah.

Third, the other fifth (or still less) of a given tractate will comprise composites that take shape around [1] Scripture or [2] themes
or topics of a generally theological or moral character. Distinguishing the latter from the former, of course, is merely formal; very
often a scriptural topic will be set forth in a theological or moral
framework, and very seldom does a composite on a topic omit all
reference to the amplification of a verse or topic of Scripture. The
proportion of a given tractate devoted to other-than-Mishnah exegesis and amplification is generally not more than 10%.

The Bavli speaks about the Mishnah in essentially a single voice,
about fundamentally few things. Its mode of speech as much as of

thought is uniform throughout. Diverse topics produce slight differentiation in modes of analysis. The same sorts of questions phrased
in the same rhetoric—a moving, or dialectical, argument, composed of questions and answers—turn out to pertain equally well to
every subject and problem. The Talmud's discourse forms a closed
system, in which people say the same thing about everything. The
fact that the Talmud speaks in a single voice supplies striking evidence for three propositions:

1. that the Talmud does speak in particular for the age in which its
   units of discourse took shape;
2. that that work was done toward the end of that long period of
   Mishnah-reception that began at the end of the second century and
   came to an end at the conclusion of the sixth century;
3. that the medium for the Talmud's message was, and could only
   have been, the hermeneutics that defined the writing and how it
   was to be read.

The hermeneutics, that is, voice of "the Talmud," authoritatively
defines the mode of analysis. The inquiry is consistent and predict-
able; one argument differs from another not in supposition but only
in detail. When individuals' positions occur, it is because what they
have to say serves the purposes of "the Talmud" and its uniform
inquiry. The inquiry is into the logic and the rational potentialities
of a passage. To these dimensions of thought, the details of place,
time, and even of an individual's philosophy, are secondary. All
details are turned toward a common core of discourse. This, I
maintain, is possible only because the document as whole takes
shape in accord with an overriding program of inquiry and comes
to expression in conformity with a single plan of rhetorical expression. Formed of compositions put together into composites, the second Talmud did not just *grow*, but rather, someone *made* it up; it is
not the outcome of an incremental and agglutinative process but of
a sustained hermeneutics that governed the work of composition
and compilation alike.

   The Bavli is a document of remarkable integrity, repeatedly insisting upon the harmony of the parts within a whole and unitary
structure of belief and behavior, we ask what the Bavli says: the one
thing that is repeated in regard to many things. To begin with, the
answer to that question requires us to see what is special about the
Bavli, which is to say, what distinguishes it from its predecessor, the
Yerushalmi. Where we can identify initiatives characteristic of the
Bavli and unusual in the Yerushalmi, there we describe the Bavli in
particular. To state the governing hermeneutics that is unique to
the second Talmud: the task of interpretation is to uncover the

integrity of the truth that God has manifested in the one and unique revelation, the Torah (oral and written). By integrity I mean not merely the result of facile harmonization but the rigorous demonstration that the Torah, at its foundations, makes a single statement, whole, complete, cogent and coherent; harmonious; unified and beyond all division. Integrity refers to a writing that is shown to be whole, complete, cogent and coherent; harmonious; unified and beyond all division.

The message of the first document of the oral Torah, the Mishnah, was the hierarchical unity of all being in the One on high. Then the right medium for that message is the Bavli on account of the character of its hermeneutics, best summarized as its quest for abstraction. Matching the Mishnah's ontology of hierarchical unity of all being is the Bavli's principle that many principles express a single one, many laws embody one governing law, which is the law behind the laws. In more secular language, the intellectual medium of the Bavli accomplishes the the transformation of jurisprudence into philosophy. How do the two documents work together to establish through many facts a single statement of the governing fact of being? The Mishnah establishes a world in stasis: lists of like things, subject to like rules. The Bavli portrays a world in motion: lists of like things form series; but series too conform to rules. The Mishnah sets forth lists, the Bavli, series.

In the comparison with the Yerushalmi we appreciate that the Bavli's quest for unity leads to the inquiry into the named authorities behind an unassigned rule, showing that a variety of figures can concur, meaning, names that stand for a variety of distinct principles can form a single proposition of integrity. That same quest insists on the fair and balanced representation of conflicting principles behind discrete laws, not to serve the cause of academic harmony (surely a lost cause in any age!), but to set forth how, at their foundations, the complicated and diverse laws may be explained by appeal to simple and few principles; the conflict of principles then is less consequential than the demonstration that diverse cases may be reduced to only a few principles.

Take for example the single stylistically-indicative trait of the Bavli, its dialectical, or moving, argument. The dialectical argument opens the possibility of reaching out from one thing to something else, not because people have lost sight of their starting point or their goal in the end, but because they want to encompass, in the analytical argument as it gets underway, as broad and comprehensive a range of cases and rules as they possibly can. The movement from point to point in reference to a single point that accurately describes the dialectical argument reaches a goal of abstraction, leaving behind the specificities of not only cases but laws, carrying us upward to the law that governs many cases, the premises that undergird many rules, and still higher to the principles that infuse diverse premises; then the principles that generate other, unrelated premises, which, in turn, come to expression in other, still-less intersecting cases. The meandering course of argument comes to an end when we have shown how things cohere. That is what we have learned about the Bavli in this comparison of the two Talmuds.

But the Yerushalmi is not the only, or even the principal, point of comparison for the Bavli. The Mishnah, to which the Bavli formally is devoted as a commentary, and which most of the Bavli really does serve as just that, surely claims a high place in the hierarchy of valid comparisons. For, after all, a writing that is attached to another document surely demands comparison and contrast with that other document. Only one point of comparison makes any difference at all: the contrast of the Bavli's and the Mishnah's fundamental intellectual agenda. These, I shall now show, are fully complementary. Both bring to expression in a huge mass of instantiations a few simple propositions, all of which come down to one statement: truth is one. The integrity of the truth forms the singular statement of the Judaism of the dual Torah, and each in its way, the Mishnah and the Bavli make that statement— and, at their foundations, that statement alone.

The Mishnah's version of the integrity of truth focuses upon the unity of all being in hierarchical ontology. A single metaproposition encompasses the multitude of the Mishnah's proposition, which is, all classes of things stand in a hierarchical relationship to one another, and, in that encompassing hierarchy, there is place for everything. The theological proposition that is implicit but never spelled out, of course, is that one God occupies the pinnacle of the hierarchy of all being; to that one God, all things turn upward, from complexity to simplicity; from that one God, all things flow downward, from singularity to multiplicity. To understand that simple statement, we begin with a definition of a metaproposition.

A proposition presents the result of an analysis of a given problem. When analyses of a variety of problems yield diverse propositions that as a matter of fact turn out to say the same one thing about many diverse things, that one thing said in many ways about many things forms not a proposition but a metaproposition. It is a proposition that derives from all subsets of propositions and states in an abstract and general way—whether explicitly or merely by indirection—the one proposition contained within many demonstrations of propositions. We know that we have identified the metapropositional program of a writing if, when we say what we think is at stake, in the most general terms, in a variety of specific syllogisms, we turn out to be saying the same thing again and again. We may test our hypothetical metaproposition by asking whether, in those many things, we may identify any other proposition to define the stakes of a demonstration; or whether some other encompassing proposition may serve as well as the one we propose over as broad a range of data as we examine. Where may we expect to find not only propositions but a statement that coheres throughout: a statement in behalf of all propositions? A coherent legal system, for one example, not only sets forth rules for diverse circumstances but, through the rules, also may lay out a philosophy of the social order, an account of what is always fair and just; then all of the cases, each with its generalization, turn out to repeat in different ways a single encompassing statement.

So too, while the author of a document makes statements about a great many subjects, a well-crafted document by a strong-minded writer will find the author saying much the same thing about all things. Then the key to good writing will be the power to make the same point again and again without boring the reader or belaboring the obvious. Indeed, an important and truly well-conceived piece of writing addressed to a long future will precipitate productive debates about not only details but what that some one thing said in many ways is meant to propose. Great writing leaves space for readers. That is the mark of a strong argument, a well-crafted formulation of a considered viewpoint, the expression of a deeply-reflected-upon attitude, or, in intellectual matters, a rigorously-presented proposition. To find out what we might imagine some one thing a writer may say about many things, we ask simply, "What is at stake if this point is validated?" or simply, "if so, so what?" If time and again we find that treatment of a given subject yields as its final and most general and abstract point a proposition that turns out also to emerge from an unrelated treatment of some other subject, altogether, then we have what I call a metaproposition, meaning, a proposition that transcends a variety of propositions and that occurs in all of them.

The Mishnah's authority repeatedly demonstrates that all things are not only orderly, but are ordered in such wise that many things fall into one classification. So one thing may hold together many things of a diverse classifications. These two matched and complementary propositions—[1] many things are one, [2] one thing encompasses many—complement each other. In forming matched opposites, the two provide a single, complete and final judgment of the whole of being, social, natural, supernatural alike. Nearly the whole of the document's tractates in one way or another repeat that simple point. The metaproposition is never expressed but it is everywhere demonstrated by showing, in whatever subject is treated, the possibility always of effecting the hierarchical classification of all things: each thing in its taxon, all taxa in correct sequence, from least to greatest.

Showing that all things can be ordered, and that all orders can be set into relationship with one another, we of course transform method into message. The message of hierarchical classification is that many things really form a single thing, the many species a single genus, the many genera an encompassing and well-crafted, cogent whole. Every time we speciate, we affirm that position. Each successful labor of forming relationships among species, e.g., making them into a genus, or identifying the hierarchy of the species, proves it again. Not only so, but when we can show that many things are really one, or that one thing yields many (the reverse and confirmation of the former), we say in a fresh way a single immutable truth, the one of this philosophy concerning the unity of all being in an orderly composition of all things within a single taxon. Exegesis always is repetitive—and a sound exegesis of the systemic exegesis must then be equally so, everywhere explaining the same thing in the same way.

Both the Mishnah and the Bavli undertake to uncover and expose, in the laws of the Torah, the philosophy that the Torah reveals. That is the upshot of the two documents' powerful and reasoned, fully-instantiated polemic: many things yield one thing, and this is that one thing. Stated in the language of revelation, the Torah through many things says one thing, through many commandments, sets forth one commandment, through diversity in detail makes a single, main point. And we know what that point is. By "the integrity of truth," in secular language, we say the same thing that we express when, in mythic language, we speak, as does Sherira Gaon at the end of a long apologetic tradition, of "the one whole Torah of Moses, our rabbi." But now, by "one" and by "whole," very specific statements are made: jurisprudence reaches upward toward philosophy, on the one side, and the teachings and rules of the Torah are wholly harmonious and cogent, on the other. In the language that I have used here, the upshot is very simple: mind is one, whole, coherent; thought properly conducted yields simple truth about complex things.

Comparing the Mishnah and the Bavli, as much as contrasting

the Yerushalmi and the Bavli, yields this conclusion. The outcome of the contrast is not merely the difference that the Yerushalmi is brief and laconic while the Bavli speaks in fully spelled out ways. Nor is it the difference that, in general, the Yerushalmi's presentations are not dialectical, and the Bavli's are, for even though that difference may in general prove fixed, on occasion the Yerushalmi will expand an argument through question and answer, parry and counterthrust, and the analogy of a duel will apply to the Yerushalmi, if not consistently. The difference comes to the surface in hermeneutics: the Bavli's composites' framers consistently treat as a question to be investigated the exegetical hypotheses that the Yerushalmi's compositions' authors happily accept as conclusive. All of the secondary devices of testing an allegation—a close reading of the formulation of the Mishnah, an appeal to the false conclusion such a close reading, absent a given formulation, might have yielded, to take the examples before us—serve that primary goal. The second recurrent difference is that the Bavli's framers find themselves constantly drawn toward questions of generalization and abstraction (once more: the law behind the laws), moving from case to principle to new case to new principle, then asking whether the substrate of principles forms a single, tight fabric. The Yerushalmi's authors rarely, if ever, pursue that chimera.

But what gives the Bavli its compelling, ineluctable power to persuade, the source of the Bavli's intellectual force is that thrust for abstraction, through generalization (and in that order, generalization, toward abstraction). To spell out in very simple terms what I conceive to be at issue: the way that the law behind the laws emerges is, first, generalization of a case into a principle, then, the recasting of the principle into an abstraction encompassing a variety of otherwise free-standing principles. The Bavli's hermeneutics contains the theology of the Judaism of the dual Torah: the correct method that yields authoritative statements. Five hermeneutical rules govern throughout the Bavli are as follows:

1. DEFINING THE TORAH AND THE CONTEXT FOR MEANING: The Torah consists of free-standing statements, sentences, sometimes formed into paragraphs, more often not; and we are to read these sentences both on their own—for what they say—and also in the context created by the entirety of the Torah, oral and written. Therefore the task is to set side by side and show the compatibility of discrete sentences; documents mean nothing, the Torah being one. The entirety of the Torah defines the context of meaning. All sentences of the Torah, equally, jointly and severally, form the facts out of which meaning is to be constructed.

2. SPECIFYING THE RULES OF MAKING SENSE OF THE TORAH: several premises govern in our reading of the sentences of the Torah, and these dictate the rules of reading. The first is that the Torah is perfect and flawless. The second is that the wording of the Torah yields meaning. The third is that the Torah contains, and can contain, nothing contradictory, incoherent, or otherwise contrary to common sense. The fourth is that the Torah can contain no statement that is redundant, banal, silly or stupid. The fifth is that our sages of blessed memory when they state teachings of the Torah stand for these same traits of language and intellect: sound purpose, sound reasoning, sound result, in neat sentences. The task of the reader (in secular language) or the master of the Torah (in theological language, in context the two are one and the same) then is to identify the problems of the Torah, whether written or oral, and to solve those problems. Knowing what will raise a difficulty, we also know how to resolve it.

3. IDENTIFYING THE CORRECT MEDIUM OF DISCOURSE, WHICH IS THE DIALECTICAL ARGUMENT: since our principal affirmation is that the Torah is perfect, and the primary challenge to that affirmation derives from the named classifications of imperfection, the proper mode of analytical speech is argument. That is because if we seek flaws, we come in a combative spirit: proof and conflict, not truth and consequence. Only by challenging the Torah sentence by sentence, at every plausible point of imperfection, are we going to show in the infinity of detailed cases the governing fact of perfection. We discover right thinking by finding the flaws in wrong thinking, the logical out of the failings of illogic. Only by sustained confrontation of opposed views and interpretations will truth result.

4. THE HARMONY OF WHAT IS SUBJECT TO DISPUTE, THE UNITY AND INTEGRITY OF TRUTH: Finding what is rational and coherent: the final principle of hermeneutics is to uncover the rationality of dispute. Once our commitment is to sustained conflict of intellect, it must follow that our goal can only be the demonstration of three propositions, everywhere meant to govern: [1] disputes give evidence of rationality, meaning, each party has a valid, established principle in mind; [2] disputes are subject to resolution; [3] truth wins out. The first proposition is most important. If we can demonstrate that reasonable sages can differ about equally valid propositions, for instance, which principle governs in a particular case, then schism affords evidence of not imperfection but profound coherence. The principles are affirmed, their application subjected to conflict. So too, if disputes worked out in extended, moving arguments, covering much ground, can be brought to resolution, as is

frequently the case in either a declared decision or an agreement to disagree, then the perfection of the Torah once more comes to detailed articulation.

5. KNOWING GOD THROUGH THE THEOLOGY EXPRESSED IN HERMENEUTICS: And, finally, in a protracted quest for the unity of the truth, detailed demonstration that beneath the laws is law, with a few wholly coherent principles inherent in the many, diverse rules and their cases—in that sustained quest, which defines the premise and the goal of all Talmudic discourse the second Talmud's writers maintain is where humanity meets God: in mind, in intellect, where that meeting takes place in accord with rules of reason that govern God and humanity alike.

7 THREE OTHER APPROACHES TO THE SYNTHESIS OF RABBINIC JUDAISM

This account of the definition and history of the formation of Rabbinic Judaism appeals for data to the character of the documents of that Judaism, read in sequence, and viewed as exemplified through the unfolding hermeneutics of those documents. It consequently represents the history of Judaism through the medium of hermeneutics. The documentary approach is only one way of defining the same Judaism and describing its history. The other approach analyzes not completed documents, read in sequence, but rather the specific sayings attributed to named authorities in those documents. This reading of all canonical writings as equally representative of each age and every circle of rabbinic Judaism further collects sayings on a given topic and arranges them for a picture of the Judaic treatment of that topic. Sayings assigned to the same name or on the same theme therefore are joined together, without regard to the time of the redaction and closure of the diverse documents in which they occur; from the compilation of sayings attributed to various authorities, we have a picture of opinions held in the time of those authorities. On that basis, we have a history that rests upon attributions. The history focuses upon the content of what is said by the named sages, rather than on the hermeneutics that the documents, read in their entirety, set forth. Hence, since a fair proportion of sages' statements concern the meaning of Scripture and define various theological propositions—e.g., sayings about ethics and morality, the covenant between God and Israel, what God requires Israel to do and the like—other syntheses of Rabbinic Judaism synthesize theology and provide accounts of theological dogmatics. We shall now examine the most important result of such

an approach, that of George F. Moore, as well as two improve-
ments on Moore's results produced by the same method, both done
in the 1970s, E. E. Urbach and E. P. Sanders. The contrast between the documentary approach, taken here, and the theological
approach to the description of Judaism, taken by all three prior
writers, will be of interest to colleagues in cognate areas of learning.

A George Foot Moore, Judaism: The Age of the Tannaim[26]

Slightly more than a half-century has passed since George Foot
Moore's *Judaism in the First Centuries of the Christian Era: The Age of the
Tannaim* made its appearance. The work was published in May
1927 and reprinted in November, had a third printing in 1932, a
fourth in 1944, and a seventh in 1954, and remains in print and
current. Not only was it an immediate success in the marketplace
but the earliest reviews accorded the book a remarkably favorite
reception. Among those of 1927 only one, F.C. Porter's, which I
shall cite at length below, raised important critical questions alongside entirely appropriate, adulatory comments. The warmest tribute, of course, is envy and imitation, and the main outlines of
Moore's argument and the principal definition of issues and methods came to be imitated in accounts of exactly the same subject,
constructed in exactly the same way, yielding exactly the same results, for the following fifty years. So for one set of reasons, Jewish
scholars of Judaism, and for another set of reasons, Christian scholars of Judaism, reached the same positive conclusion. Moore had
said the last word, which now needed only to be repeated by scholars proposing to say their own last word.

Moore assembles sayings on various subjects out of the so-called
Tannaite writings. He makes use of sources which speak of people
assumed to have lived in the early centuries of the Common Era,
even when said sources derive from a much later or a much earlier
time. For Moore, "Judaism" is a problem of ideas, and the history
of Judaism is the history of ideas abstracted from the groups that
held them and from the social perspectives of said groups. Moore
states, "The aim of these volumes is to represent Judaism in the
centuries in which it assumed definitive form as it presents itself in
the tradition which it has always regarded as authentic. These pri-

---

[26] *Judaism in the First Centuries of the Christian Era: The Age of the Tannaim.* By George
Foot Moore. Cambridge, 1927: Harvard University Press. I-III.

mary sources come to us as they were compiled and set in order in the second century of the Christian era..." The evidence he adduces derives from, and therefore represents, altogether too wide a range of varieties of Judaism, over too long a period of time. Much of the evidence for "Judaism" in Moore comes from, and faithfully portrays, either the age long before 70 or the period four or five centuries after the formation of the Mishnah in 200. More important: a vast amount of material derives from circles which cannot be deemed at all concentric with the social and intellectual group behind Mishnah. Thus Moore describes many kinds of "Judaism" as if they formed a single concept.

Moore's work to begin with is not really a work in the history of religions at all—in this instance, the developmental and formative history of a particular brand of Judaism. His research is in theology. It is organized in theological categories. Moore presents a synthetic account of diverse materials, (deriving from diverse sources, as I said) focused upon a given topic of theological interest. There is nothing even rhetorically historical in the picture of opinions on these topics, no pretense of systematically accounting for development and change. What is constructed as a static exercise in dogmatic theology, not an account of the history of religious ideas and—still more urgent—their unfolding in relationship to the society of the people who held those ideas. Moore in no way describes and interprets the religious world-view and way of life expressed, in part, through the ideas under study. He does not explore the interplay between that world-view and the historical and political context of the community envisioned by that construction of a world. So far as history attends to the material context of ideas and the class structure expressed by ideas and institutions alike, so far as ideas are deemed part of a larger social system and religious systems are held to be pertinent to the given political, social, and economic framework which contains them, Moore's account of dogmatic theology to begin with has nothing to do with religious history, that is the history of Judaism in the first two centuries of the Common Era.

When "Judaism" is made to refer to the exegetical compilations of the rabbis of the fourth and fifth centuries—and much later—as well as the writings of the "sectaries at Damascus" (as Moore calls them), then the term "Judaism" stretches so far, covers so much diversity, as to lose all definitive use. Evidence from the fifth century of the Common Era and from the first or second century before it—six hundred years—serves no more naturally to describe a single relation (if also no less) than the poetry of the age of

Beowulf and that of our own day serves to describe a single language (if also no less).

Frank C. Porter's review points to two principal flaws in Moore's
account of Judaism, first, the claim that the "Judaism of the
Tannaim" was normative, and second, the systematic aversion to
discussion of the Judaism revealed by the legal texts:

> The Judaism which Professor Moore describes with such wealth of
> learning is that of the end of the second century of our era, and the
> sources which he uses are those that embody the interpretations and
> formulations of the law by the rabbis, chiefly from the fall of Jerusalem,
> 70 A.D., to the promulgation of the Mishnah of the Patriarch Judah,
> about 200 A.D. When Moore speaks of the sources which Judaism has
> always regarded as authentic, he means "always" from the third cen-
> tury A.D. onward. It is a proper and needed task to exhibit the reli-
> gious conceptions and moral principles, the observances, and the piety
> of the Judaism of the Tannaim. Perhaps it is the things that most
> needed to be done of all the many labors that must contribute to our
> knowledge of that age. But Professor Moore calls this Judaism "norma-
> tive"; and means by this, not only authoritative for Jews after the work
> of the Tannaim had reached its completion in the Mishnah, but nor-
> mal or authentic in the sense that it is the only direct and natural
> outcome of the Old Testament religion. It seems therefore, that the
> task here undertaken is not only, as it certainly is, a definite, single, and
> necessary one, but that other things hardly need doing, and do not
> signify much for the Judaism of the age of Christian beginnings. The
> book is not called, as it might have been, "The Judaism of the
> Tannaim," but Judaism in the First Centuries of the Christian Era:
> The Age of the Tannaim. Was there then no other type of Judaism in
> the time of Christ that may claim such names as "normative," "nor-
> mal," "orthodox"? The time of Deuteronomy was also the time of
> Jeremiah. The religion of revelation in a divinely given written law
> stood over against the religion of revelation in the heart and living
> words of a prophet. The conviction was current after Ezra that the age
> of prophecy had ended; the Spirit of God had withdrawn itself from
> Israel (I, 237). But if prophecy should live again, could it not claim to
> be normal in Judaism? Where, in the centuries after Ezra, are we to
> look for the lines of development that go back, not to Ezra and Deuter-
> onomy, but to Jeremiah and Isaiah? R.H. Charles claims the genuine
> succession for his Apocalypses. The Pharisees at least had the prophets
> in their canon, and it is claimed by many, and by Moore, that the
> rabbis were not less familiar with the prophets than with the Penta-
> teuch, and even that they had "fully assimilated" the teaching of the
> prophets as to the value of the cultus (II, 13), and that their conception
> of revealed religion "resulted no less from the teaching of the prophets
> than from the possession of the Law" (I, 235). Christians see prophecy
> coming back to Judaism in John the Baptist and in Jesus, and find in
> Paul the new experience that revelation is giving in a person, not in a
> book, and inwardly to each one through the in-dwelling Spirit of God,
> as Jeremiah had hoped (31:31-34). And now, finally, liberal Judaism

claims to be authentic and normal Judaism because it takes up the lines that Jeremiah laid down....

It would require more proof than Professor Moore has given in his section on "History" to justify his claim that the only movements that need to be traced as affecting religion are these that lead from Ezra to Hillel and Johanan ben Zakkai and Akiba and Judah the Prince. Great events happened during the three centuries from Antiochus IV to Hadrian, events which deeply affected Judaism as a religion. But of these events and their influence Moore has little to say. It is of course in connection with these events that the Apocalypses were written.

Porter's second criticism of Moore seems to me still more telling. He points out that Moore almost wholly neglects the Tannaitic legal corpus—Mishnah itself:

In [Moore's] actual exposition of the normative, orthodox Judaism of the age of the Tannaim comparatively little place is given to Halakah. One of the seven parts of his exposition is on observances; and here cultus, circumcision, Sabbath, festivals, fasts, taxation, and interdictions are summarily dealt with; but the other six parts deal in detail with the religion and ethics, the piety and hopes, of Judaism, matters about which the Haggada supplies most of the material, and for which authority and finality are not claimed. The tannaite (halakic) Midrash (Mechilta, etc.) contains a good deal of Haggada together with its halakic exegesis, and these books Moore values as the most important of his sources (I, 135ff.; II, 80). The principles of religion and morals do indeed control the interpretation of certain laws, so that Halakah is sometimes a source for such teachings, and "is in many instances of the highest value as evidence of the way and measure in which great ethical principles have been tacitly impressed on whole fields of the traditional law" (I, 134). This sounds as if the ethical implications constituted the chief value of the Mishnah for Moore's purposes. But these are not its chief contents. It is made up, as a whole, of opinions or decisions about the minutiae of law observance. It constructs a hedge of definitions and restrictions meant to protect the letter of the law from violation, to make its observance possible and practicable under all circumstances, and to bring all of life under its rule.

The Jewish scholar, Perles, in a pamphlet with which Moore is in sympathy, criticized Bousset, in Die Religion des Judentums, for using only books such as Bacher's, on the Haggada, and for expressing a preference for haggadic sources; whereas the Halakah in its unity, in its definitive and systematic form, and its deeper grasp upon life is much better fitted to supply the basis of the structures of a history of the Jewish religion. Moore agrees with Perles' criticism of Bousset's preference for the later, haggadic, Midrashim; but it is not because they are halakic that he gives the first place to the early Midrash. "It is this religious and moral element by the side of the interpretation of the laws, and pervading it as a principle, that gives these works [Mechilta, etc.] their chief value to us" (I, 135). Perles insists on the primary importance of the Halakah, not only because it shows here and there the influence of prophetic ethics, but because throughout as it stands, it is the principal work of the rabbis, and the work which alone has the character of authority, and because, concerned as it is with ritual, cultus, and the law (Recht), it has decisive influence upon the whole of life. This applies peculiarly to the religion of the Tannaim. The Haggada neither begins nor ends with them, so that Bousset ought not, Perles thinks, to have used exclusively Bacher's work on the Haggada of the Tannaim, but also his volumes on the Haggada of the Amoraim, as well as the anonymous Haggada which Bacher did not live to publish. It is only in the region of the Halakah that the Tannaim have a distinctive place and epoch-making significance, since the Mishnah, the fundamental text of the Talmud, was their creation.

Would Perles be satisfied, then, with Moore's procedure? Would he think it enough that Halakah proper, observances, should occupy one part in seven in an exposition of the Judaism of the Tannaim, considering that in their classical and distinctive work Halakah practically fills sixty-two out of sixty-three parts? Moore agrees with Perles that there is no essential distinction between earlier and later Haggada (I, 163), and that the teachings of the Tannaim about God and man, morals and piety, sin, repentance, and forgiveness are not only also the teachings of the later Amoraim, but run backward, too, without essential change into the Old Testament itself. There is no point at which freedom and variety of opinion and belief, within the bounds, to be sure, of certain fundamental principles, came to an end, and a proper orthodoxy of dogma was set up. But orthodoxy of conduct, of observance, did reach this stage of finality and authority in the Mishnah; and the tannaite rabbis were those who brought this about. It is in accordance with Moore's chief interests in haggadic teachings that he does not confine himself to sayings of the Tannaim, but also quotes freely from the Amoraim; how freely may be seen by the list that ends Index IV.

Professor Moore's emphasis upon his purpose to present normative Judaism, definitive, authoritative, orthodox, would lead one to expect that he would give the chief place to those "jurisdic definitions and decisions of the Halakah" to which alone, as he himself sometimes says, these adjectives strictly apply. We should look for more about the Mishnah itself, about its systematic arrangement of the laws, its methods of argument and of bringing custom and tradition into connection with the written law, and more of its actual contents and total character, of those actual rules of life, that "uniformity of observance" which constituted the distinction of the Judaism of the rabbis.

True, the history of a religion and the dogmatics of that religion are going to relate to one another. But a description of dogmatics of seven centuries or more and an account of the contents thereof simply do not constitute a history of the religion which comes to formal ideological expression in dogmatic theology. So Moore did not do what the title of his book and of his professorship ("professor of the history of religion") promises, even though in his work he discusses numerous matters bearing historical implication.

B Ephraim E. Urbach, The Sages[27]

Ephraim E. Urbach, professor of Talmud at the Hebrew University and author of numerous articles and books on the Talmud and later rabbinic literature, here presents a compendious work intended "to describe the concepts and beliefs of the Tannaim and Amoraim and to elucidate them against the background of their actual life and environment." When published in Hebrew, in 1969, the work enjoyed immediate success, going into a second edition within two years; an English-language edition followed shortly thereafter. The work before us has been accurately described by M.D. Heer (Encyclopaedia Judaica 16:4): "He [Urbach] outlines the views of the rabbis on the important theological issues such as creation, providence, and the nature of man. In this work Urbach synthesizes the voluminous literature on these subjects and presents the views of the talmudic authorities." The topics are as follows: belief in one God; the presence of God in the world; "nearness and distance—Omnipresent and heaven;" the power of God; magic and miracle; the power of the divine name; the celestial retinue; creation; man; providence; written law and oral law; the commandments; acceptance of the yoke of the kingdom of heaven; sin, reward, punishment, suffering, etc.; the people of Israel and its sages, a chapter which encompasses the election of Israel, the status of the sages in the days of the Hasmoneans, Hillel, the regime of the sages after the destruction of the Temple, and so on; and redemption. The second volume contains footnotes, a fairly brief and highly selective bibliography, and alas, a merely perfunctory index. The several chapters, like the work as a whole, are organized systematically, consisting of sayings and stories relevant to the theme under discussion, together with Urbach's episodic observations and comments on them.

In the context of earlier work on talmudic theology and religion. Urbach's contribution is, as I said, a distinct improvement in every way. Compared to a similar, earlier compendium of talmudic sayings on theological subjects, A. Hyman's *Osar divré hakhamin ufitgamehem* (1934), a collection of sayings laid out alphabetically, according to catchword, Urbach's volumes have the advantage of supplying not merely sayings but cogent discussions of the various

---

[27] *The Sages. Their Concepts And Beliefs.* By Ephraim E. Urbach. Translated from the Hebrew by Israel Abrahams. Jerusalem: The Magnes Press, The Hebrew University, 1975. Two volumes—I. Text: pp. XXII and 692. II. Notes: pp. 383.

sayings and a more fluent, coherent presentation of them in essay form. Solomon Schechter's *Some Aspects of Rabbinic Theology* (1909, based on essays in the *Jewish Quarterly Review* printed in 1894-1896) covers exactly what it says, some aspects, by contrast to the much more ambitious dimension of the present work. The comparision to George Foot Moore's *Judaism in the First Centuries of the Christian Era: The Age of the Tannaim* (1927-1930) is somewhat more complex. Moore certainly has the advantage of elegant presentation. Urbach's prose, in I. Abraham's English translation, comes through as turgid and stodgy, while Moore's is the opposite. Morton Smith comments on Moore's work, "Although it too much neglects the mystical, magical and apocalyptic sides of Judaism, its apology for tannaitic teaching as a reasonable, humane, and pious working out of biblical tradition is conclusive..." (*Encyclopaedia Judaica* 12:293-4; compare *Harvard Library Bulletin* 15, 1967, pp. 169-179). By contrast to Moore, Urbach introduces sayings of Amoraim into the discussion of each category, and since both Urbach and Moore aim to present a large selection of sayings on the several topics, Urbach's work is on the face of it a more comprehensive collection.

Urbach's own comments on his predecessors (I, pp.5-18) underline the theological bias present in most, though not all, former studies. Wilhelm Bousset and Hugo Gressmann, Die Religion des Judentums im späthellenistischen Zeitalter (1926) is wanting because rabbinic sources are used sparingly and not wholly accurately and because it relies on "external sources," meaning apocryphal literature and Hellenistic Jewish writings. Urbach's own criticism of Moore, that "he did not always go deeply enough into the essence of the problems that he discussed," certainly cannot be leveled against Urbach himself. His further reservation is that Moore "failed to give an account of the origin of the beliefs and concepts, of their struggles and evolution, of their entire chequered course till their crystallization, of the immense dynamism and vitality of the spiritual life of the Second Temple period, of the tension in the relations between the parties and sects and between the various sections of the Sages themselves." This view underlines the historical ambition of Urbach's approach and emphasizes his view of his own contribution, cited at the outset: to elucidate the concepts and beliefs of the Tannaim and Amoraim against the background of their actual life and environment. Since that is Urbach's fundamental claim, the work must be considered not only in the context of what has gone before, in which, as I said, it emerges as a substantial step forward, but also in the setting of its own definition and understanding of the historical task, its own theory of how talmudic ma-

terials are to be used for historical knowledge. In this regard it is
not satisfactory.

There are some fairly obvious problems, on which we need not
dwell at length. Urbach's selection of sources for analysis is both
narrowly canonical and somewhat confusing. We often hear from
Philo, but seldom from the Essene Library of Qumran, still more
rarely from the diverse works assembled by R.H. Charles as the
apocrypha and pseudepigrapha of the Old Testament, and the like.
If we seek to describe the talmudic rabbis, surely we cannot ask
Philo to testify to their opinions. If we listen to Philo, surely we
ought to hear—at least for the purpose of comparison and contrast—from books written by Palestinian Jews of various kinds. The
Targumim are allowed no place at all because they are deemed
"late." Within a given chapter, the portrayal of the sources will
move rapidly from biblical to Tannaitic to Amoraic sources, as
though the line of development were single, unitary, and harmonious, and as though there were no intervening developments which
shaped later conceptions. Differentiation among the stages of
Tannaitic and Amoraic sayings tends to be episodic. Commonly,
slight sustained effort is made to treat them in their several sequences, let alone to differentiate among schools and circles within
a given period. Urbach takes with utmost seriousness his title, the
sages, their concepts and beliefs, and his "history," topic by topic,
reveals remarkably little variation, development, or even movement. One looks in vain for Urbach's effort to justify treating "the
sages" as essentially a coherent and timeless group.

Does the world-view of the talmudic sages emerge in a way
which the ancient sages themselves would have recognized? From
the viewpoint of their organization and description of reality, their
world-view, it is certain that the sages would have organized their
card-files quite differently. We know that is the case because we do
not have, among the chapters before us, a single one which focuses
upon the theme of one of the orders, let alone tractates, within
which the rabbis divided and presented their various statements on
reality, e.g., Seeds, the material basis of life; Seasons, the organization and differentiation of time; Women, the status of the individual; Damages, the conduct of civil life including government;
Holy Things, the material service of God; and Purities, the immaterial base of divine reality in this world. The matter concerns not
merely the superficial problem of organizing vast quantities of data.
The talmudic rabbis left a large and exceedingly complex, well-
integrated legacy of law. Clearly, it is through that legacy that they
intended to make their fundamental statements upon the organiza-

tion and meaning of reality. An account of their concepts and beliefs which ignores nearly the whole of the halakhah surely is
slightly awry.

Has Urbach taken account of methodological issues important in
the study of the literary and historical character of the sources? In
particular, does he deal with the fundamental questions of how
these particular sources are to be used for historical purposes? The
answer is a qualified negative. On many specific points, he contributes sporadic philological observations, interesting opinions and
judgments as to the lateness of one saying as against the antiquity of
another, subjective opinions on what is more representative or reliable than something else. If these opinions are not systematic and if
they reveal no uniform criterion, sustainedly applied to all sources,
they nonetheless derive from a mind of immense learning. Not all
judgment must be critical, and not all expression of personal taste
systematic. The dogmatic opinions of a man of such self-evident
mastery of the tradition, one who, in addition, clearly is an exemplar of the tradition for his own setting, are important evidence for
the study and interpretation of the tradition itself, particulary in its
modern phase.

Yet we must ask, if a saying is assigned to an ancient authority,
how do we know that he really said it? If a story is told, how do we
know that the events the story purports to describe actually took
place? And if not, just what are we to make of said story and saying
for historical purposes? Further, if we have a saying attributed to a
first-century authority in a document generally believed to have
been redacted five hundred or a thousand years later, how do we
know that the attribution of the saying is valid, and that the saying
informs us of the state of opinion in the first century, not only in the
sixth or eleventh in which it was written down and obviously believed true and authoritative? Do we still hold, as an axiom of
historical scholarship, ein muqdam umeuhar ["temporal considerations do not apply"]—in the Talmud?! And again, do not the sayings assigned to a first-century authority, redacted in documents
deriving from the early third century, possess greater credibility
than those first appearing in documents redacted in the fifth, tenth,
or even fifteenth centuries? Should we not, on the face of it, distinguish between more and less reliable materials? The well-known
tendency of medieval writers to put their opinions into the mouths
of the ancients, as in the case of the Zohar, surely warns us to be
cautious about using documents redacted, even formulated, five
hundred or a thousand or more years after the events of which they

speak. Urbach ignores all of these questions and the work of those who ask them.

Urbach's work brings to their full realization the methods and suppositions of the past hundred years. I cannot imagine that anyone again will want, from these perspectives, to approach the task of describing all of "the concepts and beliefs of the Tannaim and Amoraim," of elucidating all of them "against the background of their actual life and environment." So far as the work can be done in accord with established methods, here it has been done very competently indeed. Accordingly, we may well forgive the learned author for the sustained homiletical character of his inquiry and its blatantly apologetic purposes:

> The aim of our work is to give an epitome of the beliefs and concepts of the Sages as the history of a struggle to instill religious and ethical ideals into the everyday life of the community and the individual, while preserving at the same time the integrity and unity of the nation and directing its way in this world as a preparation for another world that is wholly perfect... Their eyes and their hearts were turned Heavenward, yet one type was not to be found among them... namely the mystic who seeks to liberate himself from his ego and in doing so is preoccupied with himself alone. They saw their mission in work here in the world below. There were Sages who inclined to extremism in their thoughts and deeds, and there were those who preached the way of compromise, which they did not, however, determine on the basis of convenience. Some were severe and exacting, while others demonstrated an extreme love of humanity and altruism. The vast majority of them recognized the complexities of life with its travail and joy, its happiness and tragedy, and this life served them also as a touchstone for their beliefs and concepts.

All of this may well be so, but it remains to be demonstrated as historical fact in the way in which contemporary critical historians generally demonstrate matters of fact. It requires analysis and argument in the undogmatic and unapologetic spirit characteristic of contemporary studies in the history of ideas and of religions. But in the context in which these words of Urbach are written, among the people who will read them, this statement of purpose puts forth a noble ideal, one which might well be emulated by the "sages"— exemplars and politicians of Orthodox Judaism—to whom, I believe, Urbach speaks most directly and persuasively, and by whom (alone) his results certainly will be taken as historical fact. The publishing success of the book and the recognition accorded its learned author are hopeful signs that the ideal of the sage of old indeed has not been lost upon their most recent avatars. It is by no means a reduction of learning to its sociological and political relevance to say that, if it were only for his advocacy of the humane and constructive position just now quoted. Urbach has made a truly formidable contribution to the contemporary theological life of Orthodox Judaism.

C E. P. Sanders, Paul and Palestinian Judaism[28]

"Palestinian Judaism" is described through three bodies of evidence: Tannaitic literature, the Dead Sea Scrolls, and Apocrypha and Pseudepigrapha, in that order. I shall deal only with the first. To each set of sources, Sanders addresses questions of systematic theology: election and covenant, obedience and disobedience, reward and punishment and the world to come, salvation by membership in the covenant and atonement, proper religious behavior (so for Tannaitic sources); covenant and the covenant people, election and predestination, the commandments, fulfillment and transgression, atonement (Dead Sea Scrolls); election and covenant, the fate of the individual Israelite, atonement, commandments, the basis of salvation, the gentiles, repentance and atonement, the righteousness of God (Apocrypha and Pseudepigrapha, meaning, specifically: Ben Sira, I Enoch, Jubilees, Psalms of Solomon, IV Ezra). There follows a brief concluding chapter (pp. 419-28, summarizing pp. 1-418), and then the second part, on Paul, takes up about a fifth of the book. Sanders provides a very competent bibliography (pp. 557-82) and thorough indexes. So far as the book has a polemical charge, it is to demonstrate (pp. 420-21) that "the fundamental nature of the covenant conception... largely accounts for the relative scarcity of appearances of the term 'covenant' in Rabbinic literature. The covenant was presupposed, and the Rabbinic discussions were largely directed toward the question of how to fulfill the covenantal obligations." This proposition is then meant to disprove the conviction ("all but universally held") that Judaism is a degeneration of the Old Testament view: "The once noble idea of covenant as offered by God's grace and obedience as the consequence of that gracious gift degenerated into the idea of petty legalism, according to which one had to earn the mercy of God by minute observance of irrelevant ordinances."

---

[28] *Paul and Palestinian Judaism: A Comparison of Patterns of Religion.* By E.P. Sanders. London: SCM Press, 1977. Pp. XVIII+627.

Sanders' search for patterns yields a common pattern in "covenantal nomism," which, in general, emerges as follows (p. 422):

> The "pattern" or "structure" of covenantal nomism is this: (1) God has chosen Israel and (2) given the law. The law implies both (3) God's promise to maintain the election and (4) the requirement to obey. (5) God rewards obedience and punishes transgression. (6) The law provides for means of atonement, and atonement results in (7) maintenance or re-establishment of the covenantal relationship. (8) All those who are maintained in the covenant by obedience, atonement, and God's mercy belong to the group which will be saved. An important interpretation of the first and last points is that election and ultimately salvation are considered to be by God's mercy rather than human achievement.

Anyone familiar with Jewish liturgy will be at home in that statement. Even though the evidence on the character of Palestinian Judaism derives from diverse groups and reaches us through various means, Sanders argues that covenantal nomism was "the basic type of religion known by Jesus and presumably by Paul..." And again, "covenantal nomism must have been the general type of religion prevalent in Palestine before the destruction of the Temple.

The stated purposes require attention. Sanders states at the outset (p. xii) that he has six aims: (1) to consider methodologically how to compare two (or more) related but different religions; (2) to destroy the view of Rabbinic Judaism which is still prevalent in much, perhaps most, New Testament scholarship; (3) to establish a different view of Rabbinic Judaism; (4) to argue a case concerning Palestinian Judaism (that is, Judaism as reflected in material of Palestinian provenance) as a whole; (5) to argue for a certain understanding of Paul; and (6) to carry out a comparison of Paul and Palestinian Judaism. Numbers (4) and (6), he immediately adds, "constitute the general aim of the book, while I hope to accomplish the others along the way." Since more than a third of the work is devoted to Rabbinic Judaism, Sanders certainly cannot be accused of treating his second goal casually.

Having described the overall shape of the work, let me make explicit the point at which I think historians of religion should join the discussion, since, it is self-evident, the long agendum of this book touches only occasionally upon issues of history, history of religions, and history of ideas. In fact, this is a work of historical theology. But Sanders' very good intention deserves the attention of students of religions who are not theologians, because what he wanted to achieve is in my view worthwhile. This intention is the proper comparison of religions (or of diverse expressions of one

larger religion): "I am of the view... that the history of the comparison of Paul and Judaism is a particularly clear instance of the general need for methodological improvement in the comparative
study of religion. What is difficult is to focus on what is to be
compared. We have already seen that most comparisons are of
reduced essences... or of individual motifs..." This sort of comparison Sanders rejects. Here I wish to give Sanders' words, because I
believe what he wants to do is precisely what he should have done
but, as I shall explain, has not succeeded in doing:

> What is clearly desirable, then, is to compare an entire religion, parts
> and all, with an entire religion, parts and all; to use the analogy of a
> building to compare two buildings, not leaving out of account their
> individual bricks. The problem is how to discover two wholes, both of
> which are considered and defined on their own merits and in their own
> terms, to be compared with each other.

Now let us ask ourselves whether or not Sanders has compared an
entire religion, parts and all, with other such entire religions.
On the basis of my description of the contents of the book, we must
conclude that he has not. For the issues of election and covenant,
obedience and disobedience, and the like, while demonstrably
present and taken for granted in the diverse "Judaisms" of late
antiquity, do not necessarily define the generative problematic of
any of the Judaisms before us. To put matters in more general
terms: Systemic description must begin with the system to be described. Comparative description follows. And to describe a system,
we commence with the principal documents which can be shown to
form the center of a system. Our task then is to uncover the exegetical processes, the dynamics of the system, through which those
documents serve to shape a conception, and to make sense, of reality. We then must locate the critical tensions and inner problematic
of the system thereby revealed: What is it about? What are its
points of insistence? The comparison of systems begins in their
exegesis and interpretation.

But Sanders does not come to Rabbinic Judaism (to focus upon
what clearly is his principal polemical charge) to uncover the issues
of Rabbinic Judaism. He brings to the Rabbinic sources the issues
of Pauline scholarship and Paul. This blatant trait of his work,
which begins, after all, with a long account of Christian anti-
Judaism ("The persistence of the view of Rabbinic religion as one of
legalistic works-righteousness," pp. 33-58), hardly requires amplification. In fact, Sanders does not really undertake the systemic description of earlier Rabbinic Judaism in terms of its critical tension.
True, he isolates those documents he thinks may testify to the state

of opinion in the late first and second centuries. But Sanders does not describe Rabbinic Judaism through the systemic categories yielded by its principal documents. His chief purpose is to demonstrate that Rabbinism constitutes a system of "covenantal nomism." While I think he is wholly correct in maintaining the importance of the conceptions of covenant and of grace, the polemic in behalf of Rabbinic legalism as covenantal does not bring to the fore what Rabbinic sources themselves wish to take as their principal theme and generative problem. For them, as he says, covenantal nomism is a datum. So far as Sanders proposes to demonstrate the importance to all the kinds of ancient Judaism of covenantal nomism, election, atonement, and the like, his work must be pronounced a success but trivial. So far as he claims to effect systemic description of Rabbinic Judaism ("a comparison of patterns of religion"), we have to evaluate that claim in its own terms.

First, throughout his "constructive" discussions of Rabbinic ideas about theology, Sanders quotes all documents equally with no effort at differentiation among them. He seems to have culled sayings from the diverse sources he has chosen and written them down on cards, which he proceeded to organize around his critical categories. Then he has constructed his paragraphs and sections by flipping through those cards and commenting on this and that. So there is no context in which a given saying is important in its own setting, in its own document. This is Billerbeck-scholarship.

Of greater importance, the diverse documents of Rabbinism are accorded no attention on their own. As we have seen in the earlier part of this chapter, Sifra powerfully states one point: the Mishnah requires an exegetical foundation. But the Mishnah notoriously avoids scriptural proof-texts. To Sifra none of the Mishnah's major propositions is acceptable solely upon the basis of reason or logic. All of them require proper grounding in exegesis—of a peculiarly formal sort—of Scripture. One stratum of the Talmuds, moreover, addresses the same devastating critique to the Mishnah. For once a Mishnaic proposition will be cited at the head of a talmudic pericope, a recurrent question is, What is the source of this statement? And the natural and right answer (from the perspective of the redactor of this sort of pericope) will be, As it is said..., followed by a citation of Scripture. Now if it is so that Sifra and at least one stratum of Talmud so shape their materials as to make a powerful polemical point against the Mishnah's autonomous authority ("logic"), indifferent as the Mishnah is to scriptural authority for its laws, then we must ask how we can ignore or neglect that polemic. Surely we cannot cite isolated pericopae of these documents with

no attention whatsoever to the intention of the documents which
provide said pericopae. Even the most primitive New Testament
scholars will concur that we must pay attention to the larger purposes of the several evangelists in citing sayings assigned to Jesus in
the various Gospels. Everyone knows that if we ignore Matthew's
theory of the law and simply extract Matthew's versions of Jesus'
sayings about the law and set them up side by side with the sayings
about the law given to Jesus by other of the evangelists and attitudes imputed to him by Paul, we create a mess of contradictions.
Why then should the context of diverse Rabbinic sayings, for example, on the law, be ignored? In this setting it is gratuitous to ask for
an explanation of Sanders' constant reference to "the Rabbis," as
though the century and a half which he claims to discuss produced
no evidence of individuals' and ideas' having distinct histories. This
is ignorant.

The diverse Rabbinic documents require study in their own
terms. The systems of each—so far as there are systems—have to
be uncovered and described. The way the several systems relate
and the values common to all of them have to be spelled out. The
notion that we may cite promiscuously everything in every document (within the defined canon of "permitted" documents) and
then claim to have presented an account of "the Rabbis" and their
opinions is not demonstrated and not even very well argued. We
hardly need dwell on the still more telling fact that Sanders has not
shown how systemic comparison is possible when, in point of fact,
the issues of one document, or of one system of which a document
is a part, are simply not the same as the issues of some other document or system. That is, he has succeeded in finding Rabbinic
sayings on topics of central importance to Paul (or Pauline theology). He has not even asked whether these sayings form the center
and core of the Rabbinic system or even of a given Rabbinic document. To state matters simply, How do we know that "the Rabbis"
and Paul are talking about the same thing, so that we may compare
what they have to say? And if it should turn out that "the Rabbis"
and Paul are not talking about the same thing, then what is it that
we have to compare?

Since this is one of the most ambitious works in Pauline scholarship in twenty-five years and since, as I just said, it does adumbrate
initiatives of considerable methodological promise, we must ask
ourselves what has gone wrong with Sanders' immense project. I
think the important faults are on the surface.

First, his book should have been subjected to the reading of two
kinds of editors, a good editor for style and a critical editor for the

planning and revision of the book. As a whole, it simply does not hang together. Sanders writes in a self-indulgent way.

Second, I think Sanders pays too much attention to the anti-Judaism of New Testament scholars. It is true, I suppose, that there is a built-in bias on the part of some of Christian scholarship on Rabbinic Judaism, leading to negative judgments based upon fake scholarship (Sanders' attack on Billerbeck is precise and elegant). But the motive for a major scholarly project must be constructive. One must love one's subject, that is, one's sources and scholarly setting.

Third, if, as I believe, Sanders has given us a good proposal on "the holistic comparison of patterns of religion" (pp. 12-24), then he should have tried to allow his book to unfold as an exposition and instantiation of his program of systemic comparison. This he does not do.

Fourth, his approach to the Rabbinic literature covers too much or too little. That is, he begins with a sizable description of methodological problems. But when he comes to the substantive exposition of the Rabbinic theology important for his larger project, Sanders seems to me to have forgotten pretty much everything he said on method. There are acres and acres of paragraphs which in sum and substance could have been lifted straightaway from Schechter, Moore, or Urbach, to name three other efforts at systematic dogmatics in early Rabbinic religion. I found the systematic theology of the Dead Sea Scrolls equally tedious but know too little of the problems of working on those sources to suggest how things might have been done differently and better. But to produce Sanders' substantive results of the theological discussions, from election and covenant to the nature of religious life and experience (pp. 84-232), we simply do not need to be told about critical problems ("the use of Rabbinic material, the nature of Tannaitic literature") laid out earlier (pp. 59-83). In all, it seems to me a bit pretentious, measured against the result.

SPECIAL TOPICS

JUDAISM IN THE LAND OF ISRAEL
IN THE FIRST CENTURY

James D.G. Dunn
(University of Durham)

1 INTRODUCTION

The description of Judaism in the land of Israel in the first century CE is beset with problems of definition, not least those of anachronistic definition.

An older generation, both Jewish and Christian, thought in terms of "normative Judaism",[1] the assumption being that the Judaism represented in rabbinic tradition already served as the norm determinative for Judaism in the first century.[2] Scholars were, of course, aware of Jewish pseudepigrapha and of Philo, but these writings had been preserved by Christians and not by the rabbis, and so could the more easily be regarded as variations on or deviations from a Pharisaic/rabbinic norm.[3] To be sure, there was also some reflection on the possibility that diaspora Judaism was a different branch of the species from Palestinian Judaism, perhaps thus providing a solution to the conundrum of what Judaism it was that the Christian Paul set his face so firmly against.[4] But the thesis simply reinforced the sense that diaspora Judaism was a divergent (and inferior) form of Judaism, whose degree of divergence itself provided a large part of the explanation of why Pauline Christianity and normative/Palestinian Judaism went their separate ways.

In the mid-twentieth century, however, the assumption of a Pharisaic/rabbinic normative Judaism recognized as such in first century Israel was shattered by the discovery of the Dead Sea Scrolls. Although the delay in publishing many of the more obviously sectarian documents has diminished their impact, they clearly include Jewish documents which predate and have been unaffected by Christianity, whose self-asserted sectarian character is evident, and which can hardly fail to be attributed to a kind of Judaism which flourished in the heart of the land of Israel up to the 60s of

---

[1] The term is particularly linked to Moore; see e.g. Sanders (1977) 34 and n.11.
[2] The assumption prevails, e.g., in Jeremias (1971) and in Safrai & Stern.
[3] See e.g. the disagreement between Bousset, Gressmann and Moore on this question (as discussed by Sanders [1977]34 and 55-6).
[4] Particularly Montefiore and Schoeps.

the first century. This in turn has resulted in a renewed interest in the pseudepigrapha[5] and an increasing recognition that they too have to be described as representing different forms of Judaism. At the same time the extent of Pharisaic influence in first century Israel has been radically questioned,[6] and the sharpness of any distinction between "Judaism" and "Hellenism", which allowed a clear demarcation between "Palestinian Judaism" and "Hellenistic Judaism" has been considerably blurred.[7] Within a broader framework we could perhaps also note that the liberal thrust of so much western scholarship, reinforced more recently by post-modern scruples, has progressively undermined the very idea of a "norm".

In consequence the last two decades of the present century have witnessed an increasing tendency to emphasize the diverse character of first century Judaism and to speak of several "Judaisms", leaving the question of their legitimacy as forms of "Judaism" unasked as being either misleading or improper.[8] Still too little explored, however, is the further or alternative question, how this quite proper modern, phenomenological description of different Judaisms relates to the self-perception of each of these several Judaisms in their own day, not to mention their evaluation of these other Judaisms.

Whether we should speak of "Palestinian Judaism" as one of the sub-heads within "Judaism" sets another series of hares running. "Palestinian" as an epithet is widely used and apparently acceptable in most circles of scholarship. But one suspects that the rationale is partly political and reflects an unwillingness to use the term "Israel" for the territory which today (since 1967) includes the occupied territories ("the west bank" of the Jordan, etc). On the other hand it is too little appreciated that the name "Palestine" only came into formal use for the territory in the second century CE, when, following the failure of the Second Jewish Revolt, the Roman colony of Aelia Capitolina was re-established and Judea was renamed Syria Palaestina. The simple expression "first century Palestinian Judaism" can thus mask more than one anachronistic understanding of the subject matter. Hence the more carefully formulated title

---

[5] See particularly Charlesworth (1983, 1985) and Sparks.
[6] Differently by Neusner (1971) and (1973) and by Sanders (particularly 1992).
[7] Particularly Hengel (1974) and (1990).
[8] E.g. Sandmel ch. 2 "Palestinian Judaisms"; Neusner (1987); Neusner, *Classical Judaism* 27-36; Segal (1987); Murphy 39. "Whereas rabbinic Judaism is dominated by an identifiable perspective that holds together many otherwise diverse elements, early Judaism appears to encompass almost unlimited diversity and variety—indeed, it might be more appropriate to speak of early Judaisms"—Kraft & Nickelsburg 2.

of the present paper—"Judaism in the land of Israel in the first century".[9]

Equally problematic has been the temporal designation attached to "Judaism". An older scholarship spoke of first century Judaism as "Spätjudentum", a usage which persisted into the late 1960s. This was an astonishing designation since it reduced Judaism to the role of serving solely as forerunner to Christianity and left a question-mark over how one should describe the next nineteen centuries of Judaism! The still more common "intertestamental Judaism" re-duced the significance of this "Judaism" to bridging the gap be-tween the (Christian) Testaments and implied a coherence ("Juda-ism") for the documents chiefly referred to which is by no means clear. The natural reaction has been to choose the opposite adjec-tive and to speak of "early Judaism", or "formative Judaism".[10] The actual period covered is of uncertain length, particularly its starting point—whether from Ezra, or from the Greek period (300 BCE), the most favoured option, or from the close of the Jewish canon (from Bible to Mishnah), or from the Maccabees, or from the emer-gence of the Pharisees as a religious force, or indeed from the be-ginnings of the reformulation of Judaism after 70 CE. The end point is more obviously 200 CE, on the grounds that the codifica-tion of the Mishnah marks the beginning of rabbinic Judaism proper. The designation, however, runs a risk similar to that for the objectionable "Spätjudentum", since it can be taken to imply that the only significance of first century Judaism was as a precursor to rabbinic Judaism.

The further alternative of designating the period 300 BCE to 200 CE as "Middle Judaism"[11] has the advantage of distinguishing the Greco-Roman period from what went before ("ancient Judaism" as 6th to 4th centuries BCE). But it raises in turn the issues of when we should start speaking of "Judaism" proper, whether "Judaism" is a concept or simply a label, and the justifica-tion for and significance of marking off the pre-exilic period ("the religion of Israel") so sharply from the still biblical "Judaism" of the return from exile.[12]

---

[9] The terms "Israel" has its own problems, as we shall see, but at least the usage here is unambiguous.

[10] So e.g. the title of the volume edited by Kraft and Nickelsburg; Neusner has also promoted the term "Formative Judaism" in the series produced by him under that title. In contrast the series of volumes edited by W. S. Green (*Approaches to Ancient Judaism*) use "Ancient Judaism" to cover everything from the post-exilic period to the early rabbis.

[11] Boccaccini.

[12] *The Anchor Bible Dictionary* completes its articles on the "History of Israel" with the Persian period and begins its treatment of "Judaism" with the Greco-Roman period (*ABD* 3.526-76, 3.1037-89).

All this points up the need to proceed cautiously if we are to avoid the danger of imposing categories and grids which might distort the evidence more than display it. In view of the confusion of definitions which has weakened earlier debate we should obviously begin with some clarification of the term "Judaism" itself. We can then indicate something of the range of belief and practice which that term may properly be used to categorise. And finally we will have to ask what it is which makes it possible to use the same category, "Judaism", for them all, what is the common ground which they share.

2 Definitions

2.1 The Term "Judaism"

What is "Judaism"? When did "Judaism" begin? If the answer were to depend solely on word occurrence in our literary sources the answer would be clear. For Ἰουδαϊσμός first appears in literature in 2 Maccabees, in three passages—2.21, 8.1 and 14.38. 2.21 describes the Maccabean rebels as "those who fought bravely for Judaism (ὑπὲρ τοῦ Ἰουδαϊσμοῦ)", 8.1 their supporters as "those who had continued in Judaism (τοὺς μεμενηκότας ἐν τῷ Ἰουδαϊσμῳ)", and 14.38 the martyr Razis as one who had formerly been accused of Judaism and who had eagerly risked body and life ὑπὲρ τοῦ Ἰουδαϊσμοῦ. Reflecting the same traditions, 4 Macc. 4.26 describes the attempt of Antiochus Epiphanes "to compel each member of the nation to eat defiling foods and to renounce Judaism".

The only other literary evidence from our period (before the end of the first century CE) is Gal. 1.13-14, where Paul speaks of his former conduct ἐν τῷ Ἰουδαϊσμῳ, and recalls how he had at that time persecuted "the church of God" and had progressed ἐν τῷ Ἰουδαϊσμῳ beyond many of his contemporaries among his people (ἐν τῷ γ°νει μου). In addition however we should note a funerary inscription from our period in Italy, which praises a woman "who lived a gracious life ἐν τῷ Ἰουδαϊσμῳ (CIJ 537).[13]

Two points call at once for comment. First, in the earliest phase of its usage there are no examples of the term being used by non-Jews. "Judaism" begins as a Jewish term of self-reference. But equally noticeable is the fact that all four sources reflect the perspective of Hellenistic (or diaspora or Greek-speaking) Judaism.

---

[13] Amir.

Thus, it is significant that the term occurs in 2 Maccabees, composed in Greek and a self-confessed "epitome" of the five volume work of Jason of Cyrene (2.26, 28), and not as a translation of some Hebrew term in 1 Maccabees. Indeed, K. G. Kuhn can find only one passage in rabbinic literature and perhaps Palestinian usage where יהדות = Ἰουδαισμός occurs, but, interestingly, in a description of the Jews in Babylon who did not change their God or their religious laws but held fast ביהדותן ("in their Judaism") (*Esther Rab.* 7.11).[14] Here we should simply note the further element of anomaly in our definitions in that we are using a term ("Judaism") to describe the religion of Jews in the land of Israel in the first century which they evidently did not use for themselves.

Second, in all cases the term "Judaism" was being used in self-definition to mark out the character of belief and practice which distinguished the referent from the surrounding culture and ethos. Such diaspora Jews lived "in Judaism" as "a sort of fenced off area in which Jewish lives are led".[15] Indeed, in 2 Maccabees the term is obviously coined as a counter to "Hellenism" (Ἑλληνισμός) (2 Macc. 4.13). That is to say, for the author of 2 Maccabees, "Judaism" is the summary term for that system embodying national and religious identity which was the rallying point for the violent rejection by the Maccabees of the Syrian attempt to assimilate them by the abolition of their distinctive practices (particularly circumcision and food laws—1 Macc. 1.60-63; so also 4 Macc. 4.26). From the beginning, therefore "Judaism" has a strongly nationalistic overtone and denotes a powerful integration of religious and national identity which marks Judaism out in its distinctiveness from other nations and religions.

This is confirmed by the other literary usage cited above—Gal. 1.13-14. For the life described there as "in Judaism" is marked by the same total commitment to traditional religious practices and by the same hostility to anything which would dilute or defile Israel's distinctiveness. The fierceness of this reaction is indicated particularly by the terms "zeal" (Phil. 3.6) and "zealot" (Gal. 1.14). These are prominent in describing Maccabean motivation (ζῆλος—1 Macc. 2.54, 58; ζηλοῦν—1 Macc. 2.24, 26, 27, 50, 54, 58; ζηλωτής—2 Macc. 4.2; 4 Macc. 18.12), where Phinehas is presented as the great role model (1 Macc. 2.26, 54; 4 Macc. 18.12) and the war-cry is "zeal for the law" (1 Macc. 2.26, 27, 50, 58; 2 Macc. 4.2). And Paul implicitly aligns himself with such fiercely nationalistic response by attributing his motivation as a persecutor

---

[14] Kuhn 3.363 and 364 n.49.
[15] Amir 39-40.

of the church to the same "zeal" (Phil. 3.6). It is equally significant
that he sets his life "in Judaism" in sharp contrast to his commission
as apostle to the Gentiles (Gal. 1.13-16), implying clearly that it was
the hostility to things "Gentile" in his "Judaism" on which he had
now turned his back.[16]

In short, so far as its earliest usage is concerned, the term
"Judaism" describes the system of religion and way of life within
which diaspora Jews lived so as to maintain their distinctive identity, and also the national and religious identity which was given its
more definitive character by vigorous resistance to the assimilating
and syncretistic influences of wider Hellenism.

2.2 "Jew, Israel, Judaize"

This finding seems to be strengthened by comparison with the
much more widespread use of the terms "Jew" and "Israel". The
term "Jew" ('Ιουδαῖος) begins of course as a way of identifying
someone from Judea ('Ιουδαία, יהודה)—"the Jews", then, as the
nation or people identified with that territory. But since Judea was
a temple state a religious identity was inextricably bound up with
ethnic identity—"the Jews" as worshippers of the God whose temple was in Jerusalem.[17] And when the Hasmoneans pushed back the
boundaries of that temple state it was natural to use "Jews" for the
people as a whole (from Galilee as well), that is, those who by birth
or conversion (proselytes) were identified as members of that people
and devotees of that temple's cult.[18] Likewise "Israel", though applicable primarily to the northern kingdom in the period of the divided kingdoms, was too precious an expression of Jewish self-identity not to be used by all who claimed to stand in the line of inheritance from the patriarchs.[19]

The point for us, however, is the one again made so effectively
by Kuhn: that is, that "'Israel' is the name which the people uses
for itself, whereas 'Jews' is the non-Jewish name for it".[20] In other

---

[16] See further my *Galatians* (Black's NT Commentary; London: A. & C. Black,
1993) *ad loc.*

[17] Hence the well known but still surprising willingness of the Roman authorities
to permit diaspora Jews to send their temple dues to Jerusalem.

[18] See e.g. Dunn (1991) 143-5 and Kraemer.

[19] "Israel implies the religious claim to be God's chosen people even when it is
used in secular contexts, with no religious emphasis, as the accepted designation"
(Kuhn 362, with examples). Zeitlin (1936) 10 notes that the prophets of Judah (the
southern kingdom) always delivered their messages in the name of the God of
Israel, never of the God of Judah.

[20] Kuhn 360; see analysis and discussion on 359-65; see further *Encyclopaedia
Judaica* 10.22.

words, "Jew" is more the term used, by (hellenistic) Jews (Philo, Josephus, Aristeas, Eupolemus, Artapanus, Hecataeus) as well as others, to distinguish the people so designated from other peoples; whereas "Israel" is a self-affirmation by reference to its own distinctively apprehended heritage. Thus, for example, the use of "Jews" in 1 Maccabees where the context is official and the tone diplomatic, but of "Israel" when it is a matter of self-designation;[21] in the Gospels "king of the Jews" is Pilate's terminology, but "king of Israel" that of the high priests (Mark 15.2, 9, 12, 26; 15.32 pars.); Paul speaks regularly of "Jew(s) and Greek(s)" as a way of categorising the whole of humanity (e.g. Rom. 2.9-10; 3.9; 10.12; 1 Cor. 12.13; Gal. 3.28), while prefering to say of himself, "I am an Israelite" (Rom. 11.1; 2 Cor. 11.22);[22] and in the rabbinic writings "Israel" and not "Jews" is the almost universal self-designation.[23] "Jews", in other words, naturally evokes the counterpart, "Gentiles", each defining itself by its exclusion of the other—"Jew" = non-Gentile, "Gentile" = non-Jew. In contrast, "Israel" has no defining antonym; it is defined by the insider, not the outsider, and by reference to its internal history, not the history of nations and peoples. In short, "Jew" betokens the perspective of the spectator (Jewish included), "Israel" that of the participant.

We might simply add that the picture is confirmed by the use of the verbal equivalent to "Judaism" and "Jew", equally infrequent in our sources as the former—ἰουδαίζειν, "to live like a Jew" (Esther 8.17 LXX; Theodotus in Eusebius, *Praep. Evang.* 9.22.5; Josephus, *War* 2.454; *Ant.* 20.38-46). In each case it describes the action of a non-Jew in undertaking observance of the distinctive Jewish customs (sabbath, food-laws, etc.) even to the extent of being circumcised (becoming a proselyte). In contrast, there is no verbal form of "Israel/Israelite". The "judaizer" starts from outside, his very action presupposes the distinction between Jew and Gentile, he crosses a boundary; whereas the "Israelite" starts from inside and so has no need to take an action equivalent to ἰουδαίζειν.

2.3 Conclusion

The upshot of all this is that great care must be taken in using the term "Judaism" to categorize the religious identity of the principal

---

[21] Kuhn 360-1.

[22] In contrast it is the Gentile Luke who has Paul say of himself "I am a Jew" not only to the Roman tribune but also to the Jerusalem crowd, speaking in Aramaic (Acts 21.39; 22.3).

[23] Zeitlin (1936) 31-2, recalling that after the failure of the bar Kokhba revolt the Jews ceased to exist as a nation.

inhabitants of the land of Israel in the first century. Of course our modern use need not be determined or restricted by ancient usage; though it can also be noted that any modern attempt to describe first century Judaism does actually share something of the spectator perspective and concern for differentiation implicit in that ancient usage. The difficulty is, however, that our use of data from the period in filling out our description is bound to reflect in part at least the attitudes which were also expressed in the term "Judaism". So we must be conscious of the strong nationalist overtones in the term's early use, and of the degree to which national and religious identity were fused in the one word, including not only differentiation from but also a certain hostility to the other nations and their religious practices. Moreover, any attempt to describe the religious identity of first century Israel will naturally want to include an insider's perspective for as many of the participants and practitioners as possible, but such an attempt is bound to jar in one degree or other with the principal defining term "Judaism". Such problems should not inhibit us from attempting a brief sketch of "Judaism in the land of Israel in the first century", but they should alert us to the complexities of using multiple sources and the danger either of mistaking the perspectives which shaped these sources or of unwittingly imposing our own.

3 THE DIVERSITY OF FIRST CENTURY JUDAISM

What counts as Judaism in the land of Israel in the first century? What falls within the scope of "Judaism"? How broad and encompassing was it, or (from our perspective) can it be as a historical description? A natural and popular response has been to look at the different groups and writings of the period. And though this approach is open to objection, as we shall see, a description of these groups and writings does form an important part of our understanding of first century Judaism, particularly of its diversity.

Our first objective, then, is, within the space available, to give some indication of the range of practice and belief covered by "Judaism" as a phenomenological description. In each case the key question is: If this too is "Judaism", what does that tell us about "Judaism"? Although much of the evidence available is fragmentary, often hostile and sometimes minimal, we have enough information to work with, and modern treatments have improved markedly in quality and reliability over the last two decades.

If we are to gain a fuller perspective on first century Judaism, however, there is another aspect which we ought not to ignore.

That is, the view of Judaism *from inside*, what these groups claimed
for themselves and thought of each other. Without taking some
account of an insider's view, a spectator's view of first century
Judaism will always be inadequate. A spectator may be content to
describe a Judaism which was richly diverse in character, but did
the insiders share that recognition of diversity, and if not how
should that fact influence our perception of first century "Judaism"?
Here too there is probably sufficient evidence in most cases, though
in comparison with the first approach the issue here has rarely been
addressed in modern discussions.

3.1 Judaism and Judaisms from Without

3.1.1 The Four "Sects"

The usual starting point has been Josephus' "four philosophies" or
"sects" (αἱρ°σεις)—not unnaturally since Josephus' way of intro-
ducing them seems to imply that they were the only groupings
among the Jews worthy of attention on the part of his readers (*War*
2.119-166; *Ant.* 18.11-25).[24] To begin with Josephus also makes
good sense since Josephus is as close to the events as we could hope
for and he is more informative than we might have expected (he
was attempting to describe and defend his native religion to his
influential Roman patrons). That such an apologetic treatment will
be biased and selective need hardly be said. But the fact remains
that the spectator perspective of Josephus is likely to give a fuller
and sounder basis for a description of first century Judaism than
any other, and there are sufficient other sources for us to be able to
recognize much if not most of Josephus' bias. In each case, however, there are major questions unresolved and continuing debate
of great vigour.

Pharisees naturally come first: Josephus always gives them first
place in his lists, and they were undisputedly the principal forerun-
ners of subsequently prevailing rabbinic Judaism. Older treatments
of them are generally unreliable, partly because of a Christian bias
which saw them as chief representatives of a legalism which served
by way of contrast to highlight the gracious character of the Christian message, and partly because of uncritical use (by both Jewish

---

[24] In reference to the debate as to whether Josephus really thought of four
rather than three philosophies or sects we might simply note that he describes the
movement begun by Judas of Galilee both as a "sect" (*War* 2.118) and as a "philosophy" (*Ant.* 18.9, 23).

and Christian scholars) of the later rabbinic traditions as evidence
of what the first century Pharisees already believed and practised.
The first of these misperceptions has been shattered in English
speaking scholarship particularly by Sanders,[25] the second by Neusner in his careful layering of the traditions to expose those which
can be traced back to the first century with the greatest confidence.[26]

The issues of continuing debate are those highlighted by Neusner and Sanders. In particular, on sources, Sanders may be justified
in objecting to Neusner's use only of attributed rabbinic traditions
to inform his picture of Pharisaic debates, but he is himself open to
criticism for bracketing out the evidence of the Gospels. And more
should certainly be made of Paul, the only self-attested Pharisee
writing in the pre-70 period.[27] The second main bone of contention
is whether the Pharisees were primarily a purity sect? Sanders objects to Neusner on this score, but concedes a good deal of key
ground while disputing its significance, and diffuses his criticism by
concentrating on the question of the Pharisees' political and social
influence.[28] But more weight surely should be given to the Pharisees' very name, generally agreed to signify "separated ones",[29] and
thus indicating a wider perception of the Pharisees as a group who
defined themeslves by their concern to keep themselves apart—a
primarily purity concern.[30]

Where the Pharisees stood out most clearly among their contemporaries and in rabbinic perspective, however, was in their meticu-
lous concern to interpret the law accurately (Josephus, *War* 1.110;
2.162; *Ant.* 17.41; *Life* 191; Acts 22.3; 26.5),[31] and in their development of a distinctive halakhic interpretation of Torah, "the traditions of their fathers" (*Ant.* 13.297, 408; 17.41; *Life* 198; Mark 7.3,
5; Gal. 1.14; the so-called "oral law"). It is no surprise that the
Judaism which survived the disaster of 70 CE, the Judaism most
closely related to the Pharisees, was a Judaism of rabbi, Torah and
Halakhah.[32]

---

[25] Sanders (1977); also (1985) index "Pharisees".
[26] Neusner (1971); also (1973).
[27] See Dunn (1990).
[28] Sanders (1992) chs. 18-19. For Neusner's own reply see his "Mr Maccoby's
Red Cow, Mr Sanders's Pharisees—and Mine", *Journal for the Study of Judaism* 23
(1991) 81-98; also "Mr. Sanders's Pharisees and Mine", *Bulletin for Biblical Research*
2 (1992) 143-69.
[29] See e.g. Schürer 2.396-7, and Cohen 162.
[30] See further Dunn (1991) 110.
[31] See particularly A. I. Baumgarten, "The Name of the Pharisees", *Journal of
Biblical Literature* 102 (1983) 413-7.
[32] See also Saldarini and Stemberger.

Little can be said of the *Sadducees* because of the paucity of evidence. They are usually said to have differed from the Pharisees by rejecting the "oral law" (on the basis of *Ant.* 13.297 and 18.17), though a minority see the basic issue separating Sadducee from Pharisee as that, once again, of purity.[33] A considerable overlap is also generally assumed between the Sadducees and the aristocratic families from whom the high priests were drawn and who controlled the Temple.[34] Since Judea/Israel was a Temple state, that placed the levers of political, religious, economic and social power firmly in their hands, to the extent permitted by Rome and the Herods.[35] It also means that so far as Jewish involvement in the death of Jesus is concerned we can speak only of the high priestly faction.[36] At the same time, despite their wealth and degree of hellenisation, their very name (if it does indeed indicate that they took their name from Zadok the priest)[37] suggests, somewhat surprisingly, an origin similar to that of the Essenes, that is, in partisan protest on behalf of the legitimate (Zadokite) priesthood. At all events their prominence and power prior to 70 CE is clear testimony to the importance of the Temple in first century Judaism.

As for the *Essenes*, there is continuing consensus that Qumran was an Essene community and that the great bulk of the Dead Sea Scrolls came from their library. But the evidence of Josephus (*War* 2.124) and Philo (*Prob.* 76) is probably sufficient to demonstrate that Qumran was only one branch of the Essenes and that other groups lived in various towns. And the disparity of the material in the scrolls is becoming steadily clearer, with only some representative of the Qumran community's own beliefs, and probably the *Covenant of Damascus* (CD) representative of the more widely dispersed Essenes.[38]

The Qumran community is the clearest example of a "sect" (in the modern sense of the word) within first century Judaism—its distinctiveness as such becoming steadily clearer as the more sectarian of the Dead Sea Scrolls (from Cave 4) are published, including strong predestinarian, dualistic and mystical features.[39] It evidently

---

[33] G. G. Porton, *ABD* 5.892-3. "In the Mishnah and Tosefta most of the disputes between the Sadducees and Pharisees (and others) concern interpretations of the laws of ritual purity" (Saldarini 233).

[34] See Sanders (1992) ch. 15.

[35] On the character, status and powers of "the Sanhedrin" see now Sanders (1992) 472-88.

[36] See e.g. Dunn (1991) 51-3 and those cited there.

[37] Schürer 2.405-7; Porton, *ABD* 5.892.

[38] Sanders (1992) 342, 347.

[39] See e.g. the texts from 1QS cited in Vermes 42-3 and the "Songs for the Holocaust of the Sabbath" on 221-30.

regarded itself as an alternative to the Jerusalem Temple (e.g. 4QFlor.; hence its withdrawal to the wilderness), determined membership by reference to its own understanding and interpretation of scripture, and applied strict rules for novitiate and continuing membership (1QS 5-9). Most like the earliest Christian movement in its sense of divine grace (1QS 11; 1QH), eschatological fulfilment and anticipation (e.g. 1QpHab, 1QSa, 1QM), it is furthest removed from the former in its strict application of purity rules and discipline.[40] If this too is Judaism it underlines the extent to which Torah and Temple were fundamental and defining characteristics of Judaism.

With Josephus' "fourth philosophy", the *Zealots*, the main dispute is whether we can properly speak of a Zealot party active prior to the first revolt (66 CE). The consensus is that we should not so speak,[41] and is probably confirmed by the fact that Paul could call himself a "zealot" without indicating membership of a political party or resistance movement.[42] Nevertheless, the name iteslf ("Zealot") indicates the claim of a continuity of tradition and piety from Phinehas and the Maccabees, where resistance to any dilution or infringement of Israel's distinctive relationship with Yahweh was the overmastering concern. If this too is Judaism, its self-understanding as the elect people of God, separated out from among the nations must also count as a fundamental defining characteristic.

3.1.2 The Other Judaisms

In talking about recognizable groups within Judaism in the land of Israel in the first century we must also mention *the Christians*. The term is again anachronistic. The name was first given in a diaspora context (Antioch) and its Latin formation ("Christiani") suggests a name first coined by the Roman authorities to identify a subset probably still perceived as essentially Jewish (like the "Herodiani").[43] Within Israel itself the only distinctive name designates them "the sect of the Nazarenes" (Acts 24.5), a group identified by reference to their founder (like Zadokites), distinctive within but not from Judaism.[44] We need not press the point, since it is now widely recognized that Jesus stood foursquare within the Judaism of his

---

[40] Newton.

[41] See Grabbe 499-500 and D. Rhoads, "Zealots", *ABD* 6.1043-54; otherwise Hengel (1989).

[42] See above pp. 231-2.

[43] A clear distinction between Jews and Christians only begins to become evident in Greco-Roman writers of the second century (Tacitus, Suetonius, Pliny).

[44] Even the description "the Way" (itself thoroughly Jewish in its emphasis on a way of life to be walked) occurs only in reference to the Christian Hellenists and the mission of Paul in Acts (9.2; 18.25-26; 19.9, 23; 22.4; 24.14, 22).

day and that the movement which sprang from him initially was entirely Jewish in character, a legitimate expression within the spectrum of first century Judaism.[45] Following the breach with Stephen and the Hellenists, a breach as much with the first Christian Jews as with a Temple centred Judaism (Acts 6-7), the Jesus disciples who remained in Jerusalem and Judea until the early 60s can quite properly be ranked together with the four groups already surveyed as a further "sect" within first century Judaism (Acts 24.5, 14; 28.22).[46] Their distinctiveness, however, was focused not in Temple or Torah (they seem to have been quite conservative in these respects, if Acts 21.20 is any guide), but in the claims they made regarding Jesus of Nazareth and the link this gave them to the developing "Christianity" beyond Israel's borders.

A survey of groups within the land of Israel in the first century cannot ignore *the Samaritans*. Unfortunately their history in this period is obscure beyond a few references (e.g. *Ant.* 17.319, 342; 18.85-89; 20.118-36; Acts 8) and their own literature is too late to help us. The fact that at various times they called themselves "Judeans/Jews" (*Ant.* 11.340), "Hebrews" (*Ant.* 11.344) and "Israelites" (in a inscription [150-50 BCE] from Delos)[47] is a further reminder of how careful we have to be in our own use of such descriptive titles. It is sufficiently clear, however, that there was already a sharp breach between Samaria and the Jews generally (as implied in Matt. 10.5; Luke 9.52-54; 10.30-37; John 4.9; 8.48). No doubt significant factors in the breach were folk memories of Samaria's hostility to Judea's reconstitution in the Persian era (Ezra 4-5; Neh. 4-6) and the sense that Samaritans were a people whose ethnic and religious identity had been gravely diluted ("apostates from the Jewish nation"—*Ant.* 11.340; contrast Ezra 9-10). But in the event the breach came to focus much more sharply and decisively on the question of the Temple and the correct place to worship God (cf. John 4.20), with the Samaritan claim for Mt Gerizim backed up by their own version of the Pentateuch.[48]

---

[45] See e.g. W. A. Meeks in Cohen 9; Cohen 124-6; Flusser xv-xvi; Charlesworth (1988); Boccaccini 15-18 and see also his n.12 and 28-9. At one point Neusner argues that "from the very beginnings the Judaic and Christian religious worlds scarcely intersected" (*Jews and Christians* x). That may be increasingly fair comment from the later stages of first century Christianity, arguably even from Paul when his distinctive mission to the Gentiles was in full flood, but not for the first 20-30 years of the movement and not for "Christianity" in Judea.

[46] See further Dunn (1991).

[47] A. T. Kraabel, *Biblical Archaeologist* 47 (1984) 44-46; and further L. M. White, "The Delos Synagogue Revisited. Recent Fieldwork in the Graeco-Roman Diaspora", *Harvard Theological Review* 80 (1987) 133-60.

[48] Ses further F. Dexinger, "Limits of Tolerance in Judaism: The Samaritan Example", in Sanders (1981) 88-114 and J. D. Purvis, "The Samaritans and Judaism" in Kraft & Nickelsburg 81-98.

Finally in trying to gain a sense of the range and diversity of Jewish groupings in first century Israel we should not forget the large amorphous body which we might here identify simply as *"Hellenists"*. Broadly speaking the term designates those influenced in significant degree by Greek language and culture. Despite the fact that "Judaism" constituted itself initially by opposition to "Hellenism", the influence of Hellenistic culture (the international culture of the day) was too pervasive for a line of total opposition to be maintained. Thus the Jews had to tolerate a Hasmonean and then Herodian court which was characteristically "Hellenistic" in style.[49] Within Jerusalem we hear of a significant number of "Hellenists", probably Jews returned from the diapora, who had their own synagogue(s), where, presumably, the language of communication was Greek (Acts 6.1, 9). Within the land of Israel there were several Hellenistic cities, notably Sepphoris and Tiberias, which were thoroughly Greek in political and social structure but included large Jewish populations.[50] These too have to be included within Judaism in the land of Israel in the first century.[51]

3.1.3 The Evidence of Apocrypha and Pseudepigrapha

In addition to these various groupings within Judaism (or forms of Judaism), we have to make room for other expressions of Judaism, most notably those found in the *pseudepigrapha*. For a grasp of first century Judaism in the land of Israel there is an immediate problem here. All four of Josephus' "sects" we know were operative in our period and territory. But with the apocrypha several of the items come from the diaspora, and the scope and datings of so much of the pseudepigrapha is unclear that we are often uncertain as to which of the writings are of relevance to us. At the same time, however, many of the documents fall into groupings or reveal trends which must have been present in our period and region, so that a broad picture can be sketched.

Most striking is the sequence of *apocalyptic writings*, particularly the Enoch corpus, 4 Ezra, 2 Baruch, the Apocalypse of Abraham,

---

[49] The ambivalence of feelings towards Herod the Great in particular, however, is illustrated by Josephus' designation of him as a "half-Jew", because of his Idumean birth (*Ant.* 14.430).

[50] See J. F. Strange, "Sepphoris" *ABD* 5.1090-3 and "Tiberias", *ABD* 6.547-9.

[51] A more detailed study would have to consider also "the Herodians" (Mark 3.6; 12.13) and possible baptismal sects, not to mention groups of bandits! (see Grabbe 501-2, 507-9 and 511-4).

and, we may add, the Apocalypse of John (Revelation).[52] These all grow out of the overmastering conviction that events of earth are determined by what happens in heaven, with the consequent desire to know these heavenly secrets. Prominent in them are angelic beings, both interpreter angels, but also glorious angels, the sight of whom is to assure the seer that he is close to the presence of the one God, but whose very glory can both enhance and threaten the exclusive majesty of the one God.[53] This is a Judaism focused in the immediacy of spiritual (revelatory) experience, but in consequence also vulnerable to "flights of fancy".

A *testamentary literature* also developed in this period (a patriarchal figure giving his last will and testament). Though only the precursors of the Testaments of the Twelve Patriarchs and the Testament of Moses fall for consideration within our concern, the fact that the format was so widespread both in Israel and in diaspora Judaism is a further reminder that the interrelatedness between the two must have been considerable. The overlap with apocalyptic literature is substantial (warning us not to operate with too strict categories), but their most distinctive feature is the desire to promote righteous living. In the Testaments of the Twelve Patriarchs the superiority of Levi over Judah (particularly *Test. Jud.* 21.2-4; 25.1) indicates a Judaism where Temple and priest are still the central defining feature.[54]

The difficulty of drawing firm lines between literary evidence from within the land of Israel and that from the diaspora is well illustrated by the *wisdom literature*. It is striking nonetheless that the only two which can be said to have originated in Hebrew (ben Sira and Baruch) both make a point of focusing universal divine wisdom explicitly in the Torah (Sir. 24.23; Bar. 4.1). Of the *stories of Jewish heroes and heroines* which must have fed popular piety wherever they were read, we might note how consistently they were portrayed as prospering precisely because of their loyalty to the food laws and refusal to eat the food of Gentiles (1 Macc. 1.62-63; Dan. 1.8-16; Tob. 1.10-13; Jud. 12.2, 6-9, 19).

Of other relevant pseudepigrapha there are two which deserve special mention. The first is *Jubilees*, a reworking of Genesis and the early chapters of Exodus, and clearly designed to promote more

---

[52] Texts of the former in Charlesworth (1983).
[53] See particularly Rowland (1982).
[54] For a review of the ongoing debate, particularly regarding the Testaments of the Twelve Patriarchs, see J. J. Collins, "The Testamentary Literature in Recent Scholarship", in Kraft & Nickelsburg 268-85.

rigorous obedience to the stipulations of the Torah. It probably comes from the early Maccabean-Hasmonean period, and is now generally regarded as a precursor of the Qumran Essenes. The second is the *Psalms of Solomon*, written in the aftermath of the Roman conquest of Jerusalem (63 BCE) and wrestling with the consequent problem of theodicy—how to square recent events with God's choice of Israel.

A major problem for us with all these documents is the question of how representative and influential they were. Although we know, for example, that portions of the Enoch corpus were evidently prized at Qumran and can see in CD 16.2-4 an allusion to Jubilees, we cannot deduce from this that they speak for substantial groupings within first century Judaism. After all, an apocalypse could have been the work of a single person and not speak for any party. At the opposite extreme it would be equally unwise to list them all as expressive of disparate Judaisms without any overlap or commonality. Just as it would be inadmissable as a procedure to identify each document with a single community, as though no subgroup could happily express the richness of its own self-perception through several different writings.[55] In particular, the breadth of the appeal of wisdom and heroic literature surely prevents us from seeing it as representative of distinctive Judaisms. Frustrating though our lack of information may be here, then, we must be content to let these writings illuminate facets of first century Judaism in the land of Israel without imposing a systematised coherence of our own.

3.1.4 Common Judaism

When all is said and done, however, the most relevant of those so far mentioned represent a very small minority within the population of the land of Israel in the first century. Josephus indicates that the Pharisees were more than 6,000 strong (at the time of Herod), the Essenes more than 4,000, and the Sadducees a small wealthy elite (*Ant.* 17.42; 18.20; 13.298). The "Christians" can have been no more than a few thousand at most within the land of Israel (even allowing for Acts 21.20). The Samaritans, of course, were a significant political entity, but should probably be placed beyond the spectrum of what may properly be called "Judaism" from a specta-

---

[55] This is a fallacy to which several NT scholars commit themselves in hypothesizing a distinctive (and distinctively) Q community.

tor perspective. And the number of "Hellenists" was no doubt a substantial minority of the population but impossible to quantify, and they could not be said to have formed a coherent party. We have no sure way of knowing how many or who the various apocryphal or pseudepigraphal writings spoke for, but that they represented distinctive groups of any significant number must be considered doubtful in view of Josephus' silence regarding them. All in all, then, the Judaisms so far described, about which we can speak with any confidence and whose distinctiveness gives at least a prima facie case for describing them as different "Judaisms", probably constituted a very small minority of the Jews living in the land of first century Israel.

It is at this point that Sanders' reminder is important, that in speaking of first century Judaism we need to speak first and foremost of the practices and beliefs of the great mass of the people, what he calls *"common Judaism"*.[56] For these other forms of Judaism are simply luxuriant or exotic growths which, from a spectator's perspective, mark them out from what in comparison may seem the more commonplace but is in fact the much more extensive flower bed or garden. It is this common "bedding" in the Judaism of the people at large which gives these diverse forms of Judaism their common denominator as "Judaism". Or to be more precise, it is because there is a Judaism more generally recognizable as constituting the life of the people (the Jews) that we can go on to speak of different versions of it practised by different groups of Jews. Elsewhere I have spoken of "the four pillars of Judaism", the point being the same: that there was a common foundation of practice and belief whi·h constituted the constant or recurring or common factors unifying all the different particular forms of first century Judaism and on which they were built.[57]

Before we turn to describe this Judaism, or, again to be more precise, these common features of Judaism, however, we have once again to remind ourselves that our phenomenological description of the diversity of first century Judaism may not represent adequately the self-understanding and perspective of any of the particular forms of first century Judaism. Before proceeding to "common Judaism", therefore, we must try to step inside and see first century Judaism in the land of Israel "from within".

---

[56] Sanders (1992) Part II.
[57] See Dunn (1991) ch. 2.

3.2 Judaism and Judaisms from Within

How do we get "inside" the Judaism(s) of our period? Obviously by reading empathetically the documents which were written within Israel during our period, particularly those that were written from a self-consciously insider perspective and in defence of their self-perception, even if in the event they speak for what may have been only small and relatively unrepresentative forms of Judaism. When we do so, at once a remarkable feature becomes apparent. For wherever we have such documents from within the Judaism(s) of the second half of the second Temple or post Maccabean period in the land of Israel we find a common theme regularly recurring— firm and unyielding claim to be the only legitimate heirs of Israel's inheritance, and sharp, hostile often vituperative criticism of other Jews/Judaisms. The same is true whether it be Qumran or Christian writings, or 1 Enoch or the Testament of Moses, or Jubilees or the Psalms of Solomon. The period was evidently marked by a degree of intra-Jewish factionalism remarkable for its sustained nature and quality of bitterness—a factionalism which included some at least of the other groups from whom we have no first hand account from the period. The point can be illustrated readily enough.

The Qumran Essenes saw themselves as alone true to the covenant of the fathers, "the sons of light", "the house of perfection and truth in Israel", the chosen ones, and so on (1QS 2.9; 3.25; 8.9; 11.7). In contrast, the political and religious opponents of the sectarians are attacked as "the wicked", "the men of the lot of Belial", "children of Satan" who have departed from the paths of righteousness, transgressed the covenant, and such like (e.g. CD 1.13-21; 1QS 2.4-5; 1QH 2.8-19; 1QpHab. 5.3-8; 4QFlor.[4Q174] 1.8). One of the chief sins for which these other Jews are condemned is the failure to recognize the Essene claim to have been given the correct insight into the Torah, and thus to be constituted as the people of the new covenant (e.g. CD 4.7-8; 1QS 5.7-11; 1QpHab 2.1-4). "Those who speak smooth things", the "deceivers" (1QH 2.14-16; 4.6-8; 4QpNah 2.7-10) are usually identified as the Pharisees, and the halakhic debates reflected in the recently published 4QMMT confirm that Pharisees were amongst the Qumran sect's disputants.

In Christian writings the confidence of being those to whom the promises had been fulfilled, the climax of God's purpose for Israel, is everywhere apparent. In Paul, in particular, the sense that Christians are "the holy ones", the elect" is strong (e.g. Rom. 1.7; 8.33;

1 Cor. 1.2; 1 Thess. 1.4) and the opposition can be excoriated as "dogs" and dupes of Satan (Phil. 3.2; 2 Cor 11.13-15). To be noted is the fact that the opposition here is also Christian—Christian Jews—factionalism within factionalism! Elsewhere we may simply recall the virulence of the opposition once again to the Pharisees in particular in Matt. 23. In John the opposition to "the Jews" is as fierce as anything we meet elsewhere (particularly John 8.44), though it is evident that John's target is the Jewish authorities of his day and that there is a large body of "Jews" in the middle ground, for whose loyalty John's Jesus and "the Jews" are in dispute. And if these references reflect a later phase in the partings of the ways between Judaism and Christianity, we may also note the degree of conflict between Pharisees and Jesus reflected in Mark 2.23-3.5 and 7.1-23, and the tradition of Jesus' conduct in defiance of Jews classifying other Jews as "sinners" (Mark 2.16-17; Matt. 11.19), traditions which certainly go back well into the pre-70 situation in Israel.[58]

The Enoch corpus gives evidence of a bitter calendrical dispute which racked Judaism probably during the second century BCE. "The righteous", "who walk in the ways of righteousness", clearly distinguished themselves from those who "sin like the sinners" in wrongly computing the months and feasts and years (*1 Enoch* 82.4-7). The accusation in *1 Enoch* 1-5 is less specific, but again draws a clear line of distinction between the "righteous/chosen" and the "sinners/impious" (1.1, 7-9; 5.6-7), where the latter are clearly fellow Jews who practised their Judaism differently from the self-styled "righteous"—"You have not persevered, nor observed the law of the Lord" (5.4).

Similarly in *Test. Mos.* 7 we find a forthright attck on "godless men, who represent themselves as being righteous" and who "with hand and mind ... touch unclean things", even though they themselves say, "Do not touch me, lest you pollute me" (7.3, 9-10). Here too we may have to recognize an attack on Pharisees, by means of caricaturing Pharisaic concern to maintain purity, though if *Aristeas* 139, 142, *War* 2.150 and Col. 2.21 are of any relevance the concern for purity and fear of defilement by touch was a good deal more widespread within first century Judaism. The point here, however, is that a Jewish document characterizes such concern as the concern of "godless men".

---

[58] See Dunn (1991) particularly chs. 6-8.

Jubilees is directed to Israel as a whole, a plea for a more rigorous observance of the covenant (see e.g. 22.10-23; 23.22-31), but includes the conviction that many sons of Israel will leave the covenant and make themselves like the Gentiles (15.33-34). Here too the calendar was a bone of contention: observance of the feast or ordinance wrongly computed counted as *non*-observance, as failure to maintain the covenant, as walking in the errors of the Gentiles (6.32-35; 23.16).

Finally we may simply note how thoroughgoing is the polemic in the *Psalms of Solomon* on behalf of those who regarded themselves as "the righteous", the "devout", against the "sinners" (e.g. 3.3-12; 4.1, 8; 13.6-12; 15.4-13). It is clear enough that "the righteous" are not Israel as a whole, but those who believed that they alone "live in the righteousness of the commandments" (14.2). Whereas the sinners are not only Gentiles or the blatantly wicked, but the Jewish opponents of the "righteous", probably the Hasmonean Sadducees who had usurped the monarchy and (in the eyes of the devout) defiled the sanctuary (1.8; 2.3; 4.1-8; 7.2; 8.12-13 etc.). When Messiah came such sinners would be driven out from the inheritance (17.23).

How serious was all this polemic? The range of opinion here is of some interest, particularly as it bears on the position of Christianity within the spectrum of first century Judaism. At one end, for example, it may be argued that the disagreements are simply those of vigorous halakhic dispute, so that Jesus and the Pharisees of his day should be seen simply as friendly disputants.[59] At the other, the polemic of Matt. 23 and John 8 would normally be regarded as indicating that a decisive breach with Judaism had already taken place. But in fact the character of denunciation and quality of vituperation is remarkably consistent across the range of literature surveyed above. We may consider, for example, the fearful curses called down on the men of Belial when the novice enters the Qumran community -

> Be cursed because of all your guilty wickedness!
> May he deliver you up for torture at the hands of the vengeful Avengers!
> May he visit you with destruction by the hand of all the wreakers of revenge!
> Be cursed without mercy because of the darkness of your deeds!
> Be damned in the shadowy place of everlasting fire! ... (1QS 2.5-10).

---

[59] This is the position of Sanders developed in his writings since (1985).

The curses against the deceitful and stubborn covenanter in 1 QS 2.11-18 are no less fierce than those against the "men of the lot of Belial". Or in *Jub.* 15.34 "there is for them (those who have made themselves like the Gentiles) no forgiveness or pardon so that they might be pardoned and forgiven from all of the sins of this eternal error". We might compare the warning against the "eternal sin" in Mark 3.29, occasioned by refusal to recognize that Jesus' exorcisms were effected by the power of the Holy Spirit. And the Johannine Jesus' castigation of "the Jews" as sons of the devil (8.44) is readily echoed in *Jub.* 15.33, 4QFlor. 1.8 and *Test. Dan* 5.6 (the last drawing on the Book of Enoch the Righteous). Perhaps most striking of all in its sustained character in the polemic reviewed above is the regular condemnation of other Jews as "sinners", given that the sinner in Jewish theology was excluded from participation in the world to come and condemned to eternal darkness (e.g. Deut. 29.18; Ps. 92.7; *1 Enoch* 98.10-16; 102.3; *Jub.* 36.9-10; *Test. Abr.* 11.11; *Pss. Sol.* 2.34; 3.11-12).[60]

How much weight should we give to such considerations? Did the Jews who wrote 1QS or the Psalms of Solomon really believe that those thus cursed or called sinners were as such indeed outside the covenant, beyond the saving righteousness of God? Did the Pharisees who criticised Jesus for eating with sinners really think that these sinners would be condemned in the final judgment, and Jesus too? That is certainly the theological logic of their language. But did they mean it? Here we might note how incipient sectarianism forces an inevitable ambivalence on the key term of the insiders' self-understanding—"Israel". Are only those "Israel" who have remained true to the covenant, as understood by the group in focus, or will God restore the wholeness of disobedient and exiled Israel in the end (in eschatological fulfilment of the pattern in Deut. 30)? We see the ambivalence, for example, in CD 3.12-4.12, where "Israel" appears on both sides of the equation—God's covenant with Israel, Israel has strayed, the "sure house in Israel", "the converts of Israel". Again in the tension in *Jubilees* between 15.34 and 22.23-31; or in the *Psalms of Solomon* between the sustained condemnation of Jewish "sinners" and the final hope for Israel in 17. 44-45 and 18.5;[61] or in Paul between the affirmation that "not all who are from Israel are Israel" and the assurance that "all Israel will be

---

[60] See further Dunn (1994); also Sanders (1977) index "the Wicked", and D. A. Neale, *None but the Sinners. Religious Categories in the Gospel of Luke* (Sheffield: 1991) 82-95.

[61] See further the sensitive discussion of Sanders (1977) 240-57; also 361, 367-74, 378 (*Jubilees*) and 398-406, 408 (*Psalms of Solomon*).

saved" (Rom. 9.6; 11.26). Perhaps the imagery of "focus" is helpful here in that so much of our literature operates with a "close-up focus" for most of the time, and only occasionally with a "long-range focus", and too little attention is given to the inconsistencies in detail which result from changing ("zooming") from one to the other.

What, we might ask alternatively, was the function of such abusive language? To condemn fellow Jews irretrievably? or was it simply the language of self-legitimation, to confirm themselves in the rightness of their own beliefs and of their crucial importance? or language of exhortation and evangelism, all the more condemnatory and fearful in order to frighten others into accepting their own beliefs and halakhoth? Here we may see the consequence of all sectarianism, or, alternatively expressed, the tendency to fundamentalism. The very affirmation of the fundamental importance of some key element of belief and practice carries with it the corollary that those who dispute or play down that key element are thereby damned. It is quite literally the curse of such incipient fundamentalism that it cannot recognize the legitimacy of alternative interpretations without denying its own. In this case first century Judaism is simply typical of the tensions between the ideal of "the pure church" and comprehensiveness which have afflicted all religions and ideologies at one time or another.

Here then is a tension constantly distorting the coherence of any description of Judaism in the land of Israel in the first century. The spectator perspective can observe the diversity of Judaism quite well, including the distinctive features of the different sub-groups, whether set against the broad sweep of common Judaism or not. But as soon as we get inside one of these Judaisms the picture changes from a comfortable comprehensiveness to a hostile jostling to remain "in" by ensuring inter alia that others are defined "out". The tension in part is between "Judaism" perceived phenomenologically and "Israel" perceived from within; but in part also between the insider's perception of an Israel of pure/purified form in the here and now and an Israel of eschatological completeness. Such tendency to sectarianism is probably inevitable, perhaps even desirable, wherever claims to ultimate truth are constitutive of identity, for it constantly recalls the larger body to its constitutive truth claim and underlines the inescapability of the tension between ideal and practice. Failure to recognize its presence in the case of first century Judaism simply makes it harder to understand the dynamic of the group interactions, including the impact of Jesus and the emergence of his "sect".

At the same time, we need to recall once again that all this argument over who constitutes Israel, all this polemic, whether evangelistic or dismissive, was going on between relatively small groups within first century Judaism. All the while "common Judaism", the potentially restored comprehensive Israel was still functioning as such. All the while that which fundamentally constituted Israel as Israel, Judaism as Judaism was still in effect. To this we therefore turn.

4 THE UNITY OF FIRST CENTURY JUDAISM

Not least of the anachronisms in which modern research into Jewish and Christian origins finds itself is the very use of the term "Judaism" in the plural (Judaisms). For nowhere in its early usage is "Judaism" used in the plural; it occurs only in the singular. "Judaism" was evidently perceived, from "outside" as well, not as a multiplicity of forms but as a singular entity; there was a something called "Judaism". We may call this "common Judaism", of which these other "Judaisms" were particular expressions, remembering that Sanders' "common Judaism" is derived principally from Josephus' spectator perspective. Or "foundational Judaism", on which these more specific superstructures were erected. What matters is that there was a recognisable genus, "Judaism", of which there were different species. It is this generic Judaism behind, below, within all these particular Judaisms with which we must now finally be concerned.

In an earlier study I spoke of "the four pillars of Second Temple Judaism"[62] and this categorisation still seems to me to provide a useful mode of description. It begins from the well recognized fact that historically Judaism has always involved a combination of three principal factors—"belief in God, God's revelation of the Torah to Israel, and Israel as the people who lives by the Torah in obedience to God".[63] The only difference for first century Judaism is that we could hardly fail to add a fourth factor—the Temple.

4.1 Temple

There can be no doubt that the Temple was the central focus of Israel's national and religious life prior to its destruction in 70 CE. It was the hub of political and economic power, the reason for

---

[62] Dunn (1991) ch. 2.
[63] *Encyclopedia Judaica* 10.387.

Jerusalem's existence in the out of the way Judean highlands. The power of the high priesthood was a major factor in Hasmoneans and Romans keeping it firmly under their control. The income generated through the sacrificial cult, the Temple tax and the pilgrim traffic must have been immense.[64] Above all, the Temple was the place where God had chosen to put his name, the focal point for the divine human encounter and the sacrificial cult on which human well being and salvation depended.[65] "Jew" was as much a religious identifier as an ethnic identifier because it focused identity in Judea, the state whose continuing distinctive existence depended entirely on the status of Jerusalem as the location of the Temple. It should occasion no surprise, then, that Sanders devotes more than half of his description of "common Judaism" in our period to an account of the Temple, its personnel, its cult and the festivals which also focused on it.[66]

We saw also that the different sects highlighted the importance of the Temple—most obviously the Sadducees, but also the Qumran Essenes, and most likely also the Pharisees, who probably, in some measure like the Essenes, sought to extend or at least live out the holiness required for the Temple more widely in the holy land.[67] Here it is important to grasp the fact that the disputes and denunciations relating to the Temple, noted in the survey of the Judaisms above, do not amount to a dispute regarding the fundamental importance of the Temple itself. On the contrary, it was precisely because the Temple was so important that disputes about its correct function were so important. It was not the Temple but its location (the Samaritans) and abuse (*Psalms of Solomon* and Qumran) which was denounced.[68] This is particularly evident in the preoccu-

---

[64] See also Jeremias (1969) particularly 21-30, 73-84 and 126-38; Mendels ch. 10.

[65] Note the comments of A. Momigliano, "Religion in Athens, Rome and Jerusalem in the First Century BC", in *Approaches to Ancient Judaism*, Vol. 5 *Studies in Judaism and Its Greco-Roman Context*, ed. W. S. Green (Atlanta: 1985) 1-18: "Jerusalem was also different from any other place because its Temple had long been the symbol of the unity of Judaism. I do not know of any other ancient god who had a sanctuary as exclusive as the Temple of Jerusalem. . . . Jerusalem was a place for pilgrims unmatched by Athens or Rome, with all their attractions" (14).

[66] Sanders (1992) chs. 5-10.

[67] This is one of the points at which Sanders criticizes Neusner, but the weight of opinion, as represented by Vermes, Cohen, Saldarini, Segal and Grabbe continues to be more supportive of Neusner; see e.g. Dunn (1991) 41-42.

[68] Arguably so also in the case of Jesus' so-called "cleansing of the Temple"; see particularly R. Bauckham, "Jesus' Demonstration in the Temple", in *Law and Religion. Essays on the Place of the Law in Israel and Early Christianity*, ed. B. Lindars (Cambridge: 1988) 72-89; C. A. Evans, "Jesus' Action in the Temple: Cleansing or Portent of Destruction?", *Catholic Biblical Quarterly* 51 (1989) 237-70.

pation with the Temple among the Qumranites (as in 11QT and the Songs of the Sabbath Sacrifice), even among a group who felt themselves distanced from its present operation.

It is true that the Christians became disengaged from the Temple as they spread beyond the coasts of Israel, the Hellenists at least. But they continued to acknowledge its symbolical and religious power (not least in Hebrews), and Paul devoted much time and energy to an affirmation of Jerusalem's importance (the collection) which must have seemed to many like a Christian equivalent to the temple tax. The destruction of the Temple in 70 CE changed things, though the hope of its rebuilding, or the building of an eschatological temple was common to important strands of both Christianity and Judaism;[69] nor did the failure of that hope to be realized prevent both rabbinic Judaism and Christianity from transforming its spiritual significance into other forms. The continuing potency of Jerusalem as a symbol of faith for both Judaism and Christianity is a continuing reverberation of the fundamental significance of the Temple all these centuries ago.

4.2 God

Belief in God as one and in God's un-image-ableness was certainly fundamental to the first century Jew. The *Shema'* was probably said by most Jews on a regular basis (Deut. 6.4, 7); Jesus was surely striking a familiar cord in the tradition attributed to him in Mark 12.28-31. And the twin commandment to acknowledge God alone and to make no images of God (Ex. 20.3-6; Deut. 5.7-10) was no doubt burnt into the heart and mind of the typical first century Jew.

Little of this actually appears upon the surface of Judaism in the land of Israel in the first century, for the simple reason that it was non-controversial and so could be taken for granted—an important reminder that the fundamental character of an item of belief and practice is not to be measured by the amount of verbiage it engenders, and that what belongs to the foundation may often be hidden from sight. But those who explained Judaism to the outsider found it necessary, as did Josephus, to point out that the acknowledgment of "God as one is common to all the Hebrews" (*Ant.* 5.112). And the abhorrence of idolatry was a common feature in all Judaism (Isa. 44.9-20; Wisd. Sol. 11-15; Ep. Jer.; *Sib. Or.* 3.8-45; 1 Cor. 8-10; 1 John 5.21; *m. Abodah Zarah*). Within first century Israel itself we

---

[69] See commentaries on Mark 11.17 and 14.58.

need only recall the violent reaction from the people at large to misguided attempts by Pilate to bring standards perceived as idolatrous into Jerusalem (*Ant.* 18.55-59) and to the attempt of Caligula to have his own statue set up within the Temple (*Ant.*18.261-72).

Since the oneness of God was an issue which proved decisive in the parting of the ways between Christianity and Judaism we should simply note that in the early decades of Christianity a passage like Matt. 4.10 was evidently cherished within Christian Jewish communities, that Paul continued to affirm that "God is one" (1 Cor. 8.6), and that the christology of John's Gospel has close parallels in the Jewish apocalyptic and mystical speculations of the time.[70] Here again the dispute is not so much whether the central Jewish creed is correct (God *is* one for both sides), but rather stems from and highlights the continuing importance of that creed for both sides.

4.3 Election

Equally fundamental was Israel's self-understanding of itself as the people of God specially chosen from among all the nations of the world to be his own. This conviction was already there in the pre-exilic period in such passages as Deut. 7.6-8 and 32.8-9. But it became a fundamental category of self-definition in the post-exilic period from Ezra onwards (Ezra 9-10), it was the undergirding motivation behind the resistance to Hellenistic syncretism in the Maccabean crisis, and it constantly came to expression in the compulsive desire to maintain distinct and separate identity from the other nations (Gentiles).[71] The attitude is expressed in extreme form in *Jub.* 15.30-32 and 22.16. But it lies behind the everyday preoccupation with purity, which was so prominent in most of the Judaisms reviewed above, and which is attested also by the large numbers of ritual baths now uncovered by archaeology.[72] Not surprisingly the same concern ties this foundation pillar into the others, since it included the fear of contamination by Gentile idolatry, as also the counteractive emphasis on the holiness of the land centred in holy Jerusalem and ultimately in the holy of holies within the Temple (hence the prohibition which prevented Gentiles from passing beyond the court of the Gentiles in the Temple area).[73]

---

[70] See Dunn (1991) ch. 11.

[71] The prophecy of Balaam in Num. 23.9 was particularly significant for Jewish self-understanding—"a people dwelling alone, and not reckoning itself among the nations".

[72] See Sanders (1990) 214-27.

[73] See e.g. my *Partings* 38-42.

As already noted earlier, "Judaism" was itself coined as an expression of ethnic and religious identity defined by opposition to the corruptive influences of the wider world. Thus it expresses, we may say, an understanding of Israel's election which in itself encourages suspicion and exclusiveness. This was the attitude which comes to the surface in the sectarian tendency of so many of the Judaisms reviewed above; the more thoroughgoing the definition and practice of the "righteousness" by which Israel should be distinguished, the more "the righteous" are required to distance themselves from and condemn others, not least other Jews, who fail to honour and observe that righteousness.[74] Ironically, however, it is the insider term "Israel" itself which proves the more comprehensive, since, unlike "Judaism", it does not begin as a term of opposition, is defined precisely not by race or status but only by electing grace (Deut. 7.6-8), and includes the task of bringing salvation to the end of the earth (Isa. 49.6). Insofar as this is recognized both by rabbinic Judaism[75] and by Christianity in the person of Paul (Gal. 6.16; Rom. 9-11), the prospects for a rapprochement between continuing Judaism and its biggest schismatic "sect" (Christianity) need not be despaired of. In contrast any attempt to retrieve "Jew" as a more comprehensive term (as in Rom. 2.28-29 and Rev. 2.9, 3.9) was probably fatally compromised by its integral nationalistic and ethnic-religious overtones. By definition a "Gentile" could not be a "Jew", but a "Gentile" might be numbered within "Israel".[76]

4.4 Torah

Finally we must speak of the Torah, as fundamental to Israel's self-understanding as any of the other three. It was the Torah which justified and explained the importance of the Temple and its cult, and which proved the more foundational and durable when rabbinic Judaism was able to transform itself from a religion of Temple and priest to one of Torah and rabbi. It was the Torah which had been given to Israel as a mark of the one God's favour to and choice of Israel, an integral part of his covenant with Israel, to show

---

[74] But see again n. 61.

[75] Neusner (1995) criticizes my earlier conclusion ([1991] e.g. 230), that the ethnic character of "Judaism" made inevitable a breach with Christianity (where Gentiles were a rapidly increasing majority), by pointing out that "in the various documents of Rabbinic Judaism . . . "Israel" forms a supernatural and religious category, not a this-worldly, merely ethnic one". When we add this to Zeitlin's observation above (n. 23) it adds further strength to my argument here.

[76] It could perhaps be noted that in the unusual *CIJ* 21 (a Roman epitaph) one Irene is described as both a "proselyte" and "an Israelite".

Israel how to live as the people of God (Deuteronomy), its significance classically expressed in the claim that universal divine Wisdom is now embodied therein (Sir. 24.23; Bar. 3.36-4.4). And it was
the Torah which served as boundary and bulwark separating Israel
from the other nations by its insistence on their maintenance of the
purity code (e.g. Lev. 20.24-26; Dan. 1.8-16; *Aristeas* 139, 142).[77]
Since the Torah was both school text book and the law of the land
we may assume a substantial level of respect and observance of its
principal regulations within common Judaism.[78]

Because of its centrality in determining what it meant to be the
people of God, devotion to Torah was bound to be a feature in the
divisions within Judaism. Again, not because the different groups
disputed its importance, but for precisely the opposite reason. It
was desire to meet the obligations specified by the Torah for Israel
as fully as possible which resulted in what was in effect a competitive dispute as to what that meant in practice. All would have
agreed that they ought to live according to the principles of "covenantal nomism",[79] but each group's claim that it was so living
carried with it the effective denial that others were doing so. In
these disputes circumcision played no role, since they were all disputes within Judaism; circumcision came into play as a boundary
marker between Jew and Gentile, as the early Christian mission to
Gentiles reminds us. But it is clear that other issues of calculating
feast days, and the right maintenance of purity (including Temple
purity), food laws and the sabbath, were usually the flash points and
make or break issues on which differences and divisions turned (e.g.
1 Enoch 82.4-7; 1QS 10.1-8; 4QHos 2.14-17; *Pss. Sol.* 8.12, 22; *Test.
Mos.* 7.10; 1 Macc. 1.62-63; Gal. 2.11-14; *Jub.* 50.6-13; CD 10-11;
Mark 2.23-3.5). Here again we should recall the seriousness of these
disputes as indicated by frequent use of the abusive epithet "sinners",[80] for a sinner was defined precisely as one who broke or
disregarded the regulations of Torah. In such polemic the need for
a group to find in the Torah its own self-affirmation had the inevitable corollary of making the Torah an instrument by means of
which one group condemned another.

---

[77] See further Dunn (1991) 23-31.
[78] Following his treatment of the Temple and associated features Sanders devotes two chapters (1992) to the theme of "observing the law of God" (190-240).
[79] The term coined by Sanders and still used by him to denote the obedience to
the law which was generally understood to be the proper response to the grace of
God given in the covenant ([1992] 262-78). Need it still be said that "covenantal
nomism" does not = "legalism"?
[80] See above §3.2.

On this point too it may be important to reflect further on the distinction between Judaism and Israel. For it could be argued that it was an overemphasis on the Torah, and on such distinctives as circumcision and food laws, which gave the term "Judaism" its national and anti-Gentile character. It was the Torah seen and emphasized in its function of separating Israel from the other nations which, we may say, transformed Israel into Judaism. Not the Torah as such, but the Torah understood to define the Jew by his difference from the Gentile. With that role demoted and diminished it might arguably be possible to reassert the primary link between Torah and Israel understood in an inclusive rather than exclusive way.

5 CONCLUSION

Questions therefore remain as to whether "Judaism" is the best name to describe the religious practices and beliefs of the people of the land of Israel in the first century CE. It was not their own name for themselves, and its origin and use during our period emphasizes the distinctive ethnic and national character of the religion it names. And if its use is unavoidable for us, in view of its long history since then, we should at least be aware of its defects for our purpose. So too we should at least hesitate before speaking of plural "Judaisms" as the too easy phenomenological response to the older view of a single normative Judaism already determinative in first century Israel. For such language is still further removed from the self-understanding of the groups described above and is in danger of obscuring the Judaism which was common to the vast bulk of Jews, the foundational practices and beliefs which the distinctive expressions of different groups and writings were intended to promote and safeguard, each in its own way.

When we focus on these groups and their diversity as attested particularly by their own writings from the period, we must constantly recall how small a minority within the land of Israel these writings actually spoke for and that some groups have left no writings (that have come down to us) which represent their views in their own terms (including the Pharisees, Sadducees, "Hellenists" and the Judean Christians). There are also writings whose constituency, its size and significance, is completely unknown to us. On the other hand, we should equally recall that the Pharisees and early Christians were among the most significant opinion formers in the influence they exercised in the event in the subsequent emergence and spread of rabbinic Judaism and Christianity.

Of those who have left a literary deposit we need to ask further whether we should take them seriously, not only in the impressiveness of their commitment, but also in the language of their condemnation of others, since the two go together. Is there a parallel with modern denominations within Christianity (in their less tolerant days), or with the splits between Orthodox, Conservative and Reformed Judaism today? Or were they rather like the orders within mediaeval Catholicism—Benedictines, Franciscans, Dominicans, and so on? And do we need to recall that divisions within denominations are often deeper than those between—liberal Catholics more readily in tune with liberal Protestants, or with Reformed Jews, than with their more conservative codenominationalists?[81] Or again, would those who penned such blood-curdling threats really have wished for the authority and power to implement their judgments, like some quasi-inquisition or a German state during the Reformation? Or was it all bluster and show, with the shared conviction untroubled at the heart of things that all were, after all, Jews and so all, deo volente, would be saved.[82] It is hard for us today who cherish human rights to enter sufficiently into such a mindset to form any coherent judgment on such questions, though the Holocaust, the break-up of former Yugoslavia and the rise of militant fundamentalism in different religions today serve as constant reminders that passionate but unbridled commitment to a cause can all too easily become a ferocious beast that seeks to devour anything that stands in its path.

Finally, we have found it important to note that the term "Israel" gives a different perspective from that implicit in "Judaism"—the perspective of the insider, laying, it is true, sectarian-like claims to the heritage of Israel as a whole, but always hoping that the purity of the sect would in due time be transformed into the restoration of the whole. Moreover, "Israel" expresses a self-identity established solely by act of divine initiative and not defined as Israel by antithesis to non-Israel. Unlike the more ethnically oriented "Judaism" ("Judaism" = resistance to "Hellenism", "Jew" = not-"Gentile"), "Israel" has the power to embrace all whose identity is likewise established by the grace of God. It is in the uncomfortable tug-of-war of its twin identity as "Judaism" and as "Israel" that both the divisive tensions within and the rich religious potential of "Judaism in the land of Israel in the first century" are to be discerned most clearly.

---

[81] Cf. the various discussions on the use of terms like "sect" in Cohen ch.5 and Saldarini particularly 70-3, 123-7.
[82] Cf. particularly Schiffman (1985).

BIBLIOGRAPHY

Y. Amir, "The Term Ἰουδαισμός: A Study in Jewish-Hellenistic Self-Identification", *Immanuel* 14 (1982) 34-41

M. Avi-Yonah & Z. Baras, ed., *Society and Religion in the Second Temple Period* (Jerusalem: 1977)

G. Boccaccini, *Middle Judaism: Jewish Thought 300 BCE to 200 CE* (Minneapolis: 1991)

W. Bousset & H. Gressmann, *Die Religion des Judentums im späthellenistischen Zeitalter* (Tübingen: 1925; 4th edition 1966)

J. H. Charlesworth, *The Old Testament Pseudepigrapha* 2 vols (New York: 1983, 1985)
, *Jesus within Judaism* (London: 1988)
, ed., *Jesus' Jewishness. Exploring the Place of Jesus in Early Judaism* (New York: 1991)

S. J. D. Cohen, *From the Maccabees to the Mishnah* (Philadelphia: 1987)

J. J. Collins, *The Apocalyptic Imagination. An Introduction to the Jewish Matrix of Christianity* (New York: 1984)

W. D. Davies, *The Gospel and the Land* (University of California: 1974)

J. D. G. Dunn, "Pharisees, Sinners and Jesus", *Jesus, Paul and the Law* (London: 1990) 61-88
, *The Partings of the Ways between Christianity and Judaism* (London: 1991)
, "Jesus and Factionalism in Early Judaism", in *Hillel and Jesus*, ed. J. H. Charlesworth (New York: 1994)

Encyclopedia Judaica: "Jew" 10.21-25; "Judaism" 10.383-97

D. Flusser, *Judaism and the Origins of Christianity* (Jerusalem: 1988)

S. D. Fraade, "Palestinian Judaism", *Anchor Bible Dictionary* 3.1054-61

M. Goodman, *The Ruling Class of Judaea. The Origins of the Jewish Revolt against Rome AD 66-70* (Cambridge: 1987)

L. L. Grabbe, *Judaism from Cyrus to Hadrian*, 2 vols (Minneapolis: 1992)

M. Hengel, *The Zealots* (Edinburgh: 1989)
, *Judaism and Hellenism* 2 vols. (London: 1974)
, *The "Hellenization" of Judaea in the First Century after Christ* (London: 1990).

R. A. Horsley & J. S. Hanson, *Bandits, Prophets and Messiahs. Popular Movements at the Time of Jesus* (New York: 1985)

J. Jeremias, *Jerusalem at the Time of Jesus* (London: 1969)
, *New Testament Theology: The Proclamation of Jesus* (London: 1971)

R. S. Kraemer, "On the Meaning of the Term 'Jew' in Greco-Roman Inscriptions", *Harvard Theological Review* 82 (1989) 35-53.

R. A. Kraft & G. W. E. Nickelsburg, *Early Judaism and its Modern Interpreters* (Atlanta: 1986).

K. G. Kuhn, with G. von Rad & W. Gutbrod, Ἰσραήλ, *Theological Dictionary of the New Testament* 3.356-91

H. Maccoby, *Judaism in the First Century* (London: 1989)

J. S. McLaren, *Power and Politics in Palestine. The Jews and the Governing of their Land 100 BC-AD 70* (Sheffield: 1991)

J. Maier, *Zwischen den Testamenten. Geschichte und Religion in der Zeit des zweiten Tempels* (München: 1990)

D. Mendels, *The Rise and Fall of Jewish Nationalism* (New York: 1992)

C. G. Montefiore, *Judaism and St. Paul* (London: 1914)

G. F. Moore, *Judaism in the First Three Centuries of the Christian Era* 3 vols. (Cambridge, Mass.: 1927-30)

J. Murphy, *The Religious World of Jesus: An Introduction to Second Temple Palestinian Judaism* (Hoboken, NJ: 1991)
J. Neusner, *The Rabbinic Traditions about the Pharisees before AD 70* (Leiden: 1971)
, *From Politics to Piety. The Emergence of Rabbinic Judaism* (Englewood Cliffs: 1973)
, *Judaism: The Evidence of the Mishnah* (Chicago: 1981)
, "Varieties of Judaism in the Formative Age", *Formative Judaism*, Second Series (Chico CA: 1983) 59-89
, *Judaism in the Beginning of Christianity* (London: 1984)
, *Jews and Christians. The Myth of a Common Tradition* (London: 1991)
, *Studying Classical Judaism: A Primer* (Louisville: 1991)
, *Children of the Flesh, Children of the Promise. Is Judaism an Ethnic Religion?* (Cleveland: 1995)
J. Neusner & E. S. Frerischs, ed., *"To See Ourselves as Others See Us". Christians, Jews and "Others" in Late Antiquity* (Chico, CA: 1985)
J. Neusner, et al. ed., *Judaisms and their Messiahs at the Turn of the Christian Era* (Cambridge: 1987)
M. Newton, *The Concept of Purity at Qumran and in the Letters of Paul* (Cambridge: 1985)
G. W. E. Nickelsburg, *Jewish Literature between the Bible and the Mishnah: A Historical and Literary Introduction* (London: 1981)
B. Otzen, *Judaism in Antiquity* (Sheffield: 1990)
J. A. Overman & W. S. Green, "Judaism in the Greco-Roman Period", *Anchor Bible Dictionary* 3.1037-54
J. Riches, *The World of Jesus. First-Century Judaism in Crisis* (Cambridge: 1990)
C. Rowland, *The Open Heaven. A Study of Apocalyptic in Judaism and Early Christianity* (London: 1982)
, *Christian Origins: From Messianic Movement to Christian Religion* (London: 1985)
S. Safrai & M. Stern, ed., *The Jewish People in the First Century* 2 vols. (Assen: 1974, 1976)
S. Safrai, ed., *The Literature of the Sages* (Assen: 1987)
A. J. Saldarini, *Pharisees, Scribes and Sadducees in Palestinian Society* (Edinburgh: 1988)
E. P. Sanders, *Paul and Palestinian Judaism* (London: 1977)
, et al. ed., *Jewish and Christian Self-Definition*, Vol. 2 *Aspects of Judaism in the Graeco-Roman Period* (London: 1981)
, *Jesus and Judaism* (London: 1985)
, *Jewish Law from Jesus to the Mishnah* (London: 1990) 214-27.
, *Judaism: Practice and Belief 63 BCE-66CE* (London: 1992)
S. Sandmel, *The First Christian Century in Judaism and Christianity* (New York: 1969)
L. H. Schiffman, *Who was a Jew? Rabbinic and Halakhic Perspectives on the Jewish-Christian Schism* (Hoboken, NJ: 1985)
, *From Text to Tradition: A History of Second Temple and Rabbinic Judaism* (Hoboken, NJ: 1991)
H. J. Schoeps, *Paul: The Theology of the Apostle in the Light of Jewish Religious History* (London: 1961).
E. Schürer, *The History of the Jewish People in the Age of Jesus Christ* 4 vols. (Edinburgh: 1973, 1978, 1986, 1987)

A. F. Segal, *Rebecca's Children: Judaism and Christianity in the Roman World* (Cambridge, MA: 1986)

——, *The Other Judaisms of Late Antiquity* (Atlanta: 1987)

P. Sigal, *The Foundations of Judaism from Biblical Origins to the Sixth Century AD* (Pittsburgh: 1980)

J. Z. Smith, "Fences and Neighbours: Some Contours of Early Judaism", in *Approaches to Ancient Judaism*, Vol. 2, ed. W. S. Green (Chico, CA: 1980) 1-25

M. Smith, "Palestinian Judaism in the First Century", *Israel: Its Role in Civilization*, ed. M. Davis (New York: 1956) 67-81

H. F. D. Sparks, ed. *The Apocryphal Old Testament* (Oxford: 1984)

G. Stemberger, *Pharisäer, Sadduzäer, Essener* (Stuttgart: 1991)

M. E. Stone, *Scriptures, Sects and Visions: A Profile of Judaism from Ezra to the Jewish Revolts* (Philadelphia: 1980)

M. E. Stone, ed. *Jewish Writings of the Second Temple Period* (Assen: 1984)

S. Talmon, ed., *Jewish Civilization in the Hellenistic-Roman Period* (Sheffield: 1991)

E. E. Urbach, *The Sages. Their Concepts and Beliefs*, 2 vols. (Jerusalem: 1979)

G. Vermes, *The Dead Sea Scrolls in English* (Penguin: 3rd edition 1987)

S. Zeitlin, *The Jews: Race, Nation, or Religion?* (Phildelphia: 1936)

——, "The Names Hebrew, Jew and Israel", *Jewish Quarterly Review* 43 (1952-53) 365-79

JESUS WITHIN JUDAISM

Bruce Chilton
(Bard College)

That Jesus and his movement may only be understood within the context of the Judaism of their time has long been a truism of scholarship. Indeed, recognition of the Judaic matrix of Christianity predates what is usually thought of as the period of critical study. John Reuchlin's recourse to Jekiel Loans at the close of the fifteenth century,[1] and Bishop Brian Walton's magisterial edition of the Jewish and Christian Bibles of his time[2] are two examples of a programmatic desire to locate the New Testament in respect of Judaism which was encouraged (but not occasioned) by the historical curiosity of the eighteenth century.[3]

A conscious historicism nonetheless provided a necessary condition of the encyclopedic registration of Judaica, usually in comparison with the New Testament. John Lightfoot's *Horae Hebraicae et Talmudicae*[4] provided a model which has been followed and developed many times since, among others by Emil Schürer (and his revisers),[5] by Paul Billerbeck,[6] by Claude Montefiore,[7] by George Foot Moore,[8] by Safrai and Stern.[9] The difficulties of comparing

---

[1] Cf. Francis Barham, *The Life and Times of John Reuchlin, or Capnion* (London: Whittaker, 1843) 53-55. Pp. 271-284 present a bibliography.
[2] *Biblia Sacra Polyglotta* (London: 1655-1657).
[3] Cf. Henning Graf Reventlow (tr. J. Bowden), *The Authority of the Bible and the Rise of the Modern World* (London: SCM, 1984).
[4] Published in Latin between 1658 and 1674, the first edition was reprinted and translated during the seventeenth century and subsequently. A convenient reprint of the 1859 Oxford edition is available: John Lightfoot, *A Commentary on the New Testament from the Talmud and Hebraica* 1-4 (Grand Rapids: Baker, 1979).
[5] See, for example, the revision of M. Black, G. Vermes, F. Millar, P. Vermes, M. Goodman, *The History of the Jewish People in the Age of Jesus Christ (175 B.C.- A.D. 135)* (Edinburgh: Clark, 1973-1987).
[6] Hermann Leberecht Strack and Paul Billerbeck (latterly with J. Jeremias and K. Adolph), *Kommentar zum Neuen Testament aus Talmud und Midrasch* 1-6 (München: Beck, 1922-1961).
[7] Claude Goldsmid Montefiore, *Rabbinic Literature and Gospel Teachings* (London: Macmillan, 1930); cf. Montefiore (with H. Loewe), *A Rabbinic Anthology* (London: Macmillan, 1938).
[8] *Judaism in the First Centuries of the Christian Era. The Age of the Tannaim* 1-3 (Cambridge: Harvard University Press, 1927-1930).
[9] S. Safrai and M. Stern with D. Flusser, W. C. van Unnik, *The Jewish People in the First Century. Historical Geography, Political History, Social, Cultural and Religious Life and Institutions*: Compendia Rerum Iudaicarum ad Novum Testamentum 1 (Assen:

the New Testament with Judaica have been discussed often and thoroughly. Essentially, two types of problem have been identified: the encyclopedic works do not provide enough by way of context to permit of a sensitive reading of Judaica, and they typically fail to do justice to the chronological development of Judaism in its considerable variety.

Neither type of problem should be taken to mean that the task of encyclopedic comparison is impossible. But both problems suggest that students of the New Testament should have recourse to the relevant works of Judaica and to competent introductions. Perhaps the dearth of readily accessible translations (until recently) helps to explain why, repeatedly during the course of the twentieth century, Jesus' relationship to Judaism has been denied or ignored. Complete denial is common in popular and/or devotional works, and makes a brief and lamentable appearance in the guise of critical scholarship with Walter Grundmann's exercise for *das Institut des jüdischen Einflusses auf das deutsche kirchliche Leben*.[10] But critical scholars more typically take the tack of Rudolf Bultmann[11] and his student, Günther Bornkamm:[12] they attempt a direct comparison of Jesus with the Prophets, ignoring the sources of the Judaism they describe as "Late." Rabbinic Judaism is held to a debased form of the religion which Jesus and the prophets of the canon upheld.

George Foot Moore's *Judaism* marks the beginning of a sea change from the encyclopedic comparison which had treated Judaism as a static entity. The advance is perhaps a function of Moore's approach of the subject matter in a thoroughly historical manner; he constantly notes that the Judaism he treats of is a variegated phenomenon.[13] But the implications of pluralism within Judaica for

---

Van Gorcum, 1974). A second volume, still under the rubric of CRINT 1, appeared in 1976, and was co-published by Fortress Press in Philadelphia. In 1987, with P. J. Tomson, Safrai brought out *The Literature of the Sages*: The Literature of the Jewish People in the Period of the Second Temple and the Talmud as CRINT 2, with van Gorcum.

[10] *Jesus der Galiläer und das Judentum*: Veröffentlichungen des Instituts zur Erforschung des jüdischen Einflusses auf das deutsche   kirchliche Leben (Leipzig: Weigand, 1940).

[11] Cf. *Jesus*: Die unsterblichen, die geistigen Heroen der Menschheit (Berlin: Deutsche Bibliotek, 1926); (tr. L. P. Smith and E. H. Lantero), *Jesus and the Word* (New York: Scribner, 1934).

[12] Cf. *Jesus von Nazareth*: Urban-Bücher 19 (Stuttgart: Kohlhammer, 1956); (tr. I. McLuckey, F. McLuckey, J. M. Robinson), *Jesus of Nazareth* (New York: Harper, 1960).

[13] See, for example, "Character of Judaism," in *Judaism* 1, pp. 110-121. Today, of course, the pluralism would be emphasized much more, and Moore's claim of the achievement of "unity and universality" (p. 111) at the close of the period would be denied.

the comparative task are not spelled out, because Moore limits himself to an ostensible description of Judaism, and leaves aside an analytic comparison with the sources of Christianity. The great problem of Moore's opus is hermeneutical, rather than methodological. Because he wrote in an environment in which the global contrast between Judaism and Christianity was simply assumed, despite his warnings against that assumption, his work has been (mis)taken as simply one more exercise in encyclopedic comparison.

Moore was especially attracted to the teachers within the rabbinic corpus to whom miraculous powers are attributed. His two best examples are Honi, called the circler, and Hanina ben Dosa (see *Judaism* 1, pp. 377-378; volume 2, pp. 222, 235-236; volume 3, 119). Honi is said to have been able to control rain by praying within a circle he drew on the ground, and Hanina is said to have brought about healing at a distance by means of prayer. Moore observes that neither Honi nor Hanina appears to have been a very influential teacher, but he locates them both within rabbinic Judaism. As he points out, even Aqiba was said to have prayed successfully for rain (*Judaism* 2, 209, 235).

In his popular work, *Jesus the Jew*, Geza Vermes takes up just these two examples within his portrait of Jesus as a "charismatic" or "Hasid."[14] Vermes differs from Moore, however, in presenting that category as an alternative to that of a rabbi. His argument is nothing if not elastic, since he even concludes that Eliezer ben Hyrcanus was a charismatic![15] Despite the wealth of halakhic and exegetical material attributed to Eliezer, Vermes makes him out as a non-rabbinic charismatic on the strength of his recourse to miraculous demonstration during the dispute over the stove of Akhnai in Baba Mezia 59b. In fact, Eliezer's alleged recourse to miracle is no more incompatible with his standing within rabbinic discussion than is Hillel's designation as a *hasid*.[16] Another sign of Vermes's conceptual embarrassment is that he suddenly refers to Hanina's teaching as "logia" (p. 77), comparable to Jesus', when in fact they are incorporated together with other teachers' wisdom within Avoth (3:9-10; 5:10) without any indication that "rabbi" and "hasid" were mutually exclusive categories.

---

[14] "Jesus and charismatic Judaism," *Jesus the Jew. An Historian's Reading of the Gospels* (Philadelphia: Fortress, 1981, from London: Collins, 1973) 69-82. The first edition appeared in 1967.

[15] In regard to Eliezer, see Jacob Neusner, *Eliezer ben Hyrcanus. The Tradition and the Man*: Studies in Judaism in Late Antiquity (Leiden: Brill, 1973).

[16] Cf. Nahum N. Glazer, *Hillel the Elder. The Emergence of Classical Judaism* (Washington: B'nai B'rith 1959)

Vermes does not explain the sources of his thought (nor, indeed, his debt to Moore), but they are plain enough. The neo-orthodox mode of Protestant thought (and, in its wake, Catholic thought) after the Second World War made Martin Buber a companion saint with Karl Barth, and the image of the prayerful Ḥasid appealed both to theologians such as Reinhold Niebuhr[17] and to historians such as Roland De Vaux and André Dupont-Sommer in their work on the Dead Sea Scrolls.[18] The picture of the sectarians of Qumran as monastic Ḥasidim has since drawn considerable criticism. Indeed, Millar Burrows remarked as early as 1955:

> Not a few scholars have identified the covenanters of Qumran with the Hasidim. The term Hasidim, however, seems to designate devout, conservative Jews in general rather than a definite sect or party. We may therefore say that the organized sect of the Dead Sea Scrolls arose among the Hasidim, but this does not yet provide a specific identification. (*The Dead Sea Scrolls*, pp. 274-275)

Vermes, at first active within the French-speaking Catholic circles which propagated the ḥasidic/Essene hypothesis, worked on the scrolls during the period in which the hypothesis was most in vogue, and he has recently been described as having "reiterated it without any essential modification ever since."[19]

The adjective "charismatic" serves in Vermes's reading to distinguish Jesus (with Ḥoni and Ḥanina) from any communal structure. It functions in the manner of Max Weber's portrait of the charismatic hero whose personality is the basis of a religious movement in its initial, revolutionary stage; if the movement continues, a settled hierarchy is the mark of its routinization.[20] It remains an unresolved issue within critical study, however, whether that paradigm of charismatic heroism can appropriately be applied to Ḥoni, Ḥanina, or

---

[17] Cf. Reinhold Niebuhr, *The Nature and Destiny of Man. A Christian Interpretation* (New York: Scribner's, 1949) II.110-114, for a commendation of "self-transcendence" which is — earlier in the volume — also attributed to Buber, I.133, II.26. In association with Niebuhr's work, it may be instructive to read Buber's *The Origin and Meaning of Hasidism* (ed. and tr. M. Friedman; New York: Horizon, 1960), especially "Spirit and Body of the Hasidic Movement," pp. 113-149.

[18] See Millar Burrows, *The Dead Sea Scrolls* (New York: Viking, 1955) 279-298, who in some ways anticipates the current period of revisionism concerning the Essene hypothesis in the study of Qumran.

[19] Philip R. Davies, "Qumran Beginnings," *Behind the Essenes. History and Ideology in the Dead Sea Scrolls*: Brown Judaic Studies 94 (Atlanta: Scholars, 1987) 15-31, 15.

[20] See Max Weber (ed. and tr. S. N. Eisenstadt), "Charisma and Institutionalization in the Sphere of Religion and Culture," *On Charisma and Institution Building*: The Heritage of Sociology (Chicago; University of Chicago Press, 1968), 251-309.

Jesus. As if in compensation for the lack of direct evidence for a portrait of Jesus as such a self-consciously heroic figure, Vermes pushed the discussion of the Aramaic locution "son of man" (בר אנשא) in a new and interesting direction. Building upon the earlier work of (and the examples already adduced by) Hugh Odeberg,[21] Vermes suggested that a speaker might refer to himself as "son of man" as a circumlocution for his own personal existence, rather than as belonging to humanity as a whole.[22]

In three respects, Vermes's portrait of the charismatic Ḥasid has been weakened since the publication of *Jesus the Jew*. First, William Scott Green has shown that Ḥoni and Ḥanina were both claimed by rabbis of a later period as of their own, so that any bifurcation of "Ḥasidim" from rabbis within the first century would not seem to be recommended.[23] (But then, Vermes's own reference to Eliezer, and Moore's to Aqiba, should already have been taken as warnings against such a bifurcation.) Second, the notion of the isolation of Galilee from Judea (and from the Greco-Roman world), which is asserted several times by Vermes without supporting evidence, has effectively been disproved by subsequent study.[24] Third, it has been demonstrated that "son of man" in Aramaic is a generic form of language in which a speaker includes himself within the realm of humanity, rather than the heroic designation of oneself as distinct from others which Vermes claimed it was.[25]

Despite the weakness of its own argument, *Jesus the Jew* has brought about a renewal of interest in the Judaic matrix of Jesus

---

[21] *The Aramaic Portions of Bereshit Rabbah*: Lund Universitets Arsskrift 36.3 (Lund: Gleerup, 1939) 92, 154-157.
[22] *Jesus the Jew*, pp. 160-191; "The 'Son of Man' Debate," *Journal for the Study of the New Testament* 1 (1978) 19-32.
[23] William Scott Green, "Palestinian Holy Men: Charismatic Leadership and Rabbinic Tradition," *Aufstieg und Niedergang der römischen Welt* II.19.2 (ed. W. Haase; Berlin: de Gruyter, 1979) 619-647, 646. At the same time, Green acknowledges, in the tradition of Moore, the distinction between miracle and tradition as a ground of authority.
[24] Cf. Eric M. Meyers, "The Cultural Setting of Galilee: The Case of Regionalism and Early Judaism," *Aufstieg und Niedergang der römischen Welt* II.19.1 (ed. W. Haase; Berlin: de Gruyter, 1979) 686-702. Vermes is specifically criticized on p. 690 (with n. 12).
[25] See Chilton, "The Son of Man: Human and Heavenly," *The Four Gospels 1992. Festschrift Frans Neirynck*: Bibliotheca Ephemeridum Theologicarum Lovaniensium (eds. F. Van Segbroeck and others; Leuven: University Press, 1992) 203-218, also available as "[בר אנשא]: Human and Heavenly," *Approaches to Ancient Judaism* (New Series), *Volume Four. Religious and Theological Studies*: South Florida Studies in the History of Judaism 81 (ed. J. Neusner; Atlanta: Scholars, 1993) 97-114.

and Christianity.[26] *The Aims of Jesus* by Ben F. Meyer signaled a fresh and vital engagement with Judaism by scholars of the New Testament.[27] Meyer focused upon the texts of the Gospels in the first instance, with a critical capacity to allow for the tendencies of development which took up from the time of Jesus. In his exegetical focus as well as in his sensitivity to literary development, Meyer presaged the work of the next decade, the most intense and critical discussion of Jesus since the last century. At the same time, Meyer never lost sight of the catalytic place of eschatology within the Judaic milieu of Jesus, and of the principal terms of reference within the Judaism of Jesus' period. Meyer's book is an enduring index of its own insight and of what was to come, as important in its time as Weiss's *Die Predigt Jesu* was in the last century.

The principal insight which Meyer offers is that Jesus is only to be understood within the medium of Judaism, but that the movement of which the New Testament is the greatest monument itself represents an understanding of Jesus (pp. 223, 239-241). Where Vermes sketched a version of early Judaism within which he attempted to categorize Jesus, Meyer located Jesus within Judaism, but then allowed of the distinctive character and logic of his movement. Vermes's Jesus is a charismatic miracle-worker whose teaching was incidental; Meyer's Jesus is galvanized by a particular and specifiable purpose which his teaching expresses and his actions effect. The focus of Jesus' aims, according to Meyer, was the restoration of Israel:

> In sum, once the theme of national restoration in its full eschatological sweep is grasped as the concrete meaning of the reign of God, Jesus' career begins to become intelligible as a unity. (*The Aims*, p. 221)

The number of the apostles who are commissioned to preach and heal is not a coincidental rounding, but corresponds to the para-

---

[26] Cf. Vermes, *Jesus and the World of Judaism* (London: SCM, 1983); *The Religion of Jesus the Jew* (London: SCM, 1993). Mention should be made of Donald A. Hagner, *The Jewish Reclamation of Jesus. An Analysis & Critique of the Modern Jewish Study of Jesus* (Grand Rapids: Zondervan, 1984), as providing a review of some of the literature. Just after the publication of Hagner's work, Harvey Falk's *Jesus the Pharisee. A New Look at the Jewishness of Jesus* (New York: Paulist, 1985) appeared. Falk defends the position of Rabbi Jacob Emden (1697-1776), which he also cites:

> the writers of the Gospels never meant to say that the Nazarene came to abolish Judaism, but only that he came to establish a religion for the Gentiles from that time onward. Nor was it new, but actually ancient; they being the Seven Commandments of the Sons of Noah, which were forgotten. (p. 19)

Together with Hagner's, Falk's book demonstrates the continuing influence of apologetic considerations within scholarly discussion.

[27] (London: SCM, 1979).

digm of the tribes of Israel (*The Aims*, pp. 153-154). Jesus and his
followers were motivated by the hope of the restoration and exten-
sion of the people of God, in that for them "the religious factor
should become absolutely decisive for the self-definition of Israel"
(p. 223).

Meyer's analysis was not, and did not pretend to be, entirely
original. Joachim Jeremias, in *Jesu Verheissung für die Völker*,[28] had
already called attention to the symmetry between (on the one hand)
the prophetic and rabbinic expectation of the eschatological exten-
sion of Israel, and (on the other hand) the radical claims attributed
to Jesus. In the view of Jeremias those attributions are correct,
while Meyer is more cautious in his assessments of authenticity.
Meyer's book would merit continued attention if its only contribution was to re-tool Jeremias's analysis for a new day. But its genuine
originality is more profound. Meyer was not trapped, as Jeremias
ultimately was, by the programmatic assumption that the Gospels
are reliable as history. Rather, Meyer freely allowed that the Gospels are tendentious, but he went on to argue convincingly that the
positions ultimately attributed to Jesus are most easily explicable on
the supposition that the theology of restoration was in fact Jesus'
aim.

Meyer elegantly rectified an anomaly within the critical study of
Jesus. The anomaly had been that, while scholars of the New Testament generally stressed the importance of developing tendencies
within the corpus, the old, encyclopedic comparisons with Judaism
were inclined to accept assertions in the Gospels at face value.
Since the Synoptic Gospels in their received forms are the products
of communities in the Hellenistic world (probably in Rome [Mark],
Damascus [Matthew], and Antioch [Luke]) which lived in tension
with Jewish institutions, it is all too easy to read a Jesus off the page
who triumphantly transcends Judaism. Vermes inadvertently yields
to that facile hermeneutic, by according primacy to stories of miracles rather than teaching, although the critical literature had long
since demonstrated that the tradition tended to emphasize and
elaborate miraculous elements as it developed. Vermes's charis-

---

[28] (Kohlhammer: Stuttgart, 1956); (tr. S. H. Hooke), *Jesus' Promise to the Nations*:
Studies in Biblical Theology 14 (London: SCM, 1958). As Jeremias himself remarks in his preface, he in turn worked out the suggestions of B. Sundkler, "Jésus
et les païens," *Revue d'Histoire et de Philosophie religieuses* 16 (1936) 462f.

matic Ḥasid is less a function of early Judaism than of some of the most anti-Judaic elements within the Gospels.[29]

The challenge of Meyer's contribution was in various ways taken up by three works during the decade which followed. Although Borg, Chilton, and Sanders worked independently, in the approaches of each a development of Meyer's perspective is evident. The need for development was pressing, because — although Meyer indeed framed his concerns with reference both to early Judaic eschatology and the emerging tendencies of the New Testament — he finally could only argue in a general way for a theology of restoration of which Jesus availed himself. His principal sources were the classical Prophets of the Bible and the Gospels' portrayal of Jesus' public ministry and teaching. Meyer left unexplored the *realia* of practice and belief which might have occasioned a career such as Jesus' within Judaism, and the particulars which distinguished him from others.

In 1984, Marcus Borg published a revised version of his doctoral dissertation, written under the supervision of George Caird at Oxford University. Entitled, *Conflict, Holiness & Politics in the Teaching of Jesus*, Borg attempted to locate Jesus' activity within the world of Judaic concerns regarding purity.[30] Building upon the phenomenological approach to religion developed by Huston Smith, Borg argues that Jesus, in the manner of shamans, the prophets, and the Buddha, acted on the basis of special insight into "the primordial tradition" which is accessible by mystical experience (see pp. 230-247).

The hypostasis of allegedly common experience into a monist "tradition," as in Smith's work (and Otto's and Eliade's before him, as well as Campbell's alongside him) has not stood up well to criti-

---

[29] At least, however, Vermes's version of the hermeneutic of transcendence is relatively sophisticated. In the case of *Jesus and the Transcendence of Judaism* by John Riches (London: Darton, Longman & Todd, 1980), we have an appeal to the old saw that Jesus set out to replace the religion which was in fact his milieu. It is not surprising, in view of the apologetic tendency of discussion which has already been noted, that Judaism becomes the cipher within a theological claim of transcendence. After all, long after *Jesus der Galiläer* was published, Grundmann continued to argue a form of his position; cf. *Die Geschichte Jesu Christi* (Berlin: Evangelische Verlagsanstalt, 1956); *Die Entscheidung Jesu. Zur geschichtlichen Bedeutung der Gestalt Jesu von Nazareth* (Berlin: Evangelische Verlag, 1972); *Die frühe Christenheit und ihre Schriften: Umwelt, Entstehung und Eigenart der neutestamentlichen Bücher* (Stuttgart: Calwer, 1983).

[30] Studies in the Bible and Early Christianity 5 (New York: Mellen, 1984). The dissertation was submitted in 1972, but the preface makes it clear that much of the distinctive matter of the book was developed afterwards.

cism among religionists.[31] Borg makes Jesus into a hero of religious experience; any consideration of the setting of his teaching within Judaism is made subsidiary to the claim that his mystical insight was profound and that it was mature at a relatively early stage in his life:

> Occasionally and remarkably, sagacity is found in younger persons, as in Jesus and the Buddha. In such instances, the vantage point is obviously not the product of the age; rather, the transformation of perception is the product of their spiritual experience. (Borg, *Conflict*, 238)

Nonetheless, Borg did begin in the central section of his book (pp. 51-199) to consider Jesus' attitude toward purity as of *primary* importance for an understanding of his ministry for the first time within critical discussion since the end of the Second World War. He held in effect that it was Jesus' particular understanding that God was creating a newly holy territory, a space for his heavenly throne, which especially put him into conflict with many of his contemporaries, notably his Pharisaic contemporaries (see pp. 93, 230-247).

But alongside a positive evaluation of Jesus' program of purity, Borg also slips into the bifurcation of Jesus and Judaism:

> Where Judaism spoke of holiness as the paradigm for the community's life, Jesus spoke of mercy. (*Conflict*, p. 128)

His appeal to the "primordial tradition" ultimately swallows up his attention to the practice of purity, so that the old apologetic antinomy, "the hermeneutical battle between mercy and holiness" (p. 142) takes over from any serious discussion of purity as a central category of Jesus' ministry. The battle is never resolved in Borg's mind, in that he does accept that "a pure heart" was Jesus' goal (p. 246). He never considers, however, that the very antinomies he

---

[31] On p. 380, Borg cites Smith's *Forgotten Truth: The Primordial Tradition* and Eliade's *Myth and Reality*. Otto's *The Idea of the Holy* is also of foundational importance to Borg's definition (p. 73). In a later work, which is in the nature of a popularization of his approach, Borg approvingly cites Eliade's *Shamanism* and Campbell's *Hero with a Thousand Faces*; cf. Borg, *Jesus, A New Vision. Spirit, Culture, and the Life of Discipleship* (San Francisco: Harper, 1987) 53. For important criticisms of the conceptions on which Borg relies, see Robert D. Baird, *Category Formation and the History of Religions* (The Hague: Mouton, 1971; Berlin and New York: Mouton de Gruyter, 1991); Guilford Dudley, "Mircea Eliade: Anti-Historian of Religions," *Journal of the American Academy of Religion* 44 (1976) 345-359; Jonathan Z. Smith, *Map Is Not Territory. Studies in the History of Religions*: Studies in Judaism in Late Antiquity 23 (Leiden: Brill, 1978); Ivan Štrenski, *Four Theories of Myth in Twentieth-Century History. Cassirer, Eliade, Lévi-Strauss and Malinowski* (Iowa City: University of Iowa and Basingstoke: Macmillan, 1987); Shlomo Biderman (ed.), *Myth and Fictions. Their Place in Philosophy and Religion* (Leiden: Brill, 1994).

reverts to, purity/mercy and outside/inside, are those which characterize the most Hellenistic strata of the Gospels (see, for example, Mark 7 and its parallels). He is doing what many early Christians did who had approached Jesus with cultural backgrounds unlike that of Jesus himself: unable to comprehend the sense of purity, they made any interest in it a "Pharisaic" anachronism, and portrayed Jesus as a triumphant herald of anti-cultic common sense. But despite his conceptual confusion, Borg set a standard for subsequent, historical discussion: if Jesus is to be understood within Judaism, there is an implicit challenge to discover his view of purity.

Chilton's book appeared in the same year as Borg's, and proceeded along a much narrower line of analysis.[32] His earlier work, on the place of the kingdom of God within Jesus' public proclamation, had suggested that exegetical traditions incorporated within the Targum of Isaiah were taken up and developed in dominical sayings.[33] A Galilean Rabbi and His Bible explores the relationship between Jesus and the Targum further. It confirms that the literary history of the Targum only commenced after the burning of the Temple in 70 C.E., but that there are verbal, contextual, and thematic associations between exegetical traditions within the Targum and Jesus' teaching.

The proposed dating of the Targum has been confirmed by subsequent discussion, and the link between targumic traditions and Jesus' teaching has generally been granted. In a work published in 1982, Chilton had suggested that the Targum of Isaiah should be understood to have developed in two principal stages.[34] A version—no doubt incomplete—of Isaiah in Aramaic was composed by a meturgeman who flourished between 70 and 135 C.E.. That work was completed by another meturgeman, associated with Rabbi

---

[32] A Galilean Rabbi and His Bible. Jesus' Use of the Interpreted Scripture of His Time: Good News Studies 8 (Wilmington: Glazier, 1984); also with the subtitle Jesus' own interpretation of Isaiah (London: SPCK, 1984).

[33] God in Strength. Jesus' Announcement of the Kingdom: Studien zum Neuen Testament und seiner Umwelt 1 (Freistadt: Plöchl, 1979), reprinted in the series "The Biblical Seminar" (Sheffield: JSOT/Sheffield Academic Press, 1987).

[34] Cf. The Glory of Israel. The Theology and Provenience of the Isaiah Targum: Journal for the Study of the Old Testament Supplements 23 (Sheffield: JSOT, 1982). It might be mentioned, in the interests of accuracy, that the date printed on the title page is an error. (Churgin's work suffered a similar fate, although the error involved misplacing his book by a decade! Cf. P. Churgin, Targum Jonathan to the Prophets: Yale Oriental Series [New Haven: Yale University Press, 1927]). In a condensed form, Chilton's conclusions are available in The Isaiah Targum. Introduction, Translation, Apparatus, and Notes: The Aramaic Bible (Wilmington: Glazier and Edinburgh: Clark, 1987) xiii-xxx.

Joseph bar Hiyya of Pumbeditha, who died in 333.[35] Throughout
the process, however, the communal nature of the interpretative
work of each meturgeman is evident; insofar as individuals were
involved, they spoke as the voice of synagogues and of schools.[36]
Given the periods of development of the Isaiah Targum, the argument that agreements between the targumic renderings and Jesus'
sayings are simply a matter of coincidence appears strained.[37]

The problem with Chilton's book is not in its findings, but in
interpreting what those findings mean.[38] Chilton himself applies his
discovery within the discussion of Jesus' use of scripture (*A Galilean
Rabbi*, 148-198). He comes to the conclusion that Jesus' method
should not be described as midrash, since there is no general plan
of commentary evident within his sayings. Rather, Jesus employed
scripture, scriptural imagery, and scriptural language (all in the
popularly received form which would later be crystallized in the
Targumim) by way of analogy. That implicit but powerful analogy
—involving both similarities and critical distinctions—was always
between what was said of God and what Jesus claimed of God as a
matter of experience.

The last third of *A Galilean Rabbi* is devoted overtly to the theological implications of Jesus' instrumental usage of scripture. The

---

[35] *The Glory of Israel*, pp. 2, 3; *The Isaiah Targum*, p. xxi. For the sections of the
Targum most representative of each meturgeman; cf. *The Isaiah Targum*, p. xxiv.

[36] The model developed for the case of the Targum of Isaiah is applied in D. J.
Harrington and A. J. Saldarini, *Targum Jonathan of the Former Prophets*: The Aramaic
Bible 10 (Wilmington: Glazier and Edinburgh: Clark, 1987) 3; R. Hayward, *The
Targum of Jeremiah*: The Aramaic Bible 12 (Wilmington: Glazier and Edinburgh:
Clark, 1987) 38; S. H. Levey, *The Targum of Ezekiel*: The Aramaic Bible 13
(Wilmington: Glazier and Edinburgh: Clark, 1987) 3, 4; K. J. Cathcart and R. P.
Gordon, *The Targum of the Minor Prophets*: The Aramaic Bible 14 (Wilmington:
Glazier and Edinburgh: Clark, 1989) 12-14. Levey's acceptance of the paradigm is
especially noteworthy, in that he had earlier argued that Targum Jonathan (espe-
cially Isaiah) should be placed within the period of the ascendancy of Islam, cf.
"The Date of Targum Jonathan to the Prophets," *Vetus Testamentum* 21 (1971) 186-
196.

[37] Of course, that does not prevent such arguments from being made; cf.
Michael D. Goulder, "Those Outside (Mk. 4:10-12)," *Novum Testamentum* 33.4
(1991) 289-302.

[38] Hence the remarkable conclusion of M. D. Hooker's review, that although
the connections posited between Jesus's teaching and the Targum were demonstrated, they were "only to be expected," cf. *New Blackfriars* 66 (1985) 550-552. Cf.
the very different conclusions of M. McNamara in *Catholic Biblical Quarterly* 47
(1985) 184-186 and 48 (1986) 329-331 and I. H. Marshall in *Evangelical Quarterly* 58
(1986) 267-270. It is odd that Professor Hooker now finds such connections pre-
dictable, when her work on the phrase "son of man" is innocent of reference to the
Targumim; cf. *The Son of Man in Mark* (London: SPCK and Montreal: McGill
University Press, 1967).

book was in fact written to some extent with a view to continuing debates concerning authority within the Church, and was published by an Anglican house as well as by a Catholic publisher. There has been a tendency to confuse the historical and literary analysis of the book (the relationship between Jesus and the Isaiah Targum) with its theological argument (that analogy is the appropriate approach to scripture within the Church).[39] Such a confused reading of the book leads to the misimpression that Chilton attributed a systematic theology to Jesus, when his stated conclusion is that Jesus employed scripture in the service of an experience of God. The question his book begs does not involve Jesus' theology of scripture, for the simple reason that the existence of such a theology is denied. Jesus' understanding of how God is experienced is the questioned which is opened, and left unresolved.

In *Jesus and Judaism*, E. P. Sanders made an attempt along the the lines of discussion prior to Vermes's contribution to make a global distinction between Jesus and his Judaic milieu.[40] Sanders essentially takes Meyer's perspective as axiomatic, and argues that Jesus was motivated by an ambient theology of the restoration of Israel.[41] His construction of the theology is more apocalyptic than Meyer would have it, in that Sanders accepts Schweitzer's contribution virtually as read.[42] In that regard, Sanders is out of step with the criticism of the simplistic eschatology which Schweitzer attributed to Jesus.[43] Borg especially in recent years has been identified with a rigorous challenge of purely temporal constructions of the kingdom of God in Jesus' teaching,[44] and it is surprising that Sanders asserts Schweitzer's position without defending it against Borg's criticisms. His treatment of the earlier criticisms of T. F. Glasson and C. H. Dodd (pp. 124-125, 154-156) does not deal with the central issue, whether there is in fact evidence of an apocalyptic scenario held by Jesus, such that he held his actions were bringing about the kingdom.

---

[39] See P. S. Alexander's review in *Journal of Jewish Studies* 36 (1985) 238-242 and, in contrast, J. Neusner's in *Journal of Ecumenical Studies* 22 (1985) 359-361.

[40] (Philadelphia: Fortress and London: SCM, 1985).

[41] See chapter 2, "New Temple and Restoration in Jewish Literature," pp. 77-90, and chapter 3, "Other Indications of Restoration Eschatology," pp. 91-119.

[42] Sanders treats of his relationship to Schweitzer on pp. 327-334.

[43] For the difficulties involved in Schweitzer's conception of Jesus' apocalypticism, see T. Francis Glasson, "Schweitzer's Influence: Blessing or Bane?" *Journal of Theological Studies* 28 (1977), also available in Chilton, *The Kingdom of God in the Teaching of Jesus*: Issues in Religion and Theology 5 (London: SPCK and Philadelphia: Fortress, 1984), 107-120.

[44] In addition to *Conflict, Holiness & Politics*, see "A Temperate Case for a Non-Eschatological Jesus," *Forum* 2 (1986) 81-102.

The issue of eschatology is subsidiary for Sanders in the end. What distinguishes Jesus from John the baptizer and Judaism generally is not his view of the kingdom: that in Sanders's opinion was commonplace. Jesus parted company with his contemporaries over the issue of repentance. Where they saw repentance as a requirement of remaining within the covenant, Jesus imagined that the kingdom of God was making itself available to all Israel, whether there was repentance or not. Specifically, he insists that Jesus offered the kingdom to the wicked without repentance.[45] Sanders has been criticized for the slim evidential basis of his claim.[46] Because a growing emphasis upon repentance is apparent as the Christian tradition developed, Sanders takes it that Jesus himself said nothing whatever about repentance (*Jesus and Judaism*, pp. 106-113). Although the weakness of the logic invoked by Sanders is obvious, two of its constituent features should be identified, because they are recurring arguments in the study of Jesus.

The first feature is the global application of "the criterion of dissimilarity," developed most articulately by Norman Perrin.[47] The criterion is pratised by isolating elements within Jesus' teaching which are characteristic of Judaism and Christianity; they are then put to the side, as likely to have been attributed to Jesus during the course of the transmission of his sayings. The residue of his teaching, everything which is "dissimilar" to what a Jewish or Christian teacher might have held, is then taken to be authentic.

The assumption of Jesus as the great original, heroically dissimilar from his environment, is intrinsic to every application of the criterion which has ever been attempted. Moreover, from Perrin onwards, there has been a willingness to discount what seems Jewish and what seems orthodox, but to embrace as authentic elements which are consistent with Gnosticism and with Greco-Roman philosophical conventions. (Crossan's work, discussed below, is an example of that trend.) Such a bias can only result in the privileging of the christology of certain wings of early Christianity, the wings within which it was fashionable to see Jesus as magus, as Cynic, and/or as transcendent Redeemer. In that those fashions were demonstrably generated after the foundation of the movement, to

---

[45] See pp. 187, 199, 206-208, 227, 322, 323, and his earlier work, "Jesus and the Sinners," *Journal for the Study of the New Testament* 19 (1983) 5-36.
[46] See Chilton, "Jesus and the Repentance of E. P. Sanders," *Tyndale Bulletin* 39 (1988) 1-18.
[47] *Rediscovering the Teaching of Jesus* (London: SCM and New York: Harper, 1967) 39.

make them the touchstone of authenticity is itself an exercise in modern christology.

Sanders's application of the criterion of dissimilarity exacerbates its inherent weakness. He is, of course, in no position to claim that a saying attributed to Jesus contradicts the necessity of repentance. The only index at his disposal to suggest that Jesus did not require repentance is that the Gospels claim he *did* require repentance! Unless one accepts that the criterion of dissimilarity is of such certainty that one might employ it to invert the stated meaning of texts, Sanders's portrait has nothing to recommend it but the allure of an antinomian Jesus.

The second constituent feature of Sanders's argument, which also illuminates much recent discussion, is the assumption that Jesus is to be understood in historical terms by means of an alleged rupture with Judaism. The coordinates of the rupture are carefully laid out, and have in fact been developed during the course of Sanders's career. On the side of Judaism, Sanders had (in *Paul and Palestinian Judaism*[48]) already defined the religion as a form of "covenantal nomism," such that "obedience to the Torah" was "the means of maintaining membership in the covenant established by God's grace."[49] Accordingly, refusing the necessity of repentance would amount to a systematic (and — one would have thought — conscious) rejection of received Judaism. On the side of Jesus, Sanders claims that his interpretation is virtually positivistic, based upon the "*certain* knowledge about Jesus" (viz., his baptism by John, his call of disciples, his characteristic activity of healing and preaching, his "attack" on the Temple, his execution; *Jesus and Judaism*, 321). The antinomy between nomistic Judaism and an overtly antinomian Jesus seems inescapable.

Sanders nonetheless insists that his reading does not involve a "polar opposition" between Jesus and Judaism (*Jesus and Judaism*, 337-340). While his Jesus indeed does not formally deny Judaism, the question of the Torah is of structural importance within Sanders's thesis:

> It is important not to oversimplify the stance of Jesus towards his contemporaries in Judaism and towards the Jewish law and tradition. He was not a wild antinomian, nor was he an anti-Jewish Jew. He confined

---

[48] *A Comparison of Patterns of Religion* (Philadelphia: Fortress and London: SCM, 1977).

[49] The actual formulation is taken from Ed Parish Sanders, "Jesus, Paul and Judaism," *Aufstieg und Niedergang der römischen Welt* II.25.1 (ed. W. Haase; Berlin: de Gruyter, 1982), 390-450, 394. The article is a succinct statement of a position developed in many different publications.

his preaching and healing to his own people, he acted in the name of
the God of the Patriarchs, and it would appear that he also observed
such commandments as those governing eating and Sabbath observance. We should repeat that the Jerusalem disciples, after his death, did
not understand him to have "abrogated" the Torah. On the other
hand, he preached the inheritance of the kingdom to those who did not
accept the yoke of the Torah, and he thus extended the salvific promises not only beyond what a supposedly ossified and stiff-necked legalism could accept, but beyond what could be reasonably inferred from
Jewish tradition and Scripture. ("Jesus, Paul and Judaism," 427-428)

The ideological antinomy is as inevitable in its influence upon interpretation as the exaggerated appeal to the criterion of dissimilarity. Wild or not, Sanders's Jesus *is* antinomian.

Of course, neither side of the antinomy is anything more than
possible, and both appear suppositious. The centrality of the covenant for Judaism is a virtual truism, but the instrumental role
which Sanders assigns to the law is more characteristic of Rabbinic
sources from the Mishnah and later than of sources of the first
century. And only the latest, most Hellenistic traditions within the
Gospels ascribe an expressly antinomian or anti-cultic intention to
Jesus. The attempt to construe Jesus' program as a conscious or
systematic rupture with Judaism, to make Jesus and Judaism into a
duality, is only feasible in theological terms, not within the discussion of Jesus as a historical figure.

A critically more feasible construction of Jesus is offered by
Richard Horsley in *Jesus and the Spiral of Violence*.[50] Horsley sets Jesus'
movement within the context of the increase in banditry within
Roman Palestine during the years leading up to the revolt which
included elements of the priestly aristocracy from 66 C.E.:

> The brigand is a symbol of resistance to injustice as well as a champion
> of justice in his righting of wrongs for the poor villagers with whom he
> remains in close contact. Moreover, brigands provide the occasions for
> supportive peasants to resist the authorities themselves.[51]

In contrast to the portrait of Jesus as a zealot, which had been
developed earlier by S. G. F. Brandon,[52] Horsley argues that Jesus
programmatically opposed violence, although he also observes that
Jesus can not be described as a pacifist on the grounds of the evidence available (*Jesus and the Spiral of Violence*, p. 319).

---

[50] *Popular Jewish Resistance in Roman Palestine* (San Francisco: Harper and Row,
1987).
[51] P. 37, and see the analysis of pp. 20-58. See also Horsley and J. S. Hanson,
Bandits, Prophets, and Messiahs (Minneapolis: Winston-Seabury, 1985).
[52] *Jesus and the Zealots. A Study of the Political Factor in Primitive Christianity* (Manchester: Manchester University Press, 1967).

As Horsley has it, Jesus' mission was to bring restoration in the midst of systematic oppression:

> ...Jesus was engaged in direct manfestations of God's kingdom in his practice and preaching, and he was confident that God was imminently to complete the restoration of Israel and judge the institutions that maintained injustice. (*Jesus and the Spiral of Violence*, p. 321)

Horsley's appealing portrait is evidently indebted to Meyer's (whose work is cited on p. 340 n. 36), but the setting of the portrait develops the hypothesis of Brandon. Horsley's analysis is more sophisticated than Brandon's, in that there is no assumption that there was a "sustained movement of violent resistance to Roman rule during the first century C.E." (p. 318). But like Brandon, Horsley projects a desire for revolution onto Jesus, who is therefore portrayed as a revolutionary (p. 326).

No argument is made to the effect that Jesus or his movement construed the purpose of his activity within political terms of reference. There is no question but that Judaism and Christianity are better understood in respect of Rome, but to conclude that any given teacher, Judaic or Christian, was motivated by political considerations, requires evidence within the texts to hand. Jesus does not need to have thought in political or social terms in order to have inspired Martin Luther King.

Horsley's contribution, along with Sean Freyne's,[53] remains useful as a guide to some of the most pressing social realities of Palestine within the first century. But in Horsley's work, as in Sanders's, a disturbing tendency of recent discussion becomes apparent. Because study over the past fifty years or so has greatly enhanced the critical appreciation of Judaism, it is sometimes assumed that what is understood of Judaism can be transferred directly to the assessment of Jesus. Sanders finds a theology of restoration in Judaism, and attributes an antinomian form of it to Jesus; Horsley knows there were bandits in Galilee, and sees their motivations (but not their tactics) reflected in the Gospels.

There are two complications in studying Jesus within the milieu of his Judaism(s). First, the range and diversity of that religion prior to the destruction of the Temple are enormous, and for the most part only indirectly attested in the surviving literature. Second, of course, the Gospels themselves only attest Jesus' movement from

---

[53] See *Jesus, Galilee, and the Gospels. Literary Approaches and Historical Investigations* (Dublin: Gill and Macmillan, 1988).

the time when separation from Judaism had become either an accomplished fact or an inevitable development. One reason for which the field is inclined to dismiss the importance of Judaism for the study of Jesus is that the evaluation of Judaic sources is no more straightforward than the evaluation of the Gospels.

The recent contribution of John Dominic Crossan attests the strength of the temptation to retreat from Judaism in the evaluation of Jesus.[54] His book may be read as an extended attempt to construct a portrait of Jesus without reference to Judaism. The attempt begins with an early complaint that scholars who have analyzed Jesus in relation to Judaism have come up with differing results:

> There is Jesus as a political revolutionary by S. G. F. Brandon (1967), as a magician by Morton Smith (1978),[55] as a Galilean charismatic by Geza Vermes (1981, 1984), as a Galilean rabbi by Bruce Chilton (1984), as a Hillelite or proto-Pharisee by Harvey Falk (1985), as an Essene by Harvey Falk, and as an eschatological prophet by E. P. Sanders (1985). (*The Historical Jesus*, p. xxvii)

Such differences are taken, not as a sign of health in an emerging sub-discipline, but as a reason to use a different foundation of analysis. Crossan opts for the model of Jesus as a popular philosopher in the vein of the Cynics (whom he characterizes as "hippies in a world of Augustan yuppies," p. 421.), since there were many non-Jews in Galilee. During the course of his description, he admits that Jesus was unlike the Cynics in his calling of disciples (pp. 349, 421), in his refusal to have those he sent carry a staff,[56] in his concern for questions of purity, in his avoidance of cities, in the limitation of his activity to Israel (pp. 421-422).

The mystery is only why Crossan clings to such an evidently faulty model. That mystery is resolved when he criticizes the understanding of Jesus as a rabbi. His criticism is based upon an elementary misunderstanding. Crossan sees rabbis during the second century as the equivalent of the papacy on the Christian side: both are hierarchical assertions of doctrinal unity which attempt to homogenize the intrinsic pluralism of their respective religious systems (p. 417). A double projection is evident here. Crossan, a liberal Catholic, sees the papacy of the twentieth century reflected in the earlier use of communion with Rome as a standard of catholic

---

[54] *The Historical Jesus. The Life of a Mediterranean Jewish Peasant* (San Francisco: Harper and Edinburgh: Clark, 1991).

[55] Crossan's reference is to *Jesus the Magician* (San Francisco: Harper and Row, 1978).

[56] P. 339. Earlier, Crossan refers to "cloak, wallet and staff" as "almost an official triad" (p. 82).

continuity. However helpful that first projection may (or may not) be, the second is unwarranted: scholarship of Rabbinic Judaism through the second century would not encourage a comparison, even an attenuated comparison, with the Vatican in its post-Tridentine form.

Crossan's confusion becomes egregious, when he goes on to compare rabbis with the priesthood in the Temple, as if they formed a united front. Evidently, his acceptance of a sociological model of a charismatic hero of religion opposed by the forces of routinization has totally overwhelmed even a gesture towards understanding the complexity of Judaism during the first century:

> In all of this the point is not really Galilee against Jerusalem but the far more fundamental dichotomy of magician as personal and individual power against priest or rabbi as communal and ritual power. Before the Second Temple's destruction, it was magician against Temple, and therefore magician against rabbi. (P. 157)

Crossan is happy to use Vermes's image of the *hasid* for that reason, but he realizes it has not worn well. As a result, he exchanges the charismatic *hasid* for a charismatic sage, borrowing the category of magician from Morton Smith (pp. 137-167).

The point has apparently escaped Crossan's notice that the teachers we call rabbis, masters (in varying degrees) of discussion and parable and exposition and judgment and ethics and purity and health and healing and other aspects of covenantal wisdom, *referred to each other as sages*. It has long been commonplace in the field to acknowledge that the formalism of a rabbinate, including a concern for succession and a notion of a syllabus to be mastered by disciples, only prevailed with the emergence of rabbis as the basis of systemic redefinition in the period after 70 C.E.[57] Such nuances are lost on Crossan, who asserts, "There was, in the world and time of Jesus, only one sort of Judaism, and that was Hellenistic Judaism..." (p. 418). Rabbinic Judaism was exclusive of Hellenistic influences; Jesus was inclusive (p. 422). Within such a typology, the fact that Jesus is called "rabbi" by his followers is simply beside the point.

Just Jesus' identity as a rabbi is taken as a suitable point of departure by John P. Meier.[58] Although Meier's book appeared

---

[57] Cf. Hayim Lapin, "Rabbi," *The Anchor Bible Dictionary* 5 (ed. D. N. Freedman; New York: Doubleday, 1992) 600-602. As a matter of interest, we might note that the earlier article of Pierson Parker, "Rabbi, Rabbouni," *The Interpreter's Dictionary of the Bible* 4 (ed. G. A. Buttrick; New York: Abingdon, 1962) 3, comes to much the same conclusion. See also Chilton, *A Galilean Rabbi*, pp. 34-35.

[58] *A Marginal Jew. Rethinking the Historical Jesus*: the Anchor Bible Reference Library (New York: Doubleday, 1991).

shortly before Crossan's, he reacts to many of its principal contentions (which had appeared in earlier works). He carefully allows for the findings of Sean Freyne in respect of the Galilean setting of Jesus' ministry, but Meier questions whether we can reasonably claim any advancement in our knowledge in calling Jesus a peasant. Modern romanticism often obscures the meaning of the term, and insofar as Jesus was a member of a peasant society, it was because he was a woodworking rabbi (pp. 278-315).[59] Crossan's usage of the so-called Apocryphal Gospels is also severely criticized in a judicious treatment of the likely chronologies and histories of composition (pp. 112-166). Finally, Meier very specifically embraces the category of "rabbi" as the suitable designation of Jesus' public ministry, and even concludes that Jesus was literate in Hebrew (p. 276, cf. n. 125 on p. 306).

Meier's volume represents the first two parts of a four part project. The first part is devoted to "issues of definitions, methods, and sources," and the second deals with "some of the linguistic, educational, political, and social background." The public ministry is to be the focus of part three, while part four is to consider Jesus' death (p. 13). Following his schema, it would seem we may only expect a detailed account of Jesus within Judaism from part three onward.

The analysis of Jesus within Judaic terms of reference has been pursued by Chilton in *The Temple of Jesus*.[60] Where *A Galilean Rabbi* developed a comparison of Jesus' citation of Isaiah with the interpretative tradition of the Targum, the focal point of *The Temple of Jesus* is Jesus' occupation of the Temple (pp. 91-111). It is argued that what Jesus did was neither a protest against sacrifice nor a prediction of the Temple's destruction, but a forceful insistence that a condition of purity in sacrifice was that Israelites should offer of their own produce in God's house. Purity, in other words, is not the extraneous matter it is often taken to be, but—as is the case within sacrificial systems generally (pp. 3-42), in the Hebrew Bible (pp. 45-67), and even in the orientation of Josephus (pp. 69-87)—a vital component within any sacrifice which is considered effective. Purity refers both to the products which are offered as well as to the gestures by which they are offered, and by attending to those pragmatic issues, sacrificial communities believe they enjoy the affective and the ideological benefits which they associate with sacrifice. Be-

---

[59] It should be noted that Crossan's analysis belies the subtitle of his book, in that he concludes that Jesus was not a peasant, but an artisan (*The Historical Jesus*, pp. 29, 46, cf. 15-19). One might suggest that Crossan has in fact written "The Life of a Judaeo-Cynic Artisan."

[60] *His Sacrificial Program Within a Cultural History of Sacrifice* (University Park: Pennsylvania State, 1992).

cause purity is a systemic concern which links sacrifice in the Temple with the domestic practice of cleanliness, it is precisely Jesus' view and practice of purity which was likely to have earned him friends and enemies both in Galilee and in Jerusalem.

Jesus, in other words, must be understood, not over and against Judaism, nor alongside it, but from within; necessarily, that implies he is to be apprehended as having a positive definition of purity. That definition is cognate with an aspect of Jesus' ministry which is usually overlooked: his programmatic concern with the issues of who is fit to sacrifice, how a person might be considered clean, when foods might be taken with whom, and what should be sacrificed (see *The Temple of Jesus*, pp. 121-136). Forgiveness for Jesus established an eschatological purity among people whose fellowship and sacrifice opened the way for the kingdom of God (pp. 130-136). That programmatic understanding explains his intentional insistence upon communal eating, and the "last supper" in particular (p. 137-154).[61]

It has been nearly sixty years since we were first warned of the peril of modernizing Jesus.[62] Jesus obviously engaged the religious dimension of purity, a dimension linking a complex of issues which proved to be crucial during his ministry (including sacrifice in the Temple, fellowship at table, the forgiveness of sins, the declaration of purity, the definition of who might be included in the eschatological banquet). Purity offers a perspective upon Jesus' activity which is not an artifact of the apologetic tradition which attempts to portray him as transcending Judaism. Rather, purity is a systemic concern within early Judaism which Jesus took up, and which his movement developed until it claimed that an alternative to purity had been established. The non-modern Jesus, the historical Jesus, is the Jesus whose passion was a purity which the Christian West has long believed is beside the point. Purity was the substance of the restoration which Meyer correctly identified as the central issue in Jesus' activity. Discussion since his seminal contribution may at last have discovered a way of speaking of Jesus' activity and of his experience of God which may reasonably claim to be more historical than apologetic. That would be a fitting result of the interest in Jesus within Judaism, which has already taught us what had been denied for a generation: that we must address the question of Jesus if we would understand Christianity.

---

[61] The latter issue is taken up further in an exegetical study, *A Feast of Meanings. Eucharistic Theologies from Jesus through Johannine Circles*: Supplements to Novum Testamentum 72 (Leiden: Brill, 1994).

[62] See Henry Joel Cadbury, *The Peril of Modernizing Jesus*: Lowell Institute Lectures (New York: Macmillan, 1937).

Bibliography

Robert D. Baird, *Category Formation and the History of Religions* (The Hague: Mouton, 1971; Berlin and New York: Mouton de Gruyter, 1991)

Francis Barham, *The Life and Times of John Reuchlin, or Capnion* (London: Whittaker, 1843)

Shlomo Biderman (ed.), *Myth and Fictions. Their Place in Philosophy and Religion* (Leiden: Brill, 1994)

Günther Bornkamm, *Jesus von Nazareth*: Urban-Bücher 19 (Stuttgart: Kohlhammer, 1956)

———, (tr. I. McLuckey, F. McLuckey, J. M. Robinson), *Jesus of Nazareth* (New York: Harper, 1960)

Marcus Borg, *Conflict, Holiness & Politics in the Teaching of Jesus*: Studies in the Bible and Early Christianity 5 (New York: Mellen, 1984)

———, *Jesus, A New Vision. Spirit, Culture, and the Life of Discipleship* (San Francisco: Harper, 1987)

———, "A Temperate Case for a Non-Eschatological Jesus," *Forum* 2 (1986) 81-102

S. G. F. Brandon, *Jesus and the Zealots. A Study of the Political Factor in Primitive Christianity* (Manchester: Manchester University Press, 1967)

Martin Buber (ed. and tr. M. Friedman), *The Origin and Meaning of Hasidism* (New York: Horizon, 1960)

Rudolf Bultmann, *Jesus*: Die unsterblichen, die geistigen Heroen der Menschheit (Berlin: Deutsche Bibliotek, 1926)

———, (tr. L. P. Smith and E. H. Lantero), *Jesus and the Word* (New York: Scribner, 1934)

Millar Burrows, *The Dead Sea Scrolls* (New York: Viking, 1955)

Henry Joel Cadbury, *The Peril of Modernizing Jesus*: Lowell Institute Lectures (New York: Macmillan, 1937)

Bruce Chilton, *A Feast of Meanings. Eucharistic Theologies from Jesus through Johannine Circles*: Supplements to Novum Testamentum 72 (Leiden: Brill, 1994)

———, *A Galilean Rabbi and His Bible. Jesus' Use of the Interpreted Scripture of His Time*: Good News Studies 8 (Wilmington: Glazier, 1984); also with the subtitle *Jesus' own interpretation of Isaiah* (London: SPCK, 1984)

———, *The Glory of Israel. The Theology and Provenience of the Isaiah Targum*: Journal for the Study of the Old Testament Supplements 23 (Sheffield: JSOT, 1982)

———, *God in Strength. Jesus' Announcement of the Kingdom*: Studien zum Neuen Testament und seiner Umwelt 1 (Freistadt: Plöchl, 1979), reprinted in the series "The Biblical Seminar" (Sheffield: JSOT/Sheffield Academic Press, 1987)

———, *The Isaiah Targum. Introduction, Translation, Apparatus, and Notes*: The Aramaic Bible (Wilmington: Glazier and Edinburgh: Clark, 1987)

———, "Jesus and the Repentance of E. P. Sanders," *Tyndale Bulletin* 39 (1988) 1-18

———, "The Son of Man: Human and Heavenly," *The Four Gospels 1992*. *Festschrift Frans Neirynck*: Bibliotheca Ephemeridum Theologicarum Lovaniensium (eds. F. Van Segbroeck and others; Leuven: University Press, 1992) 203-218, also available as "אנש[א] בר: Human and Heavenly," *Approaches to Ancient Judaism* (New Series), *Volume Four. Religious and Theological Studies*: South Florida Studies in the History of

Judaism 81 (ed. J. Neusner; Atlanta: Scholars, 1993) 97-114
, *The Temple of Jesus. His Sacrificial Program Within a Cultural History of Sacrifice* (University Park: Pennsylvania State, 1992)
John Dominic Crossan, *The Historical Jesus. The Life of a Mediterranean Jewish Peasant* (San Francisco: Harper and Edinburgh: Clark, 1991)
Philip R. Davies, *Behind the Essenes. History and Ideology in the Dead Sea Scrolls*: Brown Judaic Studies 94 (Atlanta: Scholars, 1987)
Guilford Dudley, "Mircea Eliade: Anti-Historian of Religions," *Journal of the American Academy of Religion* 44 (1976) 345-359
Harvey Falk, *Jesus the Pharisee. A New Look at the Jewishness of Jesus* (New York: Paulist, 1985)
Sean Freyne, *Jesus, Galilee, and the Gospels. Literary Approaches and Historical Investigations* (Dublin: Gill and Macmillan, 1988)
T. Francis Glasson, "Schweitzer's Influence: Blessing or Bane?" *Journal of Theological Studies* 28 (1977), also available in Chilton, *The Kingdom of God in the Teaching of Jesus*: Issues in Religion and Theology 5 (London: SPCK and Philadelphia: Fortress, 1984) 107-120
Nahum N. Glazer, *Hillel the Elder. The Emergence of Classical Judaism* (Washington: B'nai B'rith, 1959)
William Scott Green, "Palestinian Holy Men: Charismatic Leadership and Rabbinic Tradition," *Aufstieg und Niedergang der römischen Welt* II.19.2 (ed. W. Haase; Berlin: de Gruyter, 1979) 619-647
Walter Grundmann, *Die Entscheidung Jesu. Zur geschichtlichen Bedeutung der Gestalt Jesu von Nazareth* (Berlin: Evangelische Verlag, 1972)
, *Die frühe Christenheit und ihre Schriften: Umwelt, Entstehung und Eigenart der neutestamentlichen Bücher* (Stuttgart: Calwer, 1983)
, *Die Geschichte Jesu Christi* (Berlin: Evangelische Verlagsanstalt, 1956)
, *Jesus der Galiläer und das Judentum*: Veröffentlichungen des Instituts zur Erforschung des jüdischen Einflusses auf das deutsche kirchliche Leben (Leipzig: Weigand, 1940)
Donald A. Hagner, *The Jewish Reclamation of Jesus. An Analysis & Critique of the Modern Jewish Study of Jesus* (Grand Rapids: Zondervan, 1984)
Richard Horsley, *Jesus and the Spiral of Violence. Popular Jewish Resistance in Roman Palestine* (San Francisco: Harper and Row, 1987)
, and J. S. Hanson, *Bandits, Prophets, and Messiahs* (Minneapolis: Winston-Seabury, 1985)
Joachim Jeremias, *Jesu Verheissung für die Völker* (Kohlhammer: Stuttgart, 1956)
, (tr. S. H. Hooke), *Jesus' Promise to the Nations*: Studies in Biblical Theology 14 (London: SCM, 1958)
Hayim Lapin, "Rabbi," *The Anchor Bible Dictionary* 5 (ed. D. N. Freedman; New York: Doubleday, 1992) 600-602
John Lightfoot, *A Commentary on the New Testament from the Talmud and Hebraica* 1-4 (Grand Rapids: Baker, 1979)
John P. Meier, *A Marginal Jew. Rethinking the Historical Jesus*: the Anchor Bible Reference Library (New York: Doubleday, 1991)
Ben F. Meyer, *The Aims of Jesus* (London: SCM, 1979)
Eric M. Meyers, "The Cultural Setting of Galilee: The Case of Regionalism and Early Judaism," *Aufstieg und Niedergang der römischen Welt* II.19.1 (ed. W. Haase; Berlin: de Gruyter, 1979) 686-702
Claude Goldsmid Montefiore, *Rabbinic Literature and Gospel Teachings* (London: Macmillan, 1930)

George Foot Moore, *Judaism in the First Centuries of the Christian Era. The Age of the Tannaim* 1-3 (Cambridge: Harvard University Press, 1927-1930)

Jacob Neusner, *Eliezer ben Hyrcanus. The Tradition and the Man*: Studies in Judaism in Late Antiquity (Leiden: Brill, 1973)

Hugh Odeberg, *The Aramaic Portions of Bereshit Rabbah*: Lund Universitets Arsskrift 36.3 (Lund: Gleerup, 1939)

Norman Perrin, *Rediscovering the Teaching of Jesus* (London: SCM and New York: Harper, 1967)

Henning Graf Reventlow (tr. J. Bowden), *The Authority of the Bible and the Rise of the Modern World* (London: SCM, 1984)

John Riches, *Jesus and the Transcendence of Judaism* (London: Darton, Longman & Todd, 1980)

S. Safrai and M. Stern with D. Flusser, W. C. van Unnik, *The Jewish People in the First Century. Historical Geography, Political History, Social, Cultural and Religious Life and Institutions*: Compendia Rerum Iudaicarum ad Novum Testamentum 1 (Assen: Van Gorcum, 1974)

E. P. Sanders, *Jesus and Judaism* (Philadelphia: Fortress and London: SCM, 1985)

, "Jesus and the Sinners," *Journal for the Study of the New Testament* 19 (1983) 5-36

, "Jesus, Paul and Judaism," *Aufstieg und Niedergang der römischen Welt* II.25.1 (ed. W. Haase; Berlin: de Gruyter, 1982) 390-450

, *Paul and Palestinian Judaism. A Comparison of Patterns of Religion* (Philadelphia: Fortress and London: SCM, 1977)

Emil Schürer (eds. M. Black, G. Vermes, F. Millar, P. Vermes, M. Goodman), *The History of the Jewish People in the Age of Jesus Christ (175 B.C.-A.D. 135)* (Edinburgh: Clark, 1973-1987)

Jonathan Z. Smith, *Map Is Not Territory. Studies in the History of Religions*: Studies in Judaism in Late Antiquity 23 (Leiden: Brill, 1978)

Morton Smith, *Jesus the Magician* (San Francisco: Harper and Row, 1978)

Hermann Leberecht Strack and Paul Billerbeck (latterly with J. Jeremias and K. Adolph), *Kommentar zum Neuen Testament aus Talmud und Midrasch* 1-6 (München: Beck, 1922-1961)

Ivan Strenski, *Four Theories of Myth in Twentieth-Century History. Cassirer, Eliade, Lévi-Strauss and Malinowski* (Iowa City: University of Iowa and Basingstoke: Macmillan, 1987)

Geza Vermes, *Jesus and the World of Judaism* (London: SCM, 1983)

, *Jesus the Jew. An Historian's Reading of the Gospels* (Philadelphia: Fortress, 1981, from London: Collins, 1973)

, *The Religion of Jesus the Jew* (London: SCM, 1993)

, "The 'Son of Man' Debate," *Journal for the Study of the New Testament* 1 (1978) 19-32

Brian Walton, *Biblia Sacra Polyglotta* (London: 1655-1657)

HISTORY OF JUDAISM: ITS PERIODS IN ANTIQUITY

G. Boccaccini
(University of Michigan)

1 PERIODS AND TERMS: THE SUBSTANCE BEHIND THE CONVENTION

The identification of a historical period, in terms of chronology and nomenclature, is always a convention, a fragile creation of human mind. It depends on the evaluative work of historians who interpret the past by giving a certain order to the indistinct mass of social and intellectual phenomena. By definition, writing history is a process of selection that produces a taxonomy.[1]

The identification of a historical period also depends on cultural, political and religious factors: the importance that an age has for the people or the class to which one belongs. The past is an essential part of human self-understanding and identity. Each generation tranfers back its intellectual baggage and according to this, for instance, defines an age as a period of gloomy decadence or glorious renaissance.

Periods and terms, therefore, are conventional but not ideologically neutral; they are sensitive to cultural, political and religious revolutions, and to developments of research. Different approaches cause the emergence of rival taxonomies. As a result of changing perspectives, some terms suddenly turn old and derogatory, others appear new and fresh. It is naive to state that since names are mere conventions, one is as bad as the other and terminological discussions are only a superfluous (and somehow boring) matter of style and personal taste. On the contrary, a choice between rival ideologies is often at stake. The history of historiography demonstrates that the replacement of a terminology is never a painless event; it means the victory of a competing framework and the contemporaneous defeat of the previous one.

What is true in any branch of history, is apparent in the study of Judaism, particularly of Judaism between the third century BCE and the second century CE. Few historical periods have claimed such a persistent and profound interest. These centuries are the common cradle of the two living faiths that we now call Christianity and Judaism, as well as the bridge where the "religious" East met

---

[1] See Gracia J.J.E. (1992)

the "philosophical" West, laying the foundations of our civilization. Precisely because of its enduring significance, this period belongs not only to scholars; the rabbi and the theologian, the philosopher and the historian, the artist and the poet, the writer and the musician, as well as the ordinary people, have looked at it with passion along the course of history, in order better to understand themselves and their own identity.[2]

The cultural hegemony exerted by the Christians was for centuries challenged only by the presence of a Jewish minority, that shared the same past events, yet arranged them in a competitive "sacred history". Even the birth and development of secular history did not mean the immediate end of religious paradigms so well established in our culture and subconsciousness. The emancipation of historical research from confessional interests and presuppositions, the open questioning of the largely "mythical" character of the Christian and Jewish sacred histories, is a contemporary phenomenon.[3] The centripetal force given by the conservative confessional taxonomies, still opposes the centrifugal force given by the achievements of critical scholarship. The lack of a shared terminology and of precise chronological boundaries to describe Judaism in antiquity is not accidental; it is consequent upon the unresolved confrontation between these divergent forces. While the old balance is definitively lost, the new one is still hard to define.

It would not make sense to propose here a new periodization and terminology if it were not required and supported by the latest achievements of scholarly research. Periods and terms are not good or bad in themselves; they appear better or worse whether they express or contradict the hermeneutical approach that one follows, and more generally, the cultural climate in which one lives. The discussion will therefore not be carried out in the abstract but historically. Step by step, I will show by which ideological contexts previous periodizations and terminologies were generated, when they established themselves, and why the time is now ripe for a "better" scientific taxonomy.

2 THE TRADITIONAL APPROACH: THE ONE JUDAISM

The idea of a single Judaism, corresponding to a single Christianity, has ruled the relationships between Christianity and Rabbinic

---

[2] A comprehensive outline of the history of research, from Josephus to the present time, is in Boccaccini G. (1992).

[3] See Garbini G. (1986).

Judaism for centuries. This framework was all the more deeply rooted because it was not an object of interconfessional debate; since the beginning instead, it was the balancing point of a difficult coexistence between the Christian and Rabbinic sacred histories.[4]

For oppressed Jews, the model served to emphasize their enduring fidelity to an ancient and unaltered tradition since Moses' time, and polemically to sanction the complete otherness of Christianity (as well as any other "deviation") compared to the one Judaism. Stating the *ab origine* presence of a normative model had a reassuring function for the identity of Jews. Anything in the past—any problem or internal contradiction in history—automatically became "non-Jewish". The most important contradiction, the birth of Christianity from within Judaism, could be removed at the very moment it appeared.

Paradoxically, in the opinion of triumphant Christians the same model served to point out the newness and uniqueness of Jesus of Nazareth, whose message was seen as grafted onto an older religion at the end of its role as a "precursor". Judaism, replaced and rendered useless by the advent of Christianity, thus became no more than a pathetic and sclerotic relict without vitality or dignity, proper to an incredulous and even "deicidal"[5] people who remained attached to old and outdated beliefs.

Although Christian and rabbinic literatures reminded of the plurality of ancient Judaism, "the Jewish sects" aroused no interest.[6] The decisive dramatic conflict between the Synagogue and the Church, each so well defined in its respective role, certainly had no

---

[4] The idea of a single Judaism is very ancient in both traditions. In the *Dialogue with Trypho* 11:1-5, Justyn already speaks of Judaism as a unit replaced by Christianity, while the treatise *Aboth* (1:1) lays the foundations of normative rabbinic tradition through the creation of a single, uninterrupted and faithful chain of transmission since Moses' times.

[5] Already in Origen (*In Mattheum* 27:25) we find the idea that Jesus' blood is not only on those who lived then, but also on all the following generations of the Jews, until the end of the world. The complex story of a conflict among rival groups in Judaism turns into the lasting fight between two static and atemporal identities: the Christians of every time and every place against the Jews of every time and every place.

[6] References to the "Jewish sects" are scattered in rabbinic and Christian documents; the most comprehensive treatments are those offered by the Christian Epiphanius (*Panarion*) and Philastrius (*Liber de haeresibus*) in the fourth century. See, respectively, Migne J.-P., ed. *Patrologia graeca*, vols. 41-42 (Paris: 1862); and Idem, ed. *Patrologia latina*, vol. 12 (Paris: 1845). Throughout the Middle Ages, a strong interest in the subject is apparent only in the work of the Karaite Yaqub al-Qirqisani (*Kitab al-anwar*) at the beginning of the tenth century. See Chiesa B. and Lockwood W. *Yaqub al-Qirqisani on Jewish sects and Christianity* (Frankfurt am Main and New York: 1984).

need of other, minor characters—in fact, they were quickly forgotten. In their triumph or distress, both the Rabbis and the Christians
had good reasons to consider themselves as the only legitimate heirs
of the one biblical Judaism, which the former claimed to have faithfully maintained and the latter to have faithfully fulfilled.

It was not until the seventeenth century that some Christian
scholars began to use the Jewish post-biblical literature and history
not only for apologetic and missionary ends, but also to gain a
better understanding of the Old and New Testaments and their
historical setting.[7] Christian theology began to admit that, to a certain extent, post-biblical Judaism served to prepare for the coming
of Jesus and the acceptance of his message. The age "from Malachi
to Jesus" then emerged as a distinct historical period: it was the
"connection" between the Old and the New Testament, the
"intertestamental age".[8]

While theological concerns pushed Christian scholars of the
eighteenth and nineteenth centuries progressively to concentrate
upon the age "when Jesus was born" (and to develop a new branch
of history, the socalled *neutestamentliche Zeitgeschichte*),[9] the new Jewish
historiography emerging from the ghettoes was instead engaged to
present this age as one of the many parts of the long, glorious, and
not yet concluded history of the Jewish people: it was the age of the
Hebrew's Second Commonwealth or the Second Temple Period.[10]

The appearance of harshly anti-Jewish attitudes in European
culture—particularly since the second half of the nineteenth century—strengthened the Christian characterization of post-biblical
Judaism as a degenerative phenomenon. Judaism "in the age of
Jesus" was a legalistic and decadent religion which turned the mer-
ciful God of the Bible into the inaccessible Lord of Torah and made
the faithful Jew a mere accountant of salvation. Judaism "in the age

---

[7] See Cartwright C. *Mellificium Hebraicum*, 5 vols. (London: 1649); and Lightfoot
J. *Horae Hebraicae et Talmudicae*, 6 vols. (Cambridge: 1658-74).

[8] Credit goes first to an English ecclesiastic, Humphrey Prideaux, who at the
beginning of the eighteenth century turned a neglected appendix of biblical history
into an autonomous historioghraphical unit, "for it may serve as an epilogue to the
Old Testament in the same manner as [...] a prologue to the New". So he wrote in
the preface in 1715 (see Prideaux H. [1716]).

[9] After hesitant attempts to present the period either as the prologue of Church
history or the epilogue of ancient Jewish history, the age eventually established
itself as a historiographical unit: "the time of Jesus" (see Langen J. [1866]) or "the
world of the New Testament" (see Hausrath A. [1868]). The masterpiece of Emil
Schürer was the synthesis of these two converging research efforts, which is demonstrated even by the easy interchangeability of the title from the first to the
following editions (see Schürer E. [1874]).

[10] See Jost I.M. (1820); Graetz H. (1853); and Wise I.M. (1880).

of Jesus" was the "background"—we might better say the "black-ground"—against which Christian novelty had to fight and triumph. The term *Spätjudentum* (late Judaism) appeared the most appropriate—chronologically and morally—to denote this period.[11]

The Second World War and the Holocaust shook even the most insulated consciences, and marked the return of post-war scholarship to the less derogatory notion of "intertestamental Judaism" or to the apparently neutral idea of "Second Temple Judaism". The single Judaism model succeeded itself, with only its most polemical traits removed. Pharisaic Judaism continued to be seen as the predominant and "normative" type of Judaism and Palestinian Judaism as an ideological unit so much homogeneous that it could be described through a "common-denominator theology".

Within this perspective, the problem of the Jewishness of Jesus had no agreement. Since Judaism and Christianity were presented as two well-defined and different ideological entities, no comparison was possible except in terms of opposition. Jesus himself was a matter of confrontation. Either he belonged to the one Judaism (and someone else was the creator of Christianity), or he was only incidentally a Jew. The one Judaism might comprise Jesus, not his movement; when the one Christianity emerged, it was no longer a Jewish phenomenon.[12]

The legacy of the single Judaism model is strong and influential, and still characterizes many contemporary scholarly works.[13] We have been provided with an established period (the age of Jesus, or the Second Temple Period) and an amazingly enduring term ("intertestamental").[14] The interest in defining a periodization, how-

---

[11] See Baldensperger W. (1900); and Bertholet A. (1909).

[12] A history of modern debate on the Jewishness of Jesus in Christianity and Judaism is in Hagner D.A. *The Jewish Reclamation of Jesus: An Analysis and Critique of the Modern Jewish Study of Jesus* (Gran Rapids, MI: 1984); and Charlesworth J.H. (1988).

[13] Some Jewish scholars keep seeing Pharisaic-Rabbinic Judaism as the predominant and "normative" type of Judaism in the first-century and the birth of Christianity as a betrayal of Judaism and of Jesus himself (see Maccoby H. [1989]). Their position parallels that of those Christian scholars who soften the Jewishness of Jesus and place Judaism and Hellenism on the same level as the two "backgrounds" that prepared the emergence of the unique Christian phenomenon (see Ferguson E. [1987]). Disturbing echoes of ancient polemics limit the contribution offered to contemporary scholarship by this kind of works. A more sophisticated and balanced attempt at reproposing the single Judaism model is that recently offered by Ed Parish Sanders through his concept of "covenantal nomism" or "common Judaism" (see Sanders E.P. [1978 and 1992]).

[14] All these terms have become interchangeable in contemporary scholarship and still title many introductions to the period (see, e.g., Maier J. [1990]; and Murphy F.J. [1991])

ever, was only marginal in the single Judaism model. The assumption was that the substance of "Judaism" (and "Christianity") does not change along with the course of history. On the one hand, Jewish-oriented terms aimed to show the continuity of Jewish history ("Second Temple Judaism") and the purity of "normative" (or "orthodox", or "common") Judaism versus the disordered spread of the "sects" and the emergence of "non-Jewish" phenomena (such as Christianity), more than to establish a periodization. On the other hand, Christian-oriented terms, such as "late" or "intertestamental", were intended to label derogatorily the *whole* Judaism more than to define a distinctive period within a single, indivisible system.

3 THE TRADITIONAL APPROACH REVISITED: MAINSTREAM JUDAISM

In these last decades, a slightly different model has gradually replaced the single Judaism model. Instead of stating the ideological unity of Judaism behind its historical differences, scholars now stress the continuity of Jewish tradition in terms of evolution. The dynamic and pluralist nature of Judaism, as well as the existence of diverse groups, are fully recognized. The claim, however, is that these groups shared sufficient common ground as to be classified as one, albeit variegated, religious tradition. "Judaism" is viewed as a developing religion which knew different stages in its history. Its unity is demonstrated not by the reference to an unchanged ideological system, but by the gradual and consistent evolution from one ideological system to the following one.[15]

Because of its flexibility, the evolutionary model seems to offer a very effective framework for the study of Judaism as the religion of the Jewish people. It softens too monolithic a view of Judaism, without denying the theological concerns of the single Judaism model over the unchanged unity of the Jewish people and religion. It gives room to differences, discontinuities, and dead possibilities before "mainstream Judaism" found its natural course. At the end of this process "the Rabbis were the winners of ancient Jewish history".[16]

The evolutionary model also offers a non-conflicting framework to the relations between Judaism and Christianity, without denying

---

[15] See Cohen S.J.D. (1987); and Schiffman L.H. (1991).
[16] Cohen S.J.D. (1987) 18. For Schiffman, "the Judaism that emerged at the end of the Talmud era [was] chosen by a kind of natural selection process in the spheres of history and religion" (Schiffman [1991] 15).

their difference and otherness. Judaism and Christianity are two distinct ideological traditions, two divergent chains of ideological systems, which happened to share one link of their developing and unitary histories. One link, among the many, of Jewish tradition became the first link of developing Christian tradition. The evolutionary model allows one to consider Jesus and his first followers as belonging to both the Jewish and the Christian tradition. Although limited to the first stage of its evolution, the Jewishness of Christianity lasted long enough to support the claim that Jesus and his followers were entirely Jewish and, at the same time, were the creators of a new religion that would flourish out of Judaism.

These features of the evolutionary model explain why it has become predominant among Jewish and Christian scholars. The possibility to consider early Christianity as part of Jewish history and also as the first stage of a new developing religion, has provided a common ground for specialists in Judaism and the New Testament and has removed any suspicion of confessional interest in the rediscovery of the Jewishness of Jesus.[17] The new ecumenical climate between Christians and Jews in the wake of the Second Vatican Council is not foreign to the success of the evolutionary model.

The development of the new hermeneutical model gave birth to a renewed terminology. In fact, the need of a periodization is more urgent in the evolutionary model that sees Judaism as a sequence of distinctive stages. The term *Frühjudentum* (early Judaism) established itself in the 1970s and early 1980s[18] as an attempt to describe the stage of Judaism contemporaneous to early Christianity: the use of the same adjective emphasized a close parallelism between the two. Until those years, the term "early Judaism" had been used in scholarship to describe the earliest phase of Judaism: the period immediately following the Babylonian exile.[19] Chronological consistency was now sacrified to the generous goal of giving the joining point of Jewish and Christian traditions the same positive and fresh connotation. As "early" Christianity was the first stage of Christian tradition, "early" Judaism defined a period within Jewish tradition which was the beginning of something no less new and fresh: rabbinic Judaism.[20] While the unity of Judaism remained untouched,

---

[17] See Flusser D. (1988); Charlesworth J.H. (1988 and 1991); Riches J (1990); Maier J. (1990); and Murphy F.J. (1991).
[18] See Maier J. (1973); and Kraft R.A. (1986).
[19] See Brown L.E. (1929).
[20] "As early Christianity signifies the origins of Christianity so early Judaism denotes the beginning of synagogal (modern) Judaism" (Charlesworth J.H. [1985] 59).

the breakdown with the polemical concerns that originated the single Judaism model could not be expressed more effectively: what once was "late" was now labeled "early".

4 THE BREAKDOWN WITH THE TRADITIONAL APPROACH: MANY JUDAISMS (INCLUDING CHRISTIANITIES)

Despite its acknowleged merits, the evolutionary model has aged quickly. In the last years, the progress of research has made scholars more conscious that Judaism—as with every religion—is to be considered neither an ideologically homogeneous unit nor an incremental, unitary tradition, but, in today's world as well as in the past, a set of parallel systems in competition. The fundamental characteristic of Judaism is its fragmentary nature; a plurality of groups, movements, and traditions of thought coexist in a complex dialectic relationship. "Whether we deal with a long period of time, such as a millenium, or a brief period of just a few centuries, the picture is the same. [...] Judaisms flourished side by side. Or they took place in succession to one another. Or they came into being out of all relationship with one another".[21]

Credit goes primarily to Jacob Neusner, to his monumental work that has already left a clear imprint ("from Judaism to Judaisms") on Judaic studies.[22] Neusner's approach has been greatly supported by recent works dealing with the history and thought of ancient Judaic systems other than rabbinic.[23] Albeit with difficulty, "noncanonical" documents have reemerged from the centuries-old oblivion to which confessional bias had relegated them. This phenomenon has given to us a new perspective of the complexity of Judaism in antiquity. The ideological differences noticed by scholars can hardly be described as nuances within one normative system or results of an evolutionary process that multiplied choices before selecting the predominant.

In the first century the Rabbinic movement was neither the normative nor the mainstream Judaism. Many other Judaisms, including the early Christian movement, were competing for the supremacy or simply for their own survival. And the Rabbis were not the "winners" predestinated by divine decree or historical necessity; they had to share the victory of survival with two other groups (the

---

[21] J. Neusner "Preface", in Neusner J. (1987) xii.
[22] See Neusner, J. (1991) 27-36.
[23] See Segal A.F. (1987); Saldarini A.J. (1988); Sacchi P. (1990); and Stemberger G. (1991).

Samaritans and the Christians). The blood-tie in particular between Rabbinic Judaism and Christianity is not a parent-child relation; the latter was not born from the former. Both are Judaisms, constituent parts of the same whole, Judaism. Taking up an effective image from Alan F. Segal,[24] we could say that they are "fraternal twins" born of the same womb.

The concept and imagery of Christianity and Rabbinic Judaism as "twins" are not new. They emerged at the turn of this century by some representatives of Reform Judaism (Isaac W. Wise) and Christianity (Robert H. Charles),[25] who used the paradigm in their common debate versus orthodox Judaism. Jewish thought comprised two opposite trends: the bad one was the legalistic trend of scribes and Pharisees that originated orthodox Judaism; the good one was the anti-nomistic trend of prophets and apocalyptic writers that originated Christianity, survived in Jewish mystical traditions and eventually produced Reform Judaism.

With its polemical aspects removed, this paradigm was occasionally taken up by some enlightened precursors of the Jewish-Christian dialogue, such as Francis C. Burkitt and James W. Parkes.[26] The contemporary stress on pluralism of ancient Judaism now gives new strength to this intuition. The "two" rival trends have become so many, complex, and interacting as to make impossible any attempt to define a good and a bad tendency. Christianity and Rabbinism knew their formative periods and became normative systems only from the second century CE onwards. Prior to that they were only two of the many Judaisms of late antiquity, two instruments of an ancient orchestra, which only the canonical myopia prevented us from identifying and enjoying.

5 Criticism of Early Judaism

As a consequence of this new understanding of Judaism, more and more scholars are getting aware of something disturbing associated with the term "early Judaism"—something that they have not noticed before.

First, denoting this period in relation to Rabbinic Judaism as its "early" phase, we symmetrically reproduce a confessional paradigm

---

[24] See Segal A.F. (1986); and Perelmuter H.G. (1989).
[25] See Wise I.M. (1880); and Charles R.H. (1914).
[26] See Burkitt F.C. "What Christians Think of Jews", *Hibbert Journal* 28 (1929-30) 261-70; and Parkes J.W. (1960).

so dear to the Christian tradition. In fact, "early Judaism"—as the period "between the Bible and the Mishnah"[27]—is to rabbinic Judaism precisely what "intertestamental Judaism"—i.e., the period "between the Old and the New Testament"—is to Christianity. Neither Rabbinic Judaism nor Christianity, however, can presume to preempt this period, which is the matrix of both, as well as the environment of many other Judaisms.

Secondly, the claimed analogy with the term "early Christianity" makes "early Judaism" an ideological term too, that is, the name of a defined variety of Judaism. The nomenclature suggests that between "early Judaism" and later "(rabbinic) Judaism" there is the same ideological continuity as between "early Christianity" and later Christianity. However, not all the Jewish movements active between the third century BCE and the second century CE can be defined as "early Judaisms", that is, they cannot be placed in a direct line of continuity with rabbinic Judaism. For example, it is difficult to reconcile the term with the apocalyptic movement or to claim that the Qumran Judaism was continuous with Rabbinic Judaism. Each Judaism has its own integrity, and not is part of an incremental, single, unitary tradition. And what does "early Judaism" stand for, if not an incremental tradition at an early stage?

Finally, there must be something wrong in a term that by definition include all the Judaisms active in the first century except early Christianity. The absence of the early Chrstian movement, even in the most recent introductions to "early Judaism" is really disturbing. It is like a well-contrived drama. The curtain rises and unveils a marvelous scene, crowded with walk-ons (Jews and Gentiles, men and women, priests and soldiers, rich and poor). The main characters (Pharisees, Sadducees, Essenes) introduce themselves, one after the other. The protagonist, however, keeps the audience waiting!

It is equally disturbing to see scholars discussing the relationship between "early Christianity" and "early Judaism". This is a comparison of incommensurable units. How can we pretend to compare a part (a type of Judaism) such as early Christianity to a whole (a set of many Judaisms—a set that should include early Christianity)? No one has ever dreamed of comparing Essenism or Pharisaism, for example, to "early Judaism"—it would immediately

---

[27] It is not by chance that this nomenclature emerged in the 1970s and early 1980s, contemporaneously with the term "early Judaism" (see Unnik W.G. [1974]; Weingreen J. [1976]; and Nickelsburg G.W.E. [1981]).

appear absurd. Likewise, we are used to discussing whether a certain document (for instance, a pseudepigraphon like the Testaments of the Twelve Patriarchs) is "Christian" or "Jewish". While dealing with a real and important problem—the ideological identification of this document—we scarsely realize that we are incorrectly using the term "Jewish" as a synonym for "non-Christian". More properly, we should discuss whether this document is Christian or belongs to *another* Jewish group. Because early Christianity, like Pharisaism or Essenism, was a first-century Judaism, all the early Christian documents belong to Judaism. Nobody, whether scholar or student, would ever ask if a certain document is Pharisaic or Jewish, Essene or Jewish—rather, if this document is Pharisaic or apocalyptic, Essene or Sadducean. Why should we not do the same when speaking of early Christianity in relation with the other Judaisms?

Separating early Christianity from the other Jewish groups is an unconscious consequence of confessional bias, of the lasting Ptolemaic idea that everything revolves around and exists in relation to early Christianity. A confessional notion imposes itself on history in the perception that Christianity is an extraneous seed miraculously planted on the ground destined for it, not one of the many fruits brought forth by the same soil. The fact that the original ground of Christianity is now claimed to have been "fertile" ("early", intellectually and morally creative) and not "sterile" ("late", intellectually and morally decadent) does not changes the terms of the problem. The internal dialectic of the Judaisms of that age will continue to be deprived of an important element until we recognize that historically Christianity is only one of the many Judaisms then active—nothing more and nothing else—and is as unique as its contemporaneous fellows.

Because the confessional bias so strongly perdures in our subconscious (if no longer in our consciousness), it is not mere chance that the term "early Judaism" is also born maimed. Once again terminological inadequacy is the agent of hermeneutic difficulty.

6 A TECHNICAL VOCABULARY OF JUDAISM

The meaning and use of the term "Judaism" in the scientific study of religion calls for reconsideration. Along the course of history this term—as every name—has borne different meanings. The *Webster's Dictionary* defines "Judaism" as "1. the Jewish religion, a monotheistic religion based on the laws and teachings of the Holy Scripture and the Talmud; 2. the Jewish way of life; observance of Jewish

morality, traditions, ceremonies, etc.; 3. Jews collectively; Jewry".[28]
In this definition, two elements are especially worth noticing. First,
by "Judaism" modern English—as well as the other modern languages—denotes both the set of all the many Judaisms by which the
Judaic religion has been formed over the centuries, and one definite
(ideologically homogeneous) Judaic system, namely Rabbinism.
Secondly, the common language presupposes an inseparable bond
between "Judaism" and the "Jews", that is, between an intellectual
phenomenon and a social entity, so much that the two terms are
almost interchangeable and the same adjective "Jewish" (or
"Judaic") refers to both.[29]

Noticing that our contemporary usage of the term Judaism is
coined on the Rabbinic view of Judaism and reflects the single
Judaism model is not surprising. After all, this view has been predominant for centuries in our culture and even in scholarship. The
definition that the *Harper's Bible Dictionary*, for example, gives to
"Judaism" does not differ from that of the *Webster's Dictionary*: "The
religion of the Jewish people from the Sinai theophany through the
present day. Up to and including modern times, Judaism professes
the belief in the one, asexual, eternal, creator God, righteous and
compassionate king, and parent, who entered into a permanent
historical relationship with the children of Israel that would culminate in eschatological redemption. The written and oral Torah per-
petually obligated the people to a detailed code of ethical and ritual
behavior".[30]

The many Judaisms model eventually meets the progressive
secularization of Western culture and marks the complete emancipation of critical scholarship from confessional presuppositions,
what neither the single Judaism model nor the evolutionary model
had carried out. Critical scholarship now openly argues that it is
anachronistic and misleading to read back the history of Judaism in
the light of Rabbinic or Christian thought. Since in our culture the
understanding of the past has been so deeply influenced by the
Christian and the Rabbinic sacred history, not surprisingly the argument opens also a gap between the common language and the

[28] V. Neufeldt, ed., *Webster's New World Dictionary of American English: Third College Edition* (Cleveland and New York: 1988) 731. See E. Ehrlich, et al., eds., *Oxford American Dictionary* (Nw York: 1980) 481: "Judaism: the religion of the Jewish peo-ple, with belief in one God and based on the teachings of the Old Testament and the Talmud".
[29] "Jewish: of or having to do with Jews or Judaism" - "Judaic: of the Jews or Judaism; Jewish". V. Neufeldt, ed., *Webster's New World Dictionary*, 726, 731.
[30] Achtemeier P.J. *Harper's Bible Dictionary* (San Francisco: 1985) 513.

language of critical scholarship. The scientific study of religion is experiencing a phenomenon that already occurred in the other branches of science: the need of a specialized taxonomy, autonomous from the common opinion, and of a technical vocabulary, autonomous from the common language. This does not mean a dismissal of religious beliefs. On the contrary, a clear distinction between the science of history, on the one hand, and religious and cultural patterns, on the other hand, is the necessary premise for a non-conflicting relation. Confessional and cultural models have dignity in themselves even though critical scholarship does not recognize any historical value to them. History does not prevent theology from inferring its truths; theology should not impose its truths backwards on history.[31]

The problem to fix the technical meaning of the term "Judaism" within a scientific taxonomy, is a problem of today. It must not be confused with the search for the "original" historical usage that the term *Ioudaismos* had first in Greek. Such philological inquiry has value for the analysis of the relations between Greeks and Jews in the Hellenistic age, but cannot solve our contemporary quest. Twenty centuries of history cannot be cancelled, nor can the development of language be artificially stopped. And it would be absurd to think that in our understanding of Judaism we should limit ourselves to the conceptual framework of ancient Greeks. We have to solve the problem and build the future on the foundations given by the entire intellectual baggage of the present, not ahistorically refusing our being modern.

Now, the contemporary use of the term "Judaism" in the common language gives us two reasonable possibilities. The first one is to use "Judaism" strictly as a synonym for "Rabbinic Judaism".[32] This implies that we should not use this term to describe comprehensively the religion of Israel before the second or third century CE, when Rabbinism became predominant. If there was "Judaism" in the first century, it was only the religion of a small group of Jews.

This choice would remove many misunderstandings, but it is far from being satisfactory. It stresses too much the discontinuity between "Rabbinic Judaism" and the earliest religion of Israel that produced the biblical documents. It also separated "early rabbinic Judaism" from the other contemporaneous religious groups, leaving

---

[31] See Schüssler Fiorenza E. "Contemporary Biblical Scholarship: Its Roots, Present Understandings, and Future Directions", in *Modern Biblical Scholarship: Its Impact on Theology and Proclamation*, ed. F.A. Eigo (Villanova, PA: 1984).
[32] This choice was made by Di Nola A.M. (1970).

us without a name to denote comprehensively the monotheistic systems created by the Jews before the emergence of Christianity and Rabbinism.

The second possibility given by th commom language is preferable: "Judaism" denotes the whole family of monotheistic systems that historically started developing from within the Jewish people. Judaism therefore describes a multifarious intellectual phenomenon, that is, the history of a religion in the plurality of its developments. Such a definition—limited to the religious sphere, yet inclusive of a great variety of intellectual phenomena—implies three major consequences.

First, Judaism needs to be studied through the same methodologies as used in the study of critical intellectual history. The distinction between religion and philosophy is an uncorrect transposition, on the historical level, of the legitimate religious belief that one must distinguish what comes from above from what comes from humans. From the viewpoint of critical scholarship, religion and philosophy are both expression of intellectual thought. What is commonplace in humanistic fields,[33] including the scientific study of religions, scholars seem hesitant about applying to Judaic (and Christian) studies. While a renewed attention to the study of ideas is noticeable, the fact of borrowing criteria commonly used in the study of the history of secular philosophy still appears so unusual as to be considered a nonconformist, even provocative intrusion. Scholars are even more reluctant to discuss the issue theoretically. So far, the only organic attempt to lay down a scientific methodology for the study of Judaic thought has been made by J. Neusner.[34] Contributions from other scholars and a wider debate will be necessary.

Secondly, a distinction is mandated between "Judaism" and the "Jewish people". Many Jews do not confess, in the present as well as in the past, any religious kind of "Judaism", although they remain ethnically and culturally Jews. Conversely, many gentiles—by means of conversion—confess, in the present as well as in the past, some types of Judaism other than Rabbinic, although they are not ethnically Jews, nor do they become such from the cultural point of view. In this perspective I find useful to introduce a distinction between the terms "Jewish" and "Judaic", that in modern English are actually synonyms. In a technical sense, "Jewish" should be used as a referent to the people, history and culture of Israel,

---

[33] See Garin E. (1959).
[34] See Neusner J. (1988 and 1989).

while "Judaic" should be used as a referent to the religion of Judaism.

Finally, Rabbinism is not the only religious system that "appeals as an important part of its authoritative literature or canon to the Hebrew Scriptures of ancient Israel, or Old Testament".[35] The same definition fits many other religious systems, such as Samaritanism, Karaism, the Phalasha Judaism and, yes, Christianity. All of them are Judaisms.

7 Christianity as a Judaism

Speaking of Christianity as a variety of Judaism may be shocking. In the first half of this century, the question as to whether the matrix of Christianity was Judaism or Hellenism was still being asked.[36] It is now widely recognized that there was no normative type of Judaism in the first century, that Jesus and his movement were constituent part of that pluralistic context, and that Rabbinic origins paralleled Christian origins. Neusner's usage of the plural, Judaisms, and Segal's imagery of early Christianity and early Rabbinic Judaism as "twins" (or brothers, sisters, siblings) have become popular patterns, even among scholars who follow the evolutionary model.[37] But there is a substantial point of disagreement. According to the evolutionary model, the Jewishness of Christianity only lasted until the Jewish religion reached the Rabbinic stage of its inner evolution. Having missed the chance to develop within "mainstream Judaism", Christianity developed as a separate religion out of Judaism and out of the Jewish people. Hence, the many Judaisms model and the "twins" imagery would be valid inasmuch as they are limited to the first century; afterwards, with the victory of mainstream Judaism, the Jewish "brother" only remained in the parent's house, while the Christian brother went away. Christianity then ceased to be a Judaism.

This approach does not make sense when one refuses the single Judaism and the evolutionary model, looks at Judaism as a set of contemporaneous systems in competition, and take seriously the generative goal of both Rabbinism and Christianity: their parallel attempt at reforming ancient Judaism. Both of them appealed to the same ancient tradition, believed themselves to be part of the same religion, and recognized the other as a competitor and not as

---

[35] Neusner J. (1991) 59=64.
[36] See Odeber H. "Ist das Christentum hellenistisch oder jüdisch?", *Zeitschrift für systematische Theologie* 17 (1940) 569-86.
[37] See Neusner J. (1987); and Shanks H. (1992).

an external threat. The question is not: When did Christianity cease to be a Judaism?, but: When and why did Christianity and Rabbinic Judaism stop considering themselves, and recognizing the other, as belonging to the same religion?[38] This question concerns the weakening of common practices as well as ethnic, cultural and sociological bonds between the two, it does not imply the cessation of their being Judaic systems.

The reference to the same legacy has never failed in both traditions. Certainly, the Christian and the rabbinic system of thought—distinct from their respective beginning—are very different from one another, and equally innovative, too. Opposite beliefs were founded on and justified by the same, open premises. Christians reinterpreted the Old Testament in the light of the New Testament; the Rabbis made the Hebrew Bible the written side of the dual Torah revealed to Moses on Sinai. Christians turned Judaism into a multinational religion; the Rabbis strengthened the idea of Judaism as the religion of the Jewish people. Christians reread the Scripture typologically as evidence of the preexistent Christ; the Rabbis developed a normative corpus of written and oral Laws as evidence of the preexistent Torah. Despite their different understandings, the two Israels never rejected their past; both of them placed themselves, and their original developments, in analogous lines of continuity and discontinuity with ancient Judaism. The debate over which of them is the more authentic development (that is, "the true Israel") belongs to confessional polemics. Everybody will agree that espousing the arguments of one of the parties certainly is not the correct way to try to suit about a contested heritage. This is all the more true before the tribunal of history. The idea of Judaism of a religion linked to a defined people, the Jews, and rooted in the obedience to the dual Torah comes to us from Rabbinism—it is merely the rabbinic interpretation of Judaism. For a historian of religion, Rabbinism and Christianity are simply different Judaisms.

What gradually failed in both Christianity and rabbinic Judaism, was the common consciousness and recognition of being part of the same religion. The gradual and reciprocal weakening of such consciousness marked the emergence of two distinct branches of Judaism, not the birth of the new religion from an elder religion. Christianity and Rabbinic Judaism continued to honor the same unrejected heritage and their common elders, while they taunted each other with having betrayed the family. After having tried long

---

[38] Cf. Dunn J.D.G. (1991).

and hard to convince one another of their own conviction to be "the true Israel", they eventually denied any reciprocal recognition. Not only they rejected their sibling, but each also tried to disinherit the other. This reciprocal excommunication affected their contemporary relations, and in Christianity caused also the emergence of harsh anti-Jewish attitudes. The more the Jews lost their interest in Christianity and identified themselves with Rabbinic Judaism while charging Christians with being a non-Jewish phenomenon, the more the gentile Christians lost their love and interest in the Jewish people. The religious debate against rabbinic Judaism ruined Christians' consciousness of the Jewish cultural and ethnic roots of their own religion. Not even this tragic process of *damnatio memoriae*, however, involved the religious bond between Christianity and ancient Judaism. While Christianity is no longer a Jewish phenomenon from the cultural and ethnic point of view, ideologically it has never ceased to be a Judaism. No longer "Jewish", Christianity is still entirely "Judaic".

8 A Scientific Taxonomy of Judaism

Having clarified what we should mean by "Judaism" (and "Judaic") and "Jews" (and "Jewish") in a technical vocabulary, it is now possible to define a consistent scientific taxonomy. As the name of a monotheistic religion—or better, the collective label of a complex set of related ideological systems—"Judaism" properly denotes the genus. Its history is connected, yet not coincident with the history of the Jewish people, not even with the history of Jews' religious beliefs. Judaism emerged from within the Jewish people since the Babylonian exile, yet developed from that ancient root and spread also out of Israel.

Since the beginning, the *genus* Judaism was made up of various contemporaneous *species*, or Judaisms—movements in competition, yet sharing a common sense of membership to the same religious community. We do not have one system of thought but many, often parallel, systems. Some of these had a short history; some flourished and developed for centuries. Each of them needs to be traced and studied diachronically, from its emergence to its decline (or enduring success), and contextualized with the support of historical, archaeological and sociological evidences. There is an ideological continuity—and then the existence of a Judaism is stated—only if an ideological tradition is developed out of the same generative idea. Sometimes the competion among *species* happened to grow up so much as to destroy any mutual recognition. Although each claimed to be faithful to the same ancient tradition, one was no longer available to recognize the "orthodoxy" of the other; the common sense of membership failed and some species grew apart from others. The parting of their ways then generated distinct (and no less pluralistic) *branches* of Judaism, such as Samaritanism, Rabbinism, and Christianity.

The history of "Judaism"—a *genus* composed of many species and developing into distinct branches—can be effectively described as a genealogical tree. Rooted in the politheistic cults of the Near East and initially limited to a small people, the "trunk" of the new monotheistic religion strengthened and then flourished in a plurality of branches—a vigorous and blooming growth up to the present day. The periodization of Judaism that is here proposed, aims to define—in a comprehensive view—the three fundamental stages of growth of the *genus*.

The first period of Judaism —that of "ancient Judaism" (sixth through the fourth century BCE)—is particularly important. The richness and pluralism of "ancient Judaism," of its many ideological *species*, is the premise of later developments. Ancient Jews created very dynamic religious systems that would successfully adapt themselves to new environments and circumstances. This is the age in which the founding documents of later Judaisms took shape: the "canonical" documents of Samaritanism, Christianity, and Rabbinism, but also some of those noncanonical writings (like the first parts of 1 Enoch)[39] that were so influential on Christian origins.

Judaism of 300 BCE to 200 CE is the second stage of growth of the genus Judaism. This period has been always defined *backwards*, either in the light of Christianity (as the "late," "intertestamental," final-point of Judaism before Jesus), or in the light of Rabbinism (as the "early," starting-point of "classical" Judaism). A comprehensive view of "Judaism" now allows an *onwards* definition. Historically, the most relevant characteristic of the period is its being the bridge between "ancient Judaism" and the main "modern" branches of Judaism emerging from antiquity: Samaritanism first, and then Rabbinism and Christianity. And what is more appropriate than "middle" to denote this transitional age? By stressing the midway-point (in place of the final- or the starting-point of confessional periodizations), "middle Judaism" states a series, "ancient-middle-modern," which is chronologically consistent and equally significant for the entire Judaic genus and for its "modern" branches.[40]

---

[39] See Sacchi P. (1990).
[40] See Boccaccini G. (1991).

The chronological boundaries of "middle Judaism" are not marked by confessional *corpora* (the Samaritan Pentateuch, the Old and the New Testament, or the Hebrew Bible and the Mishnah), but by two events significant for the entire history of Judaism: the meeting with the Hellenistic world after Alexander the Great and the ultimate parting of the ways between Rabbinism and Christianity by the end of the second century CE.

As a purely historical periodization, "middle Judaism" does not describe an organic and homogeneous system of thought, much less a theology or a spiritual category. To refer to the plurality of its ideological movements—the numerous *species* active in the period (including early Christianity and early rabbinic Judaism)—we shall use the plural and speak of "middle Judaisms" or "middle Judaic" movements.

While "ancient Judaism" denotes a set of species and "middle Judaism" had to face the already growing branch of Samaritanism, "modern Judaism" (the third stage of growth of the *genus* Judaism, up to and including the present time) distinguishes itself for being exclusively a set of branches (each including numerous species). Writing the history of "modern Judaism" means tracing the history of these "modern" branches, by giving a specific term and an appropriate periodization to each of them, from its birth as a species within ancient and/or middle Judaism to its parting and development as an autonomous branch. It is beyond the scope of this article the identification and classification of all the modern branches of Judaism up to the present day; Samaritanism, Christianity and Rabbinism are only the first branches generated by the trunk of Judaism. A comprehensive framework and a consistent methodology have been here offered, however. In fact, the history of each branch reproduces on a small scale that of the entire *genus*. New species were born within each branch and branches parted into further branches. Christianity and Rabbinism in particular would be estremely prolific in both species and branches. The generative power of Judaism does not show signs of exhaustion, yet.

9 A Comprehensive Approach

The study of a period in Judaism implies a twofold task: the diachronic analysis of the *species* flourishing in that limited period of time, and the synchronic analysis of their relations through a holistic comparison of their competing systems. A common-denominator methodology that joins records of different *species*, is absolutely misleading; it assumes a unity that never existed, and makes us see the one where we have the many.

The object of a history of middle Judaic thought, therefore, is not the identification and synchronic study of the one Judaism as witnessed by the Jewish sources of the time (as in the single Judaism model), nor the identification and diachronic study of an overlapping phase in the evolution of Jewish and Christian religions (as in the evolutionary model). Object of a history of middle Jewish thought is the identification and diachronic study of many parallel Judaisms (including Christianities) in themselves and in the context of their complex synchronic relations.

A hard and fascinating work is before us: hundreds of texts—one of the most impressive amounts of literature coming to us from antiquity—still need to be classified, document by document, as ideological records of different Judaisms. The greatest obstacle is that sources have come down to us grouped into confessional corpora, or canons (the Samaritan Pentateuch, the Hebrew Bible, the Old and the New Testament, the Pseudepigrapha, etc.). In our Christian-influenced civilization, such confessional division gave birth to a confessionaly divided scholarship with clear boundaries between Christian and Judaic, canonical and noncanonical studies. A century of historical method has not been able to modify this perspective at its roots. To a large extent, each corpus still lives its own separate, self-sufficient existence, with its own specialists, journals, bibliographies, and audience. The fact that a document belongs to one or another corpus largely determines its being popular (or conversely, neglected) in public opinion as well as in scholarship. The canonical status, more than any intrinsic historical value, is the best warranty of success: it secures a high frequency of editions and commentaries, and the presence in the programs of universities and seminaries.

Christian and Judaic studies still remain two distinct and often noncommunicating fields of research. Each requires a different training and is housed in different departments; each addresses a different audience, has its own initiates and is represented by different professional associations. Since early Christianity is supposed to be a "non-Jewish" phenomenon (or, at the most, a negligible Jewish sect), the scholar of Judaism generally is not professionally interested in the knowledge of Christianity. The opposite is more frequent, yet optional still; New Testament scholars are expected to be familiar with, not specialists in "early" Judaism. For some time the specialist in "intertestamental" or "early" Judaism has become a welcomed guest at conferences of biblical or Judaic studies, but as a professor is a luxury that only the richest universities can afford. The student has to ply between the departments of biblical and

Judaic studies and between the departments of history and philosophy, if he or she wants to study Daniel and the New Testament, Philo and Josephus, the Dead Sea Scrolls and the early Rabbinic documents, the Apocrypha and the Pseudepigrapha. And at the university library he or she would find middle Judaic sources cataloged into different files and sheltered in different sections (if not in different buildings).

Some will object that there is now a growing awareness that "Christian" and "Jewish" sources cannot be studied apart from one another, and canonical documents in isolation from the noncanonical. But so serious a problem as the existence of the corpora cannot be solved by weak answers.

Weak answer is that of balancing the specific weight of each corpus by giving an introduction, distinct research instruments and even a "common-denominator" theology to the previously deprived collections. Canons and corpora make sense only in relation to later epochs and ideologies; they are absolutely misleading in their prejudicial interposition between the sources (their author, their age, and their ideological horizons) and the modern interpreters. What is the value of studying and teaching sources within a framework that creates *a posteriori* affinities while separates originally related texts? A confessional criterion for collecting sources, be it even the legimate love for the founding documents of one's own religious tradition, is not a criterion for understanding their original content.

Another example of weak answer is that of summing competences, so that the specialist of one corpus also becomes specialist of another and, listing the numerous and significant connections that unite canonical and noncanonical, or "Jewish" and "Christian" corpora, then triumphantly proclaims how the knowledge of one corpus helps to understand the other.[41] The search for literary and ideological parallels does not produce a comprehensive understanding of the period; the comparison between (later!) corpora is a poor and anachronistic substitute for the necessary comparison between parallel Judaisms. When we compare the New Testament with the Pseudepigrapha or the Dead Sea Scrolls, we waste our time comparing noncommensurable entities that did not even exist in the

---

[41] Although still fashionable, this long and glorious methodological tradition — usually involving the New Testament and another, more or less contemporaneous Jewish corpus (be it rabbinic literature, the Dead Sea Scrolls, or the Pseudepigrapha) — is now openly questioned by scholars who labeled it as an inconclusive "parallelomania". See Sandmel S. "Parallelomania", *Journal of Biblical Literature* 81 (1962) 1-13.

first century. The New Testament is a very selective collection of ancient Christian sources; the Dead Sea Scrolls are the result of an archeological discovery; and the Pseudepigrapha have no ideological homogeneity, being a modern miscellany of extracanonical writings.

The problem will not be solved but when the focus of attention is shifted from the corpora to the age in which the constituent writings were composed, and documents are freed from the cage of their respective corpora and rearranged according to purely historical criteria. In so doing, the interpreter should not be afraid of or surprised at finding forgotten connections or unexpected distances, new hierarchies or unsettling marginalities, supporting roles elevated to protagonists and protagonists reduced to supporting roles. The goal is not to study one or another corpus but to describe the period in its complexity, using all the material available without confessional presuppositions and artificial distinctions between canonical and noncanonical, Christian and Judaic studies.

It is impossible to understand any ideological movement of middle Judaism (including early Christianity) apart from a *comprenhensive* view of the period, and a *comprehensive* view of middle Judaism cannot be reached without a comprehensive view of all its constituent parts (including early Christianity). This means that a common training, common competences, and a common sharing of scholarly results are required to all those who deal with the period. The New Testament scholar and the specialist in "early" Judaism shall be replaced by a new figure, that of the specialist of middle Judaism. One may have a particular expertise in one or another middle Judaism (Essenism, early Christianity, Pharisaism, etc.), in one or another body of literature (Old Testament Pseudepigrapha, New Testament, Dead Sea Scrolls, etc.), but the task of the specialist in middle Judaism is the same: identyfing and comparing Judaic systems.

10 CONCLUSION

Judaic and Christian studies are gradually converging toward a more comprehensive and inclusive approach to the period of Judaism between 300 BCE and 200 CE. The concept of "late" monolithic Judaism, which constituted the background of the one Christianity, has been lately replaced by the view of an "early" pluralistic period that was both the beginning of a new stage in the inner evolution of Judaism and the first, or "Jewish," phase of Christianity. Now, the period is turning into something even more complex: the historical setting of many rival contemporaneous Judaisms (including early Christianity). With the varieties of its ideological systems, "middle Judaism" marks the passage from "ancient Judaism" to the distinct existence of the two major branches of "modern Judaism": Christianity and Rabbinism.

Such terminological revolution signals the ultimate parting of critical scholarship from confessional presuppositions by establishing a scientific taxonomy and a technical vocabulary in the study of Judaism. It also opens the way to a comprehensive approach to the period, shifting the focus of attention from the *corpora* to the ideological movements and overcoming the traditional and misleading distinction in scholarship between Christian and Judaic studies.

BIBLIOGRAPHY

Baldensperger W. *Das spätere Judenthum als Vorstufe des Christenthums* (Giessen: 1900).
Bertholet A. *Das religionsgeschichtliche Problem des Spätjudentums* (Tübingen: 1909).
Boccaccini G. *Middle Judaism: Jewish Thought, 300 BCE to 200 CE* (Minneapolis: 1991).
Boccaccini G. *Portraits of Middle Judaism in Scholarship and Arts: A Multimedia Catalog from Flavius Josephus to 1991* (Torino, 1992).
Brown L.E. *Early Judaism* (Cambridge: 1929).
Charles R.H. *Religious Development Between the Old and the New Testament* (London and New York: 1914).
Charlesworth J.H. *The Old Testament Pseudepigrapha and the New Testament* (Cambridge: 1985).
Charlesworth J.H. *Jesus Within Judaism* (New York: 1988).
Charlesworth J.H., ed. *Jesus' Jewishness: Exploring the Place of Jesus Within Early Judaism* (Philadelphia: 1991).
Cohen S.J.D. *From Maccabees to the Mishnah* (Philadelphia: 1987).
Di Nola A.M. "Ebrei, religione degli. La religione post-esilica e la nascita del giudaismo", in *Enciclopedia delle religioni*, ed. M. Gozzini, vol. 2 (Firenze: 1970) 953-83.
Dunn J.D.G. *The Partings of the Ways Between Christianity and Judaism and Their Significance for the Character of Christianity* (London and Philadelphia: 1991).
Ferguson E. *Backgrounds of Early Christianity* (Grand Rapids, MI: 1987]).
Flusser D. *Judaism and the Origins of Christianity* (Jerusalem: 1988).
Garbini G. *Storia e ideologia nell'Israele antico* (Brescia: 1986); English trans. by John Bowden, *History and Ideology in Ancient Judaism* (London: 1988).
Garin E. *La filosofia come sapere storico* (Bari: 1959).
Graetz H. *Geschichte der Juden von den ältesten Zeiten bis auf die Gegenwart*, 11 vols. (Leipzig: 1853-76)
Gracia J.J.E. *Philosophy and Its History: Issue in Philosophical Investigation* (Albany NY: 1992).
Hausrath A. *Neutestamentliche Zeitgeschichte*, 3 vols. (Heidelberg: 1868-74).

Kraft R.A. and G.W.E. Nickelsburg, eds. *Early Judaism and Its Modern Interpreters* (Philadelphia: 1986).

Jost I.M. *Geschichte der Israeliten seit der Zeit der Maccabäer bis auf unsere Tage*, 9 vols. (Berlin: 1820-28).

Langen J. *Das Judenthum in Palästina zur Zeit Christi* (Freiburg im Bresgau: 1866).

Maccoby H. *Judaism in the First Century* (London: 1989)

Maier J. *Zwischen den Testamenten. Geschichte und Religion in der Zeit des zweiten Tempels* (München: 1990).

Maier J. and J. Schreiner, eds. *Literatur und Religion des Frühjudentums* (Würzburg: 1973).

Murphy F.J. *The Religious World of Jesus: An Introduction to Second Temple Palestinian Judaism* (Hoboken, NJ: 1991).

Neusner J. *The Systemic Analysis of Religion* (Atlanta: 1988).

Neusner J. *The Ecology of Religion: from Writing to Religion in the Study of Judaism* (Nashville: 1989).

Neusner J. *Studying Classical Judaism: A Primer* (Louisville: 1991).

Neusner J., W.S. Green, and E.S. Frerichs, eds. *Judaisms and Their Messiahs at the Turn of the Christian Era* (Cambridge: 1987).

Nickelsburg G.W.E. *Jewish Literature Between The Bible and the Mishnah* (London: 1981)

Parkes J.W. *The Foundations of Judaism and Christianity* (Chicago: 1960).

Perelmuter H.G. *Siblings: Rabbinic Judaism and Early Christianity at Their Beginnings* (New York: 1989)

Prideaux H. *The Old and New Testament Connected in the History of the Jews, and Neighbouring Nations; from the Declension of the Kingdoms of Israel and Judah to the Time of Christ*, 2 vols. (London: 1716-18).

Riches J. *The World of Jesus: First-Century Judaism in Crisis* (Cambridge: 1990).

Sacchi P. *L'apocalittica giudaica e la sua storia* (Brescia: 1990).

Saldarini A.J. *Pharisees, Scribes and Sadducees in Palestinian Society: A Sociological Approach* (Wilmington, DE: 1988).

Sanders E.P. *Paul and Palestinian Judaism: A Comparison of Patterns of Religion* (Philadelphia and London: 1978).

Sanders E.P. *Judaism: Practice and Belief, 63 BCE - 66 CE* (London and Philadelphia: 1992).

Schiffman L.H. *From Text to Tradition: A History of Second Temple and Rabbinic Judaism* (Hoboken, NJ: 1991).

Schürer E. *Lehrbuch der neutestamentliche Zeitgeschichte*, (Leipzig: 1874); from the 2nd ed. under the title: *Geschichte des jüdischen Volkes im Zeitalter Jesu*.

Segal A.F. *Rebecca's Children: Judaism and Christianity in the Roman World* (Cambridge, MA: 1986).

Segal A.F. *The Other Judaisms of Late Antiquity* (Atlanta: 1987).

Shanks H., ed. *Christianity and Rabbinic Judaism: A Parallel History of Their Origins and Early Development*, (Washington, DC: 1992).

Stemberger G. *Pharisäer, Sadducäer, Essener* (Stuttgart: 1991).

Unnik W.C. van, ed. *La littérature juive entre Tenach et Mishna* (Leiden: 1974).

Weingreen J. *From Bible to Mishnah: The Continuity of Tradition* (Manchester and New York: 1976).

Wise I.M. *History of the Hebrew's Second Commonwealth with Special Reference to Its Literature, Culture, and the Origin of Rabbinism and Christianity* (Cincinnati: 1880).

GENERAL INDEX

INDEX TO BIBLICAL AND TALMUDIC REFERENCES

HANDBUCH DER ORIENTALISTIK

Abt. I: DER NAHE UND MITTLERE OSTEN

ISSN 0169-9423

Band 1. Ägyptologie
1. *Ägyptische Schrift und Sprache.* Mit Beiträgen von H. Brunner, H. Kees, S. Morenz, E. Otto, S. Schott. Mit Zusätzen von H. Brunner. Nachdruck der Erstausgabe (1959). 1973. ISBN 90 04 03777 2
2. *Literatur.* Mit Beiträgen von H. Altenmüller, H. Brunner, G. Fecht, H. Grapow, H. Kees, S. Morenz, E. Otto, S. Schott, J. Spiegel, W. Westendorf. 2. verbesserte und erweiterte Auflage. 1970. ISBN 90 04 00849 7
3. HELCK, W. *Geschichte des alten Ägypten.* Nachdruck mit Berichtigungen und Ergänzungen. 1981. ISBN 90 04 06497 4

Band 2. Keilschriftforschung und alte Geschichte Vorderasiens
1-2/2. *Altkleinasiatische Sprachen [und Elamitisch].* Mit Beiträgen von J. Friedrich, E. Reiner, A. Kammenhuber, G. Neumann, A. Heubeck. 1969. ISBN 90 04 00852 7
3. SCHMÖKEL, H. *Geschichte des alten Vorderasien.* Reprint. 1979. ISBN 90 04 00853 5
4/2. *Orientalische Geschichte von Kyros bis Mohammed.* Mit Beiträgen von A. Dietrich, G. Widengren, F. M. Heichelheim. 1966. ISBN 90 04 00854 3

Band 3. Semitistik
Semitistik. Mit Beiträgen von A. Baumstark, C. Brockelmann, E. L. Dietrich, J. Fück, M. Höfner, E. Littmann, A. Rücker, B. Spuler. Nachdruck der Erstausgabe (1953-1954). 1964. ISBN 90 04 00855 1

Band 4. Iranistik
1. *Linguistik.* Mit Beiträgen von K. Hoffmann, W. B. Henning, H. W. Bailey, G. Morgenstierne, W. Lentz. Nachdruck der Erstausgabe (1958). 1967. ISBN 90 04 03017 4
2/1. *Literatur.* Mit Beiträgen von I. Gershevitch, M. Boyce, O. Hansen, B. Spuler, M. J. Dresden. 1968. ISBN 90 04 00857 8
2/2. *History of Persian Literature from the Beginning of the Islamic Period to the Present Day.* With Contributions by G. Morrison, J. Baldick and Sh. Kadkanī. 1981. ISBN 90 04 06481 8
3. KRAUSE, W. *Tocharisch.* Nachdruck der Erstausgabe (1955) mit Zusätzen und Berichtigungen. 1971. ISBN 90 04 03194 4

Band 5. Altaistik
1. *Turkologie.* Mit Beiträgen von A. von Gabain, O. Pritsak, J. Benzing, K. H. Menges, A. Temir, Z. V. Togan, F. Taeschner, O. Spies, A. Caferoglu, A. Battal-Tamays. Reprint with additions of the 1st (1963) ed. 1982. ISBN 90 04 06555 5
2. *Mongolistik.* Mit Beiträgen von N. Poppe, U. Posch, G. Doerfer, P. Aalto, D. Schröder, O. Pritsak, W. Heissig. 1964. ISBN 90 04 00859 4
3. *Tungusologie.* Mit Beiträgen von W. Fuchs, I. A. Lopatin, K. H. Menges, D. Sinor. 1968. ISBN 90 04 00860 8

Band 6. Geschichte der islamischen Länder
5/1. *Regierung und Verwaltung des Vorderen Orients in islamischer Zeit.* Mit Beiträgen von H. R. Idris und K. Röhrborn. 1979. ISBN 90 04 05915 6
5/2. *Regierung und Verwaltung des Vorderen Orients in islamischer Zeit.* 2. Mit Beiträgen von D. Sourdel und J. Bosch Vilá. 1988. ISBN 90 04 08550 5
6/1. *Wirtschaftsgeschichte des Vorderen Orients in islamischer Zeit.* Mit Beiträgen von B. Lewis, M. Rodinson, G. Baer, H. Müller, A. S. Ehrenkreutz, E. Ashtor, B. Spuler, A. K. S. Lambton, R. C. Cooper, B. Rosenberger, R. Arié, L. Bolens, T. Fahd. 1977. ISBN 90 04 04802 2

Band 7.
Armenisch und Kaukasische Sprachen. Mit Beiträgen von G. Deeters, G. R. Solta, V. Inglisian. 1963. ISBN 90 04 00862 4

Band 8. Religion
1/1. *Religionsgeschichte des alten Orients.* Mit Beiträgen von E. Otto, O. Eissfeldt, H. Otten, J. Hempel. 1964. ISBN 90 04 00863 2
1/2/2/1. BOYCE, M. *A History of Zoroastrianism. The Early Period.* Rev. ed. 1989. ISBN 90 04 08847 4
1/2/2/2. BOYCE, M. *A History of Zoroastrianism. Under the Achaemenians.* 1982. ISBN 90 04 06506 7
1/2/2/3. BOYCE, M. and GRENET, F. *A History of Zoroastrianism. Zoroastrianism under Macedonian and Roman Rule.* With F. Grenet. Contribution by R. Beck. 1991. ISBN 90 04 09271 4
2. *Religionsgeschichte des Orients in der Zeit der Weltreligionen.* Mit Beiträgen von A. Adam, A. J. Arberry, E. L. Dietrich, J. W. Fück, A. von Gabain, J. Leipoldt, B. Spuler, R. Strothman, G. Widengren. 1961. ISBN 90 04 00864 0

Ergänzungsband 1
1. HINZ, W. *Islamische Maße und Gewichte umgerechnet ins metrische System.* Nachdruck der Erstausgabe (1955) mit Zusätzen und Berichtigungen. 1970. ISBN 90 04 00865 9

Ergänzungsband 2
1. GROHMANN, A. *Arabische Chronologie und Arabische Papyruskunde.* Mit Beiträgen von J. Mayr und W. C. Til. 1966. ISBN 90 04 00866 7
2. KHOURY, R. G. *Chrestomathie de papyrologie arabe.* Documents relatifs à la vie privée, sociale et administrative dans les premiers siècles islamiques. 1992. ISBN 90 04 09551 9

Ergänzungsband 3
Orientalisches Recht. Mit Beiträgen von E. Seidl, V. Korošc, E. Pritsch, O. Spies, E. Tyan, J. Baz, Ch. Chehata, Ch. Samaran, J. Roussier, J. Lapanne-Joinville, S. Ş. Ansay. 1964. ISBN 90 04 00867 5

Ergänzungsband 5
1/1. BORGER, R. *Das zweite Jahrtausend vor Chr.* Mit Verbesserungen und Zusätzen. Nachdruck der Erstausgabe (1961). 1964. ISBN 90 04 00869 1
1/2. SCHRAMM, W. *[Einleitung in die assyrischen Königsinschriften, 2:] 934-722 v. Chr.* 1973. ISBN 90 04 03783 7

Ergänzungsband 6
1. ULLMANN, M. *Die Medizin im Islam.* 1970. ISBN 90 04 00870 5
2. ULLMANN, M. *Die Natur- und Geheimwissenschaften im Islam.* 1972. ISBN 90 04 03423 4

Ergänzungsband 7
GOMAA, I. *A Historical Chart of the Muslim World.* 1972. ISBN 90 04 03333 5

Ergänzungsband 8
KORNRUMPF, H.-J. *Osmanische Bibliographie mit besonderer Berücksichtigung der Türkei in Europa.* Unter Mitarbeit von J. Kornrumpf. 1973. ISBN 90 04 03549 4

Ergänzungsband 9
FIRRO, K. M. *A History of the Druzes.* 1992. ISBN 90 04 09437 7

Band 10
STRIJP, R. *Cultural Anthropology of the Middle East. A Bibliography.* Vol. 1: 1965-1987. 1992. ISBN 90 04 09604 3

Band 11
ENDRESS, G. & GUTAS, D. (eds.). *A Greek and Arabic Lexicon.* (*GALex*) Materials for a Dictionary of the Mediæval Translations from Greek into Arabic.
Fascicle 1. Introduction—Sources—' – '-kh-r. Compiled by G. Endress & D. Gutas, with the assistance of K. Alshut, R. Arnzen, Chr. Hein, St. Pohl, M. Schmeink. 1992. ISBN 90 04 09494 6
Fascicle 2. '-kh-r – '-ṣ-l. Compiled by G. Endress & D. Gutas, with the assistance of K. Alshut, R. Arnzen, Chr. Hein, St. Pohl, M. Schmeink. 1993. ISBN 90 04 09893 3

Band 12
JAYYUSI, S. K. (ed.). *The Legacy of Muslim Spain.* Chief consultant to the editor, M. Marín. 2nd ed. 1994. ISBN 90 04 09599 3

Band 13
HUNWICK, J. O. and O'FAHEY, R. S. (eds.). *Arabic Literature of Africa.*
Volume I. *The Writings of Eastern Sudanic Africa to c. 1900.* Compiled by R. S. O'Fahey, with the assistance of M. I. Abu Salim, A. Hofheinz, Y. M. Ibrahim, B. Radtke and K. S. Vikør. 1994. ISBN 90 04 09450 4

Band 14
DECKER, W. und HERB, M. *Bildatlas zum Sport im alten Ägypten. Corpus der bildlichen Quellen zu Leibesübungen, Spiel, Jagd, Tanz und verwandten Themen.* Bd.1: Text. Bd. 2: Abbildungen. 1994. ISBN 90 04 09974 3 (Set)

Band 15
HAAS, V. *Geschichte der hethitischen Religion.* 1994. ISBN 90 04 09799 6

Band 16
NEUSNER, J. (ed.). *Judaism in Late Antiquity.* Part One: The Literary and Archaeological Sources. 1995. ISBN 90 04 10129 2

Band 17
NEUSNER, J. (ed.). *Judaism in Late Antiquity.* Part Two: Historical Syntheses. 1995. ISBN 90 04 10130 6

Band 18
OREL, V. E. and STOLBOVA, O. V. (eds.). *Hamito-Semitic Etymological Dictionary.* Materials for a Reconstruction. 1995. ISBN 90 04 10051 2

Band 19
AL-ZWAINI, L. and PETERS, R. *A Bibliography of Islamic Law, 1980-1993.* 1994. ISBN 90 04 10009 1